Gender, Culture,
and
Consumer Behavior

Gender, Culture, *and* Consumer Behavior

Edited by

Cele C. Otnes
University of Illinois at Urbana-Champaign

Linda Tuncay Zayer
Loyola University Chicago

Routledge
Taylor & Francis Group
New York   London

Routledge
Taylor & Francis Group
711 Third Avenue
New York, NY 10017

Routledge
Taylor & Francis Group
27 Church Road
Hove, East Sussex BN3 2FA

Printed in the United States of America on acid-free paper
Version Date: 20111012

International Standard Book Number: 978-1-84872-946-9 (Hardback)

Library of Congress Cataloging-in-Publication Data

Gender, culture, and consumer behavior / editors, Cele C. Otnes and Linda Tuncay-Zayer.
    p. cm.
    Summary: "When considering how we should introduce this volume, we reflected on our own lives as women who both grew up in America, but whose heritages are distinct. We are both daughters of male liberal arts professors who provided most of the family income, while our mothers focused on child-rearing and community activities, as well as by-choice educational pursuits and forays into the working world. Linda is a first-generation American whose parents emigrated to the U.S. in 1970. Cele's ancestors were early U.S. settlers whose families relied on hard work and the G.I. Bill to fend off blows dealt by the Depression. We decided to offer examples of how gender, culture, and consumption intersect in memories that demonstrate the dramatic and dynamic changes in these three areas over our lifetimes"-- Provided by publisher.
    Includes bibliographical references and index.
    ISBN 978-1-84872-946-9 (hardback)
    1. Consumer behavior. 2. Consumer behavior--Cross-cultural studies. 3. Consumption (Economics)--Social aspects. I. Otnes, Cele. II. Tuncay-Zayer, Linda.

HF5415.32.G457 2012
658.8'342--dc23   2011040319

Visit the Taylor & Francis Web site at
http://www.taylorandfrancis.com

and the Psychology Press Web site at
http://www.psypress.com

To Mark and Emily

To Tristan

Contents

SECTION II Media, Advertising, and Gender

SECTION III   Gender, Culture, and the Market

Preface

When considering how we should introduce this volume, we reflected on our own lives as women who both grew up in America, but whose heritages are distinct. We are both daughters of male liberal arts professors who provided most of the family income, while our mothers focused on child-rearing and community activities, as well as by-choice educational pursuits and forays into the working world. Linda is a first-generation American whose parents emigrated to the United States in 1970. Cele's ancestors were early U.S. settlers whose families relied on hard work and the G.I. Bill to fend off blows dealt by the Depression. We decided to offer examples of how gender, culture, and consumption intersect in memories that demonstrate the dramatic and dynamic changes in these three areas over our lifetimes. Here is Cele's memory of the parties her parents would host when her father served as a department chair at Louisiana State University in the 1960s and 1970s:

> My mother would start preparing weeks in advance. I would find menus written in longhand for various combinations of canapés and hors d'oeuvres with the *New York Times Cookbook, River Road Recipes,* and *C'est Si Bon* (it was Baton Rouge, after all) earmarked and spread out on the kitchen table. Exotic (to me) ingredients like Melba toast, Worcestershire sauce, and artichoke hearts would make an appearance. Since my parents didn't drink anything but wine, my father would make the requisite trip to the liquor store and oddly shaped bottles filled with mostly amber liquids would appear. My mother would dig out her bartender's guide from the top drawer of our buffet, as well as colored toothpicks, party trays, and the like. Then there would be the sweets—a huge part of entertaining in the South. For a few days prior to the party, the kitchen counter would rock on its foundation from the constant whir of the mixer, and I would hover around hoping to lick the beaters while amazing concoctions such as rum cake, pecan bars, and the like would emerge. Of course, the ultimate decision was what my mother would wear. I remember a Kelly-green maxi-gown with white straps in the early 1970s that looked great with her red hair (washed and set that afternoon at the beauty shop). My dad, of course, stayed out of the kitchen (parties were typically on a Friday night so as not to interfere with LSU football); his preparations basically consisted of

shaving and changing out of the sport coat, slacks, and tie he wore to work and into another permutation of the same. After it was over, my mother and I did the lion's share of the cleanup, and he would make a beeline for the recliner to relax in front of Johnny Carson.

And Linda remembers this incident:

Growing up, I most distinctly remember holidays where my mom would spend all day preparing handmade Turkish goodies, like baklava, lamb kebabs, and eggplant, presented eloquently on fine china in the dining room. And while it may seem somewhat paradoxical, the singular message from my mom for my two sisters and me was in fact not about being a good homemaker or mother as she had spent most of her own life doing. Instead, it was on the importance of higher education in order to be independent, career-focused women. The key was to be able to stand on our own, and if that meant that love, marriage, and children came later, so be it. Indeed, both of my sisters became medical doctors. In high school, I remember sitting at the kitchen table with my parents discussing what my college major would be. At this "negotiation," after several unsuccessful proposals on my part ranging from journalism to sociology, we settled on business. Two years into college, I told them I wanted to be a professor. I saw the relief in their faces as they felt their little girl had grown up and made the right choice.

Cut to the early 2000s. The dessert chef in the Otnes household is Cele's husband Mark, who can often be found making homemade pie crust the day before a dinner party. Likewise, in Linda's home, her husband Alan is often cooking dinner and playing with their son while she is working on research or preparing her lectures.

Although most people might argue that the constructs of gender, culture, and consumption may be unrecognizable from one generation to the next, what strikes us as particularly true is that these days, changes occur at a dizzying rate. Consider these recent examples: A Canadian family sparks a national debate when they decide to keep the sex of their child private to the outside world and encourage all of their three children to shun gender role norms. Across the globe, some Arab women are marrying in elaborate Western gowns, but only in the privacy of their own homes; in many of their countries, they will be arrested if seen unveiled or driving a car. Likewise, although European men have long embraced a more varied color palette with respect to clothing and have engaged in spa and beauty treatments traditionally eschewed by North American males, metrosexuality (Tuncay, 2006; Tuncay & Otnes, 2008a,b) now blurs the boundaries of gender-appropriate marketplace behavior. At the same time, traditional masculinity continues to be portrayed in our culture through such shows as *Entourage* and *Mad Men,* among others, although oftentimes intricately intertwined with new forms of masculinity and femininity. And, of course, celebrities from Chaz Bono to Lady Gaga are reenergizing the dialogue about how gender, culture, and consumption interact.

In sum, the time seemed ripe to gather together current research that could provide a stimulating sample of the rich tapestry of gender issues emerging across the globe in a variety of spheres. It is a truism that gender is a compelling topic within most humanities and social science disciplines. Yet we are fortunate that over the past 20 years, it has received increasingly focused attention among a growing and dedicated group of scholars in marketing and consumer behavior. The wonderful summary of gender research in this field by Bettany, Dobscha, O'Malley, and Prothero that appeared in *Marketing Theory* in 2010 correctly attributed much of the sustained interest in gender to the tireless efforts of Janeen Arnold Costa, whose inaugural conference on gender and consumer behavior in 1991 helped lay the foundation for what is now a securely concrete and consistent (but also evolving) interest in the discipline. A review of this literature is beyond the scope of this preface; however, Bettany and colleagues' article is an excellent starting point, and most chapters in this volume also review subtopics of gender, consumption, and culture.

Even as we were in the process of soliciting active and prolific authors for this book, we were only half aware of how varied and intriguing their submissions would be. Mirroring our own (and especially Linda's) interest, as well as current research trends, is the fact that six out of sixteen chapters explore some aspect of masculinity. Yet the chapters also offer insights into areas that traditionally focus on gender differences and gender roles (in particular, advertising) and also pave new pathways by actually engaging men in the study of gender issues. Furthermore, we include topics where interest is clearly on the rise—namely, sustainability, fan culture, and intersectionality. Our contributors are housed in departments of advertising, communication, and marketing. And while they reside in North America, Europe, Eurasia, and Australasia, their own ethnic heritages extend even further out around the globe, as their biographies attest.

In sum, we believe this volume can serve as a resource for students at all college levels. To facilitate the experiences of those new to the area, we offer a glossary containing key terms for each chapter at the end of the volume as well. We believe the book is appropriate for an interdisciplinary audience, including use in any introductory course in gender studies, as well as in upper level communication, advertising, consumer culture, and consumer behavior courses. We hope to serve as a resource for general readers as well.

This book is organized into five sections:

Feminist Theory and Discourses
Media, Advertising, and Gender
Gender, Culture, and the Market
Masculine Discourses
New Directions

In Section I, Catherine Coleman offers a sociohistoric inquiry of women's so-called vulnerability in the marketplace, while Hope Jensen Schau and Margo Buchanan-Oliver discuss how female fans of the popular *Twilight* saga negotiate discourses of sexuality and gender. In Section II, Lorna Stevens and Pauline Maclaran explore the feminist discourses surrounding the notion of the carnal feminine as represented in the popular *Sex and the City* movies. We then offer our own research on men's responses to idealized portrayals of masculinity and find that their experiences range from vulnerability to achievement. Next, Michelle Nelson and Alexandra Vilela examine advertising and gender issues as they provide an extensive review of gendered persuasion and processing of messages in advertising. In the last chapter on media, advertising, and gender, Jacqueline Lambiase, Tom Reichert, Mark Adkins, and Michael LaTour examine the issue of media literacy by exploring men's and women's interpretations of fashion advertisements.

In Section III, Gokcen Coskuner-Balli and Burçak Ertimur examine value cocreation within the context of gender and consumption. Helen Woodruffe-Burton and Katie Ireland add to the discussion on gender and the market as they examine the discourses of narcissism and the body in relation to female gym addictions. In the next chapter, Angeline Close examines gender roles, gift-giving, and resistance to the Valentine's Day ritual.

Section IV, which focuses on masculine discourses, begins with Jacob Ostberg's discussion of the themes of status and masculinity in the context of men's fashion in Sweden. Next, Steven Chen provides a fascinating glimpse into the emergence of *soushokukei danshi,* or a form of Japanese masculinity characterized by feminine consumption and an emphasis on comfort and leisure. Nacima Ourahmoune adds to the global perspective on masculinity by exploring men's engagement in intimate lingerie consumption rituals in France. Next, Robert Harrison, Jim Gentry, and Suraj Commuri examine the production and consumption associated with the lives of single fathers in the United States.

The last section of the book addresses new directions for gender, culture, and consumer behavior research and includes a chapter by Susan Dobscha and Andrea Prothero, who examine the intersection of sustainability, consumption, production, and feminist discourses. Next, Ahir Gopaldas and Eileen Fischer offer an illuminating discussion on intersectionality, culture, and consumer behavior. Finally, we are grateful that Janeen Costa and Gary Bamossy eloquently offer their reflections on the progression of gender and consumer behavior research. We are very proud of the compilation of research presented, and hope readers find it equally intriguing, and that these chapters will spark discussion, debate, and scholarship.

REFERENCES

Bettany, Shona, Susan Dobscha, Lisa O'Malley, & Andrea Prothero (2010). Moving beyond binary opposition: Exploring the tapestry of gender in consumer research and marketing. *Marketing Theory, 10* (March), 3–28.

Tuncay, Linda (2006). Conceptualizations of masculinity among a "new" breed of male consumers. In Lorna Stevens & Janet Borgerson (Eds.), *Gender and consumer behavior* (Vol. 8). Edinburgh, Scotland: Association for Consumer Research (online version, n.p.).

Tuncay, Linda, & Cele Otnes (2008a). The use of persuasion management strategies by identity-vulnerable consumers: The case of heterosexual male shoppers. *Journal of Retailing, 84* (December), 487–499.

Tuncay, Linda, & Cele Otnes (2008b). Exploring the link between masculinity and consumption. In Tina M. Lowery (Ed.), *Brick & mortar shopping in the 21st century* (pp. 153–168). Mahwah, NJ: Lawrence Erlbaum Associates.

Acknowledgments

We wish to extend our thanks to those who helped make this book possible. First, we thank our contributors for their excellent work and their willingness to put up with our requests pertaining to style and content. We also thank our contributors for serving as friendly reviewers of each other's work, as well as other reviewers (Mary-Agnes Parmentier and Elizabeth Crosby). We thank our research assistants, Drai Hassert and Srinivas Venugopal, for their work on the indices for this book. We are also sincerely grateful to Anne Duffy, our editor at *Psychology Press,* who embraced the idea for this book with enthusiasm. We also thank our project editor, Judith Simon, and marketing assistant, Jennifer Sefa-Boakye, for their help in making this book possible. Along those lines, we thank the anonymous reviewers of our original proposal for this volume and hope they find the final product enjoyable and enlightening. We also thank our colleagues within our departments and within the field of consumer behavior/consumer culture studies who have supported us with discussions of this volume, and by suggesting authors we could invite. We thank our families—especially our husbands, who have transcended many of the hard-and-fast tenets of American masculinity that defined their fathers' generations and are true partners in our lives. We also thank our children—Cele's daughter Emily, whose head will soon be swimming with the cultural/consumption/gender opportunities that going to college will offer, and Linda's son Tristan, who, while still a toddler, has changed her life forever. Both of us would also like to extend a special thank-you to our parents, who have inspired us. Finally, we thank our graduate assistants for their help and our students who enrich our lives every day. We are also grateful to have found each other at the University of Illinois and to continue our friendship and working relationship through this project and in the years to come.

Cele C. Otnes
University of Illinois at Urbana-Champaign

Linda Tuncay Zayer
Loyola University Chicago

About the Editors

Cele C. Otnes is the Investors in Business Education professor of marketing at the University of Illinois at Urbana-Champaign. She received her PhD from the University of Tennessee, Knoxville, her MA in advertising from the University of Texas at Austin, and her BA in English literature from Louisiana State University. Her research focuses on ritualistic consumption and how ritual practices by retailers and providers impact consumer experience. With Elizabeth Pleck, she is coauthor of *Cinderella Dreams: The Allure of the Lavish Wedding* (University of California Press, 2003) and, with Tina M. Lowrey, coeditor of *Contemporary Consumption Rituals: A Research Anthology.* Her work has appeared in numerous journals in marketing, advertising, and anthropology. She has served on the executive board of the Association of Consumer Research, as cochair of the Gender, Marketing and Consumer Behavior Conference (with Jonathan Schroeder in 2000), and as cochair of the Association for Consumer Research Conference (2012). She has taught courses on the undergraduate, MBA, and/or doctoral level in consumer behavior, consumer insights, marketing theory, and retailing. She is active in her church and enjoys yoga, cooking, traveling, and colleagues, and the challenge of parenting a creative and articulate teenager.

Linda Tuncay Zayer is associate professor of marketing at Loyola University Chicago. She received her PhD from the University of Illinois at Urbana-Champaign, MBA from the University of Notre Dame, and BS from Indiana University. Her research interests include how cultural discourses influence consumers. In particular, she examines how gender impacts identity, persuasion, and shopping behavior. Zayer's dissertation examined how men negotiate their gender identities in the marketplace. She has published in journals such as the *Journal of Consumer Research, Journal of Retailing,* and *Qualitative Market Research,* among others. She currently serves as the treasurer for the Consumer Culture Theory Consortium and the vice president of communications for the Consumer Behavior Special Interest Group of the American Marketing Association. In addition to working in academia, she owns a marketing consulting company, tealeaf consulting, and works with both small and large businesses.

About the Contributors

Mark Adkins, PhD, is a master group facilitator, program manager, and researcher who has facilitated hundreds of events for large groups of senior executives and general officers and managed multimillion dollar technology development programs. Since 1986, Dr. Adkins has been teaching, implementing, and conducting research in the fields of communication and information systems. His work in network technology has been used to develop Cyber Operations, a collaboration within the U.S. Department of Defense, and coordination of operations among all arms of the U.S. armed forces.

Gary J. Bamossy has a PhD from the University of Utah and is professor at Georgetown University. Prior to joining Georgetown, he was professor of marketing at the University of Utah. He has published widely in the field of globalization and consumer culture and is coeditor with Janeen Costa of *Marketing in a Multicultural World: Ethnicity, Nationalism and Cultural Identity.* He has coauthored many bestselling marketing textbooks that have been translated around the globe and has published articles in the *Academy of Management Journal, Journal of Consumer Psychology, Journal of Business Research,* and others.

Margo Buchanan-Oliver is professor of marketing and a director of the Center of Digital Enterprise (CODE) at the University of Auckland. Her current research focuses on sociocultural perceptions of digital technologies, the politics of the body, and the semiotics of representation. She has published in leading marketing journals and is a frequent peer reviewer.

Steven Chen is assistant professor of marketing, Fullerton's Mihaylo College of Business and Economics, at California State University. Before joining Cal State Fullerton, Steven received his BA in studio arts and a PhD in marketing management from the University of California-Irvine. Stemming from his background in art and design, Steven's principal research interest lies in the area of design thinking and new product development. His additional research interests include masculine consumption, Asian pop cultural flows, and stigma. Steven's research has been accepted in scholarly journals such as the *Journal of Product Innovation Management* and the *Journal of Business Research.*

Angeline G. Close is assistant professor of advertising at the University of Texas at Austin. Dr. Close obtained a PhD in business administration (marketing) from the University of Georgia's Terry College of Business in 2006. Her research focuses on *event marketing*—namely, how consumers' experiences at sponsored events influence attitudes and consumer behavior. Her research explains engaging consumers with events, uncovering drivers of effective event sponsorships, how entertainment impacts affect toward events/purchase intention toward sponsors, the role of sponsor–event congruity, and why consumers may resist events. Dr. Close's work has been published in the *Journal of the Academy of Marketing Science, Journal of Advertising Research,* and *Journal of Business Research,* among others.

Catherine A. Coleman is assistant professor of strategic communication in the Schieffer School of Journalism at Texas Christian University and works in the areas of advertising, marketing communications, and consumer behavior. Her research focuses on representation, vulnerability, and empowerment in advertising and marketing, particularly as these issues relate to gender and race, and on voice and engagement in consumer practices. She has a PhD from the Institute of Communications Research at the University of Illinois and is a graduate of Sewanee: The University of the South. She is a recipient of the distinguished American Association of University Women dissertation completion fellowship, and she has received the James Webb Young fund and the Verdell Frazier Award for Women, both at the University of Illinois. She has worked in marketing and advertising positions for the Health Sciences Group of the National Center for Supercomputing Applications (NCSA) at the University of Illinois, eVidient/GE Americom, and TMP Worldwide; she has experience in political polling and consulting in Washington, DC, and as a prevention specialist for sexual assault prevention.

Suraj Commuri is a member of the faculty in the School of Business at the University at Albany (State University of New York). He obtained his PhD from the University of Nebraska-Lincoln. His previous research has appeared in the *Journal of Marketing, Journal of Consumer Research,* and *Journal of Macromarketing.*

Gokcen Coskuner-Balli is assistant professor of marketing at Chapman University. Coskuner-Balli's research explores sociocultural shaping of consumer–market relationships. She is particularly interested in the ways in which these relationships are embedded in new meaning systems and social networks that are generated by marketplace dynamism in contemporary consumer culture. Her current research examines issues of masculinity and consumption—more specifically, the changing roles of men and fathers and the mobilization of marketplace resources to construct (alternative) masculinities. Coskuner-Balli's work has been published in the *Journal of Consumer Research, Journal of Consumer Culture,* and *Association of Consumer Research.*

Janeen Arnold Costa has a PhD from Stanford University and is marketing professor emerita at the University of Utah. She has published widely in many journals in consumer behavior. She was one of the early scholars to focus on the topic of gender and consumption and founded the Gender and Consumer Culture Conference in 1991, which held its 10th meeting in 2010. She is the editor of *Gender and Consumer Behavior* (Sage 2004) and has published in the *Journal of Consumer Research, Journal of Marketing,* and *Consumption, Markets and Culture,* among others.

Susan Dobscha is associate professor of marketing at Bentley University in Waltham, Massachusetts. Her research interests include sustainability and gender issues in marketing and consumer culture. Her work has appeared in the *Harvard Business Review, Journal of Public Policy and Marketing, Journal of Macromarketing,* and *Consumption, Markets, and Culture.* She served as cochair of the 9th ACR Conference on Gender, Marketing, and Consumer Behavior and is currently the associate editor for critical marketing and qualitative methodology for the *European Journal of Marketing.*

Burçak Ertimur is assistant professor of marketing at Fairleigh Dickinson University. Professor Ertimur's research interests center on the ways in which marketers and consumers interact in value cocreation processes and the implications for brand management and corporate

reputation management. Her current research on a new type of coproduction activity, "consumer-generated advertising," has been supported
by the Marketing Science Institute and received recognition by the
Society for Marketing Advances and the Academy of Marketing Science.
She has also presented her research papers at major conferences.

Eileen Fischer is professor of marketing and the Max and Anne
Tanenbaum Chair of Entrepreneurship and Family Enterprise at the
Schulich School of Business at York University. She received her PhD
from Queen's University in Kingston, Ontario in 1988. She is interested in
how consumers and entrepreneurs navigate their culturally constituted
milieus as they strive to achieve their goals. Her work has been published
in the *Journal of Consumer Research, Journal of Retailing, Journal of
Business Venturing, Journal of International Business, Entrepreneurship:
Theory and Practice, Consumption, Markets and Culture,* and a range
of other outlets. She currently serves as associate editor for both the
Journal of Consumer Research and *Journal of Business Venturing*. She is
also an editorial board member for a range of consumer research and
entrepreneurship journals.

James W. Gentry is the Maurice J. and Alice Hollman Professor of
Marketing at the University of Nebraska-Lincoln. He obtained his DBA
from Indiana University and has taught at Kansas State University,
Oklahoma State University, University of Wisconsin, and University of
Nebraska. His primary research area is consumer research, especially
focusing on family and gender issues. He is the North American editor of
the *Journal of Consumer Behavior.*

Ahir Gopaldas is a PhD candidate in the Department of Marketing at
the Schulich School of Business at York University in Toronto, Canada.
Integrating psychological and sociological concepts and methods, his
research portfolio aims to theorize and encourage environmental, fiscal,
and social responsibility in consumer culture. His dissertation, "Essays
on Consumption," was awarded the Association of Consumer Research
and Sheth Foundation dissertation award for public-purpose research
in 2010.

Robert L. Harrison is assistant professor of marketing at the Haworth College of Business at Western Michigan University. He obtained his PhD from the University of Nebraska-Lincoln. His primary research interests fall under the umbrella of consumer culture theory, particularly as it relates to family and gender issues, and holiday consumption. His research work is published, or forthcoming, in the *Journal of Advertising, Journal of Macromarketing,* and *Marketing Theory.*

Katie Ireland currently works as an account director for e-Dialog, an eBay company, which is an integrated digital marketing solutions provider. Her role focuses on building sustainable client relationships by facilitating the effective use of customer behavioral data to support operations, communications, and strategy. Katie's specialties include extensive experience within 1:1 direct online and off-line media planning, execution, and evaluation as an expert to retailer and consumer packaged goods (CPG) clients. Prior to her role at e-Dialog, she spent 4 years at dunnhumby, the data and marketing consultancy behind the success of the Tesco Clubcard. During this time, she worked with numerous blue chip clients, living and working in Europe, Asia, and North and Central America.

Jacqueline Lambiase teaches in Texas Christian University's Schieffer School of Journalism as associate professor of strategic communication. Her research focuses on gendered portrayals in advertising and mass media, on strategic uses of social media, on public relations ethics, and on other subjects explored through qualitative and rhetorical analyses. These studies have been published in refereed journals, including the *Western Journal of Communication, Language @ Internet, Journalism and Mass Communication Quarterly,* and the *Journal of Current Issues and Research in Advertising,* as well as in two coedited books with Tom Reichert: *Sex in Advertising: Perspectives on the Erotic Appeal* and *Sex in Consumer Culture: The Erotic Content of Media and Marketing.*

Michael S. LaTour is professor of marketing and Beam research fellow at the University of Nevada, Las Vegas. He earned his PhD, with honors, at the University of Mississippi. Prior to his arrival at UNLV in the fall of 2004, he was the Torchmark professor of marketing at Auburn University. His research interests focus on consumer memory, psychophysiological response to advertising, and gender issues in advertising. His research has appeared in or is forthcoming in a variety of highly ranked journals, including the *Journal of Consumer Research, Journal of Marketing, Journal of Advertising, Journal of Advertising Research*, and *Journal of the Academy of Marketing Science*.

Pauline Maclaran is professor of marketing and consumer research at Royal Holloway, University of London. Her research interests focus on cultural aspects of contemporary consumption, and she adopts a critical perspective to analyze the ideological assumptions that underpin many marketing activities, particularly in relation to gender issues. Her publications have appeared in internationally recognized journals such as the *Journal of Consumer Research, Psychology and Marketing, Journal of Advertising*, and *Consumption, Markets & Culture*. She has coedited various books, including *Marketing and Feminism: Current Issues and Research, Critical Marketing: Defining the Field*, and the *Handbook of Marketing Theory*. She is also editor in chief of *Marketing Theory*, a journal that promotes alternative and critical perspectives in marketing and consumer behavior.

Michelle R. Nelson is associate professor of advertising at the University of Illinois at Urbana-Champaign, where she received her PhD in 1997. Nelson's research, professional marketing communication experience, and teaching focus on intracultural (including gender) and international advertising and consumer behavior. She conducted research and worked in Denmark and England before assuming academic responsibilities in the United States. Nelson has published more than 40 book chapters and articles in journals such as the *Journal of Advertising, International Journal of Advertising, Journal of Advertising Research, Journal of Consumer Psychology, Sex Roles*, and *Journal of Cross-Cultural Psychology*. She is associate editor for the *International Journal of Advertising* and serves on the editorial board of the *Journal of Advertising*.

Jacob Ostberg is associate professor at The Center for Fashion Studies, Stockholm University, and holds a PhD in marketing from Lund University, Sweden. His current research projects explore discourses of masculinity in advertising and popular culture and how these discourses, alongside representations of class, are utilized in consumers' identity projects. Previous research has looked into consumers' handling of contrasting discourses of food and health as well as brands as cultural resources, and consumer tribes. His work has appeared in *Advances in Consumer Research; Consumption, Markets and Culture; Journal of Global Fashion Marketing; Journal of Marketing Management;* and *Marketing Theory,* as well as in several book chapters and books.

Nacima Ourahmoune is assistant professor in marketing at Reims Management School (RMS, France). Nacima received her doctoral degree in marketing from ESSEC Business School, Paris, France. Nacima obtained an MSc in politics (IEP and Exeter Univ.), an MSc in Management (HEC, Paris), an MSc in research in marketing (Paris 1 La Sorbonne University), and an MBA focused on the luxury sector. Nacima was previously a consultant in strategy and a marketer in the luxury industry in Paris. She contributes on a regular basis to various consultancy projects, using qualitative methods and bringing a cultural focus to managerial issues. Her academic research tackles sociocultural aspects of consumption and of branding, especially the way in which masculinities are constructed by the fashion market and reshaped by consumers' discourses and practices. Her work has been presented in 20 international conferences and published in *Advances in Consumer Research* and the forthcoming *Marketing Theory.*

Andrea Prothero is associate professor of marketing at University College Dublin, Ireland. Prior to moving to UCD in 1999, Andy lectured at universities in Wales and Scotland and she earned her PhD from the University of Cardiff. Andy's research broadly explores the area of marketing in society. Specific research projects have focused, for example, on advertising to children, motherhood and consumption, and sustainable consumption. The area of sustainability marketing has been a key focus of Andy's work since the early 1990s and she has published widely in this area. Andy was the guest editor of a special issue on green marketing in the *Journal of Marketing Management* in 1998. She currently serves as associate editor for the global policy and the environment track for the *Journal of Macromarketing* and as associate editor for the sustainability track for the *Journal of Marketing Management.* She has published in *Consumption, Markets and Culture,* the *European Journal of Marketing, Journal of Business Research, Journal of Consumer Culture, Journal of*

Macromarketing, Journal of Marketing Management, and *Journal of Public Policy and Marketing.*

Tom Reichert is professor in the Department of Advertising and Public Relations, Grady College of Journalism and Mass Communication, at the University of Georgia, where he teaches advertising courses. His research interests include social marketing and the content, effects, and strategic uses of sexual information in marketing communication. He authored *The Erotic History of Advertising* and coedited *Sex in Advertising: Perspectives on the Erotic Appeal.* His research has appeared in a variety of journals, including the *Journal of Advertising, Journal of Current Issues and Research in Advertising,* and *Journal of Communication.*

Hope Jensen Schau is associate professor of marketing and Susan Bulkeley Butler fellow and holds the Gary M. Munsinger Chair in Entrepreneurship and Innovation at the Eller College of Management, University of Arizona. She earned her PhD from the University of California, Irvine. Her research focuses on the impact of technology on marketplace relationships, branding, identity-salient consumption practices, and collaborative consumption. She has published in the *Journal of Consumer Research, Journal of Marketing, Journal of Retailing, Journal of Advertising,* and *Journal of Macromarketing.*

Lorna Stevens has been in academia since 1994 and, prior to that, spent 10 years working in the book publishing industry in Ireland and the UK. Her research interests lie in the areas of feminist perspectives and gender issues in marketing, consumer behavior, and consumption and the media. She is particularly interested in women's consumption of magazines and advertising texts, and the wider social and cultural context that frames women's reception of media texts generally. How womanhood is represented in such texts and how representations of women, including symbolic archetypes of womanhood, are interpreted by women consumers are of particular interest. She has published in the *Journal of Consumer Behavior, Journal of Advertising,* and *Journal of Strategic Marketing,* among others.

Alexandra M. Vilela received her PhD from the University of Wisconsin-Madison in 2006 and is assistant professor of advertising of the Mass Communication and Communication Studies Department at Towson

University in Maryland. Vilela's current research is focused primarily on cause-related marketing, corporate social responsibility, gender, global issues in advertising, and social strategic communication campaigns (philanthropy/charity and civic engagement volunteering). Her professional experience is varied. Prior to arriving in the United States, Vilela worked for more than 10 years in advertising, marketing, public relations, and journalism in South America and Europe.

Helen Woodruffe-Burton joined academia following a career in the banking and computing industries. Prior to joining Newcastle Business School, she was director of the graduate school at the University of Cumbria and she has also worked at Lancaster University Management School and the University of Salford. During this time, she has developed her work as an interpretive consumer researcher, writing extensively on consumer behavior as well as on issues relating to methodology and reflexivity. Helen cochaired the 10th International Conference on Gender, Marketing and Consumer Behavior in 2010 (with Lisa Peñaloza, EDHEC Business School), sponsored by the Association for Consumer Research (ACR). An elected fellow of the Chartered Institute of Marketing and a chartered marketer, Helen is also a member of the UK Academy of Marketing and the ACR.

Section I

Feminist Theory and Discourses

1

Construction of Consumer Vulnerability by Gender and Ethics of Empowerment

Catherine A. Coleman

> Thank you, ignorance.
> Thank you for starting the conversation...
> And thank you for making all of us realize that we still have a
>   long way to go.
>
> **Nike advertisement (created by Wieden & Kennedy)**
> *The New York Times, Sunday, April 15, 2007*

INTRODUCTION

A tradition of market discourse—of women in the marketplace and of the market as a gendered concept—has positioned women as particularly vulnerable. Various feminist evaluations of consumer society have asserted that women have been exploited by stereotypical imagery and by marketplace values (Bordo, 1993; Friedan, 1977; Kilbourne, 1999; Wolf, 1992). Within the framework of advertising and marketing theories, vulnerability is not associated with white adult male consumers, but rather with groups considered weak and, in marketplace contexts, often emotional and irrational—and female (or otherwise marginalized, as by being poor or Black).

This chapter offers a sociohistoric inquiry into prevailing discourses on gender and consumption that seeks to challenge the implicitness, infused in popular and scholarly thought, of women's vulnerability in the marketplace and to offer an ethical framework through which to approach gender and vulnerability. Consumer research defines vulnerability by socioeconomic and demographic variables such as gender, race, age, and income (for a critique of this practice, see Baker, Gentry, & Rittenburg, 2005). Advertising images of (and targeted toward) these so-called vulnerable groups have been feared in contemporary critiques as major moral threats (Scott, 2005). While sometimes acknowledging the complex interactions of consumers with advertising and with the market, such critiques tend to emphasize and extend assumptions of group weakness (Andrews, 1996), despite a lack of empirical evidence to support such assumptions (Bristor & Fischer, 1993; Frenzen & Davis, 1990; Ringold, 2005).

While scholars have begun to reevaluate the discourses that question women's autonomy and intelligence and presume their vulnerability in the marketplace (Bristor & Fischer, 1993; Scott, 2005), dialogues of disempowerment affect not only the practices of marketing but also the legal and ethical determinations of those practices that, instead, may suppress women's opportunities even while claiming to protect them. Thus, while criticisms of marketing and advertising practices and the industry's treatment of vulnerable audiences are important, it is equally critical to question the ways in which vulnerability is constructed through gender and the effects of such definitions as they are implemented in formal and structural ways.

The intent of this chapter is to examine prevailing discourses of gender and vulnerability, to develop understanding of how these discourses influence the construction of consumer vulnerability, and to propose a dialogic ethics of empowerment in discourses of gender and consumption. I examine previous literature and the construction of vulnerability in the context of a gendered market legacy. To ground this discussion in real circumstances, I examine prevailing discourses of gender and vulnerability through two historical cases. The first case involves the regulation of Plan B contraceptives in the United States and is a powerful example of how the construction of women as vulnerable can limit their access to resources and their ability to make informed choices in the market.

The second case, involving Don Imus's remarks about the Rutgers women's basketball team and Nike's response, shows how long-standing prejudices at the intersection of race and gender persist and how the market can be a space for countervailing voices of empowerment. With these circumstances in mind and having demonstrated the impact of defining women as vulnerable, I propose a dialogic ethics of empowerment as an appropriate alternative to historically dominant approaches to gender and vulnerability.

This work focuses on discourses of women as particularly vulnerable and does so consciously to explore the impact of long-standing and deeply ingrained conceptions of the female consumer; however, these characterizations have also meant that, until recently, masculinity and consumption have been underexplored (Holt & Thompson, 2004; Schroeder & Zwick, 2004; Zayer, 2010). As with femininity, sweeping characterizations of masculinity contribute to the marginalization of those who may not adhere to dominant gender roles for men. This work, while focusing on the disempowerment of women, speaks in many ways to the disempowerment of those whose voice and agency are marginalized and usurped.

CONSTRUCTING GENDER AND POWER

The power to define which groups are vulnerable is the power to define meaning and position within a society (Brummett, 1994; Clawson & Trice, 2000) and is the capacity either to uplift or to denigrate these groups (Gilliam, Iyengar, Simon, & Wright, 1996; Peffley, Hurwitz, & Sniderman, 1997). Yet a satisfactory understanding of vulnerability in consumer realms has remained elusive and, in large part, has been based on demographic and socioeconomic variables. With few exceptions (DeLorme, Huh, & Reid, 2006), being elderly, young, female, poor, a minority, or urban (a term generally used to mean poor minorities in urban centers) makes up the defining categories of vulnerability (Andreasen, 1975; Benet, Pitts, & LaTour, 1993; Blair & Hyatt, 1995; Hill, 2005; Kilbourne, 1999; Pechman, Levine, Loughlin, & Leslie, 2005; Sautter & Oretskin, 1997; Smith & Cooper-Martin, 1997; Stern, Russell, & Russell, 2005; Wolf, 1992) and is the focus of concerns over persuasive attempts by and the targeting practices of marketers and advertisers. As one article points out, "Heretofore consumer vulnerability has been equated to *who* experiences vulnerability, with the implication that some categories of people, because of their membership in a defined class, are *always* vulnerable" (Baker et al., 2005, p. 128). This practice has continued despite a lack of empirical evidence to support sweeping characterizations of vulnerability by gender, age, and minority status (Baker et al., 2005; Ringold, 2005).

The emphasis on demographics has led to a critique of scholarship on vulnerable consumers as deterministic and reductionist, neglecting a wide range of complex social and cultural forces. Similar criticisms have been made of traditional characterizations of gender. Scholars have demonstrated that the complexities of gender have long been underexplored. As Schroeder (2003) writes, "Gender is much more than a demographic, personality, or 'individual differences' variable—it is a basic cognitive construct, cultural category and political concept that intersects with the entire realm of consumer behavior" (p. 1).

Gender researchers today understand gender to be a fluid, culturally based concept associated with masculinity and femininity and consider sex to be biological categories of male and female (Bettany, Dobscha, O'Malley, & Prothero, 2010; Palan, 2001; Zayer, 2010). However, discourses of vulnerability have not clearly attended to these distinctions and have conflated gender and sex by lumping gender with demographic and socioeconomic variables such as age and income while also relying on long-standing historical prejudices about gender roles. This has been a particularly problematic practice because gender is a complex and contested domain that, when reduced to one perspective or to generalizations, can "mask a wide diversity of perspectives" (Fischer & Bristor, 1995, p. 535). This emphasis on gender as a demographic variable has influenced not only the production and reinforcement of women as vulnerable, but also how gender and vulnerability are defined in popular and scholarly discourse.

Legacy of the Rational Market and the Irrational Consumer

Frequently, membership in a vulnerable class is equated with irrationality. Andreasen (1975) has been credited with bringing issues of the urban (minority) poor in the United States to the attention of consumer researchers, arguing that marketing and advertising have an important role in improving their situation. In doing so, he explores the argument frequently lodged against the disadvantaged and particularly the poor that they act irrationally and, in doing so, are implicit in their own disadvantage. Andreasen's work on minority poor is informative, as similar prejudices are often reflected in discourses of a gendered marketplace that contrast a rational, masculine production sphere with an emotional, feminine consumer space.

The traditional legacy of advertising in economic and legal discourse in the United States is one of democratic and rational debate. It assumes advertising provides an important public service by offering proper information for the marketplace to flourish through rational and informed decision processes—a view upheld, for example, in the United States Supreme Court in *Bigelow v. Virginia* (1975), a right-to-know case involving abortion clinic advertising and again under the doctrine of free speech in *Virginia Board of Pharmacy v. Virginia Citizen's Consumer Council, Inc.* (1976). But in the expansive history of advertising and marketing theory, these cases, while they are precedents, only offer one view of the marketplace. Conflicting concepts of advertising—as catering to consumers' rational capacities and as manipulating consumer desires—reflect deep-seated historical depictions of the marketplace that envision seductive consumption environments as contrasted with the organization and rationality of production spheres.

This terminology further perpetuates criticisms of masculine biases that portray consumers as passive and feminine (Bristor & Fischer, 1993; Hirschman, 1993; Ramsay, 1996; Schroeder & Borgerson, 1998; Scott, 2005). Men are constructed as rational producers and portrayed as marketers and advertisers with power over the persuasion environment; women are treated as emotional consumers, with assumed weaknesses to persuasive appeals, who lack agency and who pose a variety of threats to themselves and to the rational masculine world (Fischer & Bristor, 1995; Hollows, 2000; Litosseliti, 2002; Neve, 2009).

Feminist Critiques

Scholars have demonstrated a tradition of discourse about women's vulnerability in the marketplace. The female consumer (in particular, the housewife) is labeled as vulnerable both through marketing and advertising and by critics. She is portrayed in submissive positions in popular media and is defined as submissive in feminist critiques. She is also historically defined as the consumer. As Neve (2009) describes it,

> Industrialization saw the development of gender roles in which the attributes of the feminine were newly defined wholly in terms of a domestic and private sphere...an unspoken underlying assumption that women were naturally and innately suited to mothering and domestic roles, including shopping. (pp. 2–3)

It was these assumptions and the relegation of women to the home against which much second wave feminist work reacted. Betty Friedan's

The Feminine Mystique (1997), first published in 1963, is often cited as the impetus for second wave feminism in the United States; it was also the first attack on advertising in the feminist literature. In it, Friedan was particularly critical of the homemaker role as stifling and unfulfilling. In this way, the second wave developed out of an initial disapproval of the housewife and the consumer and incorporated an element of antimarket ideology that emanated largely from the politics of many of the new feminists (Scott, 2005). Hollows (2000) argues that "consumption can be derided by aligning it with 'feminine' qualities and femininity can be derided by aligning it with consumption. Furthermore, the female consumer enslaved by her desire for goods has been seen as politically dangerous" (p. 115). Under their arguments, for example, no advertisement was acceptable for feminism based on Marxist/Freudian principles, by which they gave advertising a certain power over women—women other than themselves—that they assumed rather than tested (Scott, 2005).

Second wave feminists did such a good job of setting themselves up as experts on the housewife that marketers were turning to them for direction and researchers were encouraging it. One article proposed, "Thus, when the copy involves a children's product, educators and psychologists may be used as consumerist experts. When the product is a household product, feminists can be brought in as consumer experts" (Laric & Tucker, 1977, p. 33). By the 1970s, a large body of literature attacking advertising's portrayal of women had begun to develop and was heavily reliant on fears of female vulnerability and on a persistent distrust of the media and its role in women's oppression (Scott, 2005). Thus, through a discourse of female consumer vulnerability, long-standing prejudices about women's position in the market were further perpetuated.

However, scholarship in the wake of second wave feminism has looked more critically at the implications of second wave feminist explanations and critiques of gender roles and has expressed a need to incorporate more diverse expressions of gender that do not isolate it from other factors of identity such as race, class, ethnicity, religion, and sexual orientation. Fischer and Bristor (1995) explain that the tendency of many feminist theories to assume commonality among women "means that many women have found little enlightenment about the conditions of their own lives, much less substantive improvements in those conditions, as the result of mainstream feminist thought" (p. 526). They further argue that Betty Friedan's corrective for women's problems—that is, that the solution would be to escape the plight of the housewife and get out of the home—"simply ignored the fact that millions of women have always worked outside their own homes, often as domestic labor for the very women whose concerns Friedan was addressing" (p. 527). The authors call for greater recognition of the complexity of gender and recognition that examining sexism independently of other biases can prioritize the already privileged and neglect to give voice to the already disenfranchised.

Thus, while marketing practitioners and scholars have acknowledged that social realities of gender are complex and relate in complex ways to the market (Bettany et al., 2010; Fischer & Bristor, 1995; Schroeder, 2003; Scott, 2005), discourse about capable women in consumer realms has been tempered by ingrained conceptions of the gendered forces of the marketplace. A tradition of market discourses has positioned women both as consumers and as vulnerable, failing to acknowledge the multiple and dynamic aspects of gender and vulnerability.

Rethinking Vulnerability

Recent scholarship in marketing and advertising has rejuvenated attention to issues of consumer vulnerability and has begun to reexamine definitions of this concept (Baker, 2009; Baker et al., 2005; Commuri & Ekici, 2008). The *Journal of Macromarketing* dedicated a 2005 special issue to vulnerable consumers, calling for a broadened understanding of the intersection of individual and structural factors in marketplace vulnerability (Hill, 2005). The first article of this issue proposes a "consumer-driven definition of consumer vulnerability" that does not fall prey to the misconception that vulnerability arises from demographic variables and avoids the paternalism often inherent in discourses of vulnerability (Baker et al., 2005). The authors provide an informative review of previous scholarship on vulnerability, but, more importantly, they place prevalent constructions of vulnerability under a critical scope and provide a sound basis from which to move forward.

Some scholars have championed the inclusion and maintenance of class-based perspectives (such as sex, education, and race) based on the notion that policy development may not be flexible enough to account for transient state-based needs (Commuri & Ekici, 2008). But other scholars have demonstrated, as this chapter does, the problematic effects of externally constructed, class-based views of vulnerability. Baker et al. (2005) make the distinction, drawn from Smith and Cooper-Martin (1997), between actual and perceived vulnerability. Perceived vulnerability is derived from expectations of what the experiences of others must be like, rather than what they truly are. The authors argue that actual vulnerability is "understood only by listening to and observing the experiences of the consumer" (p. 128) and only through that understanding can marketers and public policy makers base their decision.

Baker et al. (2005) propose a definition of consumer vulnerability that works to account for the complexity of consumer vulnerability and behavior that stems from various interactions of states, characteristics, and situations. Further, they assert that conceptions of vulnerability must be drawn from consumers themselves, allow for consumer agency, and acknowledge that regulatory responses to protect consumers can also inhibit agency. Drawing from Baker et al. (2005), others have suggested the opportunity to develop new and expanded perspectives that account for the complexity of interactions or relationships that drive vulnerability in the marketplace (Baker, 2009; Shultz & Holbrook, 2009).

Shultz and Holbrook (2009) question whether the sustenance of modern socioeconomic systems is contingent on the factors that lead to vulnerability in others. Power and the perception of it are important determinants of consumer behavior. Those in positions to regulate messages in the marketplace, whether formally or informally, have a real effect on consumer vulnerability. Henry (2005) found that the experience of power influences consumption practices through its effect on the experience of social class and on self-concept. Baker et al. (2005) argue that policy response can affect consumer experience of vulnerability by either facilitating or impeding consumer agency (see also Baker, 2009). The situation becomes complex indeed if the very same systems that define vulnerability are in fact its main contributors.

CONSTRUCTING THE VULNERABLE WOMAN

Previous scholarship demonstrates that both consumers and gender are represented, constructed, and contested in complex and subtle ways through scholarly, marketing, and popular discourse and through media systems such as advertising (Cayla & Peñaloza, 2006; Grow, 2008; O'Guinn

& Shrum, 1997). To illuminate ways in which conceptions of women as particularly vulnerable affect market and consumer practices in subtle and profound ways, I offer two examples. The example of Plan B contraceptive debates in the United States demonstrates how fears about female sexuality and female vulnerability can lead to structures of regulation that further disempower women. This case is entwined with the loud voices that set the dialogue for debates about abortion (for a consumer behavior perspective on abortion in America, see Patterson, Hill, & Maloy, 1995).

However, it is not the intention of this work to engage in a debate or draw conclusions about abortion, but rather to focus on the discourse and practices of the FDA, an agency charged with consumer protection, in a case over the marketing and market availability of a product and to ask whom it is protecting and what logic or fears are driving this protection. The example of Nike's advertising response to offensive comments by radio shock jock Don Imus in 2007 against Rutgers University's women's basketball team demonstrates a moment in a longer history of the relationship of Nike marketing to women and to Black communities that offers themes and debates of disempowerment and empowerment.

Plan B and Female Sexuality

Plan B (a product of Teva Pharmaceutical Industries Ltd., formerly Barr Pharmaceuticals and formerly Women's Capital Corporation) was approved as a prescription form of emergency contraception on July 28, 1999. However, because it works best when taken within 24 hours and should be taken within 72 hours of intercourse to be effective, it must be obtained quickly (GAO-06-109, 2005; Harris, 2006; Schorn, 2009). On this basis, the manufacturer applied for over-the-counter (OTC) status for the drug in 2001. *The New York Times* called the issue of FDA approval for OTC sales of Plan B contraceptives one of the most contentious in the agency's 100-year history, a significant statement about a regulatory body with oversight of a quarter of the U.S. economy (Harris, 2006).

The issue is politically charged and debates over the drug are conflated with those over abortion, with many of the arguments for legal restrictions mimicking similar concerns over women's ability to make rational, agentic choices (Manian, 2009). Proponents of Plan B argue the drug works much like regular contraceptive pills in preventing ovulation or fertilization (Harris, 2006), thereby decreasing the likelihood of abortions (Healy, 2006); opponents argue that it is a "chemical abortion" (Schorn, 2009).

Because Plan B does not terminate an established pregnancy, but rather is an emergency contraceptive and is not related to RU-486, commonly known as the "abortion pill" (Harris, 2009), the debate revolves around a small percentage of cases when a fertilized egg could form if a woman has unprotected sex during ovulation and the drug potentially could prevent a fertilized egg from becoming implanted (Harris, 2006; Schorn, 2009), though this possibility is contested. The journal of the Catholic Health Association published findings that Plan B only works as a contraceptive and does not prevent implantation of a fertilized egg ("Catholic Journal Says Plan B Does Not Cause Abortions," 2010). While acknowledgment of the debates over abortion and issues affecting the approval of Plan B is necessary, the intention in this chapter is not to argue for or against the approval of this drug for OTC use or to discuss abortion rights and wrongs, but rather to explore the discourses of women's vulnerability both implicit and explicit in the debate and in the U.S. government's handling of decisions surrounding this drug.

Imagine a scenario in which a woman needs Plan B on a weekend but cannot gain access to her doctor until Monday morning. As Dr. Susan Wood, former head of the FDA's Office of Women's Health and one of the scientists in the agency arguing for Plan B OTC approval, indicated,

> If it's safe, and it is, and effective, it's more effective the quicker you have it. This is why it needs to be over-the-counter…Getting to a physician to get a prescription, getting that prescription to the pharmacy and getting it filled takes time, as we all know. (Schorn, 2009)

On this basis and on the belief that Plan B and similar drugs were important options in the cases of rape, broken condoms, missed birth control pills, or unprotected sex, various individuals and organizations argued for the OTC availability of Plan B.

In 2001, a citizens' petition backed by over 60 women's health organizations was filed with the FDA requesting approval for direct OTC access to Plan B and similar prescription-only contraceptives (United States Government Accountability Office [GAO], 2005; *Tummino v. Torti*, 2009). The petition was accompanied by affidavits from health officials, including one from the chair of a World Health Organization task force that had conducted the most comprehensive trials on Plan B at that time; it was further endorsed by the American Medical Association, the American College of Obstetricians and Gynecologists, the American Public Health Association, and the American Academy of Pediatrics (Schorn, 2009; *Tummino v. Torti*, 2009). An application by the manufacturer of Plan B soon followed.

In 2002, officials from the FDA met to discuss the anticipated application by the manufacturer of Plan B requesting that the marketing status of the drug be switched to OTC, which they received in 2003 (GAO-06-109, 2005). According to a report originally aired November 27, 2005, and again in 2009 on CBS's *60 Minutes* (Schorn, 2009), that same year an anti-abortion-rights gynecologist, Dr. David Hager, received a request from the Bush White House asking him to serve alongside two other anti-abortion-rights physicians on the FDA advisory committee that was to review Plan B's OTC application. Two FDA advisory committees, made up of outside experts such as medical professionals and researchers, voted unanimously that Plan B would be safe for OTC use and voted 23 to 4 in favor of the proposed switch from prescription to OTC without age or point-of-sale restrictions. Further, the joint advisory committee voted 27 to 1 that "Plan B could be appropriately used as recommended by the label and that the actual use data were generalizable to the overall population, including adolescents" (GAO-06-109, 2005, p. 14; *Tummino v. Torti*, 2009).

Nonetheless, despite these recommendations by the FDA's own scientists, the acting director of the Center for Drug Evaluation and Research (CDER) signed a "not-approvable" letter. While the FDA is not legally compelled to follow the recommendations of the joint advisory board, this was the only one of 23 other prescriptions-to-OTC switch applications the FDA had received between 1994 and 2004 for which the FDA went against the recommendation of the advisory committee. The FDA's rationale cited concerns about the product's safety for women under 16 (again, despite evidence suggesting its safety for adolescents and approval of the drug for OTC use by health organizations such as the American Academy of Pediatrics). Even after Barr Pharmaceuticals, the manufacturer of Plan B, submitted an amended application for OTC use for women 17 years of age and older, the FDA delayed action and later rather arbitrarily approved OTC use for women 18 years of age and older (GAO-06-109, 2005). Further, access was limited to behind-the-counter sales and required controversial identification checks ("Plan B Morning After Pill," 2011).

Court records later charged that this decision to approve nonprescription use for women over 18 was a political bargaining tool to appease Senators Hillary Clinton and Pat Murray from further impeding the confirmation of the incoming FDA commissioner out of concern for the capricious decision making in the Plan B case (*Tummino v. Torti*, 2009, p. 24). The Family Research Council and various other groups also sued the FDA based on the argument that the FDA had yielded to political pressure in its decision, but their concern was improper political pressure by Senators Clinton and Murray (Fagan, 2007). Thus, despite the side of the issues upon one might fall, it becomes increasingly clear that politics has molded the debate and outweighed science and even women's health in these deliberations.

In August 2005, the FDA's assistant commissioner for the Office of Women's Health, Dr. Susan Wood, resigned in protest of the FDA leader's refusal to allow OTC access to emergency contraceptives despite the FDA's own scientists' recommendations and of its forestalling of further decisions on the matter (Wood, 2005; "FDA Official Quits," 2005). The GAO was asked to investigate the matter and its investigation identified four unusual aspects of the FDA's review process:

- The officials who normally would have been responsible for signing an action letter disagreed with the not-approvable decision and thus did not sign it.
- The GAO found an unusual level of involvement by high-level management (GAO-06-109, 2005). The appointment of the anti-abortion-rights gynecologist Dr. David Hager was one such example (Schorn, 2009). Hager argued in committee meetings that the use of Plan B may increase a woman's risk of sexually transmitted diseases, contrary to the 40 studies reviewed by the advisory panel demonstrating that Plan B leads neither to an increase in cases of sexually transmitted diseases nor to riskier sexual behaviors (Schorn, 2009). A *New York Times* article suggested FDA officials were working "to appease the administration's constituents" (Harris, 2006), and court proceedings further indicated White House involvement (*Tummino v. Torti*, 2009).
- The GAO discovered conflicting accounts of whether or not the decision to approve the application was made before the reviews were completed (GAO-06-109, 2005). Sworn depositions of some of the agency's staff members indicated their belief that the FDA's political

appointees were not going to approve the application, regardless of the scientific evidence (Harris, 2006).

- The FDA was found to have followed a review process that was inconsistent with its traditional practices and to have used a novel rationale. The GAO's review of 67 other OTC switch applications indicated that the Plan B decision was not typical. While the FDA does have the right to make decisions independently of its advisory committees, "recommendations of an advisory committee that are strongly supported by the FDA's review staff have rarely, if ever, been overturned at the highest level of the agency, as they were both in the decision to reject nonprescription status for Plan B" (Wood, 2005, p. 1651) and through the repeated delays they imposed in the process.

Nonetheless, the not-approvable decision was made on a basis of concerns over "the potential impact that the OTC marketing of Plan B would have on the propensity for younger adolescents to engage in unsafe sexual behaviors" (GAO-06-109, 2005, p. 5), despite the FDA review staff's conclusion that these concerns could not be supported. An actual use study demonstrated that the "frequency of unprotected sex did not increase, condom use did not decrease, and the overall use of effective contraception did not decrease [with the use of Plan B]" (*Tummino v. Torti*, 2009, p. 10); these studies were supplemented with research indicating that young adolescents could safely use Plan B as an OTC drug. Further, Plan B has been marketed as a nonroutine backup method of birth control in cases of sexual assault, missed birth control pills, and unprotected sex and through advertisements such as, "I chose a condom but it broke. I have a second chance with Plan B contraception."

Bernadine Healy, MD, health editor for *U.S. News & World Report* and former CEO of the Red Cross, said that these arguments were "a fancy way of saying access to contraceptives would drive young women to reckless sex...[S]purious concerns both about women's sexual behavior and about abortion fuel the seemingly endless tempest surrounding...[the] lawful use of [a] drug" (Healy, 2006). In response to this "despicable treatment of women at the hands of the FDA" (Healy, 2006), the American College of Obstetricians and Gynecologists (AGOG) launched a morning-after prescription-writing campaign called "Ask Me" designed to educate women about emergency contraception and to provide them with on-hand prescriptions—in effect creating something similar to an OTC option (ACOG, 2006; Healy, 2006). The FDA, for its part, continued to drag its feet.

In 2009, a district court judge determined that "the FDA repeatedly and unreasonably delayed issuing a decision on the emergency contraceptive for suspect reasons...[and] political considerations...were not the only evidence of a lack of good faith" (*Tummino v. Torti,* 2009, p. 1). The judge remanded the decision to the FDA over the denial of the citizen petition to make Plan B and similar drugs available for OTC use without age restrictions; the judge further ordered the FDA to lower the age of OTC access from 18, which the agency had assigned arbitrarily, to 17. (In fact, FDA review staff and scientists had determined that Plan B was safe OTC without age restriction, but in an effort to get compliance from the FDA, the manufacturers had resubmitted a request with the age limit of 17 rather than the original no age limit.) Yet still, according to a motion for civil contempt filed in 2010, the FDA failed "to make any meaningful efforts to comply" with the 2009 decision; the finding was that the FDA had acted "in bad faith and in response to political pressure" and the FDA was directed to reconsider its denial of the citizen petition (*Tummino v. Hamburg,* 2010, p. 1).

The sometimes subtle and other times blatant discourse aimed at controlling women's sexuality and health decisions continues even after proceedings have repeatedly demonstrated that politics, and not science or even fair deliberation, have dominated. In early 2011, *Fox News* reported:

> Less than 2 years after the Food and Drug Administration approved Plan B, the so-called "morning after pill" for over-the-counter access by women 17 years of age and older, the drug's maker is now seeking to lift the age restrictions on the controversial product. (Brandt, 2011)

Never mind that the original petition for OTC access to women of all ages was originally filed years earlier and was not approved by the FDA in what the GAO determined to be misguided proceedings. In response to this application and after years of debate, the FDA, under Commissioner Margaret Hamburg, M.D., concluded, "There is adequate and reasonable, well-supported, and science-based evidence that Plan B One-Step is safe and effective and should be approved for nonprescription use for all females of child-bearing potential" (Hamburg, 2011). Yet, in a surprising and unprecedented move, the U.S. Department of Health and Human

Services (HHS) Secretary Kathleen Sebelius overruled the FDA's decision (Sebelius, 2011; Stein, 2011). While President Obama has insisted he did not intervene in the HHS decision (Favole, 2011), others have pointed to election politics (Stein, 2011). Of concern for this chapter is not the ultimate decisions, but rather the manner in which they have been made.

Concerns over women's ability to use emergency contraceptives safely, whether they would use Plan B as a license for promiscuity and to engage in unsafe sexual behaviors, or that it could even lead to sexual abuse ("Plan B Morning-After Pill," 2011) continue to dominate discussions. These concerns are tied very closely to the marketing and market availability of the drug and therefore to women's access to it and their ability make informed choices. Nowhere is it clear that women's voices, varied as they may be, were considered for decisions that clearly were not made on scientific evidence but rather through political structures of protectionism heavily influenced by dominant discourses over women's sexuality.

Don Imus and Nike at the Intersection of Race and Gender

Did He Just Say That? Don Imus on Race and Gender

On April 3, 2007, 35 years after Title IX was passed in the United States, in the CBS radio broadcast and MSNBC simulcast of his daily radio show, *Imus in the Morning,* Don Imus said of the Rutgers University women's basketball team:

> That's some rough girls from Rutgers. Man, they got tattoos and…That's some nappy-headed hos there. I'm gonna tell you that now, man, that's some—woo. And the girls from Tennessee, they all look cute, you know, so, like—kinda like—I don't know.

The show's producer, Bernard McGuirk, responded, "A Spike Lee thing" (quoted from Cooky, Wachs, Messner, & Dworkin, 2010, p. 140).

Days later, in spite of ratings hikes his show had been enjoying over the previous year (Johnson, 2007) and after repeated calls from various activist organizations, the program's key sponsors pulled their support and MSNBC cancelled its simulcast, followed by CBS, which fired Imus on April 12 (Cooky et al., 2010). Imus's language reportedly was reiterated in a roll call by a police sergeant and an officer addressing two African

American and one Latina officers at a Brooklyn precinct (Herbert, 2007). Imus's remarks were not simply "some idiot comment meant to be amusing," as Imus said in his apology (Carr, 2007, as quoted in Cooky et al., 2010, p. 147); they were used to affect the position of women in real ways.

Scholarship has demonstrated the perpetuation of blatant and subtle prejudices across race and gender in various media (Kern-Foxworth, 1994) and in cross-cultural settings (Paek, Nelson, & Vilela, 2011). Coltrane and Messineo (2000) demonstrate how, despite years of criticism and calls for improvement in representations and even amid the popularity of such programs as *The Cosby Show,* 1990s television advertising tended to "portray White men as powerful, White women as sex objects, African American men as aggressive, and African American women as inconsequential" (p. 363). Tracing the circumstances within a longer legacy of stereotypes that become apparent whenever Black women excel in sports, a *New York Times* story on the Imus media event quoted author Paula Giddings: "We have been perceived as token women in Black texts and token Blacks in feminist texts" (Rhoden, 2007, p. D7).

Cooky et al. (2010) argue that the media packaged the "race stories" in such a way as to construct a unitary Black community and silenced voices of knowledge at the intersection of race, gender, and sexuality. The study found that rarely did the stories mention Imus's remarks about the cute opposing team and suggestions that the women were not attractive enough on the basketball court (see also Givhan, 2007). Because Imus cast these women with racial slurs, race became the salient aspect of the controversy over the sexist and sexualized aspects of his comments, and "other ways of knowing," such as those at the intersection of race, gender, and sexuality, "are obscured" (Cooky et al., 2010, p. 156). The entire issue became obscured when, 8 months later, Imus was back at the microphone on his *Imus in the Morning* show alongside Karith Foster, who some dubbed his "Black sidekick" ("Mouth From the South," 2007). More recently, *Newsweek* named Imus number seven on its Power 50 list for the combined $11 million he brings home from his contracts with ABC radio and Fox Business ("Newsweek's Power 50," 2010).

In response to Don Imus's remarks and the controversy surrounding them, Nike took out a full-page ad in the Sunday, April 14, *New York Times.* The ad, developed by Wieden & Kennedy, intended to show support for the Nike-sponsored team:

Thank you, ignorance.
Thank you for starting the conversation.
Thank you for making an entire nation listen to the Rutgers'
team story. And for making us wonder what other great
stories we've missed.
Thank you for reminding us to think before we speak.
Thank you for showing us how strong and poised 18- and
20-year-old women can be.
Thank you for showing us that sport includes more than the
time spent on the court.
Thank you for unintentionally moving women's sport forward.
And thank you for making all of us realize that we still have a
long way to go.
Next season starts 11.16.07.

Nike's U.S. media-relations director, Dean Stoyer, was quoted in *Advertising Age* as saying, "We believe the elevated conversations around racism, sexism, inequality and disrespect in America need to move forward and not disappear when the events…are no longer front-page news" (Thomaselli, 2007). He further pointed out that Imus's name was absent to keep the focus on the issues and not on the event. Nike followed with a campaign that included billboards, a website with videos and a forum for women to share sports stories, and television and web ads in which some 18 of their female spokespersons shared unscripted monologues about their achievements.

The themes of the campaign reflected concepts that had emerged in interviews Nike conducted with 175 teenage females around the country and, with the unscripted format used by Wieden & Kennedy, they reflected themes of power and inequality faced by professional athletes. While Nike acknowledged the branding efforts that accompanied the campaign aimed at the women's market, of which they held almost 20% worldwide, Nike representatives and spokespersons indicated that they were also trying to offer a platform for women and girls (Sandomir, 2007).

While "Nike has a history of support for women's sports" and was honored in 2007 by the Advertising Women of New York for "10 years of getting it" (Howard & Petrecca, 2007), the history is a sorted, contested one both internally and externally. Similarly, the company has a long-standing relationship with Black communities and athletes that demonstrates themes of both inclusion and exclusion, support and oppression. In particular, scholars looking at the development of Nike's marketing and advertising messages point to the company's inclusiveness and positive representations of African Americans, women, and the disabled, while other scholars point to the company's scandals with foreign factory workers, particularly young women, and to the commodification of race and gender.

Nike's foreign and production practices and implications of globalization are of great import and have been explored elsewhere in the media and in popular and in scholarly work (Dukcevich, 2001; Goldman & Papson, 1998; LaFeber, 1999; Stabile, 2000) and, more recently, through Nike's own research ("Nike: Malaysian Factory Violates Major Rights," 2008; Boot, 2008). For differing and more comprehensive treatments of Nike's relationship with women, see, for example, Grow (2008) and Cole and Hribar (1995); for scholarship on Nike's relationship with Black communities, see Andrews (1996), Denzin (1996), and Wilson and Sparks (1996). The circumstances surrounding Don Imus's remarks and Nike's communication practices provide an opportunity to examine discourses and vulnerability and empowerment at intersections of race and gender, demonstrating the complexity of both gender discourses and vulnerability.

Nike has garnered the attention of consumers and scholars alike for its ability to capture the popular imagination and for its use and creation of cultural symbolism. Nike began as a running-shoe company, and its early imagery was dominated by White male runners and messages of the technical benefits of the shoes (Strasser & Becklund, 1993). Marketers and advertisers had long been criticized for failing to provide positive representations of African Americans in mainstream media. When Nike signed Michael Jordan and, more clearly when the company placed him front and center in its advertising and promotion, it marked a significant departure from Nike's previous image. Yet critics argued that Nike co-opted Black cultural symbolism and connected with more violent components of the hip-hop community. An alternate interpretation is that African American communities used Nike shoes to articulate meanings through the brand not initially intended by the company (Coleman, 2010). Nike has also offered significant markers of empowerment in American and global cultural symbolism. Despite Nike's roots as a White man's running shoe company, the company has had a long, genuine though sordid history with African-American communities and—as others have developed and I will reiterate here—with women, as well.

"If You Let Me Play": Nike and the Women's Market

Grow (2008) argues that Nike's women's advertising provides a feminist antenarrative within the larger, patriarchal structure of the organization and its other brand communications. As previously discussed content analyses indicate, advertising representations of women into the 1990s continued to typecast them into a limited number of domestic and sexual roles and neglected to reflect a diversity of women's points of view (Grow, 2008). Though Title IX legislation was passed in 1976, it had been poorly implemented and women's professional sports still exhibits little stronghold (Grow, 2008). At the same time, however, Nike had been eyeing the female market since Reebok had been able to capture a large portion of it during the aerobics revolution (Katz, 1994; Strasser & Becklund, 1993), and the company entered the female market space with its women's sub-brand amidst the limited representations of the 1990s.

Grow (2008) traces the development of Nike women's advertising within the parent brand, whose campaigns are "replete with masculine signifiers from sweating, muscle-bound male athletes, to body copy predicated on vigorous competition, with the 'Just Do It' tagline as the ultimate signifier of this masculine promise" (p. 314). The author tells a story of sub-brand rebellion against a patriarchal parent brand. The women's sub-brand became a source of tension that was expressed through the women's advertising and ultimately expressed the experiences of the female advertising creative team working on the campaign.

As had been the case with much of Nike's advertising, the women's advertising created by Wieden & Kennedy was developed from personal experience and cultural understanding rather than from market research. In a series of campaigns that Grow (2008) calls "empowered community," the female creative team resisted the masculine-dominated narratives and strategies of the parent company. Despite increasing sales and strong responses from female consumers, Nike's upper management did not fully acknowledge the female creative team's accomplishments and relegated them to print media and limited placements; they wanted them to use prettier models and they expressed concerns that the campaigns were "pinkifying the brand" (Grow, 2008, p. 328).

Nonetheless, these campaigns, according to Grow, challenged the social constraints imposed by current portrayals of femininity. She posits that "early Nike women's advertising became the 'opening' to express the stories of women's lives, creating a 'new dialogue.' At the same time that dialogue achieved Nike's marketing objective by increasing market share among women" (p. 337). These campaigns expressed women's experiences of inequality, countered and expanded the limited representations available to women, and paved the way for other campaigns "to speak female truths" (Grow, 2008, p. 340) such as Dove's *Campaign for Real Beauty*. These early women's campaigns also paved the way for the *Body Parts* campaign of 2005 and their response to Don Imus's sexist and racist comments.

That is, even within the context of a complex, global corporation often characterized by traditional patriarchal structures, resistant counternarratives can develop and can present, "much like Nike's women's advertising...'multiple ways of telling stories'" (Boje, 2001, as quoted in Grow, 2008, p. 317). Some scholars have argued that Nike's advertisements reflected the values advanced by feminism and provided a space to challenge media norms of gender (Grow, 2008; Grow & Wolburg, 2006; Scott, 1993). Other scholars contend that while Nike's narratives of empowerment may offer deep, authentic appeals, they impede political action and offer commodity, instead, as a means to equality and fulfillment (Cole & Hribar, 1995). Given this, no satisfactory framework has been offered by which to understand and critique marketers such as Nike, regulators such as the FDA, and any entity in a position of power and the publics over which they often are said to have such a tremendous influence. I propose an ethics rooted in the interpretive domain of human relationships and through the symbolism we create, as an appropriate framework for understanding consumer vulnerability. Oppression denies fulfillment of humanness. Dialogue, which is built upon coparticipation, is not simply communication but also the tool for liberation (Christians, 2008).

DIALOGIC ETHICS OF CONSUMER VULNERABILITY

Marketers and advertisers have long been criticized for violating various ethical standards, and scholars have examined ethical concerns through a variety of lenses to look at "what is done to consumers" and "what is done by consumers" (Holbrook, 1994, p. 566). Research also addresses more specific issues such as ethics and sexuality, representation and stereotyping, harmful products, and targeting of specific audiences (Gould, 1994; Haefner, 1991). Borgerson and Schroeder (2005) suggest an ontological approach to representation in advertising, arguing that discourses of marketing and advertising influence and are influenced by cultural knowledge, including values, stereotypes, and norms.

This approach acknowledges the complexities of representation in the interaction of persons and messages, and it politicizes the consequences by suggesting that "every representation has the potential to construct the way societies see other cultures and genders" (Borgerson, 2002). While their view influences this chapter, with their approach, power remains in the hands of marketing and advertising practitioners to supply more just representations and avoid bad faith. This is not a sufficient framework for understanding consumer vulnerability because it is rooted in social and historical context and circumvents the exertion of power inherent in the very act of defining vulnerability.

Advertising and marketing policies tend to proceed on utilitarian perspectives that prioritize individual liberties and grant the greatest happiness or greatest good for the greatest number (Christians, 2007). But a utilitarian ethic is not sufficient for considering vulnerable audiences because vulnerability displaces autonomy. Modern Western philosophies on persuasion, also the context for modern advertising theory, reference Greek and Roman classical rhetoricians, drawing heavily in particular from Aristotle, and apply them to the modern political and economic processes. But Aristotle's teachings have been handed down and translated into modern theory in specific ways that may neglect the range of interpretation and, in particular, the interpretive domain of Aristotle's work.

Communications scholar Christians (1997) writes of a more complex Aristotelian system of communication that affords greater opportunity for ethical engagement and discussion. Of Aristotle's three features, the biological (body), rational (mind), and symbolic (interpretive), Christians focuses on the interpretive domain as that which "confirms we are moral beings with an orienting system beyond the senses yet one differing from logic" (pp. 10–11) and is rooted in community and relationship in community.

Thus, Aristotle's legacy, at least in implicating an interpretive domain in the communication process, offers the opportunity not only to contemplate a more complex view of rhetorical communications, but also to treat all parties involved in the communication as constitutive of the communication itself. Power is not only in the hands of a speaker, but is in all parties through a dialogic exchange. As one scholar notes, "The Greek legacy to us includes some ideas about the relationship between power and rhetoric, as well as the ways in which popular culture is related to both...[Changes] in theory may be part of changes in *power*" (Brummett, 1994, p. 51). This dialogue is an important component of market exchange.

Generally widespread and accessible modern theories of consumer society recognize that consumption does more than fulfill our physical needs: it addresses in large part our cultural needs, our need to have meaning, and our need to have power in the process of created and shared meaning, much of which is created by and passed through our cultural imagery and discourses (Baker, 2009; Belk, 1988). A dialogic ethic brings us to a place of respect for the historical processes of meaning, for the contemporary moment of a globalized and technological world where monocultural perspectives are insufficient, and to a place in ethical debate where the social and historical processes of defining vulnerability are not just useful in exploring the concept but are necessary. Arnett, Fritz, and Bell (2009) argue that "dialogic ethics is the meeting place for learning in an age of difference" (p. 81).

As the rejoinder to individualistic rationalism, ethics is bound in "our mutual human existence across cultural, racial, and historical boundaries" (Christians, 2004, p. 235). The various derivations of dialogic ethics share an understanding of selfhood called to duty through relation or dialogue with community. While the deontological frameworks of Buber and Levinas offered a counter to Nietzsche's ethical relativism and influenced the development of dialogic ethics, Buber's focus on person-to-person interaction and the inescapable subjective interpretation of the other in Levinas's framework do not offer theory that adequately deals with social institutions and therefore do not provide a framework for demanding institutional and structural change in globalized, multicultural societies (De Lima & Christians, 1979; Murray, 2002).

Three other versions of dialogic ethics—discourse ethics, feminist ethics, and communitarian ethics (Christians, 2007)—come closer to an ethics that can deal adequately with vulnerability and empowerment in complex social structures. The discourse ethics of Habermas places ethics in public communication practices. Ethics is dialogic rather than monologic and is derived from "communicative action—the process of giving reasons for holding or rejecting particular claims" (Christians, 2007, p. 123). However, Habermas has been challenged for failing to be "deeply holistic, gender inclusive, or culturally constituted" and discourse ethics more generally as being ethnocentric (Christians, 2007, p. 128).

Feminist discourses have been one significant and revolutionary way in which a dialogic approach to inclusion has affected change. Feminist social ethics, for example, is rooted in human social relationships and experiences with the language of caring and understanding. It "situates the moral domain within the general purposes of human life that people share across cultural, racial, and historical boundaries" (Christians, 2007, p. 124). Yet, an ethic of caring still insinuates a dependence relationship that is problematic beyond the interpersonal. Communitarian ethics acknowledges sociocultural influence on existence and meaning. Human identity is developed in the social realm and fulfillment is achieved in community.

In its basic form, communitarianism is political theory that argues that a politics of individual rights fails to acknowledge identity formed through historical and cultural processes and is therefore incapable of offering human fulfillment (Christians, 2004, 2007). However, the political agenda of communitarianism is predicated on a dialogic view that can only be maintained in context of a larger political structure that works within the same belief system. Thus, while these versions of the dialogic move us toward the "transnational and cross-cultural in a way utilitarianism is unable to match conceptually" (Christians, 2007, p. 126), they are not sufficient to understand vulnerability in these contexts.

Instead, I propose a dialogic ethics that not only allows for but also anticipates multiculturalism, pluralism, and transformation; the notion of liberation through dialogue, not as an act of violence, but naming and therein transforming the world; the importance of voice, or the ability to be a part of naming the world; and the concept of responsibility as centered not only in the individual, but also in the social (Freire, 2006). Dialogue, in this sense, is a human encounter "mediated by the world, in order to name the world" (Freire, 2006, p. 89). For change or transformation or liberation to occur, it has to emanate from the social-historical reality of the Subject, thereby binding it in social action (De Lima & Christians, 1979). That is, "it is as transforming and creative beings that humans…produce not only material goods—tangible objects—but also social institutions, ideas, and concepts. Through their continuing praxis, men and women simultaneously create history and become historical-social beings" (Freire, 2006, p. 101). In dialogic encounters, where authentic lingual and symbolic utterance is not just expressive but is also constitutive of humanness, simply being open to another's perspective is insufficient; rather, participation in dialogue requires active listening and contribution to uncover truths.

If we are willing to relinquish our worship of Enlightenment interpretations of "rational" reasoning, we may legitimately expand the tools of the interpretive domain. The construction of vulnerability with a reliance on deep-seated historical biases and failing to account for the complex and multiple ways that people experience gender and their own vulnerabilities is implicit in the failure to acknowledge our own humanness, as is indicative of marginalizing discourse. Dialogic ethics offers a framework that insists on people's agency in creating their own worlds while at the same time acknowledging the structures of power through which they must navigate. That is, it allows for and requires that women have a voice in defining their position in the world, while at the same time acknowledging that their voices must have the possibility of resonating through institutional and cultural structures such as government regulatory bodies and popular and scholarly discourses.

For example, nowhere was it clear in the regulation of Plan B contraceptives that those most affected by the decision processes of the FDA were given a voice in the seemingly arbitrary definition of their vulnerability. In contrast, while Don Imus's remarks demonstrated the still prevalent, marginalizing conceptions of women at the intersection of race, Nike's response demonstrated the potential for empowering female counternarrative within a male-dominated structure.

Dialogic ethics brings us to a place where multiple and multicultural meanings are nurtured and, indeed, required. And it requires us to engage in dialogue that encourages critical consciousness and empowers us by giving us the tools of our own liberation and humanness. Dialogic ethics allows us to acknowledge and navigate personal and community empowerment and the social systems of power and ideology.

CONCLUSION: AN ETHICS OF EMPOWERMENT

A great deal of scholarly work has demonstrated the problematic representations of various groups, including women. These representations are deeply rooted in historical circumstances that position women, in particular, as vulnerable consumers—vulnerable through their positions in the home, through their irrational desires, and through their incapacity to make informed choices about their own bodies—and that situate women in contrast to the masculine, rational production sphere. These representations obscure the varied experiences of men and women in relation to masculinity and femininity and as they navigate production/consumption spheres. These representations have very real consequences as those in positions of power—whether formal as in regulatory agencies, structural as with marketers, or through any voices defining the circumstances—have the ability to construct meaning and position within societies.

However, there are spaces, both from within the dominant cultural systems and in the margins, for alternative voices to be heard. As scholars have distinguished (Baker et al., 2005; Smith & Cooper-Martin, 1997), perceived vulnerability is based on expectations of the experiences of others, rather than on their true circumstances. Dialogic ethics offers a framework for listening to and engaging with the experiences of others and for interrogating the circumstances of vulnerability. It offers space for empowerment such that assumptions about women's vulnerabilities and commonalities (Fischer & Bristor, 1995) do not marginalize identities and experiences that may exist in intersections with gender, race, ethnicity, class, culture, and other factors and such that "other ways of knowing" (Cooky et al., 2010) are not obscured.

REFERENCES

(ACOG) American Congress of Obstetricians and Gynecologists (2006). AGOC steps up efforts to get emergency contraception to women. AGOC News Release, May 8, http://www.acog.org/from_home/publications/press_releases/nr05-08-06-1.cfm

Andreasen, Alan R. (1975). *The disadvantaged consumer.* New York, NY: Free Press.

Andrews, David (1996). Deconstructing Michael Jordan: Reconstructing postindustrial America. *Sociology of Sport Journal, 13* (Supplement), 315–318.

Arnett, Ronald C., Janie M. Fritz, & Leeanne M. Bell (2009). *Communications ethics literacy: Dialogue and difference.* Thousand Oaks, CA: Sage Publications.

Baker, Stacey Menzel (2009). Vulnerability and resilience in natural disasters: A marketing and public policy perspective. *Journal of Public Policy & Marketing, 28* (Spring), 114–123.

Baker, Stacey Menzel, James W. Gentry, & Terri L. Rittenburg (2005). Building understanding in the domain of consumer vulnerability. *Journal of Macromarketing, 25* (December), 128–139.

Belk, Russell (1988). Possessions and the extended self. *Journal of Consumer Research, 15* (September), 139–168.

Benet, Suzanne, Robert E. Pitts, & Michael LaTour (1993). The appropriateness of fear appeal use for health care marketing to the elderly: Is it OK to scare granny? *Journal of Business Ethics, 12* (January), 45–55.

Bettany, Shona, Susan Dobscha, Lisa O'Malley, & Andrea Prothero (2010). Moving beyond binary opposition: Exploring the tapestry of gender in consumer research and marketing, *Marketing Theory, 10* (December), 3–28.

Bigelow v. Virginia (1975). 421 U.S. 809.

Blair, M. Elizabeth, & Eva M. Hyatt (1995). The marketing of guns to women: Factors influencing gun-related attitudes and gun ownership by women. *Journal of Public Policy & Marketing, 14* (Spring), 117–127.

Boot, William (2008). Nike supports migrant workers in Malaysia. *The Irrawaddy,* August 7, http://www.irrawaddy.org/article.php?art_id=13766

Bordo, Susan (1993). *Unbearable weight: Feminism, Western culture, and the body.* Berkeley, CA: University of California Press.

Borgerson, Janet (2002). Ethical issues of global marketing: Avoiding bad faith in visual representation. *European Journal of Marketing, 36*(5/6), 570–595.

Borgerson, Janet L., & Jonathan E. Schroeder (2005). Identity in marketing communications: An ethics of visual representation. In Allan J. Kimmel (Ed.), *Marketing communication: New approaches, technologies and styles.* Oxford, England: Oxford University Press.

Brandt, John (2011). FDA considers over the counter status for "morning after" pill for girls under 17. *Fox News Online,* http://www.foxnews.com/politics/2011/02/22/fda-considers-counter-status-morning-pill-girls-17/

Bristor, Julia M., & Eileen Fischer (1993). Feminist thought: Implications for consumer research. *Journal of Consumer Research, 19* (March), 518–536.

Brummett, Barry (1994). *Rhetoric in popular culture.* New York, NY: St. Martin's Press.

Catholic journal says Plan B does not cause abortions (2010). *National Catholic Reporter,* March 31, http://ncronline.org/news/catholic-journal-says-plan-b-does-not-cause-abortions

Cayla, Julien, & Lisa Peñaloza (2006). The production of consumer representations. In Connie Pechmann & Linda Price (Eds.), *Advances in consumer research.* Duluth, MN: Association for Consumer Research, 33, 458–461.

Christians, Clifford G. (1997). The ethics of being in a communications context. In Clifford Christians & Michael Traber (Eds.), *Communication ethics and universal values* (pp. 3–23). Thousand Oaks, CA: Sage Publications.

Christians, Clifford G. (2004). *Ubuntu* and communitarianism in media ethics. *Ecquid Novi, 25* (November), 235–256.

Christians, Clifford G. (2007). Utilitarianism in media ethics and its discontents. *Journal of Mass Media Ethics, 22* (2/3), 113–130.

Christians, Clifford G. (2008). Universals and the human. In Kathleen Glenister Roberts & Ronald C. Arnett (Eds.), *Communication ethics: Between cosmopolitan and provinciality* (pp. 5–21). New York, NY: Peter Lang.

Clawson, Rosalee A., & Rakuya Trice (2000). Poverty as we know it. *Public Opinion Quarterly, 64* (Spring), 53–64.

Cole, Cheryl, & Amy Hribar (1995). Celebrity feminism: Nike style post-Fordism, transcendence, and consumer power. *Sociology of Sport Journal, 12,* 347–369.

Coleman, Catherine A. (2010). *Disempowering through definition: A dialogic ethic for understanding consumer vulnerability through Nike's "Mike and Spike" advertising and African American consumer history.* PhD dissertation, Institute of Communication Research, University of Illinois.

Coltrane, Scott, & Melinda Messineo (2000). The perpetuation of subtle prejudice: Race and gender imagery in 1990s television advertising. *Sex Roles, 42* (March), 363–389.

Commuri, Suraj, & Ahmet Ekici (2008). An enlargement of the notion of consumer vulnerability. *Journal of Macromarketing, 28* (June), 183–186.

Cooky, Cheryl, Faye L. Wachs, Michael Messner, & Shari L. Dworkin (2010). It's not about the game: Don Imus, race, class, gender and sexuality in contemporary media. *Sociology of Sport Journal, 27,* 139–159.

De Lima, Venicio A., & Clifford G. Christians (1979). Paulo Freire: The political dimension of dialogic communication. *Communication, 4,* 133–155.

DeLorme, Denise E., Jisu Huh, & Leonard N. Reid (2006). Age differences in how consumers behave following exposure to DTC advertising. *Health Communication, 20*(3), 255–265.

Denzin, Norman K. (1996). More rare air: Michael Jordan on Michael Jordan. *Sociology of Sport Journal, 13* (Supplement), 319–324.

Dukcevich, Davide (2001). Disaster of the day: Nike. *Forbes,* February 22, http://www.forbes.com/2001/02/22/0222disasternike.html

Fagan, Amy (2007). Family groups sue FDA over contraceptive. *The Washington Times,* April 13, http://www.washingtontimes.com/news/2007/apr/13/20070413-010923-9684r/

Favole, Jared A. (2011). Obama says he didn't intervene over Plan B. *The Wall Street Journal,* December 8, http://online.wsj.com/article/SB10001424052970203413304577086472287736982.html

FDA easing access to 'morning after' pill. *The New York Times,* April 22, A14, http://www.nytimes.com/2009/04/23/health/23fda.html

FDA official quits over morning-after decision. (2005). *Associated Press,* August 31, http://www.msnbc.msn.com/id/9145033/ns/health-womens_health/

Fischer, Eileen, & Julia Bristor (1995). Exploring simultaneous oppressions: Toward the development of consumer research in the interest of diverse women. *American Behavioral Scientist, 38* (February), 526–536.

Freire, Paulo (2006). *Pedagogy of the oppressed* (30th anniv. ed.). New York, NY: Continuum.

Frenzen, Jonathan, & Harry Davis (1990). Purchasing behavior in embedded markets. *Journal of Consumer Research, 17* (June), 1–12.

Friedan, Betty (1997). *The feminine mystique* (10th ed.). New York, NY: W. W. Norton & Company.

GAO-06-109 (2005). Food and Drug Administration: Decision process to deny initial application for over-the-counter marketing of the emergency contraceptive drug Plan B was unusual. United States Government Accountability Office Report to Congressional Requesters, November 14, 1–58, http://www.gao.gov/products/GAO-06-109

Gilliam, Franklin D., Jr., Shanto Iyengar, A. Simon, & O. Wright (1996). Crime in black and white: The violent, scary world of local news. *Harvard International Journal of Press/Politics, 1,* 6–23.

Givhan, Robin (2007). Marion Jones, a success on the glamour track, too. *The Washington Post,* October 14, M01.

Goldman, Robert, & Stephen Papson (1998). *Nike culture.* Thousand Oaks, CA: Sage Publications.

Gould, Stephen J. (1994). Sexuality and ethics in advertising: A research agenda and policy guideline perspective. *Journal of Advertising, 23* (September) 73–80.

Grow, Jean (2008). The gender of branding: Early Nike women's advertising and a feminist antinarrative. *Women's Studies in Communication, 31* (Fall), 312–343.

Grow, Jean, & Joyce M. Wolburg (2006). Selling truth: How Nike's advertising to women claimed a contested reality. *Advertising and Society Review, 7*(2).

Haefner, Margaret J. (1991). Ethical problems in advertising to children. *Journal of Mass Media Ethics, 6*(2), 83–92.

Hamburg, Margaret (2011). Statement from FDA Commissioner Margaret Hamburg, M.D. on Plan B One-Step. U.S. Food and Drug Administration, December 7, www.fda.gov/ NewsEvents/Newsroom/ucm282805.htm Harns, Gardiner (2009).

Harris, Gardiner (2006). FDA approves broader access to next-day pill. *The New York Times,* August 25, http://www.nytimes.com/2006/08/25/health/25fda.html

Healy, Bernadine (2006). Ask and you shall receive. *U.S. News and World Report,* May 14, http://health.usnews.com/usnews/health/articles/060522/22healy.htm

Henry, Paul C. (2005). Social class, market situation, and consumers' metaphors of (dis) empowerment. *Journal of Consumer Research, 31* (March), 766–778.

Herbert, Bob (2007). Words as weapons. *The New York Times,* April 23, A19.

Hill, Ronald Paul (2005). In this special issue on vulnerable consumers. *Journal of Macromarketing, 25* (December), 127.

Hirschman, Elizabeth C. (1993). Ideology in consumer research, 1980 and 1990: A Marxist and feminist critique. *Journal of Consumer Research, 19* (March), 537–555.

Holbrook, Morris B. (1994). Ethics in consumer research: An overview and prospectus. *Advances in Consumer Research, 21,* 566–571.

Hollows, Joanne (2000). *Feminism, femininity, and popular culture.* Manchester, England: Manchester University Press.

Holt, Douglas B., & Craig J. Thompson (2004). Man-of-action heroes: The pursuit of heroic masculinity in everyday consumption. *Journal of Consumer Research, 31* (September), 425–440.

Howard, Theresa, & Laura Petrecca (2007). News and notable. *USA Today,* April 23, p. 6B.

Johnson, Peter (2007). Imus left in "a no-win position"; backlash hits CBS, advertisers, wife. *USA Today,* April 12, p. 2D.

Katz, Donald (1994). *Just do it: The Nike spirit in the corporate world.* Holbrook, MA: Adams Media Corporation.

Kern-Foxworth, Marilyn (1994). *Aunt Jemima, Uncle Ben, and Rastus: Blacks in advertising.* Westport, CT: Greenwood.

Kilbourne, Jean (1999). *Deadly persuasion: Why women and girls must fight the addictive power of advertising.* New York, NY: Free Press.

LaFeber, Walter (1999). *Michael Jordan and the new global capitalism.* New York, NY: W. W. Norton & Company.

Laric, Michael V., & Lewis R. Tucker (1977). Toward socially responsible advertising: The concept testing panel approach. *Business & Society, 17* (March), 27–34.

Litosseliti, Lia (2002). "Head to head": Gendered repertoires in newspaper arguments. In Lia Litosseliti & Jane Sunderland (Eds.), *Gender identity and discourse analysis* (pp. 129–148). Amsterdam, the Netherlands: John Benjamins Publishing Company.

Manian, Maya (2009). The irrational woman: Informed consent and abortion decision-making. *Duke Journal of Gender Law & Policy, 16,* 223–292.

Mouth from the South (2007). *The Dallas Morning News,* December 12, p. 17.

Murray, Jeffrey W. (2002). The other ethics of Emmanuel Levinas: Communication beyond relativism. In Sharon L. Bracci & Clifford G. Christians (Eds.), *Moral engagement in public life: Theorists for contemporary ethics*. New York, NY: Peter Lang Publishing, Inc.

Neve, Monica (2009). Advertising and the middle-class female consumer in Munich, c. 1900–1914, *Business and Economic History, 7*, 1–9.

Newsweek's power 50 (2010). *Newsweek, 156,* November 8, p. 37.

Nike: Malaysian factory violates major rights (2008). *MSNBC,* August 1, http://www.msnbc.msn.com/id/25970840/ns/business-world_business/

O'Guinn, Thomas C., & L. J. Shrum (1997). The role of television in the construction of consumer reality. *Journal of Consumer Research, 23* (March), 278–294.

Paek, Hye-Jin, Michelle R. Nelson, & Alexandra M. Vilela (2011). Examination of gender-role portrayals in television advertising across seven countries. *Sex Roles, 64,* 192–207.

Palan, Kay M. (2001). Gender identity in consumer behavior: A literature review and research agenda, *Academy of Marketing Science Review, 1* (10), 1–37.

Patterson, Maggie Jones, Ronald Paul Hill, & Kate Maloy (1995). Abortion in America: A consumer-behavior perspective. *Journal of Consumer Research, 21* (March), 677–694.

Pechman, Cornelia, Linda Levine, Sandra Loughlin, & Frances Leslie (2005). Impulsive and self-conscious: Adolescents' vulnerability to advertising and promotion. *Journal of Public Policy & Marketing, 24* (Fall), 202–221.

Peffley, Mark, John Hurwitz, & Paul Sniderman (1997). Racial stereotypes and Whites' political views of Blacks in the context of welfare and crime. *American Journal of Political Science, 41* (January), 30–60.

Plan B morning after pill; 17-year olds could get emergency contraceptive without prescription (2011). *New York Daily News,* February 14.

Ramsay, Iain (1996). *Advertising, culture and the law: Beyond lies, ignorance and manipulation*. London, England: Sweet & Maxwell.

Rhoden, William C. (2007). The unpleasant reality for women in sports. *The New York Times,* April 9, p. D7.

Ringold, Deborah Jones (2005). Vulnerability in the marketplace: Concepts, caveats, and possible solutions. *Journal of Macromarketing, 25* (December), 202–214.

Sandomir, Richard (2007). Nike puts women back on the pedestal. *The New York Times,* August 24, p. D2.

Sautter, Elise Truly, & Nancy Oretskin (1997). Tobacco targeting: The ethical complexity of marketing to minorities. *Journal of Business Ethics, 16* (July), 1011–1017.

Schorn, Daniel (2009). The debate over Plan B: Did religion play a role in an FDA Decision? *60 Minutes,* February 11, accessed April 3, 2011.

Schroeder, Jonathan E. (2003). Guest editor's introduction: Consumption, gender and identity. *Consumption, Markets and Culture, 6* (January), 1–4.

Schroeder, Jonathan E., & Janet L. Borgerson (1998). Marketing images of gender: A visual analysis. *Consumption, Markets & Culture, 2* (June), 161–201.

Schroeder, Jonathan E., & Detlev Zwick (2004). Mirrors of masculinity: Representation and identity in advertising images. *Consumption, Markets & Culture, 7* (January), 21–52.

Scott, Linda M. (1993). Fresh lipstick—Rethinking images of women in advertising. *Media Studies, 7* (Winter/Spring), 141–155.

Scott, Linda M. (2005). *Fresh lipstick: Redressing fashion and feminism*. New York, NY: Palgrave.

Sebelius, Kathleen (2011). A statement by U.S. Department of Health and Human Services Secretary Kathleen Sebelius. U.S. Department of Health and Human Services, December 7, www.hhs.gov/news/press/2011press/12/20111207a.html

Shultz, C., & M. Holbrook (2009). The paradoxical relationship between marketing and vulnerability. *Journal of Public Policy & Marketing, 28* (Spring), 124–127.

Smith, N. Craig, & Elizabeth Cooper-Martin (1997). Ethics and target marketing: The role of product harm and consumer vulnerability. *Journal of Marketing, 61* (July), 1–20.

Stabile, Carol A. (2000). Nike, social responsibility, and hidden abode of production. *Critical Studies in Media Communication, 17* (June), 186–204.

Stein, Rob (2011). Obama Administration refuses to relax Plan B restrictions. *Washington Post,* December 7, www.washingtonpost.com/national/health-science/2011/12/07/glQAFSHicO_story.html?tid-pm-pop

Stern, Barbara B., Cristel Antonia Russell, & Dale W. Russell (2005). Vulnerable women on screen and at home: Soap opera consumption. *Journal of Macromarketing, 25* (December), 222–225.

Strasser, J. B., & Laurie Becklund (1993). *Swoosh: The unauthorized story of Nike and the men who played there.* New York, NY: HarperBusiness.

Thomaselli, Rich (2007). Nike builds campaign out of Imus fallout. *Advertising Age,* April 23, p. 12.

Tummino v. Hamburg. (2009). CV-05-0366(ERK/VVP).

Tummino v. Torti. 603 F. Supp. 2d 519 (E.D.N.Y. 2009).

Virginia State Board of Pharmacy v. Virginia Citizens' Consumer Council (1976). 425 U.S. 748.

Wilson, Brian, & Robert Sparks (1996). "It's gotta be the shoes": Youth, race, and sneaker commercials. *Sociology of Sport Journal, 13* (Supplement), 398–427.

Wolf, Naomi (1992). *The beauty myth: How images of beauty are used against women.* New York, NY: Doubleday.

Wood, Susan F. (2005). Women's health and the FDA. *New England Journal of Medicine,* October 20, 1650–1651.

Zayer, Linda Tuncay (2010). A typology of men's conceptualizations of ideal masculinity in advertising. *Advertising & Society Review, 11*(1).

2

"The Creation of Inspired Lives":[1] Female Fan Engagement With the Twilight Saga

Hope Jensen Schau and Margo Buchanan-Oliver

INTRODUCTION

The *Twilight* brand is provocative. Rivaling even the *Harry Potter* brand in both U.S. and international book sales, the *Twilight* saga—encompassing books (four texts authored by Stephenie Meyer and published 2005–2008), films, events, music, "fanpire" magazines, vampiric products (energy drinks, female sanitary products, washing powder, automobiles), and promotional collateral—is a global phenomenon with an audience that dramatically skews female. It is easy to suggest that this magnitude of female fan commitment is simply due to it being a female-driven brand narrative, but so are many others (*Pride and Prejudice, The Joy Luck Club, Sex and the City, Hannah Montana*), which although popular, never reached the *Twilight* brand-fueled frenzy or the type, tenor, and magnitude of this community's fan engagement. *Twilight* is more akin to pop cultural phenomena such as *Star Trek, Xena: Warrior Princess,* and *Buffy the Vampire Slayer,* where fans persist for years in a state of enthusiasm that other popular media vehicles (*Casablanca, The Wizard of Oz, Iron Man, The Hangover, Shrek*) cannot achieve and in which highly unique engagement types (reading groups, conventions, camps, fan fiction, fan poetry, fan art, tattoos, body jewels) are fostered.

Our present research examines the *Twilight* brand community through its brand-authored texts (novels and films), in-depth, in-person fan interviews, e-mail and chat interviews with fans, online fan forums, and participation in corporeal events (book signings and conventions). Our research question is, "Why do girls and women aged 7 to 70 engage with the *Twilight* brand on multiple levels and do so with such passionate commitment?" The answer may surprise you. We demonstrate that the *Twilight* phenomenon is an artful mixture of Gothic Romanticism; liminalities of character, identity, and sexuality; and contemporary sociocultural resonance—all packaged in a particular women's genre that offers moral instruction explicitly focused on sexual control and conduct. As such, *Twilight* provides a discursive platform for girls and women to explore issues of feminism, sexuality, and normative gender roles.

The cultural imaginary of the vampire is, as Auerbach (1995) notes, at the heart of the American national experience: "what vampires are in any generation is a part of what I am and what my times have become" (p. 1). Consequently, for second wave feminists, imaginative engagement with the figure of the vampire may enable a breaking of the reactionary boundaries of essentialist restriction, enabling readers of vampiric texts to become creative mutations whose dangerous mobility enables ascendancy over patriarchal institutions. For third wave feminists, the play of contradictory and ambivalent heterosexual, homosexual, and homoerotic vampire enactment in these sociocultural texts may celebrate diversity of sexual experience, female empowerment, and gender freedoms.

As in previous research tackling the intersection and interaction of gender and the marketplace (Catterall, Maclaran, & Stevens, 2000; Costa, 2000; Dobscha & Ozanne, 2000; Scott, 2000), this chapter explores gender expressions within a media brand and the discourses surrounding them. We will show that brand enthusiasts are energized by Bella's haphazard navigation of disparate role expectations and her perpetual liminality. For example, the coven of vampires that Bella (human/food) joins suppress their predatory instincts and dietary imperatives, favoring compassion, reason, and defensive combat over aggression, apathy, bloodlust, and hunger. In essence, the data reveal that it is precisely Bella's liminality and her quest for equality against almost insurmountable odds that make her a compelling heroine and a touchstone, or rallying point, for brand fans. Fans are quick to address gender identity strategy and use it toward negotiating their own social roles and understanding a postfeminist perspective (Johnson, 2007).

The data show the manner in which feminist discourses are collectively negotiated, intertwined, and reconstituted (Gill, 2007). In fact, *Twilight* fans, through the collective discourses we present, acknowledge that the brand makes them think, often for the first time, about the compromises and trade-offs of being a contemporary woman. *Twilight* enthusiasts use the brand as a platform to negotiate feminism and socially prescribed female roles (Mulvey, 1975): good girl, independent woman, lover, wife, and mother. *Twilight* offers fans a paradoxical interplay of feminist and antifeminist discourses characteristic of postfeminist media culture (Friedberg, 1993). Throughout the saga, the female self is deferred in favor of the primacy of good intentions toward humanity, highlighting the problem of femininity as a quintessential pathology when defined in patriarchic discourses (Moscucci, 1990). Such concentration alludes to the, at times, elusive concept of fourth wave feminism, which fuses notions of female connectedness, social justice, and mutuality.

In order to highlight the contextual nature of the *Twilight* phenomenon, we will be tacking directly between the prior literature and the data. The chapter will begin with a brief overview of our field site and methodology, followed by a discussion of the findings as they connect to the (re)current literature on vampirism, feminism, consumption, and fan engagement and brand community.

FIELD SITE

Twilight is a series of four published books written by first-time author Stephenie Meyer that chronicle the romance between a human, Bella Swan, and a vampire, Edward Cullen. It is an epic tale of love, loss, and heroism. It is a coming-of-age narrative with a gothic twist. The *Twilight* saga, as it is called, spawned a new literary genre: teenage vampire romance. In 2009, Stephenie Meyer was ranked number 26 in terms of power on *Forbes* "The Celebrity 100" list, falling in 2010 to number 59 (Pomerantz & Rose, 2010). She is cited by *Forbes* as the second most successful author (measured in sales) of 2010 behind James Patterson, a bestselling author of more than 70 books spanning adult and young adult genres over four decades (Smilie, 2010). *Twilight* is a global phenomenon. The series made Stephenie Meyer a supernova author and one of the most influential women in Hollywood (Finke, 2009).

The fan base is predominantly female, ranging in age from approximately 7 to 70 and varying in degrees of engagement from reading the texts and later watching the movies to modifying their bodies with *Twilight*-themed images and quotations. There is a strong tradition of collective, collaborative consumption within the *Twilight* fan base. We will show in the findings that the fan group meets the criteria for being a brand community, exhibiting consciousness of kind, rituals and traditions, and moral responsibility (Muñiz & O'Guinn, 2001). The brand community is manifest online, offline, and convergently. The fans participate in online discussions (forums, message boards, and blogs), online events (fan art contests), and off-line events (conventions like *Twilight* proms, book signings, reading groups).

DATA AND METHODOLOGY

The data consist of the *Twilight* saga (composed of four official novels and an unauthorized draft novel), three feature films (with another in production and yet another film planned), literary and film criticism of the *Twilight* media products, naturalistic and participant observation in three online fan discussion forums, fan-created videos, e-mail and chat interviews with forum participants and videographers, and face-to-face interviews with *Twilight* fans. The data were iteratively collected and thematically coded and recoded following the hermeneutic tradition. Data collection took place over 4 years and is part of a larger data set on female fan engagement. This subset of data was collected through a theoretical sampling of forum posts regarding feminism and feminists and snowballing of face-to-face interviewees. Table 2.1 contains information regarding informants cited within this chapter.

FINDINGS

Collective, Collaborative, and Communal Brand-Oriented Consumption

Collective consumption occurs quite literally when consumers use the brand together. It can take many shapes: sharing a meal or drink with

TABLE 2.1

Informants

Pseudonym	Age	Occupation	Data Source
Bailey	17	High school student	Interview
Tausha	31	Medical management	Forum, interview
Miranda	27	Software designer	Interview
Claudia	37	Entrepreneur	Interview
Daniela	20	College student	Interview
Denise	19	College student	Interview
Sasha	23	Retail buyer	Interview
Miranda	41	Educator	Interview
Caitlin	26	Media buyer	Interview
Brenda	44	Manager	Interview
Kathy	25	Event planner	Interview
Cyndi	21	College student	Interview
Nikki	Unknown	Unknown	Forum
Katy	32	Physical therapist	Interview
Patricia	51	Clinical psychologist	Interview
Megan	21	College student	Interview
Courtney	22	College student	Interview
Hillery	26	Sports management	Interview
Rochelle	39	Program administrator	Interview
Stevie	31	College professor	Interview
Lexi	17	High school student	Interview
Jody	35	Stay-at-home mom	Interview
Devonne	19	College student	Interview
Delores	56	Unknown	Forum

friends, playing video games with others either proximally or online, enjoying music or television with others, or going to an amusement park with family. In the case of *Twilight*, collective consumption is manifested as reading the books in book clubs, participating in online forums, attending conventions and book signings, watching the movies together, and hosting and attending themed events.

Collaborative consumption occurs when consumers work together with other consumers and/or producers to construct the brand and its meaning. This can also take many shapes, including painting ceramics at a studio like Color Me Mine, producing a fan-made movie trailer, personalizing a shoe on Nike.com, or designing and/or buying a T-shirt on Threadless.com. For *Twilight*, consumers create vigilante marketing (Muñiz & Schau, 2007) such as unpaid advertisements and trailers, engage in textual poaching (Jenkins, 1992) such as writing their own narratives around the characters, develop and perform interpretations of the brand text, and generate visual artistic works such as graphic designs, sketches, and paintings.

One form of collective, collaborative consumption is brand communities. Muñiz and O'Guinn (2001) define brand communities are enduring (not single use) collectives that are centered on the brand and demonstrate three markers: a consciousness of kind, rituals and traditions, and a sense of moral responsibility for one another. The attributes that distinguish brand community members from traditional consumers include their connection to the brand offering, their relation to other brand consumers, and their willingness to participate in the evolution of the brand. Consumer researchers have investigated a host of consumer collectives organized around market-mediated cultural products (Muñiz & Schau, 2007). These collectives can be categorized as primarily experience based (Bagozzi & Dholakia, 2006; Cova & Cova, 2002; McAlexander, Schouten, & Koenig, 2002), lifestyle based (Goulding & Saren, 2009), opposition ideology based (Thompson, Rindfleisch, & Arsel, 2006), brand based (Martin, Schouten, & McAlexander, 2006; Muñiz & O'Guinn, 2001; Muñiz & Schau, 2005), or web community based (Szmigin & Reppel, 2004). This work demonstrates that all such collectives exhibit community-like qualities, as understood in sociology, and address identity-, meaning-, and status-related concerns for participants.

The *Twilight* phenomenon has rapidly embedded itself into the hearts and discourses of a predominantly female legion of passionate and active fans. It is not unlike other brand-oriented communities that consumer researchers have examined before in terms of tone, tenor, roles, and social architecture. It is, however, rather unique in terms of the idiosyncratic thrust of the discourse and the almost exclusively female participation in sexual identity contemplation. As author of the *Twilight* saga, Stephenie Meyer not only inspires passion and devotion in individual readers, but also importantly incites and nurtures collective engagement in multiple formats with *Twilight* in the form of a brand community demonstrating the markers identified in Muñiz and O'Guinn (2001): consciousness of kind, rites and rituals, and moral responsibility.

Consciousness of kind is exhibited within the community as members profess their affinity to the brand and their membership in the fan community. Online they create signature files identifying their membership in the community, often using the team discourse popular in the community: Team Edward and Team Jacob. These teams indicate the fan's favorite male character and the one that she supports in winning Bella's affection: Team Edward supports the vampire's rights to Bella's heart while Team Jacob supports the werewolf's claim. This staking behavior is a way for brand community members to situate themselves in the collective (Schau, Muñiz, & Arnould, 2009).

Rites and rituals can be found in the community, where fans are encouraged to write confessional narratives that relate to the brand text, stand in queues to see each film at the midnight opening, participate in *Twilight*-themed events like the brand-oriented prom convention, and recite the text in common parlance. These behaviors are ritualistic and cross nearly all the collective consumption sites for the brand.

Moral responsibility is clear in the community. The ritualized confessional narratives garner substantial empathy and members are willing to go to great lengths to comfort one another. For example, one 17-year-old prom attendee shared that her boyfriend was controlling like Edward and other fans offered kind words and advice on the spot. Like the Saab owners who helped one another out if they saw a Saab broken down on the side of the road (Muñiz & O'Guinn, 2001), *Twilight* fans routinely discuss times when they went out of their way to help another fan, even if they did not specifically know her. Bailey states:

> Last week I saw this girl at my school who sometimes wears *Twilight* shirts looking for her cell phone. I stopped and let her use my phone to call hers. We tracked the sound down and she located her phone. Since then I invited her to hang out with my friends during free period. (interview 11/02/2008)

In short, the *Twilight* fan group is a brand community that recognizes one another as belonging, has brand-based, narrative-oriented factions embedded in the community, and communally engages with the brand. It also has traditions and members demonstrate moral responsibility to one another.

The Horror of It

Twilight epitomizes the horror genre and "horror [is] by definition a woman's genre...[as] Jane Austen's *Northanger Abbey* reminds us" (Auerbach,

1995, p. 3). In the *Twilight* community, fans speak openly of the gendered nature of horror in general and *Twilight* in particular. One "Twi-hard" community member expresses the appeal of the horror genre as definitively gendered:

> Horror is at once beseeching and revolting. It resonates with us [women] because we are romantic and romance is fraught with pleasure, vulnerability and pain. The thrill of sex leads directly to the pain of childbirth and the chronic burden of others' needs forever overshadowing our own. We are riddled with self-sacrifice and unfulfilled promises. Our lives are gothic tales. (Tausha, post 02/14/2006)

Another *Twilight* fan echoes the assertion that horror is a female genre:

> Women have it tough. We are forced to carry the burden of desire, the consequences of carnal delights. Men are not. They enjoy freely. They can elect to share the responsibilities and are noble if they do. We are condemned to know pleasure as tied to pain…Horror is that balance: pleasure and pain. It helps reinforce morality and a woman's place. For a woman to know pleasure is to risk death. In order to enjoy the abandon we must embrace the doom. (Miranda, interview 05/25/2010)

Both Miranda and Tausha demonstrate that the genre uniquely resonates with women and is inextricably linked to social roles, societal norms, and gender politics. Claudia places *Twilight* firmly within the horror genre:

> *Twilight* is a classic horror tale. The female is willingly ravaged, enters a liminal and dark space, and then exists in a state of perpetual moral vigilance. She must defy her nature to obtain pleasure. She must temper pleasure with obligation and social contract. She becomes [a] benevolent monster. (interview 02/10/2009)

In essence, fans aver that horror is part and parcel of the *Twilight* appeal and that both phenomena are inherently gendered.

The Vampire and Moral Coding

The vampire's popularity has waxed and waned since its literary inception in the nineteenth century (Auerbach, 1995; Twitchell, 1981, 1985). The traditional appeal of the vampire lies in its sociocultural liminality as an exemplum of the undead and as predatory seducer and despoiler of the human species. Despite the forbidden sexual and psychological attractions of such an unbounded (anti)hero, the salutary moral of historical vampire tales has been one of return to social order and repression: "They are the morality plays of our time" (Dresser, 1989, p. 139). Daniela, a *Twilight* fan, reiterates this point:

> The books are about morality. Bella is charged with navigating right and wrong while simultaneously occupying multiple positions and juggling a host of different perspectives: daughter and parent (she parents her parents in many ways), daughter and lover, human and vampire, human and were-wolf, werewolf and vampire…And Bella floats between these positions. They [these multiple perspectives] highlight the complexity of morality, pitting so many needs against one another. (interview 01/06/2010)

Daniela affirms that *Twilight* is an apt forum through which to grapple with morality and moral ambiguity. She directly references liminality and multiplicity of roles as a catalyst for thinking through morality. She also goes on to suggest that vampires are uniquely suited to highlight moral complexity because "vampires look like mortal humans but are actually undead with super strength. They can be male or female, but are in many ways gendered [as] females. They pay heavily for their sexuality. They must keep their sexuality carefully guarded from society." In this extract, Daniela recalls the earlier vampire literature in which the vampire is a creature who hides in the shadows of the physical world (symbolically rep-resenting the psychosexual recesses of the id) and whose sexual needs are accomplished by rapine and assault under the cover of darkness. Denise describes the conundrum for Edward:

> Imagine. Edward wants so much to make love to Bella, but he knows that he would destroy her if he tried while she was still human. He literally would work himself into a frenzy and consume her. He'd ravage her, bite her, infect her with the vampire venom and likely drain her dry. "The wages of sin are [sic] death," as they say. (interview 11/07/2008)

In *Twilight*, Edward keeps Bella chaste, sometimes against her will. He carefully guards her soul because, as a vampire, his is already lost. Edward is the moral arbiter of the text.

The *Twilight* texts mirror the realities of contemporary society. *Twilight* vampires no longer inhabit the crypt and the cemetery—traditional zones of liminality between this world and the next. They inhabit the world of the high school; they are suburban and domestic creatures participating in the ordinary consumption rituals of consumer society. The *Twilight* myth may also be recognized as a reflection of more literally sexually prudent times and therefore as counterbalanced by contemporary concepts of a new form of asceticism. Sasha explains:

> Twilight is so sexy. The tension and the chronic state of foreplay make it so delectable. Edward is re[s]trained and the anticipation builds…If only real guys would commit hours at a time to kissing and foreplay and build up intimacy over months and years instead of always trying to score…it seems every at-bat has to be a homerun. It isn't a game I can win. These guys are working against me. (interview 02/18/2009)

For Sasha, Edward is an idealized lover who does not impose the pressure that males in her own life do. Edward's rules of abstinence are sexy against the state of constant longing. The fear of personal ruin that looms over Bella if Edward even momentarily succumbs fosters a tension-filled romantic space that perpetuates desire, rather than abates it. Sasha's experience of the game is that it cannot be won. The men she knows have conflicting goals and do not appear to honor hers. Edward is willing and able to sacrifice his (and Bella's) will to keep Bella safe.

This message of "be safe" is a double entendre, simultaneously meaning, from Edward's perspective, "'Be safe' while I am away" and "'Be safe' while we are together." This "be safe" notion in the text resonates strongly with the fans. Fans tattoo that message on their bodies, create fan art (like the *Twilight*-designed shoes), and participate in numerous threads based on the "be safe" quote. (See Figures 2.1 and 2.2.) The irony that safety can be imposed and maintained by Edward, the predator, does not go unnoticed by the fans. Another quote from the text dialogue emphasizes this point: "And so the lion fell in love with the lamb. What a stupid lamb. What a sick masochistic lion." (See Figures 2.3–2.5.)

Vampire anxieties are now no longer solely of a sexually rapacious nature but also comprise the anxieties of the sexually primed that incorporate abstinence from sexual contact on moral grounds or because of the fear of

FIGURE 2.1
Fan's "be safe" tattoo.

FIGURE 2.2
Fan's "be safe" shoes.

STDs and AIDS. In a postmodern inversion of the originating gothic tale, *Twilight*'s vampires act as moral encoders against the exchange of blood/semen outside of marriage and show themselves as stronger than humans in their ability to manage and guard their sexuality. Miranda explains the nature of toxins in relation to sexuality in *Twilight*:

FIGURE 2.3
Lion and lamb fan art.

Vampires have venom, like snakes and other predators. Edward vigilantly protects Bella from the venom. In the first book he actually sucks James' [vampire] venom out [of] her to keep her alive and mortal...They [Edward and Bella] can't have sex while she's human. If Edward let his guard down in the throes of passion he would infect her and possibly kill her...[it's] all complicated by the fact that Bella cannot control her [carnal] instincts. (interview 05/25/2010)

Edward's venom is analogous to HIV. It is transmitted through intimate contact. It enters your bloodstream. It infects you. It is potentially lethal at worst and at best can keep you in an undead vampiric state throughout eternity. The inversion comes in who is charged with controlling the disease transfer. In most Judeo-Christian contemporary societies, the

FIGURE 2.4
Lion and lamb tattoo.

onus is upon the woman to fend off male advances and protect her virtue (Moscucci, 1990). Here, we have the female sexual aggressor.

The Enduring Appeal of the Vampire

In its emphasis on the vampire as the force of moral arbitration and sexual abstinence, Meyer's *Twilight* series differs in this one respect from other contemporary vampire tales. Anne Rice's seminal "vamp-lit" novel, *Interview with the Vampire* (published in 1976), and L. J. Smith's four-novel series, *The Vampire Diaries* (first novel published in 1991), both obtained cult status conforming to the gothic/erotic themes of earlier vampire literature: transformation, alienation, seduction, the dread of mortality, the

FIGURE 2.5
Fan's lion and lamb "stupid lamb" tattoo.

battle between good and evil. Smith's central plot of a high school girl whose affections are contested by two vampire brothers evolves into a contest between paranormal species in Meyer's 2003 novel. The commercial success of Meyer's *Twilight* novels begot the first *Twilight* movie in 2008 (others were released in 2009, 2010, and 2011) and the spawning of the recent TV series *True Blood* (2008), which is based on Charlaine Harris's *The Southern Vampire Mysteries*, *The Vampire Diaries* (2009), and Richelle Mead's six *Vampire Academy* novels (optioned for the cinema in 2010). This most recent resurgence of vampiric stories is idiosyncratic of the current cultural moment.

In the space of 7 years this proliferation of vampiric interest appears to echo ideas of nineteenth century Romanticism (a reaction against the scientific rationalization of nature, a focus on sublimity of experience, and the elevation of folk myths), which are also in sociocultural evidence at the beginning of the twenty-first century. As Twitchell (1981) recounts,

Before the nineteenth century the vampire seems to have only folkloric existence…with each new civilization and each new generation refashioning and recreating the vampire until he emerges as the Western monster we recognize today: a demonic spirit in a human body who nocturnally attacks the living, a destroyer of others, a preserver of himself. (p. 7)

The vampire came to this pass as the avatar of the devil: a dead human body whose "entrapped soul lived eternally under the devil's control" (Twitchell, 1981, p. 8), unable to experience death and condemned to search for life-perpetuating blood, in an extension of early primitive warrior myth and an inversion of the Christian myth of communion in which the drinking of blood was a restorative appropriation of the power of the "Other"—be it the enemy or the god (Twitchell, 1981).

The sexual lure of the "Other" is also referenced in the popularity of the figure of the vampire, itself a character in the wider gothic novel genre that burgeoned in the eighteenth century. In this genre, characters commonly form a family—literally or figuratively—and an older, paternal male plays the victimizer of a virgin (Twitchell, 1985), thereby committing a sexual transgression "in violation of social convention" (p. 41). By the late nineteenth century, such monstrous transgressors could erupt from within (Mr. Hyde) or arrive from distant lands (Dracula) but could not be controlled. Acting as a proxy for sublimated and socially prohibited fears and desires, these fantastic monsters are doppelgangers acting independently of the central self and it is the vampire who emerges in twentieth and early twenty-first century culture to embody both the sexual excitement and the sexual anxiety of the "Other." Such excitements and anxieties extend to both male and female vampiric figures (see Twitchell's 1985 typology of the figure of Lamia—the devouring female, pp. 141–159).

Freedom From Constraint

Not all females involved in the narratives (characters or fans) are victims, passively waiting to be seduced. Some want to be Dracula's bride and volunteer to experience his monstrous, unnatural life, which grants freedom from mortality and from sexual and social norms: "All forbidden sexual practices come into play—oral, necrophiliac, incestual [*sic*], homosexual" (Dresser, 1989, p. 152). These eternal freedoms and sexual experiences are what Bella, the human protagonist in *Twilight,* wants from Edward, the vampire, when she contemplates her willing transformation from human to vampire and from virgin to wife and states, "I want to be a monster, too." As Caitlin shows:

> Bella is the sexual aggressor in the story. She cannot control her desires as well as Edward can. She wants sex before marriage. Edward wants a consummated monogamous marriage. He tells Bella that real sexual pleasure can only occur after she too is a vampire, a monster. (interview 03/12/2010)

For Caitlin, *Twilight* reifies Dresser's theory. Importantly, she further remarks, "It's weird that the books are all about repressing sexual desire, but they are the most sexually charged books I've ever read. Abstinence is distinctly sexy."

As Dresser (1989) notes, the vampire's story provides a "positive fantasy outlet for...feelings of aggression and sexuality. The vampire represents power" (p. 145). This can be represented as a power over self: "I wish I had more control over my life. I don't want to be afraid of everything; vampires have very little to fear unless they attract too much attention" (p. 155). However, more commonly, it refers to the power appropriated by sexual domination: "being enslaved by the vampire...and submitting to him" and experiencing the "twin contradictory thrills of helplessness and power" (p. 155). Donna reflects that "Bella is vulnerable to Edward in that he can kill her, but powerful in that she can make herself irresistible. That is an incredible power and [a] huge vulnerability" (interview 06/09/2009). Likewise, Sabina notes, "It is clearer in the movies as they show her exposing her neck that the thrill is in submission but it is also powerful because it holds the promise of immortality and physical perfection" (interview 07/05/2009).

For followers of the genre, the vampire product both "affirms and resists culturally and historically determined discourses of sexuality" (Schopp, 1997, p. 232) and power. It is on the record that the vampire has always turned to women to "perform the extreme implications of [his] monstrosity," needing women to "act out" his nature (Auerbach, 1995, p. 7). However, Schopp (1997) and Craft (1988) note alternative performances of desire, arguing that Dracula's initial (and forbidden) homoerotic desire for a male (Jonathan Harker) is reified in his heterosexual rapacity, which performs "a history of men using women to mediate their homosocial or homoerotic desires" (Schopp, p. 235). Whether heteronormatively or trangressively, the vampire provides a cultural and psychological space for the subversion of social order and for experiencing sublimated and conscious desires, constituting a "mirror that reflects shifting cultural desires and fears" (Schopp, p. 232). As Brenda, an avid "Twi-hard," remarks,

> All my life I'm told to guard my sexuality and give it as a gift to that one special man in this one culturally condoned heterosexual way...Vampires allow us to explore ambisexuality, they bite and gain pleasure from both genders indiscriminately. Carlyle turns Edward first then Esme, his mate [into vampires]. He confronts almost uncontrollable bloodlust, lust, in both [situations]. We fear that sort of sexual honesty. We repress that in our society. Here, a "straight" man is prohibited from even recognizing another man's physical attractiveness...but while we get a glimpse of sexual freedom Meyer's vampiric vision has heterosexual monogamous vampire mates. (interview 03/17/2010)

The cultural imaginary of desire inherent in the narrative of the vampire may never be gratified in the everyday sexual existences of vampire devotees, but can be potently sublimated and/or enjoyed via the enabling and projective mirrors of textual, visual, and cinematic performance. Kathy explains:

> It is so damn sexy the way Bella and Edward are in a state of chronic foreplay. I get so hot reading the books that I almost jump my boyfriend when I put the book down...better than pornography because it's intimacy, not just what goes in where. (interview 08/16/2009)

The allure is in the denial and specifically in the denial of the climax. The foreplay is perpetual. The kisses take up pages of text and still leave the characters wanting. Cyndi offers a confessional tale:

> I used to have this boyfriend back when the book first came out. We used to make out all the time. We thought about more. We talked about all the physical things we wanted to do but never did them. It was probably one of, if not the, hottest relationships I ever had. Of course it ended because he is not Edward and his patience wore out. (interview 11/10/2008)

Cyndi cherished the restraint while acknowledging the desire. Denial and abstinence characterized her hottest relationship.

In contemporary texts, vampires and their buffed bodies have become the new pornography. Visually represented and textually described as eroticized, bodies (Owen, 1999) and faces undergo both male and female gazes to emerge as icons of the consumption gaze of contemporary society. We have remade vampires as consumption products answering our changing sexual and market needs. One online poster to a thread entitled, "Vampires: Cold and Sparkly and Very Sexy," describes this physical perfection and the obsession with it:

> In the books, Stephenie goes into great detail on how physically perfect the vampires are...They have zero percent body fat, chiseled muscles, perfect bone structure and they sparkle in the sun like a tempting mirage. As I was reading I was just picturing it and getting hotter and hotter. The stills [pictures] and movies are even worse...Visually stunning and very erotic. Like other romance genres it is almost soft-core [pornography]. I found myself lusting heavily after a teenage boy. Yikes. (Nikki, posted 04/11/2010)

The poster and other texts in the thread note the lust that the vampire body produces in its female consumers because it is so intensely described in the narrative and so artfully and seductively photographed in the visual products.

Isolation and Alienation

The vampire can also represent an "Other"—one outside the tribe, the solitary hunter of the tribe's women, the troubled soul, alienated in the midst of society. Dresser (1989) notes fans' feelings of empathy for the despair of the vampire, who is "one who wishes to love and to be loved...The vampire has been forced to lead this dreadful half-life" (pp. 150–151). These feelings memorialize the archetypical Byronic/Romantic hero of nineteenth century fiction and project the realities of existential angst and dislocation for contemporary consumers of vampire texts.

This latter is what Jackson (1981, p. 19) calls a state of "paraxis" in which the real and the unreal intersect and in which the fantastic affirms and challenges the conventions of the world creating a space of "alterity" where social norms can be challenged. Claudia discusses how *Twilight* deals with "Otherness":

> It is a little strange how all the characters are in some way outside the normal social sphere. Bella's dad is a bachelor who enjoys being alone. His best friends are native Americans self-segregating and living on a reservation. Bella's mom is an itinerant woman following her baseball player husband on the road. The vampires take refuge in their homes, their forest, and are self-segregated at school. Bella is clumsy and doesn't fit into any clique

easily. Jacob is suspicious of his friends and alienated from his pack before he turns into the werewolf. And yet the sexual tension flies through and among them. The desire to be intimate with the other reigns. It is something we all can relate to. (interview 02/11/2010)

As Claudia highlights, the status of the "Other" and sexual attraction are intertwined. But it is her description of Bella's fragmented family, her mother's absence, her father's psychological and physical distance, Bella's own exclusion from populist mainstream high school society and her marginal interest in cars that also speaks to the attraction of the vampire tale for the contemporary reader of the *Twilight* texts. Not only is the nominal vampire family isolated and marked as "Other" but so are the human "victim"/protagonist, Bella, and her family. No longer is the figure of the vampire the only "Other" delineated from society; the humans in this text are also dislocated and existentially adrift. They are as monstrous in their self-sufficiency as the vampire was historically and, just as in previous tales, such monstrosity must be constrained and normalized into the hegemony of the community. Katy describes Bella's status as key to her resonance with fans:

Bella is neither girl or woman, nor child or parent. She is both. Just like she sits on the cusp of turning into a vampire for a sustained period, Bella occupies the no man's land. She is between categories and consistently marginalized. (interview 06/14/2009)

Katy shows Bella as some category-defying other, but on closer inspection, *Twilight* is riddled with liminal characters: vampires who are dead yet alive, werewolves who are individual and yet operate as a collective pack, women who are not warriors but who heroically triumph over legions of murderous vampires, mothers and fathers who act like children, a coven of vegetarians who eat animals, and so on. Otherness and difference may well be tolerated because no one sits in a stable position.

This is the isolation to which Auerbach speaks in discussing her own vampire addiction in the mid-twentieth century. Her addiction to the vampire myth mirrored a personal social alienation that led to a liberating attraction for the myth delivering her "protection against a destiny of girdles, spike heels, and approval" (1995, p. 4) from the socially and gendered norm.

In such ways, consumers of the vampire product make of it what they will. As a mirror on which to project their own fears and fantasies, as an enabling device for actual or fictive transgression, as an entity through which they can cocreate narrative spaces in which their conscious experiences of the world perform or resist the workings of their unconscious. The administrator of the Twi-mom's forum posts: "*Twilight* is a way to keep the ecstatic memories of obsessive first love alive. It reminds you of what your current relationship can be." Dana asserts, "No, I'm not ever going to face choosing between a vampire and a werewolf mate, but I will be making other trade-offs and *Twilight* gives me some tools to use" (interview 04/12/2010).

Feminism and/in *Twilight*

The *Twilight* brand provides a media-based platform to think through the complexities of femininity and of the different incarnations of feminism. Patricia describes the need for *Twilight:*

> *Twilight* is useful. Like *Sex and the City, Twilight* gives fans a way to think through womanhood, sex, family, feminism...it sparks serious discussion...and the need for *Twilight* will never go away. Girls and women will always be negotiating their "difference" and their roles in society. (interview 11/23/2009)

Because the liminality is never fully resolved, there is ample opportunity for engagement and for continued engagement. The fan discourse is supported by the *Twilight* narrative, which leaves room for fans to write themselves into the story and to locate resonating themes (Derecho, 2006) to extend their brand engagement. In short, these data reveal that the liminalities are the key attributes of fan engagement. Furthermore, the primarily female enthusiasts of the brand grapple with fundamental issues surrounding femininity, expected roles, and modes of feminist resistance (Whelehan, 1995). Megan demonstrates the institutional element in terms of Bella and her position in her family of origin:

> The fact that she was adamant that she become a vampire was somewhat of a feminist move, but overall I don't believe she was a feminist. She fell into the female role a lot, especially with her dad...I feel like Edward definitely

wears the pants in their relationship. Things don't happen unless Edward wants them to. (interview 07/3/2009)

Interestingly, despite prevalent assertions that they have never really considered themselves feminists or even read feminist theories, the fans' discussions map rather closely onto third wave feminism that recognizes and asserts multifold gender positions (Henry, 2004). Courtney describes it like this: "Bella is me. She faces these choices all the time to be a 'good girl' and still bust the place up with passion. She is both. Feminism doesn't have to mean living without romance and enjoying womanhood" (interview 12/02/2009).

Twilight provides a distinct opportunity to contemplate, discuss, and work through social constructs (Harré & Gillett, 1994) and negotiate lived practices (Rodriguez, 2003). Hillery explains:

> I think the only time I thought much about feminism is when I was talking to friends about the *Twilight* series. We dissect Bella's actions. We relate them to our own lives. We work through our issues with *Twilight*…it is a catalyst for discussion. (interview 12/08/2009)

Schopp (1997) notes that it is "striking that women produce so many of the [vampire] products that…work out homoerotic desire" (p. 241) and suggests that writers like Rice (and Meyer?) are revising traditional notions of masculinity and male/male relations in order to explore sexual alternatives and socially proscribed roles and for "reconfiguring desire." Rochelle comments on this:

> I read the Rice vampire series after *Twilight* and I think there are a lot of similarities. The vampires play with gender. Carlyle turned Edward [into a vampire] with essentially a kiss…and intimacy of the nth degree…The Rice vampires are more overt in their homoerotic behaviors, but the vampire is ambiguous sexually. It is interesting. They are beautiful…metrosexuals who flirt and occasionally engage in intimate contact with other vampires of the same sex. It is incredibly sexy. Guys being [intimate] together…I'm left out of the equation but it is a turn on…I sort of get the threesome fantasy guys obsess about. (interview 03/10/2010)

Rochelle is turned on by the guys' homoerotic scenes. She equates this to the male obsession of being intimate with two females simultaneously. In essence, she flips her gender identification through the vampiric lens.

However, as Heywood and Drake (2004) assert, with third wave feminism comes not only the normalization of alternative sexualities in mass culture but also acknowledgment that "power understood as possessed by individuals has become inaccessible to almost everybody" (p. 18). Do *Twilight*'s female fans comprehend themselves as mired in a social and economic context that involves "relative gender equality in the context of economic downward mobility" (p. 15)? Are their paraxic desires and concerns not only with transgressions/liberations from sexual norms but with social positions of economic liminality and transgressions of corporate and state power? Stevie comments,

> Bella is so very vulnerable. Her parents don't have much money. The Cullens can afford everything. Bella and her dad live in a modest house. The Cullens live in a modern mansion. Bella needs financial aid to attend college and the Cullens drive fancy sports cars and go to private universities. Bella's dad fishes and probably bowls. The Cullens study music and fine arts. I wonder how much of her infatuation with Edward is the trappings of class? (interview 3/14/2010)

Certainly, the *Twilight* female protagonist, Bella, can be read as building on second wave feminist struggles to balance the personal and the professional, to overthrow patriarchal institutionalization and control, and to combat sexual violence. Her actions inscribe a challenge to palindromic (AVE/EVA) and essentialist perceptions of woman in order to escape the culturally encoded and binary oppositions of mind/body through which women have been historically constrained.

Bella's spectacular physical adroitness and her militant ability to battle evil also affirm second wave feminism. She is an exemplum of a sister "doing it for [herself]" as she performs her psychological and bodily activism against the constraints of societal and familial norms. Lexi, a high school athlete, puts it this way, "Bella is strong. She does her own thing. She makes her own choices. She is a kickass heroine who ultimately saves the day. Feminist—YESSSSSS!" (interview 04/19/2010).

But it is perhaps her ability to collectivize, to unify and pacify the diverse races represented in the *Twilight* worldview that marks her as a third wave hero(ine). Bella's liminal status is demonstrated throughout the various stages of the novels: She is the only human who can repel the mind control of the vampires, thereby enabling her to interact and anticipate their actions; she is a willing sexual and life partner to the eternal Edward; and she is the human/vampire birthmother to the monstrously gifted female child, Renesmee. A boundary spanner between human and nonhuman species, Bella collectivizes and pacifies the previously warring werewolf and vampire clans against the forces of greater darkness; she incorporates her clan's (human) familial activities with those of the nonhuman. Bella's ability to include diversity performs third wave's politics of hybridity (Heywood & Drake, 1997), as exemplified in her (gendered) performance when her daughter, Renesmee, is brought forth, a messianic product of hybrid liminality. Jody ponders:

> Bella is the glue that holds the story together. She is what unifies the characters...she is technically not like all the other creatures in the story, yet she shares similar plights. She works the boundary area between werewolf and vampire, between human and immortal. (interview 03/12/2010)

Woman, Myth, and Transformation

But let us return to nineteenth century beginnings. Just as *Twilight*'s vampires have their genesis in Victorian anxieties, desires, and concerns, so too do conceptions of the New/True Woman. As Auerbach (1982) details, the Victorian era saw the aggrandizement of the "true woman" as a figure sanctifying family and fueled the legislative triumphs of the "new woman," who galvanized society, because conservatives and radicals alike believed in woman's transforming power. She traces woman's rebirth of mythic potential in the popular culture of the age and brings forth a heroine who restores herself to "appropriate the powers of the destroying male" (p. 15).

In these myths, the victim transforms into the demon or, as Auerbach (1982) conceives it, an angel. These are angels who accrete to themselves the male characteristics of mobility, freedom, and the power of transformation. In essence, a woman liberates herself from the domestic and gendered restrictions of Coventry Patmore's "Angel in the House" to become a "demonic angel" (p. 186), appropriating all the magic left in the world and remaking herself. Citing Adrienne Rich (1976), Auerbach argues that myth is a response to the environment and the interaction between the mind and its external world. Myth, then, is always a source of contemporary strength.

The *Twilight* cultural product, via its main female characters Bella and Renesmee, enables female consumers to paraxically reify matrilineal power outstripping male power. Devonne puts it this way:

> Bella is this normal girl who hooks up for eternity with a vampire. She becomes the strongest one of them all on her terms...Through her insistence to have sex while she is still human she creates Renesemee—a being so extraordinary that she stumps and trumps the vampires. (interview 11/26/2009)

Devonne shows how Bella is able to subvert the order through the oldest institution, motherhood. Likewise, through reading and memorializing the myths of the past inherent in the variant *Twilight* texts, female readers of *Twilight* texts can actively cocreate a transformative performance space for normative and transgressive sexual and gender desires. Through fantastic liminality, *Twilight* opens the discursive space for girls and women actively to negotiate femininity and normative gender roles through the *Twilight* saga. The brand serves as a vehicle to contemplate women's potential and place in the world. In this way the "cultural myth [of the vampire] interacts with history, by giving shape to the lives that are history's [her story's] substance" (Auerbach, 1982, p. 3). Figure 2.6 features a fan, Delores, who has devoted considerable real estate to *Twilight* tattoos, which she feels directly relate to her experiences. She has indeed written her life onto the *Twilight* brand and then transferred back to her corporeal self.

CONCLUSION

While it would be easy to dismiss the *Twilight* phenomenon as yet another vampire tale or Harry Potter clone, this research demonstrates that *Twilight* is neither of these. Likewise, it might be tempting to claim that *Twilight* is no different from any other media brand that centers on a heroine's perspective, but then why do not *Hannah Montana* or *Desperate Housewives* inspire the same level and tenor of fan discourse about gender performance? A keyword search of the four largest *Desperate Housewives* fan forums and the two largest *Hannah Montana* fan forums finds few and

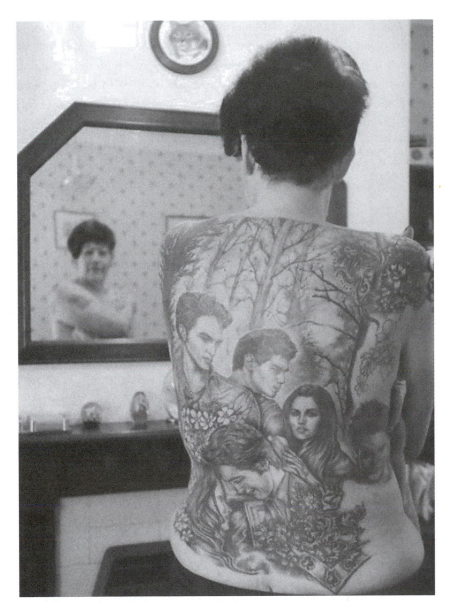

FIGURE 2.6
Fan's life story in *Twilight*-themed tattoos.

sparse references to feminism or feminist: *DH* had a total of 26 posts and no dedicated threads containing those words and *HM* had a total of five posts and no thread titles, while across the top three *Twilight* fan forums the words appear in 1,118 posts and are in the title of 41 threads.

What accounts for the relative emphasis on feminism in the *Twilight* fan community? Perhaps it is that the sexual prohibitions and tensions inherent in the figure(s) of the *Twilight* vampire(s)—male/male, female/male, and female/female relations—allow for fissures to be explored in the heteronormative rocks of gender identity and social code. As we have shown, the members of the *Twilight* brand community have used *Twilight* as a platform for contemplating their existence and a muse for creating inspired lives.

NOTE

1. Auerbach, 1984, p. 4 (commenting on Carlyle).

REFERENCES

Auerbach, Nina (1982). *Woman and the demon: The life of a Victorian myth.* Cambridge, MA: Harvard University Press.

Auerbach, Nina (1995). *Our vampires, ourselves.* Chicago, IL: University of Chicago Press.

Bagozzi, Richard P., & Utpal M. Dholakia (2006). Antecedents and purchase consequences of customer participation in small group brand communities. *International Journal of Research in Marketing, 23* (March), 45–61.

Catterall, Miriam, Pauline Maclaran, & Lorna Stevens (2000). Marketing and feminism: An evolving relationship. In Lorna Stevens, Miriam Catterall, & Pauline Maclaran (Eds.), *Marketing and feminism: Current issues and research* (pp. 1–15). London, England: Routledge.

Costa, Janeen Arnold (2000). Gender and consumption in a cultural context. In Lorna Stevens, Miriam Catterall, & Pauline Maclaran (Eds.), *Marketing and feminism: Current issues and research* (pp. 255–275). London, England: Routledge.

Cova, Bernard, & Veronique Cova (2002). Tribal marketing: The tribalization of society and its impact on the conduct of marketing. *European Journal of Marketing, 36*(5/6), 595–620.

Craft, Christopher (1988). "Kiss me with those red lips": Gender and inversion in Bram Stoker's *Dracula*. In Margaret L Carter (Ed.), *Dracula: The vampire and his critics* (pp. 167–194). Ann Arbor, MI: UMI Research.

Derecho, Abigail (2006). Different approaches: Fan fiction in context. In Karen Hellekson & Kristina Busse (Eds.), *Fan fiction and fan communities in the age of the Internet* (pp. 61–78). Jefferson, NC: McFarland and Company, Inc.

Dobscha, Susan, & Julie Ozanne (2000). Marketing and the divided self: Healing the nature/woman separation. In Lorna Stevens, Miriam Catterall, & Pauline Maclaran (Eds.), *Marketing and feminism: Current issues and research* (pp. 239–254). London, England: Routledge.

Dresser, Norine (1989). *American vampires: Fans, victims and practitioners.* New York, NY: W. W. Norton and Company.

Finke, Nikki (2009). Nikki Finke's power list. *Elle Magazine* (October 16): http://www.elle.com/Pop-Culture/Movies-TV-Music-Books/Nikki-Finke-s-Power-List

Friedberg, Anne (1993). *Window shopping: Cinema and the postmodern.* Los Angeles, CA: University of California Press.

Gill, Rosalind (2007). Postfeminist media culture: Elements of a sensibility. *European Journal of Cultural Studies, 10*(2), 147–166.

Goulding, Christina, & Michael Saren (2009). Performing identity: An analysis of gender expressions at the Whitby Goth Festival. *Consumption Markets & Culture, 12* (February), 27–46.

Harré, Rom, & Grant Gillett (1994). *The discussive mind.* London: Sage.

Henry, Astrid (2004). *Not my mother's sister: Generational conflict and third-wave feminism.* Bloomington, IN: Indiana University Press.

Heywood, Leslie, & Jennifer Drake (1997). We learn America like a script: Activism in the third wave; or, enough phantoms of nothing. In Leslie Heywood & Jennifer Drake (Eds.), *Third wave agenda: Being feminist, doing feminism* (pp. 40–54). Minneapolis, MN: Minnesota University Press.

Heywood, Leslie, & Jennifer Drake (2004). "It's all about the Benjamins": Economic determinants of third wave feminism in the United States. In Stacy Gillis, Gillian Howie, & Rebecca Munford (Eds.), *Third wave feminism: A critical exploration* (pp. 13–23). New York, NY: Palgrave Macmillan.

Jackson, Rosemary (1981). *Fantasy: The literature of subversion.* New York, NY: Methuen.

Jenkins, Henry (1992). *Textual poachers: Television fans and participatory culture.* London, England: Routledge.

Johnson, Merri Lisa (2007). *Third wave feminism and television: Jane puts it in a box.* New York, NY: IB Tauris.

Martin, Diane, John Schouten, & James McAlexander (2006). Claiming the throttle: Multiple femininities in a hyper-masculine subculture. *Consumption, Markets & Culture* (September), 171–205.

McAlexander, James H., John W. Schouten, & Harold F. Koening (2002). Building brand community. *Journal of Marketing, 66* (January), 38–54.

Moscucci, Ornella (1990). *The science of woman: Gynecology and gender in England 1800–1929.* Cambridge, England: Press Syndicate of Cambridge Press.

Mulvey, Laura (1975). Visual pleasure and narrative cinema. *Screen, 16*(3), 6–18.

Muñiz, Albert M., Jr., & Thomas C. O'Guinn (2001). Brand community. *Journal of Consumer Research, 27* (March), 412–432.

Muñiz, Albert M., Jr., & Hope Jensen Schau (2005). Religiosity in the abandoned Apple Newton brand community. *Journal of Consumer Research, 31*(March), 737–747.

Muñiz, Albert M., Jr., & Hope Jensen Schau (2007). Vigilante marketing and consumer-created communications. *Journal of Advertising, 36* (Fall), 35–50.

Owen, A. Susan (1999). Vampires, postmodernity, and postfeminism: *Buffy the Vampire Slayer. Journal of Popular Film and Television, 27* (Summer), 24–31.

Pomerantz, Dorothy, & Lacey Rose (2010). The celebrity 100 rankings. *Forbes,* July 19.

Rich, Adrienne (1976). *Of woman born: Motherhood as experience and institution.* New York, NY: Norton.

Rodriguez, Juana Maria (2003). *Queer Latinidad: Identity practices, discursive spaces.* New York: NYU Press.

Schau, Hope Jensen, Albert M. Muñiz Jr., & Eric J. Arnould (2009). How brand community practices create value. *Journal of Marketing, 73* (September), 30–51.

Schopp, Andrew (1997). Cruising the alternatives: Homoeroticism and the contemporary vampire. *Journal of Popular Culture, 30*(4) (Spring), 231–243.

Scott, Linda (2000). Market feminism: The case for a paradigm shift. In Lorna Stevens, Miriam Catterall, & Pauline Maclaran (Eds.), *Marketing and feminism: Current issues and research* (pp. 16–38). London, England: Routledge.

Smilie, Dirk (2010). The highest paid authors, *Forbes,* August 19: http://www.forbes.com/2010/08/19/patterson-meyer-king-business-media-highest-paid-authors.html

Szmigin, Isabelle, & Alexander E. Reppel (2004). Internet community bonding: The case of Macnews. *European Journal of Marketing, 38*(5/6), 626–640.

Thompson, Craig J., Aric Rindfleisch, & Zeynep Arsel (2006). Emotional branding and the strategic value of the doppelganger brand image. *Journal of Marketing, 70* (January), 50–64.

Twitchell, James B. (1981). *The living dead: A study of the vampire in Romantic literature.* Durham, NC: Duke University Press.

Twitchell, James B. (1985). *Dreadful pleasures: An anatomy of modern horror.* New York, NY: Oxford University Press.

Whelehan, Imelda (1995). *Modern feminist thought: From second wave to "postfeminism."* Edinburgh, Scotland: University Press.

Section II

Media, Advertising, and Gender

3

The Carnal Feminine: Consuming Representations of Womanhood in a Contemporary Media Text

Lorna Stevens and Pauline Maclaran

INTRODUCTION

This chapter is derived from a prior study we conducted that explored women's identification with carnality and nature in contemporary television advertisements. To explore this identification, we drew on the age-old social and cultural underpinnings of this association in order to reveal and begin to understand what we argued was the ubiquitous conflation of womanhood with the body in Western media texts. Furthermore, we argued that media texts such as advertisements served as myth carriers that reinforced deep-seated cultural meanings and that these were indelibly imprinted on our collective cultural psyches. (For a more detailed discussion of the carnal feminine, refer to our earlier study: Stevens & Maclaran, 2008.) In the earlier study we debated whether or not we should be concerned about the all-pervasive "carnal feminine" in our culture, viewing it as an age-old discrimination against women (Paglia, 1992) or embracing it as symptomatic of a positive, postmodern "return to the body" in cultural studies and women's studies. This latter perspective arguably serves to validate women's bodies and thereby women's lives (Davis, 1997).

Building from the primary study, we now turn our attention to a different kind of media text: the film *Sex and the City* and its much-anticipated sequel,

Sex and the City 2. Based on the U.S. television series of the same name, the original 2008 film offered a heady mix of fashion, fun, friendship, and sex set against the backdrop of New York City. The second film was released in 2010.

We argue that both films are highly significant in terms of contemporary representations of womanhood, in that they trace (and perhaps encapsulate) what has become a defining zeitgeist in embodied femininity as it is currently portrayed in popular media texts. This spirit, which we might perceive as an aspect of the "carnal feminine," has been described in primarily negative ways by feminist commentators as arguably having a detrimental effect on women's advancement in contemporary Western society. It is further suggested by Walter (2010) that it has a particularly harmful effect on young women, primarily because it equates young women's empowerment and liberation with sexual excesses and separates sex from emotional intimacy, thus paving the way for the "pornification" of sex in our culture.

Of course, the conflation of women's liberation with sexual licentiousness is not new, and indeed it has been a dominant ideology in young women's magazines such as *Cosmopolitan* since the 1970s, largely thanks to Helen Gurley Brown's influential book, *Sex and the Single Girl* (1962), and the lifestyle (and version of women's liberation) that it celebrated. However, there is a sense that this has escalated in recent years. This phenomenon has been variously described as retrosexism (Whelehan, 2000), porno-chic (McNair, 2002), sexual subjectification (Gill, 2003), raunch culture (Levy, 2005), and, more recently, as a hypersexual culture that hails the return of sexism (Walter, 2010) and the triumph of the one-dimensional woman (Power, 2009).

To contribute to this debate and consider its implications in relation to gender, culture, and consumer behavior, we propose to deconstruct the two films, in order to explore the consumer behavior they celebrate and the gendered nature of that consumer behavior. We will also unpack the underlying cultural values that are being valorized in these texts.

We hope that our analysis will enable us to understand better how the three dynamics of gender, consumer behavior, and culture interplay with one another in the marketplace to create all-pervasive, dominant texts that draw on past and present practices and performances of femininities. First, we explore the concept of the carnal feminine in more detail, showing how this reinforces associations between women, their appetites, and shopping in contemporary consumer culture. Then we discuss feminist debates around the concept, before going on to give an overview of the *Sex and City* genre (hereafter referred to as *SATC*). Next, we present our analysis as to how the "carnal feminine" underpins the two films in relation to plot, main characters, costumes, and settings, discussing the problematic this underpinning motif creates. We finish our chapter with a deeper look at the intersection of the carnal feminine and the marketplace. In so doing, we highlight how the marketization and commodification of the female body may be encouraging what Walter (2010) describes as the hypersexualization of Western culture and the restriction of choice for women, rather than increasing empowerment and freedom for them.

THE CARNAL FEMININE

Popular culture often portrays women as being controlled by their bodily desires. The "carnal feminine" narrative in media texts such as advertisements, films, and popular television programs often manifests itself as an identification of women with carnality; they are experiential bodies intimately engaging with the marketplace. The "carnal feminine" is an ancient narrative that depicts women as being prey to their bodily appetites (Stevens & Maclaran, 2008). The word *carnal* is from the Latin *carnalis,* from *caro carnis,* meaning "flesh." The definition of "carnal" is "of the body or flesh; worldly." Its secondary meaning is also noteworthy: "worldly, sensual, sexual" (*Oxford English Dictionary*). The "carnal feminine" thesis argues that femininity in Western culture has been traditionally associated with the body and its attendant weaknesses and excesses. By extension, men have been traditionally regarded as being "naturally" more rational than women, and thus they have had the ability to transcend their bodies' urges. Women, however, are not able to do this, as they are at the mercy of their needs, wants, and desires (Joy & Venkatesh, 1994).

According to Marina Warner (2000), the identification of women with carnality, instinct, and passion is an ancient one that contrasted strongly with women's opposite, men, who were identified with reason, control, and spirituality. Camille Paglia (1992) offers an equally persuasive account of the gendered dualism at the heart of human civilization: the tussle between nature (the feminine and women) and culture (the masculine and men). These dualisms are deeply embedded and have had important implications for how masculinity and femininity have been experienced historically and continue to be experienced. We argue that this legacy lives on in contemporary cultural representations of gender.

In Western culture, furthermore, the mind was deemed to be more important than the body, and thus it was "privileged" over the body. Womanhood had a dangerous, appetitive, and volatile nature; unlike men, women were at the mercy of their mortal bodies, subject to the body's frailties and vagaries, and buffeted by their feminine natures (Bordo, 1993; Davis, 1997; Schiebinger, 2000; Showalter, 1987).

The idea that women are at the mercy of their desires and are powerless to resist the temptations offered by the marketplace has a long history in marketing and consumer culture. Nava (1997) describes the emergence of glamorous and luxurious department stores in nineteenth century Paris. These stores offered women the freedom and space to engage in the pleasures of consumption and spectacle, as well as enjoy social encounters in elegant surroundings. These feminine spaces were described in contemporary accounts as encouraging women to behave in uncontrollable ways, however, because they unleashed a dangerous aspect of feminine nature. Words such as "passions," "temptations," "seductive," and "desire" were often used to describe women's shopping behaviors, and indeed women's lack of self-control in their pursuit of pleasure was observed with some anxiety by male commentators as signifying "a fear of nature out of control" (Huyssen in Nava, 1997, p. 77). The French novelist Emile Zola, for example, in his book, *The Ladies' Paradise,* wrote about the "longing covetous gaze" of women shoppers, using erotic language to convey the heightened excitement these retail spaces provoked in women. Elsewhere, he describes women sale-shoppers as aggressive and voracious in their lust for a bargain (in Nava, 1997, p. 76).

The notion that women's shopping behavior is always in danger of spinning out of control was demonstrated in Eugen Bleuler's *Textbook of Psychiatry* in 1924. In his book, Bleuler offered the first account of compulsive buying or "oniomania," from the Greek term combining *onios* (for sale) and *mania* (insanity). He stated that compulsive buying behavior always involved women; they were frivolous and always caused debt, due to their constant pursuit of pleasure. He also identified this propensity with female hysteria, which, thanks to Freud, was a concept enjoying much popularity at that time.

More recently, Campbell (1997), among others (see, for example, Otnes & McGrath, 2001), has noted that shopping is an activity that is gendered as feminine and thus is associated with women. He also describes the ideologies surrounding male and female shopping behaviors, which have served to legitimize gendered shopping behaviors. For women, the dominant narrative is that going shopping (as distinct from doing shopping, a functional form of shopping) is a leisure activity that provides considerable (and, at times, unrestrained) pleasure.

The perception that women enjoy shopping and may be inclined to overindulge in such activities is one that continues to hold sway. In fact, the notion that women are predisposed to engage in unbridled consumption is a powerful and indeed dominant one in contemporary consumer culture generally. It is a narrative that often depicts women as "consummate consumers" ruled by their bodies' appetites and unable to resist the lure of carnal pleasures (Belk, 1998; Belk & Costa, 1998). Typically, these carnal appetites are those associated with sex and food. Often the two drives combine in popular depictions of womanhood, so that women are shown consuming food and other products in ways that suggest lust, seduction, sexual climax, and autoeroticism (Stratton, 1996). The notion that women's "animal" appetites are always in danger of spiraling out of control thus continues to endure in Western culture (Bordo, 1993; Orbach, 1978, 2002; Urla & Swedlund, 2000; Wolf, 1991), and shopping is often represented as the ideal means for women to satisfy their lust for pleasure.

FEMINISM AND THE CARNAL FEMININE

Debates around the notion of the "carnal feminine" also reflect the differences and disjuncture between second and third wave feminism. From a second wave feminist perspective, the "carnal feminine" stems from the mind/body Cartesian dualisms such as culture/nature and mind/body that associate the body and nature with the feminine and also devalue these categories against their superior masculine counterparts (mind and culture). These carnal associations are created by a patriarchy-dominated culture where women's bodies are objectified and commoditized through advertising and marketing machines that create concomitant problems of eating and body image disorders. Third wave perspectives, emerging in the 1990s, collapsed such binary divisions, taking poststructuralist/postmodern positions that celebrate (sexual) difference and defy objectification through revalidating the body as a means of empowerment. For example, Swan (2005) describes the use of glamour when teaching MBA classes as a way to disrupt the traditional disembodied masculine subject of academic life.

Thus, third wave feminism redefined feminism for a new generation of women who, unlike their mothers, had grown up taking the gains of the women's movement for granted (Henry, 2004, 2008). Whereas their second wave predecessors fought many collective battles for women's rights in the workplace and over their own bodies (e.g., contraception and abortion, respectively), this new generation of "girlie feminists" is seen as more individualistic and concerned with dress, pleasure, sex, and family, areas often trivialized by the "old feminists" (Scott, 2005, p. 324). Describing the second wave as "victim feminism" with its focus on women's vulnerability and lack of agency (Henry, 2008), third wavers focus on a woman's right to pleasure, especially her right to explore and determine her own sexuality and display her body however she chooses. This is not just echoing the second wave liberal feminist attitude of "doing it like a man," but is rather a celebration of all things feminine and thus a type of hybridized feminism derived from both liberal and cultural feminisms.

Some argue that this third wave perspective stifles wider sociopolitical critique and confines it to individual identity creation in the marketplace (e.g., Catterall, Maclaran, & Stevens, 2005; Power, 2009). Others argue, however, that it represents a generational rebellion and the protective tendency of mothers to censure their daughters for breaking new ground, especially if it is of a sexual nature (Henry, 2004, 2008; Scott, 2005). Indeed, Scott (2005) makes the point that this censure can be likened to the early suffragettes' condemnation of the flappers in the 1920s, who similarly celebrated pleasure and femininity.

Power (2009), however, makes a particularly scathing analysis of how "liberating" feminism has gone hand in hand with the notion of "liberating" capitalism to such an extent that "almost everything turns out to be 'feminist'—shopping, pole-dancing, even eating chocolate" (p. 27). Arguing that contemporary media portrayals suggest that the height of female achievement culminates "in the ownership of expensive handbags, a vibrator, a job, a flat and a man—probably in that order" (p. 1), Power suggests that this "one-dimensional woman" is no more emancipated than her predecessors. She has become the slave of a neoliberal marketplace logic that emphasizes individualism and feeds the desire to acquire more material possessions at the expense of any broader collective political action (see also Catterall et al., 2005). Walter (2010) would concur with this view. She argues that the current hypersexual culture "has reflected and exaggerated the deeper imbalances of power in our society" (p. 8). She goes on to suggest that without economic and political change we are not experiencing the equality we sought; rather, she believes that we are witnessing "a stalled revolution" (p. 9).

SEX AND THE CITY AS A WOMAN'S GENRE

In many ways, *SATC* encapsulates third wave feminist perspectives and their problematics. This groundbreaking TV series of sex and single women has spawned a whole genre of TV series and films, all of which celebrate the lives of affluent young women with their fashionable clothes and chic friends, who spend their leisure time "drinking lattes in cafes and cocktails in hotel bars, having sex with strangers—sometimes good, sometimes weird, sometimes bad—without much emotional engagement" (Walter, 2010, p. 51).

SATC as a genre elicits many mixed responses from its audience, which is almost exclusively women. Love it or hate it (and most men adopt the latter position), it has firmly left its mark emblazoned on contemporary popular culture, not least since it foregrounds consumption as a means of expressing gender (Zayer et al., forthcoming). Not only has it become a favored topic for heated dinner party debates, but it is also the subject of endless blogs on feminist websites. In these blogs, it is not unusual for discussants to take a confessional approach, acknowledging *SATC* to be a guilty pleasure, something publicly dismissed as shallow and silly but privately consumed as engaging and entertaining.

Why such strong reactions and such guilt? While guilt often goes hand in hand with women's consumption of women's genres, we suggest that we need to interrogate these ambivalent reactions and search for the gendered assumptions that give rise to them. After all, as Andy Cohen (Bravo TV show executive/host and friend of Sarah Jessica Parker) is reported to have said, "Given the amount of actually stupid/ridiculous movies that come out every year, I was amazed by the degree of vitriol leveled at a good one (of very few) that celebrates women" (www.feministe.us).

It is well documented that terms like "frivolous" and "trivial" are usually reserved for female-oriented media forms and that "chick flicks" are always judged more harshly than their male equivalents—firmly positioned and trivialized as low, inferior culture rather than significant, worthy, high culture, and perceived to have little literary or artistic merit (see Lury, 1996, and Hollows, 2000, for a fuller discussion of this issue). While postmodern perspectives have challenged this view and have heralded a reevaluation of popular culture (McRobbie, 1994; Storey, 1998), nevertheless this perception persists in cultural studies.

Despite the fact that this is a chick flick, then, and thus is inherently lightweight in cultural terms, when we look below the surface glitter and gossip, *SATC* has been groundbreaking in many ways. First of all, it is centered on women's experiences and, importantly, frank discussions of these experiences, particularly in relation to sex, a previously taboo area for public consumption. A film devoted to women talking, let alone about sex, challenges both cinematic conventions (Power, 2009) and the devaluation of "small talk" in our culture (Alexander, Burt, & Collinson, 1995).

Ultimately, *SATC* is about female friendship and the bonds between women that prove stronger than any created with men. Reincke (1991) highlights how women laughing with other women threaten male dominance much more than women laughing at men. In this respect, *SATC* also raises the specter of the single woman. Nelson (2008, p. 83) argues that "the single woman is a loaded figure in American history, one around which heated political and cultural debates about women's place in society have often centered."

SATC continuously disrupts traditional ideas about older women, fashion, morals, rights, and sex, providing a space for discourse that challenges the heteronormativity of mainstream media (Gennaro, 2007). It also raises questions about the institution of marriage and issues around womanhood and freedom against the backdrop of a changing social landscape (Zayer et al., forthcoming). Each character is working through her own feminist issues: Charlotte is coping with the pressures of being the perfect mother; Miranda is trying to find a balance between family life and her high-powered corporate career; Samantha is countering the suppression of woman's sexuality; and Carrie is setting her own rules and expectations in a nontraditional marriage.

While as a genre *SATC* can be acclaimed for breaking many conventions and taboos, it faces recurrent criticisms that it is not only superficial and trite, but also racist and sexist, in that it is only concerned with the rights and experiences of a certain class of women (White, privileged). In particular, it is accused of epitomizing the materialism and fashion lust that some see as Western women's continuing oppression (Wolf, 1991). Through its presentation of a hedonistic, aspirational consumer lifestyle

(Konig, 2008), *SATC* offers up a diluted and commodified feminism that many argue is meaningless (McRobbie, 2009; Power, 2009; Walter, 2010).

We continue now to explore the intersection of gender and consumption in a more detailed analysis of the films *Sex and the City* (premiered May 12, 2008) and its sequel, *Sex and the City 2* (premiered May 27, 2010). In order to do this analysis, both authors watched the two films independently several times each, undertaking a thematic analysis in relation to the carnal feminine and how this construction maps onto consumer desires. We then compared and contrasted our findings, agreeing on core motifs, themes, and key scenes through a "to-ing" and "fro-ing" process.

This was essentially a multilayered discourse, as Hirschman (1998) observes with regard to conducting research of this nature. The method draws on Hirschman's work on common-culture readers and readings and compares this to expert readers and readings. With regard to the latter, she writes: "Expert readers are those who have been socialized into a second ideological perspective which they may choose to apply to interpreting textual products, in addition to using their common-culture knowledge" (p. 261). The emphasis in such research approaches is to produce interpretations that may challenge or subvert common-culture ones, deconstructing that which is taken for granted in texts.

This approach is particularly prevalent in feminist literary approaches, where feminist researchers actively read against the grain of texts in order to expose and challenge their underlying ideologies. Feminist literary approaches have been adopted with aplomb by researchers such as Barbara Stern and Elizabeth Hirschman in our field. Typically, these analyses, while grounded in common culture and everyday life, also draw on higher level, ideological abstractions to unravel the layers of meanings in texts. It should also be noted that both authors belong to the same interpretive community (see Fish, 1980, for a full discussion of this construct), which can be summarized as a feminist and interpretive one. This perspective therefore influenced our individual readings of the two films, as well as the collective readings that emerged through discussions with one another. As interpretive researchers, we acknowledge that we do not assume our collective interpretation of the two films to be the only and right one. The presentation of our findings is organized under four key aspects of film analysis: (1) plot, (2) main characters, (3) costumes, and (4) settings.

ANALYSIS

The Plot

The plot of *SATC* revolves around labels and love, about dressing up and styling the body, and about responding to the body's urges and imperatives. Initially, it is the "love" side of the coin to which the audience is introduced. Carrie Bradshaw, the narrator, is a writer and columnist who documents her friends' relationships with men. Charlotte is looking for the perfect man, finds him, changes her religion, and adopts a child when they are "reproductively challenged." Miranda is a disciple of "tough love" who adopts a no-nonsense approach to relationships but then becomes pregnant and moves to Brooklyn with her househusband partner, Steve, and their son, Brady. Samantha meets a man who combines "sex and love" and she journeys with him to Hollywood to make him a star. Carrie has been looking for a big love, and she finds that in Mr. Big.

The main plot of *SATC* focuses on Carrie's relationship with Mr. Big. Carrie reveals that she has a whimsical, romantic, wistful side to her nature in her narratorial musings, but she also is very much grounded in the material world, with all its glorious trappings. This is particularly apparent in her relationship with Mr. Big, who is a man of considerable means. Carrie makes no secret of the fact that she wants the fairytale ending. She is easily persuaded to take part in the *Vogue* feature on weddings, which her editor says will prove "to single girls everywhere that there can be a happy ending, even after 40!" Her pleasure in posing in couture wedding dresses makes it clear that the fairytale has a powerful appeal for her. We see her wistfully reading a book of love letters by famous men, and when she gently chides Mr. Big for not writing her love letters, he says "Does a love fax count? I'm sure my secretary sent you one…I'm not the romantic type."

Carrie, on the other hand, is. When she agrees to become part of the *Vogue* wedding dress feature as the 40-year-old bride to be, her fairytale dream is on the verge of coming true: a designer wedding dress, a wealthy Prince Charming, and a palace in real estate heaven. She is Cinderella, about to be "carried away" by the man of her dreams. In this regard she perfectly embodies the two most sacred tenets of American culture: romantic love and excessive consumption (Otnes & Pleck, 2003). Furthermore, drawing on this study, Carrie's materialism demonstrates the legitimization of consumption as an expression of perfection. However, the perfection she imagines is about to disappear in reality. When faced with this lavish wedding with all its trappings, Mr. Big gets cold feet and jilts Carrie at the altar.

This catastrophic event in the film results in a complete loss of control by Carrie. She abandons the masquerade of fashion, fantasy, and fixing and retreats to a darkened room, in order to lick her wounds in private. Significantly, her first sign of recovery is having a laugh, at Charlotte's expense, when the carnality of life re-presents itself and provides them all with some lavatory humor. This down-to-earth episode marks the turning point for Carrie in the first film and enables her to reenter the world of the body, albeit a female body that in the context of feminine consumer culture is constructed, contrived, and costumed. Eventually, she does get her man (and in keeping with the Cinderella story they are brought together again by a pair of exquisite shoes!), but this is a simpler, low-key affair, in which Carrie dispenses with all the trappings of a fairytale wedding and has a much less ostentatious one instead.

The second film continues to build on the themes presented in the first film and thus centers on the friendships of the four women and their relationships with men. The film is set 2 years after *SATC* finishes. Carrie is getting used to an unconventional marriage with Mr. Big, with no children and no cooking at the top of her agenda. Charlotte grapples with the challenges of toddler tantrums and a voluptuous, bra-less Irish nanny. Miranda struggles with a sexist new boss who silences her at every opportunity, while househusband Steve enjoys quality time with their young son, Brady. Samantha comes to the rescue of the girls when she gets the chance to take her friends on a luxury, all-expenses-paid public relations vacation to Abu Dhabi. The trip offers the friends the opportunity to escape from their responsibilities and indulge in some downtime with one another in lavish and luxurious surroundings. Much of the humor in *SATC2* centers on Samantha's efforts to stave off menopausal symptoms after she is deprived of her HRT drugs and supplements at Abu Dhabi airport.

The film also develops cultural themes merely hinted at in *SATC*, particularly in its privileging of White, Western culture in comparison to "the Other"—in this case, Middle Eastern culture. Its main focus is the comparative freedoms of women, particularly in relation to the body, clothing, and, in Samantha's case, sexual behavior. The climax of the Abu Dhabi adventure is that they are chased by irate local men because Samantha breaks the strict dress code rules for women. The rescue of the girls by local women who provide them with shelter reveals that women in Abu Dhabi are not so different from Western women after all: They share a love of labels.

The Main Characters

Our first vision of Carrie, the lead character, walking down a New York street in a pale pink tutu, clearly positions her as a childlike woman, and her predominant mood is one of flirty girlishness and a somewhat contrived kookiness, primarily visible in terms of her pick-and-mix style of dressing and her childlike enthusiasm for life. She is the dressed-up carnal feminine, with her appetite for labels and love, both of which reside in the realm of the body. However, this is a carefully contained carnality; her sexual appetite and musings are more akin to the romance novel than to the sex manual. She is Scarlett O'Hara, affecting coyness but breathlessly swept away by the worldly, adventurous, and amorous charms of the ruthless but lovable rake, Rhett Butler (aka Mr. Big). He also happens to be fabulously wealthy and powerful, a not insignificant detail for such a material girl. While her appetite for labels and Mr. Big may seem excessive, her appetites elsewhere are carefully controlled; indeed, hers is a highly disciplined and somewhat fragile looking body, very slim and toned.

Carrie's obsession with fashion underlines her dedication to her body. It is an ongoing creative project for her, very much framed within feminine consumer culture that celebrates the beauty fix and the pleasures of dressing up. Indeed, in her passion for fashion, she recalls that famous icon Barbie, and she certainly has as many outfits. She joyfully immerses herself in a feminine space that is defined by the never-ending impetus to construct and reconstruct versions of femininity continually, through the judicious use of props that facilitate the "elaborate masquerade" of the beauty system (Radner, 1995, p. xiii). In her narcissistic preoccupation with dressing her body, she is a woman who arguably "reproduces herself for herself, not for others" (Radner, 1995, p. xii). (See Chapter 8 in this volume for further discussion of narcissism.) Carrie also expects her friends to share her passion for the body regime to which she subscribes, horrified when they are perceived to be letting their bodies go, through overeating (as in the case of Samantha at one stage in *SATC*) or underexercising (as in the case with Charlotte when she gives up jogging due to concerns over her baby when she becomes pregnant).

Miranda is the female body that assumes androgynous form. She is a career woman, a successful lawyer known for her direct, ballsy, no-nonsense approach to life and relationships. She inhabits a man's world and to succeed in that world she underplays her sexuality. Crop-haired and partial to power dressing, she is the 1990s woman who has succeeded by being one of the guys, and this includes her attitude to sex. Embracing the third wave feminist model, she behaves in the same ways as the men around her, which includes having a casual, no-strings-attached, emotionally disengaged approach to sex, summed up by her phrase "Bye— great sex!" Miranda believes she is in control of her body and that she can marshal it to do her bidding, be it disguising her body by dressing as an asexual, professional career woman or being a sexually liberated, promiscuous woman enjoying the rich pickings of sexual licentiousness provided by the free and easy mores of New York City in the 1990s. But her body has bigger plans for her. One of her sexual encounters results in her getting pregnant and suddenly her simple, functional approach to sex results in the ultimate biological result: a baby!

Miranda's submission to her pregnant state and subsequent commitment to Steve marks the beginning of a change in priorities. Her tussle with the carnal feminine, the body, is over and she returns to her body and her roles as lover and mother, which are now more real to her than the high flying life of a corporate lawyer. Her submission to the imperatives of the body is perhaps summed up by her rueful comment in relation to her appetite for food, when she jokes that she has got her body's appetite for food under control: She has discovered spandex underwear!

Samantha, "libidinous and liberated from seemingly all constraints" (Greven, 2008, p. 43), is the "carnal feminine" personified in all its glory. She is a woman with a voracious appetite for sex, who has sex at every opportunity. She is womanhood as sexual subject rather than sexual object, the *Cosmo* woman incarnate. When sex is not available, she turns to that other stalwart of the carnal feminine, food, devouring excessive amounts of it when her sex life is constrained by her partner's busy working schedule. Like Miranda, her attitude to sex underlines the third wave feminist position that men and women are fundamentally the same when it comes to sex, given half a chance, and that liberation means having lots of sex, with as little emotional investment as possible. When sex is in short supply, she finds sexual excitement in voyeuristically and lasciviously consuming the spectacle of her lusty male neighbor's sexual activities. In so doing she observes, "He's me! Five years ago!" thus underlining her view that men and women are no different in these matters.

The "carnal feminine" representations of womanhood often manifest joyous, irreverent, celebratory, and comedic aspects, and Samantha exemplifies these traits. She is a sassy, voluptuous, sensual person who embraces life with gusto and says yes to everything. (Carrie notes at one stage that the word "no" is not in Samantha's vocabulary!) She is also a very successful and wealthy public relations person who therefore meets men on equal terms at all levels. Women who are unapologetically excessive in terms of their appetites often suffer their comeuppance in popular media texts such as books, films, and advertisements; in Samantha's case, the ultimate comeuppance is ageing. While she is aware that she is "50 and fabulous," she attributes this to various interventions such as Botox and her arsenal of HRT medications and supplements that stave off menopause, but when these are taken from her at Abu Dhabi airport in *SATC2*, her body proceeds to act its menopausal age. At all levels, then, Samantha is the carnal feminine: her body defines her and, at times, it defies her too!

Charlotte is the fragrant, sweet-natured foil to the carnal feminine. She is wholesome, conservative, romantic, and somewhat prissy, easily shocked by the antics of her more extrovert friends. She is hyperfeminine, a woman who defines her femininity in old-fashioned terms. Her personality, physical persona, and style of dressing recall the heyday of the domestic goddess of the 1950s, a feminine prototype that brought glamour and the domestic sphere together. She is a wide-eyed innocent who embodies traditional values when it comes to sex and relationships.

Her relationship with her body is to keep it in check, just as she does her behavior. However, her surprise pregnancy enables the "unruly body" to take center stage in Charlotte's life, and the body thus earns its place at the center of her being and reproductive nature. As with all women who control their animalistic natures, the refined Charlotte is ripe for a fall, and fall she does, in spectacularly vulgar fashion, when she unwittingly imbibes water while in Abu Dhabi, thus setting a catastrophic train in motion, "lavatorially" speaking. Her collapse from coiffed to caught short provides a wonderfully carnivalesque, carnal moment in *SATC2,* and the laughter it provokes enables Charlotte to assume her rightful place as a member of the carnal feminine sisterhood. The mask (and masquerade) of hyperfemininity slips, and it turns out that Charlotte is not so ladylike after all! So the body reigns supreme over our four heroines, mocking vanity, folly, and pride, as each of the characters struggles to negotiate identity and choice within a binary system that ultimately belittles and punishes the female body for its biological excesses and lack of control.

Costumes

The pivotal role of fashion in *SATC* is best exemplified by Carrie's voiceover introduction to the first film: "Year after year, 20-something women come to New York City in search of the two Ls: labels and love." As if to emphasize this point and the fact that labels take precedence over love, more than 300 different ensembles were used during the course of the first film (Donahue, 2008).

In this respect, the films take their lead from the *SATC* TV series that has been described as "television's hottest catwalk," and the clothes, shoes, and accessories are equal stars of the show—the "fifth character," according to Bruzzi and Church Gibson (2008, p. 115). Throughout both films there is an endless parade of exclusive designer labels and couturier outfits. Indeed, the four lead characters are never on any occasion seen in the same clothing, a fact that ensures their continuous and very embodied identification with the dynamic world of fashion and that emphasizes their insatiable appetites for new creations—the "carnal feminine" materialized.

Dress and appearance are used to depict character, as Bruzzi and Church Gibson (2008) highlight. Carrie is the romantic heroine and writer who chooses appropriately eccentric mixtures of vintage chic and designer labels to create her own unique style, a fashion mix that has become *SATC*'s trademark. Miranda power dresses as befits her career in the world of corporate law, where she has to work hard to be taken seriously by her male boss. Samantha, the most extroverted of the four, has a glitzy image, reflecting her status as a public relations agent. Her costumes hark back to the dramatic appeal of a *Dallas* or *Dynasty* 1970s/1980s look, with padded shoulders and plunging necklines. Charlotte's clothing also evokes nostalgia, but recalls the more demure look of 1950s glamour as epitomized by Jackie Kennedy. This style of dressing, a conservative style of dress that includes hair bands, single strands of pearls, and Burberry mackintoshes, reinforces Charlotte's preppie background.

Despite an overall emphasis on individual styles, the four characters together offer their audience a continual spectacle with their elaborately designed costumes. This sense of the spectacular can be seen as challenging the elegance traditionally associated with femininity (Bruzzi & Church Gibson, 2008). It also refutes the "male gaze" in that it is primarily for women. As Radner (1995) notes, the pleasure of dressing up is a pleasure that is generated outside the scene of heterosexuality. This exemplifies the third wave feminist position whereby "dressing up equals fun, and fun equals empowerment" (Konig, 2008, p. 140). From this perspective, even shoes can be empowering, particularly Carrie's penchant for Manolo Blahniks—shoes that have been referred to as a source of power, making women simultaneously stylish and alluring while also "imperious and goddess like" (Niblock, 2008, p. 145). Carrie's placement of her favorite shoes in the dressing room that Mr. Big has had built for her in the new apartment serves to underline the role of fashion as a means of enabling a woman to put her stamp on things (and on places).

The links between desire, empowerment and purchasing power underpin *SATC*, and nowhere more explicitly than in the jewelry auction in *SATC*, when Samantha covets the flower ring and subsequently bids $55,000 for it, only to be outbid by an anonymous buyer. Later, when her actor husband gives it to her as an anniversary present, she is lukewarm, revealing: "I wanted to buy this for myself. That meant something to me—to be able to do that. And then he buys it for me…now every time I look at it I see him, not me." This moment resonates with a market mantra that conflates financial independence with self-worth for women, famously encapsulated in the L'Oreal slogan, "Because you're worth it," with its concomitant principle of self-gifting. The message is clear: Women do not need a man to buy them presents; sisters are doing it for themselves.

There are many similar challenges to cultural norms where costume plays a role. For example, in relation to fashion and the older woman, there is an unforgettable moment in the second film when a shop assistant suggests a particular outfit might be too young a look for Samantha, who vehemently retorts, "I am 52 and I will rock this dress!" This defiance of narrow fashion stereotyping is reiterated throughout *SATC* with Carrie's creative juxtapositioning of designer labels and vintage buys, a juxtapositioning that has initiated completely new trends in "cool" fashion around the notion of creative individualism.

There are two memorable incidents, one in each film, where dress becomes a more intricate part of the plot and elaborates on the tensions inherent in the carnal feminine. Carrie submits to pressure from her boss at *Vogue* to have her wedding featured in the magazine. It subsequently becomes what her partner, Mr. Big, refers to as a "circus" with all the lavish trappings of the fantasy white wedding, itself a powerful symbol of excess in consumer culture (Otnes & Pleck, 2003). Carrie is delighted when she is offered the opportunity to wear an extravagant creation by Vivienne Westwood. She explains to Mr. Big, who is horrified that the guest numbers have increased to 200, "It's the dress—the dress upped the ante."

The second and arguably most dramatic "dress" moment is during the girls' trip to Abu Dhabi, when Samantha defies the local female dress codes and exposes too much bare flesh, only to receive a hostile censuring and indeed chase from the local men. As her friends try to hurry her away to safety, she drops her purse and a bunch of condoms falls out, causing further consternation and anger. "Yes, I like sex!" Samantha shouts at the growing crowd as they make their escape, aided by the local women, who give them shelter and reveal the latest New York fashions under their abayas. This supposedly empowering moment, when cultural differences fall away to reveal that they all share a love of fashion, has been heavily critiqued because it is perceived to be reinforcing a "discourse of Western enlightened values" (McRobbie, 2009, p. 27) through its implication that all Middle Eastern women want to look like Western women.

This implication reinstates a "hierarchy of civilization and modernity" as a discourse "which celebrates the freedoms of fashion-conscious 'thong-wearing' Western girls in contrast to those young women who wear the veil" (McRobbie, 2009, p. 27). It also serves to reinforce the carnal feminine in that the Middle Eastern women, while their bodies are fully concealed and to an extent erased by their dark robes, are no different underneath it all; they are still bodies, and their bodies are as adorned in branded clothing as those of their Western counterparts. The moment thus suggests that underneath the surface of apparent difference, all women are the same, but the sameness that is celebrated is not so much the female body per se, but rather the trappings of femininity, the stamp of commoditized, branded clothing, which serves to denote their shared identity as women.

Settings

The rhetorical power of cityscapes to evoke the imagination is well recognized (Sadler & Haskins, 2005). New York City enjoys iconic status in this regard, symbolizing material success and entrepreneurial opportunity. It is the epitome of a glamorous and exciting lifestyle and provides an evocatively upbeat and hedonistic backdrop for *SATC*. Indeed, so famous has it now become as a setting for *SATC* that tourists can choose from any number of different tours to take them around the *SATC* hotspots. Whether the four protagonists are shopping, drinking, eating, or romancing (usually in that order!), New York City offers up its unique sense of vitality and style—the perfect consumer paradise within which to locate the fashionable four and their escapades. As Sadler and Haskins (2005, p. 209) highlight, "More than any other show, *SATC* portrays its characters as consumers of expensive goods and services. Internally, the characters might have problems, but the city with its boutiques and restaurants is always there to comfort them."

From Carrie's new luxury penthouse apartment on Fifth Avenue, with its breathtaking views of the New York skyline, to the Museum of Modern Art's restaurant, where she announces her engagement, the continuous stream of chic consumerist settings is designed to enhance our associations of the four women as consummate consumers of independent means. Perhaps the ultimate symbol of this persona is Carrie's closet, a recurrent motif in both the TV series ("I like my money where I can see it, hanging in my closet!") and the films, to the extent that merchandising for the show promotes an app called *Carrie's Closet* for the iPhone, which lets its users photograph and share favorite fashions with friends (www.warnerbros.com).

When Carrie walks into the rooftop penthouse that Mr. Big, her partner, is going to buy for them, her initial reaction is "I've died and gone to real estate heaven...Nirvana! Hello, I live here!" before she realizes that the closet is too small for her vast collection of clothes and shoes. Mr. Big, however, comes to the rescue, promising to redesign it to her wishes. In many ways, the size of Carrie's closet represents the materialization of her insatiable appetite for fashion, reinforcing "her deep and involved relationship with the contents of her walk-in wardrobe" (Konig, 2008, p. 140). In the second film, the couple have moved into another, smaller apartment but, according to Carrie, they have "kept a little bit of heaven," as the shot pans to another enormous walk-in closet.

The settings almost invariably place the protagonists in consumption situations. These settings provide appropriate places for them to engage in female bonding and have intimate discussions about their various relationships. A wide range of "consumptionscapes" unfold in both films, offering Sunday brunches, bistro menus, or opportunities for leisurely browsing and shopping. When Carrie phones Samantha to tell her about her impending marriage, she is window shopping for designer labels at the same time. Even when their discussions are in a more private setting, the friends are usually eating or drinking. In the famous feminist moment in *SATC2* when Miranda and Charlotte confess to their fears of and dissatisfactions with motherhood, they are quaffing alcohol as quickly as their confessions are tumbling out. It is in these ways and in many similar moments throughout both films that the associations between empowerment and consumption are seamlessly conflated and cemented.

Some less empowering moments are found, however, when the setting shifts from New York City, as it does in *SATC2* when the action moves to the shopping mecca of Abu Dhabi, where the girls are in their consumerist element but out of their cultural depth, as we have already highlighted. Some critics even blame this change of setting for the generally negative reviews of the second film. As already highlighted, this setting, despite its consumerist ethos, did not sit comfortably with their New York brashness and overt displays of sexuality.

There is a particularly cringe-worthy moment when they all take to the stage in an Abu Dhabi karaoke bar to sing "I Am Woman," a remake of Helen Reddy's 1970s feminist anthem, their singing fuelled by copious amounts of the champagne they have been imbibing all evening. Again, while this scene is intended to show a bonding with the local women, many of whom also start to sing, it comes across as culturally insensitive on a number of levels. Their wry observation that the belly dancers are clearly exempt from the strict female dress code laws is noteworthy, but overriding this detail is the fact that there is the ethnocentric assumption that our four protagonists are the empowered ones. This ignores the fact that many would argue that materialism and fashion lust are Western women's oppression, not their freedom.

DISCUSSION

Our analysis shows how *SATC* simultaneously reinforces associations of the "carnal feminine" with female empowerment through the marketplace while limiting women in terms of their bodies—most significantly because of their potential lack of control over their bodies. Of course, the many tensions played out in the films between these two states—empowerment versus lack of control—are the very reasons that the genre has a huge female following. These are themes that resonate strongly for women in consumer culture, as we have highlighted, given that they underline the concept that women's culture revolves around "a discourse of constructability" (Radner, 1995, p. 176). We can even extol *SATC* for the various reasons we mentioned earlier: the fact that it validates women's talk and concerns and women's bonds is no small step for womankind. As a new genre in contemporary popular culture, it does indeed disrupt traditional views of femininity and challenges many existing assumptions about ageing women and women's sexuality more generally.

Despite this, we suggest we also have reason to be concerned and take heed of McRobbie's (2009) warning that new forms of gender power are most likely to be found inside a popular culture that emphasizes neoliberalist tropes of personal freedom and choice. These taken-for-granted tropes operate as disciplinary technologies under the guise of self-management. As we have indicated, the management of womanhood is nothing new, and indeed it is deeply embedded in all cultures, even if it is presented in a language that insidiously suggests empowerment and self-determination, as is the case in Western culture. As Radner (1995) notes, being a woman means accepting that we are perpetually on a cycle of rewriting a body "that must be continuously rewritten, kept up, and made over" (p. xiii).

Like Bridget Jones and Ally McBeal before them, the girls in *SATC* reclaim the pleasures of femininity that second wave feminism is perceived to have suppressed—in particular, their own sexuality. The "carnal feminine" is given pride of place. This is very evident in our analysis of *SATC* and its often bawdy approach to the girls' open discussions of their sexual exploits. As a new breed of women, sometimes referred to as postfeminist, they confidently air their anxieties, compare their desires, avoid testosterone-fueled aggressive masculinity, and dress to please themselves (McRobbie, 2009). Yet, although they may not be slaves to men, they are most certainly slaves to the market, a market that many now allege is driving the resexualization of women's bodies through its appropriation of discourses of freedom and empowerment (Evans, Riley, & Shankar, 2010; Gill, 2003; McRobbie, 2009; Power, 2009; Walter, 2010).

Walter (2010) notes that concepts of individual choice and empowerment have been co-opted by what she describes as a "hypersexual" culture, highlighting how the choice and empowerment that are alluded to are often restricted to extremely narrow definitions of women's choices and women's freedoms. These so called choices and freedoms often manifest themselves in reductionist options for young women such as glamour modeling, lap and pole-dancing, and other soft-porn activities, which have become commonplace in our culture and on many of our high streets in the UK. Indeed, Walter writes that "all aspects of the current hypersexual culture are often now seen as proof of women's growing freedom and power" (2010, p. 5).

Female sexuality has thus been equated with (and reduced to) the sexual objectification against which second wave feminists fought, defined by the terms of the sex industry. Walter (2010) believes this has had a profound effect on young women's ambitions and aspirations, particularly young women from deprived social backgrounds. In fact, she suggests that this hypersexual culture "weighs especially heavily on women with few options in life" (p. 123). Walter offers further evidence of what Power (2009) calls "the pornification of culture" in the spate of sex memoir books and TV dramas in the UK that document the sexual exploits of women, some of whom work in the sex industry, notably Belle de Jour's *The Intimate Adventures of a London Call Girl,* which serves to underline the nonchalant normalization of prostitution in the UK. One might also add here the prostitutionalization of normality; indeed, Walter argues that "there has been a cultural shift towards embracing sex with no emotional commitment" (p. 93). It is interesting to note that this attitude bears more than a passing resemblance to Helen Gurley Brown's *Sex and the Single Girl* (1962) and *Cosmopolitan* magazine's "sex ethic" mantra of the 1970s. However, this time it is more authoritative, aggressive, and imperious, fueled by the explosion of pornography throughout our culture (Walter, 2010).

Moreover, this resexualization of women's bodies reinforces a very limited, White, heterosexual femininity for slim bodies, a femininity that is only accessible to those who can afford the purchases to create "the look" (Evans et al., 1995; Orbach, 1978, 2002). As Konig (2008) comments on Carrie and *SATC,* "Parker has become a stiletto-heeled role model for women in our time, click-clacking her way through the politics of fashion, nimbly stepping over any unsightly issues pertaining to the roles played by wealth and privilege" (p. 140).

To conclude, in her materialism, Carrie demonstrates that how we live our lives is indelibly linked to how we *spend* our lives, with the acquisition of consumer goods central to that process. Her priorities, until she is forced to reassess them, very much legitimize excessive consumption as an essential ingredient if one is to have a perfect life. Furthermore, the ongoing construction of womanhood is firmly framed in pleasurable, narcissistic, and *carnal* terms: "Women seek pleasure and construct identities as a fragmented, inter-textual process that works upon, against, and through the body" notes Radner (1995, p. xiv), and we argue that this is certainly the case in *SATC* and *SATC2*. We hope we have shown in this chapter that both films celebrate a central motif in the collective experience of women in consumer culture, that the body must be at the center of our identity projects, and that we cannot escape the body, the omnipresent "carnal feminine." It is a dominant motif of embodied femininity that is forever woven into the fabric of our cultural consciousness, and it defines us, contains us, and, ultimately, we suggest, it may constrain us as women.

REFERENCES

Alexander, Monty, Max Burt, & Andrew Collinson (1995). Big talk, small talk: BT's strategic use of semiotics in planning its current advertising. *Journal of the Market Research Society, 37*(2), 91–102.

Belk, Russell, W. (1998). In the arms of the overcoat: On luxury, romanticism, and consumer desire. In Stephen Brown, Anne-Marie Doherty, & Bill Clarke (Eds.), *Romancing the market* (pp. 41–55). London, England: Routledge.

Belk, Russell W., & Janeen A. Costa (1998). Chocolate delights: Gender and consumer indulgences. In Eileen Fischer & Daniel L. Wardlow (Eds.), *Proceedings of the fourth conference on gender, marketing and consumer behavior* (pp. 179–193). San Francisco, CA: Association for Consumer Research.

Bleuler, Eugen (1924). *Textbook of psychiatry* (A.A. Brill, Trans.), New York: Dover Publications, Inc.

Bordo, Susan (1993). *Unbearable weight: Feminism, Western culture and the body.* London, England: Berkeley.

Bruzzi, Stella, & Pamela Church Gibson (2008). "Fashion is the fifth character": Fashion, costume and character in *Sex and the City.* In Kim Akass & Janet McCabe (Eds.), *Reading* Sex and the City (pp. 115–129). London, England: I. B. Tauris.

Campbell, Colin (1997). Shopping, pleasure and the sex war. In Pasi Falk & Colin Campbell (Eds.), *The shopping experience* (pp. 166–176). London, England: Sage Publications.

Catterall, Miriam, Pauline Maclaran, & Lorne Stevens (2005). Postmodern paralysis: The critical impasse in feminist perspectives on consumers. *Journal of Marketing Management,* 21(5-6), 489–504.

Davis, Kathy (1997). *Embodied practices: Feminist perspectives on the body.* London, England: Sage Publications.

Donahue, Wendy (2008). *Sex and the City* fashion stake a starring role on the movie. *Chicago Tribune,* May 18, (accessed Dec. 16, 2011, http://archives.chicagotribune.com/2008-05-18/features/0805/40465_1_carrie-gladiator-sandals-moet-chandon).

Evans, Adrienne, Sarah Riley, & Avi Shankar (2010). Technologies of sexiness: Theorizing women's engagement in the sexualization of culture. *Feminism and Psychology, 20*(1), 114–131.

Fish, Stanley (1980). *Is there a text in this class?* Cambridge, MA: Harvard University Press.

Gennaro, Stephen (2007). *Sex and the City:* Perpetual adolescence gendered feminine? *Nebula, 4.1* (March), 246–275.

Gill, Rosalind (2003). From sexual objectification to sexual subjectification: The resexualization of women's bodies in the media. *Feminist Media Studies, 3*(1), 100–106.

Greven, David (2008). The museum of unnatural history: Male freaks and *Sex and the City.* In Kim Akass & Janet McCabe (Eds.), *Reading* Sex and the City (pp. 33–48). London, England: I. B. Tauris.

Gurley Brown, Helen (1962). *Sex and the single girl.* New York: Bernard Geis Assoc., Inc.

Henry, Astrid (2004). *Not my mother's sister: Generational conflict and third-wave feminism* Bloomington, IN: Indiana University Press.

Henry, Astrid (2008). Orgasms and empowerment: *Sex and the City* and the third wave feminism. In Kim Akass & Janet McCabe (Eds.), *Reading* Sex and the City (pp. 65–82). London, England: I. B. Tauris.

Hirschman, Elizabeth C. (1998). When expert consumers interpret textual products: Applying reader response theory to television programs. *Consumption, Markets & Culture, 2*(3), 259–304.

Hollows, Joanne (2000). *Feminism femininity & popular culture.* Manchester, England: Manchester University Press.

Huyssen, A. (1986). *After the Great Divide: Modernism, mass culture and postmodernism.* London, England: Macmillan.

Jour, Belle de (2005), *The intimate adventures of a London call girl*, London: Weidenfeld & Nicolson.

Joy, Annamma, & Alladi Venkatesh (1994). Postmodernism, feminism, and the body: The visible and the invisible in consumer research. *International Journal of Research in Marketing, 11*(4), 333–357.

Konig, Anna (2008).*Sex and the City*: A fashion editor's dream? In Kim Akass & Janet McCabe (Eds.), *Reading* Sex and the City (pp. 130–143). London, England: I. B. Tauris.

Levy, Ariel (2005). *Female chauvinist pigs: Women and the rise of raunch culture.* London, England: Pocket Books.

Lury, Celia (1996). *Consumer culture.* Cambridge, England: Polity Press.

McNair, Brian (2002). *Striptease culture: Sex, media and the democratization of desire.* London, England: Routledge.

McRobbie, Angela (1994). *Postmodernism and popular culture.* London, England: Routledge.

McRobbie, Angela (2009). *The aftermath of feminism.* London, England: Sage Publications.

Nava, Mica (1997). Women, the city and the department store. In Pasi Falk & Colin Campbell (Eds.), *The shopping experience* (pp. 56–91). London, England: Sage Publications.

Nelson, Ashley (2008). Sister Carrie meets Carrie Bradshaw: Exploring progress, politics and the single woman in *Sex and the City* and beyond. In Kim Akass & Janet McCabe (Eds.), *Reading* Sex and the City (pp. 83–95). London, England: I. B. Tauris.

Niblock, Sarah (2008). "My Manolos, my self": Manolo Blahnik, shoes and desire. In Kim Akass & Janet McCabe (Eds.), *Reading* Sex and the City (pp. 144–148). London, England: I. B. Tauris.

Orbach, Susie (1978). *Fat is a feminist issue: The anti-diet guide to permanent weight loss.* New York, NY: Berkeley Books.

Orbach, Susie (2002). *Susie Orbach on eating.* London, England: Penguin Books.

Otnes, Cele & McGrath, Mary Ann (2001). Perceptions and realities of male shopping behavior. *Journal of Retailing, 77*, (1)(Spring), 111–137.

Otnes, Cele C., & Elizabeth H. Pleck (2003). *Cinderella dreams: The allure of the lavish wedding.* Berkeley, CA: University of California Press.

Oxford English Dictionary (2000 edition). Oxford: Clarendon Press.

Paglia, Camille (1992). *Sexual personnae: Art and decadence from Nefertiti to Emily Dickinson.* Harmondworth, England: Penguin.

Power, Nina (2009). *One dimensional woman.* Winchester, UK: Zero Books.

Radner, Hilary (1995). *Shopping around: Feminine culture and the pursuit of pleasure.* London, England: Routledge.

Reincke, Nancy (1991). Antidote to dominance: Women's laughter as counteraction. *Journal of Popular Culture, 24*(4), 27–39.

Sadler, William J., & Ekaterina V. Haskins (2005). Metonymy and the metropolis: Television show settings and the image of New York City. *Journal of Communication Inquiry, 29*(3), 195–216.

Schiebinger, Londa (Ed.) (2000). *Feminism and the body.* Oxford, England: Oxford University Press.

Scott, Linda (2005). *Fresh lipstick: Redressing fashion and feminism.* New York, NY: Palgrave.

Showalter, Elaine (1987). *The female malady: Women, madness, and English culture, 1830–1980.* New York, NY: Pantheon Books.

Stevens, Lorna & Pauline Maclaran (2008). The carnal feminine: Womanhood, advertising and consumption. In Stefania Borghini, Mary Ann McGrath & Cele C. Otnes (Eds.), *European Advances in Consumer Research*, Vol. 8, July, Duluth MN: Association for Consumer Research 2008, 169–174.

Storey, John (1998). *Cultural theory and popular culture: A reader.* Hemel Hempstead, England: Prentice Hall.

Stratton, Jon (1996). *The desirable body: Cultural fetishism and the erotics of consumption.* Manchester, England: Manchester University Press.

Swan, Elaine (2005). On bodies, rhinestones, and pleasures: Women teaching managers. *Management Learning, 36*(3), 317–333.

Urla, Jacqueline, & Alan C. Swedlund, (2000). The unsettling ideals of the feminine body in popular culture. In Londa Schiebinger (Ed.), *Feminism and the body* (pp. 397–428). Oxford, England: Oxford University Press.

Walter, Natasha (2010). *Living dolls: The return of sexism.* London, England: Virago Press.

Warner, Marina (2000). The slipped chiton. In Londa Schiebinger (Ed.), *Feminism and the body* (pp. 265–292). Oxford, England: Oxford University Press.

Whelehan, Imelda (2000). *Overloaded: Popular culture and the future of feminism.* London, England: Women's Press Ltd.

Wolf, Naomi (1991). *The beauty myth.* London, England: Vintage Books.

Zayer, Linda Tuncay, Katherine Sredl, Marie-Agnes Parmentier, & Catherine Coleman (forthcoming). Consumption and gender identity in popular media: Exploring discourses of domesticity, authenticity, and sexuality. *Consumption, Markets and Culture.*

4

Climbing the Ladder or Chasing a Dream? Men's Responses to Idealized Portrayals of Masculinity in Advertising

Linda Tuncay Zayer and Cele C. Otnes

INTRODUCTION

Past gender research with regard to advertising has progressed through two main stages (Stern, 1999). The first wave highlighted the pervasiveness of gender stereotypes and sexist portrayals of females in advertising (Courtney & Whipple, 1983). Stern (1999) posits this wave largely did not account for the complexities that exist within people of the same sex, but instead focused on biological dichotomization. She further argues that representations in advertising convey norms and cultural expectations. Thus, men and women may take away different meanings from texts, not necessarily because of their biological maleness or femaleness, but rather in large part because of cultural conditioning.

In this vein, second wave scholars sought to understand differences among and across groups of women. For example, Ford and LaTour (1993) demonstrate women's differential responses to female role portrayals in ads. Moreover, due to pressure from the feminist movement, advertisers began to examine whether portrayals of women reflected women's lived experiences. In addition, men increasingly became commodified and discourses of masculinity began to shift as men began to "look at themselves and other men as objects of consumer desire" (Mort, 1988, p. 98).

Current gender research in advertising directly addresses the notion that individuals bring different cultures and life histories to the process of interpreting ads (Mick & Buhl, 1992), often using reader-response theory as a foundation because advertising can be viewed as a type of text. Moreover, consumers may use the visual text of idealized images in ads to "test" their possible selves (Markus & Narius, 1986; Scott, 1994). That is, personal identity clearly plays a significant role in how advertising is interpreted. Thus, because gender is a key part of a person's identity, it impacts the meaning-making process (Stern & Holbrook, 1994).

Using reader-response theory as a basis for the current study, this research addresses this principal research question: How do men interpret and respond to ideal depictions of masculinity in advertising? This research is important for several reasons. First, gender roles are observed, formed, and reinforced through a variety of sources, such as peers, family members, and, importantly, through advertising and media. Due to the significant influence of advertising on a consumer's conceptualization of gender, this research will explore the underlying interactions between the reader and the ad, particularly with regard to men's varied interpretations of masculinity. The context of advertising is powerful because as Easthope (1986) points out, "Men do not passively live out the masculine myths imposed by the stories and images of dominant culture...But neither can they live completely outside the myth since it pervades the culture. Its coercive power is active everywhere." (p. 167). Moreover, Schroeder and Zwick (2004) discuss how contemporary advertising links masculinity and consumer lifestyles: "Men have long been encouraged by advertising representations to take charge as consumers to construct flawless masculine identities" (p. 45).

Thus, men not only form personal conceptualizations of masculinity but also do so within broader cultural ideologies—with advertising serving as one of the primary forces to shape these ideologies. There is a distinct link between the cultural codes imbued in advertising, the meanings consumers take away from these ads, and how consumers live their lives (both in and out of the marketplace). This issue is especially relevant in the United States, where, for example, past scholars have found that U.S. broadcast television is more commercialized than in the UK (Katz & Lee, 1992).

Second, this research is important because there is still much to learn about the relationship between men's gender identities and advertising response. While past research investigated sex differences (comparing men and women) with regard to information processing (Darley & Smith, 1995; Meyers-Levy, 1989; Meyers-Levy & Sternthal, 1991; Putrevu, 2004), information processing confidence (Kempf, Laczniak, & Smith, 2006; Kempf, Palan, & Laczniak, 1997), values (Brunel & Nelson, 2000), and even message order effects (Brunel & Nelson, 2003), few studies examine advertising responses and interpretations within or between a group of male participants (for an exception, see Zayer, 2010).

Exploring the construction of masculinity among and across men is important for two reasons. First, there is a lack of extensive research and theory examining men as gendered individuals (Kimmel & Messner, 2001), especially within the context of advertising (see Bordo, 1999; Garst & Bodenhausen, 1997; Elliott & Elliott, 2005; Gulas & McKeage, 2000; Schroeder & Zwick, 2004, for exceptions). Next, by examining advertising response and interpretation across men, we can begin to understand the complexity of their experiences. To this point, in their study of open versus closed ads, Yannopoulou and Elliott (2008) state that few studies explore "real consumers' interpretations of advertising texts" (p. 10).

Thus, it is clear that there is gap in the literature with regard to how men respond to depictions of ideal masculinity in advertising. It is especially important to gain an understanding of this issue from the perspective of men themselves because their collective interpretations ultimately constitute, in part, the broader discourses of masculinity today.

LITERATURE REVIEW

This literature review first details various aspects of the central construct of masculinity. Next, we provide a brief review of past research on gendered depictions in advertising. Finally, we offer reader-response theory as a theoretical template in order to ground the interpretive approach employed in this study.

Discourses of Masculinity

Gender roles are culturally derived behaviors linked with masculinity and femininity (Palan, 2001). Past scholars note that masculinity and femininity are "a bricolage of scattered meanings and shifting significances" (Kacen, 2000, p. 345). Masculinity is neither a stable construct nor one that is consistently constructed or enacted by individuals (Cornwall & Lindisfarne,

1994). Rather, it changes over time, not only within the individual but also collectively as a discourse in society. Moreover, while masculinity can be described as the socially constructed way to be a man, women can embrace and display various tenets of masculinity as well (Halberstam, 1998). Several factors can influence a person's conceptualization of masculinity, including class (Breward, 1999; Holt & Thompson, 2004), race and ethnicity (DiPiero, 2002; Irwin, 2003; Wallace, 2002), sexuality (Forrest, 1994), religion (Boyarin, 1997), and historical context (Doyle, 1995) as well as age, education, and even geography (Beynon, 2002).

Others scholars define masculinity as a presentation (Goffman, 1971) in which men are actors on a stage following a script on how to be a man. Socialization forces such as family, peers, school, and media prescribe and validate the behaviors perceived as appropriate for these roles. Thus, some scholars conceptualize gender as a space that inculcates rigid codes of culturally accepted behavior for men and women.

Gender, Advertising, and Social Comparison

As evidenced by a surge of research emerging in this area in the last decade, academia and industry alike recognize the importance of the male consumer and the study of masculinity. For example, Schroeder and Zwick (2004) examine advertising images of the male body and contribute to an understanding of advertising as a representational system by illuminating tensions and contradictions in masculine discourses represented in three contemporary ads. Other scholars conduct content analyses to compare gender depictions cross culturally (Cheng, 1997) or to explore how men are depicted in print ads (Kolbe & Albanese, 1996).

Moreover, many studies explore how women and adolescents compare themselves to advertising images (Chan & Prendergast, 2008; Hogg, Bruce, & Hough, 1999; Martin & Gentry, 1997; Martin & Kennedy, 1994; Richins, 1991; Smeesters, Mussweiler, & Mandel, 2010). These studies mostly apply social comparison theory or a drive to self-evaluate (Festinger, 1954) as their conceptual template. For instance, Richins (1991) examines how young women compare themselves to physically attractive models. She finds that among her participants, social comparison leads to raised standards of attractiveness and lowered satisfaction with their own appearance.

Most pertinent to our research, a few studies investigate how men engage in social comparison to models. For instance, Grogan, Williams, and Conner (1996) find that both men and women are negatively impacted in terms of lowered self-esteem after viewing photos of models. Through a series of experiments, Gulas and McKeage (2000) demonstrate that men experience a lowered sense of self-esteem after exposure to idealized images of financial success as depicted by male and female models. Moreover, Garst and Bodenhausen (1997) find that men who ascribe to less traditional gender roles are significantly impacted by gendered advertising. These androgynous men, or men who display high levels of both masculine and feminine characteristics, sanction more traditional attitudes after they view traditionally masculine models, illustrating the malleability of some men's gender role attitudes. Thus, while past research focused on sex differences and comparisons of attractiveness and body image by females within the context of social comparison theory, more recent work has examined comparisons by men.

Reader-Response Theory

Reader-response theory is important to the present research because readers take an active part in formulating what text means to them. Iser (1980) posits the reader is a cocreator who goes beyond simply the written word and constructs a meaning rooted in his or her experience. However, there is consensus in meaning because reading is also based on collective conventions. Thus, it is possible to categorize people according to similar reading strategies and communal responses (Scott, 1994). While a reader's own response may be subjective, the collective interpretation of these responses transforms into cultural knowledge (Bleich, 1980).

The theoretical lens of reader-response has been used effectively in past advertising and consumer behavior research. For example, Mick and Buhl (1992) conduct a phenomenological inquiry of how three brothers experience a set of five magazine ads and develop a framework that explains how individuals assign meaning to texts based on their situated histories and life projects. Along these lines, Hirschman and Thompson (1997) find that consumers employ particular interpretive strategies in consumer–media relationships in their study of a cross section of men and women ranging from 6 to 53 years of age. Yannopoulou and Elliott (2008) also discuss how interpretive communities (such as those based on class and gender) share similarities in reading strategies of advertising text.

Researchers rely on the reader-response approach to illuminate themes pertaining to advertising responses, even with regard to idealized images in advertising (Elliott & Elliott, 2005). In fact, McQuarrie and Mick (1999) state that reader response theory offers "the rich and complex interplay between elements of the ad and consumer responses" (p. 37). Extending this work, our study adheres to the reader-response tradition and focuses on the meanings and shared interpretations that male consumers take away from ads.

METHOD

We employ an interpretive approach, utilizing in-depth interviews and projective techniques, to explore men's interpretations of ideal masculinity in advertising. Specifically, we focus on responses within a cohort of 20 Generation X men (born between 1965 and 1981), who are educated and living in the Midwest. When recruiting informants, two interviewers (one man and one woman, both in this cohort) personally contacted men of appropriate age and then used a snowball sampling technique to acquire additional informants. Because conceptions of masculinity vary greatly across cultures (Beynon, 2002), we restricted our informants to men born and raised in North America (in fact, all but one was born and raised in the United States, with one man born in Canada). Because responses to masculine depictions are largely unexplored by advertising and marketing scholars, it is appropriate to pursue a more intensive and in-depth exploration into a generational cohort of consumers. Moreover, advertisers and marketers are conscious of the economic power wielded by Generation X consumers; some analysts predict that the segment will be one of the primary drivers of economic recovery in the United States. (Wong, 2010). At the end of the chapter, Appendix A offers further biographical information on the informants.

When interviewing informants, we relied on a semistructured interview format and also offered each the same set of ads as projective aids (McGrath, Sherry, & Levy, 1993; Whyte, 1984). Projection is a technique used to discover meanings that are sometimes inaccessible by direct measurement techniques; as such, it enables people to attribute or acknowledge characteristics of stimuli (or of themselves) that they might otherwise overlook or that the researcher might not be able to access (McGrath et al., 1993).

Both projectives and in-depth interviews are appropriate in addressing our research question because they uncover the experiences of the individual while often revealing the importance or roles or social and cultural contexts in informants' experiences with phenomena. The interviewers followed the recommendations set forth by McCracken (1988) by allowing the respondents to answer questions freely and in their own words. The goal was to let the informants explain their ideals of masculinity as they perceive and experience these ideals. However, the interviews did follow a semistructured format to gather insights and make comparisons across responses to key questions.

After a general discussion of ideals of masculinity and of what it means to make comparisons to advertising, informants were shown a series of 16 ads that they were asked to rank in order from most reflective to least reflective of their own ideals of masculinity. We then used the ad that each man ranked as most ideal as the starting point for our discussion with him about his own reactions to the idealized images in the set of ads. Ads were selected by surveying the top five men's magazines in terms of circulation according to *Advertising Age: Playboy, Maxim, Men's Health, ESPN,* and *Sports Illustrated.*

To enhance the diversity of images in the sample (e.g., by including an ad portraying a father role), two ads from magazines targeting women were incorporated. It is not surprising that the ads from men's magazines had to be supplemented; scholars have noted the limited and typically stereotypical portrayals of men in today's media and the lack of nurturing father figures in advertising (Gentry & Harrison, 2010). We made every effort to incorporate ads across brands and product categories, as well as those that tapped into historical and contemporary themes of masculinity. Admittedly, however, the set of ads we shared with informants is obviously not exhaustive. Moreover, we made sure to engage in a more general dialogue of gender and social comparison to advertising with our informants; the use of 16 ads was supplementary and did not limit the men's discussions.

The first round of interviews ranged from 1 to 1.5 hours in length. In addition, we conducted follow-up interviews lasting approximately 20 minutes after conducting an initial analysis of the interview transcripts, to further probe key issues that arose during the first interview. At the conclusion of the interviews, the informants' names were put into a lottery for two $25 gift cards.

All interviews were transcribed, yielding approximately 300 pages of single-spaced text. The researchers referred to extant research in this area to discover and elaborate upon parallels with past research and also probed the text for the emergence of new themes through a process called dialectical tacking (Strauss & Corbin, 1998). Following data analysis, several themes emerged that pertained to the principal research question for this study: How do men interpret and respond to depictions of ideal masculinity in advertising? Specifically, a typology of responses emerged that was supported by interviews conducted by both the male and female interviewer. To illustrate the findings, direct quotes are provided within the text and in Table 4.1.

FINDINGS

Six themes emerge from the analysis with regard to how men respond to ad depictions of ideal masculinity: skepticism, avoidance, indifference, enhancement, striving, and chasing. These responses fall along the continuum similarly to what Elliott and Elliott (2005) find in their study of male body images in advertising. They state that there are multiple expressions of masculinity in society and advertising, in particular, and that these options can be experienced as "an opportunity or as a threat" (p. 6). The emergent themes do not support an assumption that men fit neatly into certain response types for all ads to which they are exposed. Instead, we find that men vary their reactions to the depictions in the ad, depending on the ad they discuss. Also, their responses reflect a snapshot in time.

Skepticism

Men who experience skepticism attempt to avoid engaging in comparison because they believe advertisements in general portray an unrealistic world. This conceptualization is reflective of the broader population's skepticism of advertising. Furthermore, in some sense it mirrors a categorization of Gen Xers as belonging to a skeptical generation as a whole (Manning-Schaffel, 2002).

For these men, assessing the attainability of the standards portrayed in any specific ad is not really a salient task for them. They portray indifference to any potential gap between an idealized state of masculinity and their actual selves and also display negative emotional responses to ads,

TABLE 4.1

Meanings of Masculinity

Themes in Responses	Masculinity Means...	Exemplary Informant Quotes
Skepticism	Authenticity: marketplace does not dictate what is real masculinity	Tom states he does not feel that advertising presents standards to live up to: I honestly would compare myself more to real people than I would an ad...when I'm looking at a model in an ad, I am like, well that's what he does for a living so who cares...
Avoidance	Vulnerability: susceptibility to feelings of inadequacy through comparisons of masculinity	Larry selects a Lipton ad as his ideal, which he states depicts a man based on his personality and intelligence rather than physical appearance. He contrasts this image to the attractive model in a Polo ad, which he states, can make you feel more threatened.
Indifference	Individuality: independence in thoughts of masculinity	Andy feels unaffected by ads depicting idealized notions of masculinity. *Interviewer:* Do they [idealized depictions in ads] bother you? *Andy:* No, they don't bother me at all... *Interviewer:* Do you feel like you have to live up to these standards of how men are portrayed in these ads? *Andy:* Me, personally, no. But I could see how others may.
Enhancement	Achievement: reaching goals of masculinity through incremental self-improvements	Mike discusses how he feels in comparison to the model in the ad he rated as most ideal: I don't really see him as being someone all that much different from either who I am or who I'll hopefully be.
Striving	Achievement: reaching goals of masculinity through substantial but attainable self-improvements	Gary reflects on an Air Force ad, wishing he had certain characteristics of the man in the ad such as endurance, strength, determination. He goes on to state: I don't know if I'm as determined as this guy but it would definitely be something to strive for.
Chasing	Elusiveness: goals of masculinity are desirable but somehow out of reach	Chris discusses his ambivalence toward the images in ads he sometimes wants to emulate but that he has not been able to fulfill yet: Some days it's different, I wanna be like this clean-cut guy with a rock-hard six pack... have all these women hang off of me, and then there are days when I don't really want that...sometimes I go "man I wish I had his six pack..."

sometimes even derogating the spokesperson. For example, Pete expresses his reaction to ads for exercise equipment that features a man expressing what he perceives to be an idealized version of masculinity: "I just think it's stupid…like the Nautilus or Bowflex or whatever. That's just ridiculous…[the] guys have the hugest muscles…it's just so totally unrealistic." Likewise, Scott states, "I don't look at it [an ideal depiction] and say I need to be that way…[it makes me feel] indifferent…you have to draw out all the garbage and realize what's real."

Scott and Pete both display a sense of skepticism toward the way in which men are portrayed and their negative reactions are reflected in using dismissive words such as "ridiculous" and "garbage." Advertisers should be concerned with these reactions because such counterarguing potentially hinders the effectiveness of ads (Beard, 2003). These informants often express irritation and frustration with media in general, akin to the high-agency negative emotional responses detailed by Fisher and Dubé (2005) in their study of gender differences in emotional advertising. Additionally, these informants mirror the deconstructing and rejecting strategy, or taking a critical stance by seeing media representations as unrealistic, that Hirschman and Thompson (1997) discuss. These informants are also akin to the female informants who display angry resistance to depictions of the "new man" in advertising by displaying annoyance and cynicism in a study by Elliott, Eccles, and Hodgson (1993).

Avoidance

While consumer skepticism toward advertising is well documented, a phenomenon that has been less researched is that of ad avoidance. In these cases, men eschew making active comparison to the models in certain ads because they feel threatened and anticipate falling short of depicted ideals. Although they recognize that a large gap exists between themselves and these portrayals, they are resigned to the fact that these ideals will always remain unattainable. Larry discusses how he prefers "real" images of men rather than ideal depictions:

> …for guys, everything is a competition, so…if you're someone like me and you go somewhere and you see this kind of person (man in ad for Polo)… attractive, fit…you feel more threatened…

He further reveals his resignation by stating, "I wish I could be like that, but you know I'm not. Some things you can't really change...I just kind of ignore it...just kind of look past it..." In order to cope, Larry shifts his standards of comparison away from attractiveness to dimensions of masculinity that are still culturally valorized, but that he apparently regards as more attainable, such as a sense of humor or intelligence.

These informants' responses are particularly interesting because past research observes that men attempt to display emotions in line with societal expectations (Leary, 1995). In certain social contexts, such as in the presence of other men, males are reluctant to show low-agency emotions, such as anxiety, envy, and vulnerability, in response to ads (Fisher & Dubé, 2005). Larry's avoidance of engaging in comparison with attractive models in ads resonates with some of the original theoretical work by Festinger (1954), who explains that if individuals perceive standards of social comparison to be extreme, they will not engage in comparison, even if the characteristics are desirable. Indeed, Lockwood and Kunda (1997) discuss instances of individuals feeling threatened if comparison results in recognizing that the target is unattainable.

However, Hirschman and Thompson (1997) find that the male informants in their study view media and advertising images as "as either being inconsequential or relatively easy to resist." (p. 52). Unlike those findings, several informants in this research expressed feelings to the contrary.

Indifference

While some informants feel threatened by the idealized masculine depictions in the ads, other informants portray an indifferent attitude. Individuals with this response perceive themselves as engaging in very little social comparison to the models. Although they recognize that some people may look to the standards held by advertising, they are themselves apathetic with regard to such comparisons or any potential gaps between an ideal state of masculinity and their actual selves. We therefore aver that, overall, these informants express a neutral response to the ad depictions. Luther claims he is rather unaffected by the idealized depictions in ads and does not engage in comparison to models: "I could see how [advertising] could affect some people. I don't think an advertisement affects who I am."

Indeed, many informants seem to exhibit what is termed the third-person effect (Davison, 1983). That is, they do not perceive that they are affected by advertising; however, they feel that other people are. Alternatively, these informants may purposefully insulate themselves from comparisons because they perceive the situation to be an "unwinnable competition," much like the behavior of some of the men in Thompson and Holt's study (2004, p. 326). While it is not clear to what extent the images in the ads impact our informants, they are, at the very least, outwardly insistent that they hold apathetic attitudes.

Enhancement

Other informants see advertising as a motivational tool to enhance a certain aspect of themselves. Men whose responses are consistent with enhancement often engage in passive comparison; that is, when engaging in comparison, they hone in on specific dimensions in select areas of the portrayal, such as clothing and hairstyles, rather than more ingrained aspects of the self. They accept that ads depict standards of how one should act and they believe these standards are attainable and within reach. These individuals often feel there is a small gap between themselves and the models and that, with a little more effort, they can attain their goals. Unlike informants who experience skepticism or avoidance, these men feel motivated when they view ads that depict ideal aspects of masculinity. For example, Bruce notes, "There are certain ads that I sometimes look at, sometimes the hairstyles that some of the guys have and see if it looks good and wonder how that may look on me...."

While past research often discusses the negative aspects of comparison to models in ads (Bower, 2001), very few studies document positive or motivating aspects of comparison. Yet considering the broader oeuvre of social comparison research, one robust finding is that comparers can feel inspired if they deem ideal standards as attainable. For example, Lockwood and Kunda (1997) find that comparisons with relevant superstar targets inspire comparers if they assess the level of superstars' success as attainable. Likewise, Mishkind, Rodin, Silberstein, and Striegel-Moore (1986) point out that the closer the actual self-image and the man's ideal self-image are in a comparison target, the more a man reports he is satisfied with his own body. In contrast—and as captured by men who demonstrate avoidance reactions—if the level of success by a model is considered beyond what a reader can accomplish, he will typically report feeling threatened. Thus, unlike men who experience avoidance, those engaged in enhancement tend to portray themselves as largely fulfilled and content, in need of only minor improvements, and displaying low-agency positive emotions (Fisher & Dubé, 2005).

Striving

Men with this type of response to idealized images engage in active comparison to models looking to seek out standards of how to be men. They often discuss their imagined selves relative to the image portrayed (Scott, 1994). While they still acknowledge large gaps between their actual and ideal selves, they feel this chasm can be bridged with hard work. Like men who experience enhancement, they display positive emotions because they deem advertising standards to be attainable. However, a key difference among men who strive is that they possess a greater sense of agency and therefore are highly motivated by ideal images of masculinity. For example, Joe states his feelings when he views an ad that he has selected as depicting ideal masculinity:

> Personally, they make me want to go out there and get in shape…I wouldn't necessarily say it makes me feel inadequate because that's not how I would feel because when I look at a magazine, I know it's a magazine, and I don't base my life off of an ad, but to the same point, it does make me want to go out there and it does create some of those needs and wants.

Thus, informants often experience high-agency emotions, such as feelings of encouragement, which are in line with societal expectations for how men should behave (Fisher & Dubé, 2005). Moreover, these informants' motivational responses provide additional support to Hirschman and Thompson's (1997) finding that some consumers find ad images aspirational.

Chasing

While some informants feel a sense of motivation in response to idealized masculine depictions in ads, others experience feelings of ambivalence about their pursuit to reach their ideal. Individuals who chase often participate in active comparison to models in ads. They seek out standards; however, they feel at odds with the fact that they can never quite attain these standards. These men recognize a large gap between their actual and ideal selves and often engage in problem-solving behavior to achieve their desired images. Ron states his desire to buy items to bring him closer to his ideal self:

> If you see somebody with cologne...and they show all these women around...yeah, you want to buy that stuff...you kind of want to be the same way...I'm probably guilty of buying because of the commercials they show.

Thus, Ron illustrates how he wishes to enact certain social roles but feels "guilty" for giving in to the advertising—displaying his ambivalence or mixed emotions in doing so (Otnes, Lowrey, & Shrum, 1997). These informants' responses are in stark contrast to Elliott and Elliott's (2005) assertion that some men who viewed ideal male bodies in advertising disassociate themselves from these depictions and do not feel emotionally impacted.

Fluid Nature of Responses

As we stated at the outset of our analysis, informants do not always elicit a consistent pattern of response styles when examining different images. Rather, they may display characteristics of several types of responses, depending upon the focal point of the ad. For example, a man who incorporates the theme of physical fitness as a salient theme in his sense of masculinity may be motivated by an ad such as one for Polo that depicts a man working out. However, that same individual may feel threatened by an ad depicting a highly successful individual, such as the man in a Hennessey ad, because an idealized masculine image, as well as a different type of product constellation (Solomon, 1988), is portrayed. These images and constellations in turn interact differently with the informants' personal histories and life projects (Mick & Buhl, 1992). Moreover, as these personal histories develop over time and their life projects evolve, readers' responses will undoubtedly change as well. Scott illustrates this point when discussing his reaction to depictions of ideal masculinity in ads, "Now, it doesn't affect me, but 10 years ago, boy, I needed to be that guy."

Thus, the ways in which individuals respond can be understood as very fluid, rather than as falling into hard-and-fast categories. To this point, past research in social comparison and advertising has shown that individuals can readily shift their standards of comparison and perceived performance levels (Richins, 1991). Moreover, while we validate some of the strategies used by informants in Hirschman and Thompson (1997), we find in addition that, within certain contexts, some men do express negative emotional responses to ads, such as feelings of vulnerability. Researchers contend that notions of masculinity have become more feminized (Patterson & Elliot, 2002) and that advertisers have made popular such archetypes as the metrosexual. As such, it is not surprising that men are experiencing and expressing heightened levels of vulnerability as masculinity becomes increasingly fragmented (Beynon, 2002).

The Link Between Response Themes and Consumers' Own Notions of Masculinity

Our analysis of the in-depth interviews offers evidence that the response themes also emerge as a vehicle for understanding men's conceptualizations of masculinity, rather than as merely a vehicle for understanding how they read ads. We offer the following propositions of what masculinity means to these informants, based on their response patterns to idealized depictions of masculinity.

First, for men who experienced skepticism, masculinity is something to be *authenticated,* and mediated messages of masculinity are perceived as sufficiently inauthentic due to their exaggerated or one-dimensional nature. Thus, for these men, one key dimension of masculinity is authenticity, or not allowing the marketplace to dictate what one believes should be real.

For men who engaged in avoidance, masculinity is highly competitive, and there are definite winners and losers. Thus, for these men, a key component of masculinity is *vulnerability.* Men are made to feel vulnerable because they can never achieve the desired status of ideal masculinity.

When our informants express an indifferent reaction to idealized images, it appears that mediated messages of masculinity do not seem to affect how they conceptualize their own sense of masculinity. Thus, for men with this response, the reaction of indifference signals that a key aspect of masculinity is equated with *individuality.*

Next, some men look to masculine depictions in ads as motivation to create a better self. Men who seek enhancement and engage in striving behavior conceptualize that they are actively climbing the ladder of masculinity in hopes of reaching their goals. Thus, a key dimension of masculinity is *achievement,* whether it is achieving incremental goals for men who seek enhancement or achieving larger transformations for informants who display striving responses.

Finally, informants who express a reaction consistent with chasing ideals experience mixed emotions as they seek to enact their ever-elusive ideals of masculinity. These responses reflect informants' perceptions that a core element of masculinity is its *elusiveness*. For a summary of the proposed meanings linked to masculinity, as well as exemplary quotes from informants, please refer to Table 4.1.

The findings presented here are rooted in past research on masculinity. For example, it is not surprising that vulnerability is a salient theme to men who experience avoidance as they conceptualize what masculinity means to them. Research consistently contends that there are rather strict rules for men's behavior. Any violation of these unwritten, but certainly viable rules, could lead to ostracization or social condemnation (Pleck, 1981). Moreover, Lindsey (1997) discusses the conflicts between the fragmented ideals of masculinity, thus making it impossible for any one man to perform all the roles successfully. This tension emerges in the theme of elusiveness by men who display chasing responses and who always fall short of their ideals. These informants also illustrate the cycle of consumption in which consumers engage to reach their ideals. For example, one informant expressed that while he knew getting a Bowflex exercise machine would not yield the same results as depicted by the muscular model in the ads, he nevertheless clings to the hope that it will aid him in his pursuit of the ideal body.

Another theme that emerges in our informants' responses is authenticity, as displayed by men who express skepticism. These informants believe the standards set by advertising are inauthentic and actively resist any media influence. They believe that they must maintain a sense of control over how they conceptualize their masculinity and that media depictions do not contribute to this conceptualization. Indeed, Clee and Wicklund (1980) discuss promotional influence as one of the ways in which consumers perceive their freedom to be threatened. Moreover, a sense of control is often labeled as a masculine norm (Harris, 1995).

Two other themes that emerge are individualism and achievement—characteristics that have long been associated with masculinity. In fact, Lindsey (1997) claims that individualism remains one of *the* central themes underlying American masculinity today. The need for achievement is described in consumer research; Otnes and McGrath (2001) note that men desire to fulfill a sense of achievement by acquiring bargains or one-of-a-kind items when they shop. In our study, some informants who experience enhancement and striving conceptualize their own sense of masculinity as laden with achievement goals and often feel motivated to reach them. In their review of consumer culture theory, Arnould and Thompson (2005) discuss how consumers "bend advertisements to fit their life circumstances rather than feeling pressured to conform to a specific ideological representation" (p. 20). Thus, it is apparent that consumers do not have to fit the stereotype of the "passive dupe" (p. 20). Rather, some informants in this study actively interpreted ads in a positive manner and use them as a tool for motivation.

IMPLICATIONS

The current research not only provides potential theoretical contributions, but also offers ethical and managerial implications for advertisers and marketers. As we state in the preface of this volume, and as many chapters contained within here attest, until recently men as consumers and as gendered beings have largely been overlooked in the social sciences and in the marketing literature in particular (see Bettany, Dobscha, O'Malley, & Prothero, 2010, for a discussion of this topic, as well as Chapters 10–13 in this volume). This study expands our understanding of men's responses to depictions of ideal masculinity in advertising by detailing key aspects of their comparison and interpretation processes in response to ideal advertising images. Our investigation is a first step in developing an in-depth understanding of the responses and meanings appropriated to masculinity by Gen X consumers. Naturally, ideals of masculinity vary according to the subset of men examined, so the current study has limitations. Exploring the discourses and responses of men in various age groups, social classes, and life stages and from a cross-cultural perspective all represent opportunities for future research. Moreover, a different subset of ads as projectives can potentially yield additional insights. In addition to enhancing a theoretical understanding of men's response, we argue that engaging men in the interpretation of depictions reveals men's own underlying conceptualizations about core tenets of masculinity. Thus, this research begins to unpack some of the current gender discourses in today's society as experienced and conceptualized by male consumers.

In addition, Bettany et al. (2010) state, "Gender research has an implicit critical agenda for social and cultural change" (p. 7). Following in the tradition of social change, this research also holds ethical implications. Although much research examines the negative impact on women and children of advertising depictions, very little is known about the impact on men. Yet our research finds that men do engage in comparisons to idealized depictions of masculinity and experience a range of emotions, including feelings of inadequacy and vulnerability. For example, while partying and being promiscuous are often depicted in advertising, Zayer (2010) finds that some men find these images to be negative portrayals of men and are turned off by them. That is, it is important to recognize that some men may react negatively or be adversely impacted by advertising images. As much as academics and some practitioners have called for responsibility in media messages targeting women and girls, attention should focus on men and boys as well. Moreover, other recent research indicates that men can experience vulnerability (Tuncay & Otnes, 2008) and feelings of isolation (Coskuner-Balli & Thompson, 2009) when engaged with marketplace-related phenomena.

This research also offers clear managerial implications because advertisers can use the contributions from this research to employ masculine themes in advertising more effectively and ethically. For example, certain types of responses from consumers, such as those verbalized by men who display the chasing response, have the potential to be problematic from a consumer welfare viewpoint. The theme of elusiveness that underlies informants' responses indicates the presence of anxiety and tension. Advertisers could emphasize aspects such as the attainability and achievement of healthy ideals to motivate consumers in a positive manner, rather than eliciting a sense of inadequacy in consumers. Men's responses to ads, as well as their consumer behaviors in general, are issues that are especially relevant in today's marketplace. For instance, the main shopper in 32% of American households is male, according to a study by Nielsen and the NPD Group (Albright, 2010). It is more important than ever for advertisers and marketers to find ways to appeal effectively to the male segment, and to do so in an ethical manner.

In summary, our research provides a theoretical contribution to the scholarship on masculinity and advertising and holds implications for advertisers and marketers who target male consumers. Furthermore, it adds to our knowledge of the vulnerability of men in consumer settings, which is an ethical consideration that should be explored in future research.

APPENDIX A: BIOGRAPHICAL INFORMATION OF INFORMANTS[a]

Informant Pseudonym	Biographical Information
Andy	28 years old, single, Caucasian, resides in suburb of large Midwestern city, completed some graduate school, earns $50–75K
Bob	26 years old, single, Caucasian, lives in large Midwestern city, college degree, earns $50–75K
Bobby	30 years old, single, Caucasian, resides in large Midwestern city, college degree, makes $75–100K
Bruce	28 years old, single, Caucasian, resides in suburb of large Midwestern city, graduate degree, earns $50–75K
Chris	22 years old, single, Caucasian, resides in rural Midwest, some college education, earns less than $25K
Doug	27 years old, engaged to be married, Caucasian, resides in rural Midwest, graduate degree, makes $75–100K
Gary	28 years old, single, Caucasian, lives in large Midwestern city, college degree, makes $25–50K
Jason	26 years old, single, Caucasian, resides in large Midwestern city, college degree, earns $25–50K; in the follow-up interview, engaged to be married
Joe	34 years old, single, Caucasian, lives in suburb of large Midwestern city, college degree, makes $25–50K
Jordan	24 years old, single, Asian American, lives in suburb of large Midwestern city, college degree, earns $25–50K
Larry	25 years old, Caucasian, engaged to be married, lives in large Midwestern city, currently earning graduate degree, makes less than $25K; in the follow-up interview, had finished graduate school and resided in a midsized city in the Midwest
Luther	25 years old, single, Caucasian, resides in rural Midwest, college degree, makes less than $25K
Mick	25 years old, married, Caucasian, lives in rural Midwest, currently earning his graduate degree, makes over $100K; in the follow-up interview, had finished graduate school and lived in a large city in the Southeast

Mike	27 years old, single, Caucasian, resides in large Midwestern city, graduate degree, earns less than $25K
Neil	24 years old, single, Caucasian, lives in suburb of large Midwestern city, graduate degree, income of $25–50K
Paul	28 years old, married with two children, Caucasian, resides in suburb of large Midwestern city, college degree, makes $50–75K
Pete	23 years old, single, Caucasian, resides in rural Midwest, currently earning his graduate degree, makes over $100K
Ron	29 years old, single, Hispanic, lives in rural Midwest, earns $25–50K
Scott	25 years old, single, Caucasian, lives in rural Midwest, currently earning graduate degree, earns $50–75K; in the follow-up interview, had finished his graduate degree and moved to a large city on the West Coast
Tom	28 years old, single, African American, lives in large Midwestern city, college degree, makes $50–75K
Victor	29 years old, single, Hispanic, resides in large Midwestern city, college degree, earns $50–75K

[a] Data from these same informants were also used for the analysis presented in the paper entitled, "A Typology of Men's Conceptualizations of Ideal Masculinity in Advertising," which was published in *Advertising & Society Review, 11*(1), 2010.

REFERENCES

Albright, Mark (2010). Marketing to men: Catering to new shopping realities. www.tampabay.com (June 29).

Arnould, Eric J., & Craig J. Thompson (2005). Consumer culture theory (CCT): Twenty years of research. *Journal of Consumer Research, 31* (March), 868–882.

Beard, Fred K. (2003). College students' attitudes toward advertising's ethical, economic, and social consequences. *Journal of Business Ethics, 48*(3), 217–226.

Bettany, Shona, Susan Dobscha, Lisa O'Malley, & Andrea Prothero (2010). Moving beyond binary opposition: Exploring the tapestry of gender in consumer research and marketing. *Marketing Theory, 10* (March), 3–28.

Beynon, John (2002). *Masculinities and culture.* Philadelphia, PA: Open University Press.

Bleich, David (1980). Epistemological assumptions in the study of response. In Jane Tompkins (Ed.), *Reader-response criticism* (pp. 135–163). Baltimore, MD: Johns Hopkins University Press.

Bordo, Susan (1999). *The male body: A new look at men in public and in private.* New York, NY: Farrar, Straus, and Giroux.

Boyarin, Daniel (1997). *Unheroic conduct: The rise of heterosexuality and the invention of the Jewish man.* London, England: University of California Press.

Breward, Christopher (1999). *The hidden consumer: Masculinities, fashion and city life 1860–1914.* Manchester, England: Manchester University Press.

Brunel, Frédéric, & Michelle Nelson (2000). Explaining gendered responses to "help-self" and "help-others" charity ad appeals: The mediating role of worldviews. *Journal of Advertising, 29* (Fall), 15–29.

Brunel, Frédéric, & Michelle Nelson (2003). Message order effects and gender differences in advertising persuasion. *Journal of Advertising Research, 43* (September), 330–341.

Chan, Kara, & Gerard P. Prendergast (2008). Social comparison, imitation of celebrity models and materialism among Chinese youth. *International Journal of Advertising, 27* (December), 799–826.

Cheng, Hong (1997). Holding up half the sky? A sociocultural comparison of gender-role portrayals in Chinese and U.S. advertising. *International Journal of Advertising, 16* (November), 295–319.

Clee, Mona, & Robert Wicklund (1980). Consumer behavior and psychological reactance. *Journal of Consumer Research, 6* (March), 389–405.

Cornwall, Andrea, & Nancy Lindisfarne (1994). *Dislocating masculinity: Comparative ethnographies.* London, England: Routledge.

Coskuner-Balli, Gokcen, & Craig Thompson (2009). Legitimatizing an emergent social identity through marketplace performances. In Ann McGill & Sharon Shavitt (Eds.), *Advances in consumer research* (Vol. 36; pp. 135–126), Duluth, MN: Asssociation for Consumer Research.

Courtney, Alice E., & Thomas W. Whipple (1983). *Sex stereotyping in advertising.* Washington, DC: Heath and Company.

Darley, William K., & Robert E. Smith (1995). Gender differences in information processing strategies: An empirical test of the selectivity model in advertising response. *Journal of Advertising, 24* (Spring), 41–56.

Davison, W. Phillips (1983). The third-person effect in communication. *Public Opinion Quarterly, 47* (March), 1–15.

DiPiero, Thomas (2002). *White men aren't.* Durham, NC: Duke University Press.

Doyle, James A. (1995). *The male experience.* Dubuque, IA: Wm. C. Brown Co.

Easthope, Antony (1986). *"What a man's gotta do": The masculine myth in popular culture.* London, England: Paladin.

Elliott, Richard, Sue Eccles, & Michelle Hodgson (1993). Re-coding gender representations: Women, cleaning products, and advertising's new man. *International Journal of Research in Marketing, 10* (August), 311–324.

Elliott, Richard, & Christine Elliott (2005). Idealized images of the male body in advertising: A reader response exploration. *Journal of Marketing Communications, 11* (March), 3–19.

Festinger, Leon (1954). A theory of social comparison processes. *Human Relations, 7* (May), 117–140.

Fisher, Robert J., & Laurette Dubé (2005). Gender differences in responses to emotional advertising: A social desirability perspective. *Journal of Consumer Research* (March), 850–858.

Ford, John B., & Michael S. LaTour (1993). Differing reactions to female role portrayals in advertising. *Journal of Advertising Research, 33* (September/October), 43–52.

Forrest, David (1994). "We're here, we're queer and we're not going shopping": Changing gay male identities in contemporary Britain. In Andrea Cornwall & Nancy Lindisfarne (Eds.), *Dislocating masculinity: Comparative ethnographies* (pp. 97–110). London, England: Routledge.

Garst, Jennifer, & Galen V. Bodenhausen (1997). Advertising effects on men's gender role attitudes. *Sex Roles, 36* (May), 551–572.

Gentry, James W., & Robert L. Harrison (2010). Is advertising a barrier to male movement towards gender change? *Marketing Theory, 10* (March) 74–96.

Goffman, Erving (1971). *The presentation of the self in everyday life.* Garden City, NY: Doubleday Anchor Books.

Grogan, Sarah, Zoe Williams, & Mark Conner (1996). The effects of viewing same-gender photographic models on body self-esteem. *Psychology of Women Quarterly, 20* (December), 568–575.

Gulas, Charles S., & Kim McKeage (2000). Extending social comparison: An examination of the unintended consequences of idealized advertising imagery. *Journal of Advertising, 29* (Summer), 17–28.

Halberstam, Judith (1998). *Female masculinity*. Durham, NC: Duke University Press.

Harris, Ian (1995). *Messages men hear: Constructing masculinities*. London, England: Taylor & Francis.

Hirschman, Elizabeth, & Craig Thompson (1997). Why media matters: Towards a richer understanding of consumers' relationships with advertising and mass media. *Journal of Advertising, 1* (Spring), 43–60.

Hogg, Margaret K., Margaret, Bruce, & Kerry Hough (1999). Female images in advertising: The implications of social comparison for marketing. *International Journal of Advertising, 18* (November), 445–473.

Holt, Douglas B., & Craig J. Thompson (2004). Man-of-action heroes: The pursuit of heroic masculinity in everyday consumption. *Journal of Consumer Research, 31* (September), 425–440.

Irwin, Robert M. (2003). *Mexican masculinities*. Minneapolis, MN: University of Minnesota Press.

Iser, Wolfgang (1980). The reading process: A phenomenological approach. In Jane Tompkins (Ed.), *Reader-response criticism* (pp. 50–69). Baltimore, MD: Johns Hopkins University Press.

Kacen, Jacqueline J. (2000). Girrrl power and boyyy nature: The past, present, and paradisal future of consumer gender identity. *Marketing Intelligence & Planning, 18*(6/7), 345–355.

Katz, Helen, & Wei N. Lee (1992). Oceans apart: An initial exploration of social communication differences in US and UK prime-time television advertising. *International Journal of Advertising, 11* (February), 69–83.

Kempf, DeAnna S., Russell N. Laczniak, & Robert E. Smith (2006). The effects of gender on the processing of advertising and product trial information. *Marketing Letters, 17* (January), 5–16.

Kempf, DeAnna S., Kay M. Palan, & Russell N. Laczniak (1997). Gender differences in information processing confidence in an advertising context. In Debbie MacInnis & Merrie Brucks (Eds.), *Advances in consumer research* (pp. 443–449), Provo, UT: Association for Consumer Research.

Kimmel, Michael, & Michael Messner (2001). *Men's lives* (5th ed.). Needham Heights, MA: Pearson Education Company.

Kolbe, Richard H., & Albanese, Paul J. (1996). Man to man: A content analysis of sole-male images in male audience magazines. *Journal of Advertising, 25* (Winter), 1–20.

Leary, Mark (1995). *Self-presentation: Impression management and interpersonal behavior*. Boulder, CO: Harper Collins.

Lindsey, Linda L. (1997). *Gender roles*. Upper Saddle River, NJ: Prentice Hall, Inc.

Lockwood, Penelope, & Ziva Kunda (1997). Superstars and me: Predicting the impact of role models on the self. *Journal of Personality and Social Psychology, 73* (July), 91–103.

Manning-Schaffel, Vivian (2002). Has Gen X fallen through the cracks? www.brandchanel. com/features_effect.asp?pf_id=136

Markus, Hazel, & Paula Nurius (1986). Possible selves. *American Psychologist, 41* (September), 954–969.

Martin, Mary C., & James W. Gentry (1997). Stuck in the model trap: The effects of beautiful models in ads on female preadolescents and adolescents. *Journal of Advertising, 26* (Summer), 19–33.

Martin, Mary C., & Patricia F. Kennedy (1994). The measurement of social comparison to advertising models: A gender gap revealed. In Janeen Arnold Costa (Ed.), *Gender issues in consumer behavior* (pp. 104–124). Thousand Oaks, CA: Sage Publications.

McCracken, Grant (1988). *The long interview.* Newbury Park, CA: Sage Publications.

McGrath, Mary Ann, John F. Sherry, Jr., & Sidney J. Levy (1993). Giving voice to the gift: The use of projective techniques to recover lost meanings. *Journal of Consumer Psychology, 2* (March), 171–191.

McQuarrie, Edward, & David Mick (1999). Visual rhetoric in advertising: Text-interpretive, experimental, and reader-response analysis. *Journal of Consumer Research, 26* (June), 37–54.

Mick, David G., & Claus Buhl (1992). A meaning-based model of advertising experiences. *Journal of Consumer Research, 19* (December), 317–338.

Mishkind, Marc, Judith Rodin, Lisa Silberstein, & Ruth Striegel-Moore (1986). The embodiment of masculinity. *American Behavioral Scientist, 29* (May/June), 545–562.

Meyers-Levy, Joan (1989). Gender differences in information processing: A selectivity interpretation. In P. Cafferata & Alica Tybout (Eds.), *Cognitive and affective responses to advertising* (pp. 219–260). Lanham, MD: Lexington Books.

Meyers-Levy, Joan, & Brian Sternthal (1991). Gender differences in the use of message cues and judgments. *Journal of Marketing Research, 28* (February), 84–96.

Mort, Frank (1988). "Boys own?" Masculinity, style and popular culture. In Rowena Chapman & Jonathan Rutherford (Eds.), *Male order: Unwrapping masculinity* (pp. 193–224). London, England: Lawrence and Wishart.

Otnes, Cele C., Tina Lowrey, & L. J. Shrum (1997). Toward an understanding of consumer ambivalence. *Journal of Consumer Research, 24* (June), 80–93.

Otnes, Cele C., & Mary Ann McGrath (2001). Perceptions and realities of male shopping behavior. *Journal of Retailing, 77* (March), 111–137.

Palan, Kay M. (2001). Gender identity in consumer behavior: A literature review and research agenda. *Academy of Marketing Science Review* (online), *10* (January), 1–37.

Patterson, Maurice, & Richard Elliot (2002). Negotiating masculinities: Advertising and the inversion of the male gaze. *Consumption, Markets, and Culture, 5* (September), 231–246.

Pleck, Joseph (1981). *The myth of masculinity.* Cambridge, MA: MIT Press.

Putrevu, Sanjay (2004). Communicating with the sexes. *Journal of Advertising, 33* (Fall), 51–62.

Richins, Marsha (1991). Social comparison and the idealized images of advertising. *Journal of Consumer Research, 18* (June), 71–83.

Schroeder, Jonathan, & Detlev Zwick (2004). Mirrors of masculinity: Representation and identity in advertising images. *Consumption, Markets and Culture, 7* (March), 21–52.

Scott, Linda (1994). The bridge from text to mind: Adapting reader-response theory to consumer research. *Journal of Consumer Research, 21* (December), 461–480.

Smeesters, Dirk, Thanas Mussweiler, & Naomi Mandel (2010). The effects of thin and heavy media images on overweight and underweight consumers: Social comparison processes and behavioral implications, *Journal of Consumer Research, 36* (April), 930–949.

Solomon, Michael R. (1988). Mapping product constellations: A social categorization approach to symbolic consumption. *Psychology & Marketing, 5* (Fall), 233–258.

Stern, Barbara B. (1999). Gender and multicultural issues in advertising: Stages on research highway. *Journal of Advertising, 28* (Spring), 1–93.

Stern, Barbara B., & Morris B. Holbrook (1994). Gender and genre in the interpretation of advertising text. In Janeen Arnold Costa (Ed.), *Gender issues in consumer behavior* (pp. 11–41). Thousand Oaks, CA: Sage Publications.

Strauss, Anselm, & Juliet Corbin (1998). *Basics of qualitative research: Techniques and procedures for developing grounded theory* (2nd ed.). Thousand Oaks, CA: Sage.

Thompson, Craig J., & Douglas B. Holt (2004). How do men grab the phallus? Gender tourism in everyday consumption. *Journal of Consumer Culture, 4* (March), 313–338.

Tuncay, Linda, & Cele C. Otnes (2008). The use of persuasion management strategies by identity-vulnerable consumers: The case of urban heterosexual male shoppers. *Journal of Retailing, 84* (December), 487–499.

Wallace, Maurice O. (2002). *Constructing the Black masculine.* Durham, NC: Duke University Press.

Whyte, William (1984). Interviewing strategies and tactics. In *Learning from the field* (pp. 97–112). Beverly Hills, CA: Sage.

Wong, Elaine (2010). Gen X and Y pave the way to economic recovery. http://www.adweek.com/news/advertising-branding/gen-x-and-y-pave-way-economic-recovery-101796

Yannopoulou, Natalia, & Richard Elliott (2008). Open versus closed advertising texts and interpretive communities. *International Journal of Advertising, 27* (February), 9–36.

Zayer, Linda Tuncay (2010). A typology of men's conceptualizations of ideal masculinity in advertising. *Advertising & Society Review, 11*(1).

5

Is the Selectivity Hypothesis Still Relevant? A Review of Gendered Persuasion and Processing of Advertising Messages

Michelle R. Nelson and Alexandra M. Vilela

INTRODUCTION

"You cannot market to men the same way that you market to women. It's not a simple transformation of changing colors, fonts, or packaging. Men and women are different biologically, psychologically and socially"... Because of these presumed differences, contemporary marketing advice suggests a segmentation approach based on gender. Consider the following characterizations from *Marketing Daily:*

> Men: A man focuses on himself—the "me." They are concrete thinkers who like to consummate, finish. Men tend to hone in, more quickly than women, on what they're looking for. Men are concrete and tend to tightly focus their awareness.
> Women: A woman focuses on the "we." View other people as a source of strength. Often think, "it depends." Women relate to the relationship between things. (Deutsch, 2010)

These descriptions of the focus (self vs. other) and the way that men and women process information sound like the predictions made from the selectivity hypothesis, proposed and tested by Meyers-Levy (1988) more than 20 years ago. The selectivity hypothesis is the most influential theoretical framework related to persuasion and gender (Kempf, Laczniak, &

Smith, 2006). It suggests that gender may be an important variable for understanding how men and women respond to communication efforts based on their gender roles (culturally derived behaviors and activities associated with masculinity or femininity that individuals choose to adopt; Palan, 2001).

Specifically, the theory proposes that male agentic roles (concern for self) and female communal roles (concern for self and others) influence message processing and persuasion. In an initial study, Meyers-Levy (1988) demonstrated that when traditional (self–other) sex roles are activated in men and women, their responses to persuasive messages match those roles. Subsequent research in the United States showed that women may respond better to other-oriented messages, and men may resonate better with help-self messages (e.g., Andsager, Austin, & Pinkleton, 2002; Brunel & Nelson, 2000). Also, because of these gender roles, women may be more motivated to understand subtle interpersonal cues and may show more sensitivity to situation-specific cues as a way to maintain relationships (e.g., Lenney, Gold, & Browning, 1983). In a persuasion context, the theoretical framework claims that women may elaborate more on message characteristics and use those cognitions to guide persuasion, whereas men are more likely to rely on single characteristics or heuristics (e.g., Meyers-Levy & Maheswaran, 1991; Meyers-Levy & Sternthal, 1991).

However, the findings overall are mixed when other researchers use the selectivity hypothesis to predict processing and persuasion. While some studies support agentic (male) versus communal (female) assumptions of the selectivity hypothesis (e.g., Andsager et al., 2002; Putrevu, 2004), others show no gender differences in generating cognitive responses (e.g., Peracchio & Tybout, 1996; Putrevu, 2004; Putrevu, Tan, & Lord, 2004). Further, some evidence suggests that the gender role assumptions of the selectivity hypothesis (based on research conducted mainly in the United States) may not hold in other cultural contexts with more egalitarian gender role social norms (e.g., Scandinavia; Nelson, Brunel, Supphellen, & Manchanda, 2006).

Given that both men's and women's roles have changed dramatically in the past 25 years, it is time to review this important theoretical framework and research related to gender and advertising response. In this chapter, we review research on gender and advertising response within and beyond the selectivity hypothesis. We also suggest areas for future research to expand our knowledge of how and when gender matters in advertising persuasion.

SEX AND GENDER: ARE THEY THE SAME?

Studies on gender differences (or similarities) in persuasion in the advertising and consumer literature use the terms sex and gender almost interchangeably and ambiguously (Fishman, Wick, & Koenig, 1999; Palan, 2001). In some cases, say critics, irrespective of the term, the construct is measured by asking respondents to indicate whether they are a male or female (Costa, 1994; Deaux, 1985). In other cases, an additional measure of sex roles (e.g., Bem, 1974, 1993) or gender identity (Fischer & Arnold, 1994) is used, which may tap into psychological characteristics or role expectations. Before we review the selectivity hypothesis model, we define these constructs and, where possible throughout our chapter, we indicate how particular studies measured sex or gender or related constructs (e.g., gender roles, gender identity).

Sex and gender differences are usually attributed to biological and/or physiological ("nature") and sociological ("nurture") characteristics. The distinction between "sex" and "gender" emerged in the mid-twentieth century. Feminists and scholars distinguish the characteristics attributed to biological differences (female and male) as sex and those characteristics that are results of cultural and social processes and expectations (feminine and masculine) as gender (Fishman et al., 1999).

Essentially, the term sex is related to biological and physiological characteristics and differences (e.g., chromosomes, hormonal profiles, internal and external sex organs) that define men and women (Fishman et al., 1999; WHO, 2004). Gender is defined as an ideology that originates from social, historical, and cultural constructs of ideas and beliefs. It is a set of cultural roles (Lerner, 1986). As such, gender characterizes the distinctions between females and males based on learned experiences instead of (or in addition to) biological differences (Costa, 1994). In this view, gender describes the characteristics that a society or culture (e.g., hierarchical relationships, historical and geographical locations, or social interactions) delineates as feminine or masculine (Fishman et al., 1999). It is related to the socially constructed roles, behaviors, influences, activities, and attributes that society considers appropriate for women and men.

Most of the stereotypic attributes and roles linked to gender are thought to arise more from sociological and cultural design than from biological endowment (Beall & Sternberg, 1993; WHO, 2004). Therefore, "sex" is the designation based on biology, while gender is socially and psychologically constructed (Wood, 1997, p. 23). Although some scholars adopt these concepts to define sex and gender, studies often report female and male differences without providing any evidence as to what causes them (e.g., biology, society, or both; Hyde, 2004). Indeed, as Bristor and Fischer (1993) point out, without providing the theoretical underpinnings or reasons, "reported gender differences (e.g., Meyers-Levy, 1988, 1989a, 1989b; Meyers-Levy & Sternthal, 1991) can appear to be biologically 'hard wired' and thus reinforce cultural stereotypes about men's and women's inherent abilities" (p. 532).

Gender Roles and Gender Identity

Gender roles refer to the culturally derived behaviors and activities associated with masculinity or femininity that individuals choose to adopt—that is, the norms applicable to individuals based on their socially identified gender (Eagly & Crowley, 1986). Based on gender schema theory, gender roles are related to social learning and experiences, which are programmed differently for each gender. Research suggests that socialization by families, social institutions (e.g., church, school), and media tends to polarize children into traditional gender role behaviors. By the time children reach adolescence, those roles are already established (Bem, 1981a, 1993). Certain traits tend to be associated with men and women as both genders are socialized in a particular way to play distinct roles within the society. Therefore, in terms of gender, men and women acquire attributes and characteristics for the roles that they occupy in society as they are also subjected to different social pressures (Bem, 1993; Eagly, 1987; Eagly, Wood, & Diekman, 2000).

The division of labor between genders also leads to distinctions in social behavior and personality. For instance, in certain cultures such as the United States, due to socialization pressures to conform to nurturing gender roles, women tend to take on more caring roles than do men. Conversely, men may be pushed to be more individualistic and aggressive than women (Bem, 1993). Some scholars discuss gender differences based on gender roles (Bem, 1993; Eagly, 1987; Eagly & Wood, 1991). They argue that gender differences and/or gender roles are based on "shared expectations (about appropriate qualities and behaviors) that apply to individuals on the basis of their socially identified gender" (Eagly, 1987, p. 12).

Traditional gender roles in Western cultures are related to the position that women and men occupy in society, the relationship between them, and the characteristics that distinguish them (Angrist, 1969). Women are more oriented to others, expressive of emotions toward others, caring, nurturing, empathetic or sympathetic, and idealistic than are men (Bem, 1993; Feshbach, 1982). Further, women tend to focus on close relationships, maintenance, and attending to others' concerns, whereas men give more emphasis to behavior related to assertiveness, aggression, and self-orientation (Bem, 1993). However, it is certain that not all women and men act alike: Not all women exhibit female characteristics or are feminine and not all men exhibit male characteristics or act masculine (Grunig, Toth, & Hon, 2000). This understanding of gender and gender roles can be expressed with "gender identity."

Gender identity refers to the degree or extent to which individuals identify with, or think of themselves as possessing, masculine or feminine personality traits. The term is interchangeable with sex-role identity (Kahle & Homer, 1985), sex-role orientation (Gentry & Doering, 1979), and sex-role self-concept (Stern, 1988), and it is related to an individual's psychological sex. Bem's (1981a) gender schema theory discusses gender identity in terms of individuals acquiring and displaying traits, attitudes, and behaviors consistent with their gender identity. Spence (1984) suggested that gender identity is multifactorial—that is, predictive only of situations in which gendered traits are likely to impact behaviors. In Western countries, gender identity is associated also with instrumental/agentic tendencies (personality traits: independence, assertiveness, competitiveness, rationality, reason, logic, individual goals) and communal/expressive tendencies (personality traits: caring, understanding, nurturing, responsibility, consideration, sensitivity, intuition, passion, communal goals) tendencies (Cross & Markus, 1993; Gill, Stockard, Johnson, & Williams, 1987).

Gender schema theory (Bem, 1981a) proposes that individuals acquire and display traits, attitudes, and behaviors consistent with their gender identity. Mainly, individuals process information about themselves and their world according to the way in which they view their psychological sex or gender identity. Through Bem's (1981b) sex role inventory (BSRI), individuals are categorized based on sex typed (masculine or feminine) or nonsex typed characteristics (androgynous or undifferentiated). The effect of gender identity on attitudes or behaviors depends on whether individuals are sex typed (or gender schematic, i.e., masculine schematic, feminine schematic). In other words, individuals (male or female or gender schematic) are more likely to be affected by their gender identity compared to non-sex-typed individuals (or gender aschematic, no gender related) (Palan, 2001). While sex-typed individuals are more likely to keep their behavior consistent with their culture's definitions of gender appropriateness, non-sex-typed individuals are more likely to cross the expected gender behavior.

In a review of advertising and marketing literature (Palan, 2001), sex is more significant than gender identity in a variety of contexts, such as product (preference) sex-typing (Allison, Golden, Mullet, & Coogan, 1980; Golden, Allison, & Clee, 1979; Kahle & Homer, 1985), gendered perception, attitudes and use of products and leisure activities (Gentry & Doering, 1977; Gentry, Doering, & O'Brien, 1978), ad recall (Gentry & Haley, 1984; Schmitt, Leclerc, & Dube-Rioux, 1988), choice and memory task (Schmitt et al., 1988), fashion attitudes (Gould & Stern, 1989), and self-descriptions, feelings, attitudes, and gift choice (Gould & Weil, 1991). Also, although the BSRI (Bem, 1974, 1981b) is commonly used in the psychology and sociology fields to assess individuals' gender identity, the majority of marketing, advertising, and consumer behavior gender studies evaluate "gender" with a binary self-report (male or female) variable (Wolin, 2003). In this chapter, we use the term "gender" to refer to the joint roles that nature and nurture influences play in individuals' sex-role expectations and gender identities.

THE SELECTIVITY HYPOTHESIS MODEL

Although advertising practitioners have considered gender as a segmentation strategy for more than 125 years (e.g., with the launch of the *Ladies Home Journal* in 1883; Modaffari, 2011), the scholarly literature related to gender and advertising is fragmented and often atheoretical. It was not until the development and publication of Meyers-Levy (1988, 1989a, 1989b) and colleagues' (Meyers-Levy & Maheswaran, 1991; Meyers-Levy & Sternthal, 1991) research on gender roles and influence on persuasion and processing (eventually codified in the selectivity hypothesis) that the study of gender and persuasion was legitimized as a theoretical mode of scholarly inquiry in advertising and consumer research. The model was hailed as the most influential theoretical framework related to persuasion and gender (Kempf et al., 2006). Indeed, its impact has expanded beyond advertising and consumer research to the understanding of travel search information (Ramkissoon & Nunkoo, 2010), website design (e.g., Tuch, Bargas-Avila, & Opwis, 2010), and financial investing (Graham, Stendardi, Myers, & Graham, 2002). Next, we review the development and main assertions from the theoretical framework before we review subsequent literature in these areas. Figure 5.1 provides our overview of the gendered predictions for persuasion and processing from the framework.

In an initial experiment, Meyers-Levy (1988) investigated whether gender differences in persuasion are related to traditional sex roles. In other words, would men be more likely to be persuaded by self-oriented ("medicinal benefits") messages and women by other-oriented ("cosmetic benefits") messages for mouthwash? To do so, she primed half of the respondents to think about agentic goals (e.g., "It's important to stand by your own convictions") or communal goals (e.g., "I try to consider others' feelings in making decisions") prior to message judgment.

Interesting results emerged. For those who do not receive a sex-role prime, there are no gender differences with respect to advertising persuasion. That is, both men and women respond more favorably to the help-self appeal for mouthwash. However, irrespective of whether the sex-role prime matches or does not match the respondent's gender (e.g., match: agentic-male, communal-female), the sex-role prime influences how men and women respond to the advertising appeals. For those who receive the prime, men are more positive about the help-self appeal than the help-others appeal and vice versa for women. What is most intriguing about the study is that the traditional sex role ad appeal preferences only emerge after respondents receive the sex-role prime, causing them to think about their respective gender and to use it to guide their persuasion. See the left side of Figure 5.1, where we have graphically depicted the predictions related to processing and persuasion from this body of literature.

In a second experiment, Meyers-Levy (1988) tested gender effects on evaluations of two products before and after respondents taste the product and receive positive or negative information from "others" (i.e., a confederate ostensibly from a previous experiment who provides the information to the group). Results show that only women used information from the "other" in addition to their own self-evaluations to assess the products after they taste the products. Men, on the other hand, do not use the

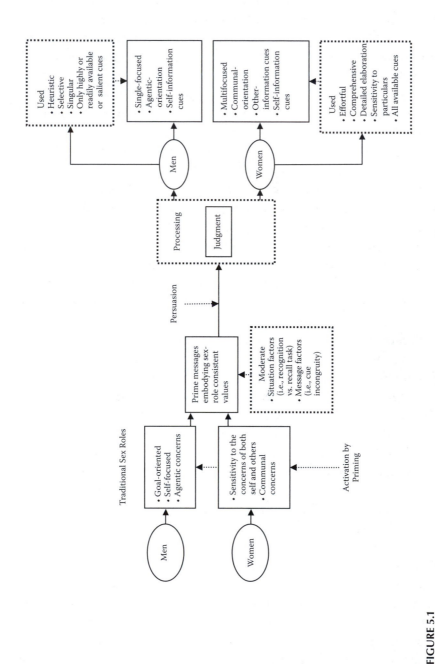

FIGURE 5.1

The selectivity hypothesis: predictions for persuasion and processing.

information from others in their product evaluations or consumption. (Please refer to the right side of Figure 5.1 for visual representation of these processing differences.) Based on the evidence from these two experiments, Meyers-Levy (1988) concludes that "the genders' sex role orientations can affect both the bases upon which they render judgments and the favorableness of their judgments" (p. 528). She questions, however, whether the processing differences (self vs. self + other) are general, and if these broader processing strategies can be applied to other situations beyond self and other-oriented processing.

Subsequent studies by Meyers-Levy (1989a, 1989b) and colleagues (Meyers-Levy & Maheswaran, 1991; Meyers-Levy & Sternthal, 1991) were designed to follow up and demonstrate processing differences across experimental stimuli and conditions. These studies show that the processing differences observed in the earlier studies are not universal and depend on several factors. For instance, Meyers-Levy and Sternthal (1991) report that women demonstrate greater processing and use of message cues than men in their evaluations of a news story and toothpaste, but only when the information presented to individuals provides sufficient attention for message cue elaboration. In this case, the moderate incongruity of some of the information cues with the overall message and product category allows women to attend better to that information, process it in depth, and use it for their product judgments. However, if the information does not allow opportunity for attention (i.e., under conditions of low message cue incongruity), then there are no differences with respect to the way that men and women process the product information. The authors speculate on several reasons for differences in message processing between men and women, particularly in terms of the gender-related psychological orientations as a result of gender socialization (e.g., agency and communion; Meyers-Levy, 1989b).

A similar study by Meyers-Levy and Maheswaran (1991) evaluates the extent of recognition of low, moderate, or highly incongruent cues about news stories embedded within an advertising description for a new *Nightline*-type news program. Respondents were asked to identify whether a series of news stories was featured in the ad, including stories not actually in the ad (i.e., "foils"). When the message cues are moderately or highly incongruous, both men and women appear to use an elaborative strategy in determining message congruity, because they demonstrate high rates of recognition and low rates of foils (i.e., picking the stories that were not actually in the ad). However, when the message cues are not very incongruous, males are more likely to select the foils rather than the actual message cues. The authors suggest that women "are more able to elaborate on and consider the particulars of message material than are males" (p. 68), but warn that this propensity will only occur when message or task factors do not encourage a particular form of processing.

Therefore, the original set of studies conducted in the late 1980s and early 1990s by Meyers-Levy and colleagues suggest that under certain conditions, men and women respond better to messages that conform to their gender identity and will also vary in the nature and use of message processing for judgments (see Figure 5.1). Across all of the experimental studies, they measured gender (biological sex), but not gender identity or sex roles. However, the authors do not suggest that the differences in message response and processing are "hard-wired" in the sexes. Instead, they test various experimental conditions to identify whether (and how) gender differences might emerge.

The Selectivity Model and Persuasion (Message Response)

As discussed in Meyers-Levy (1988), gender differences at the behavioral, motivation, and social levels influence how individuals perceive or view their roles or identity. In this way, men from cultural contexts such as the United States may be motivated by achievement needs and agentic goals. In contrast, women may be more concerned with both self and others and are thought to be dependent, relational, warm, and nurturing (Deaux, 1984; Gefen & Straub, 1997). They are motivated by personal and online interaction (Chiu, Lin, & Tang, 2005), affiliation needs, and expressive and communal goals (Bakan, 1966). As discussed earlier, Meyers-Levy (1988) demonstrates that when traditional (self–other) gender roles are activated in women and men, their responses to persuasive messages suit those roles. She does not predict or find, however, that these findings would hold when gender roles are not primed.

First, some scholars argue that men and women respond differently to persuasion efforts in general. For example, long before the inception of the selectivity hypothesis, Worchel and Cooper (1976) suggested that women are taught to be submissive as part of their socialization and therefore are more susceptible to being persuaded. In addition, some research finds that men in the United States are more likely than women to exhibit psychological reactance to persuasion efforts (Joubert, 1990; Seemann, Buboltz, Jenkins, Soper, & Woller, 2004)—the phenomenon known as the boomerang effect (e.g., Brehm & Brehm, 1981). These differences are explained according to the ways in which men and women in the United States are socialized in their respective opportunities to engage in "free" behaviors. In an advertising context, Vilela and Nelson (2006) find that men (but not women) are *less* likely to indicate they would purchase the product than they were prior to the campaign or at a 2-week delay after being exposed to a cause-related marketing (CRM) campaign for Cheerios cereal. This finding suggests that the men react against the "help others" CRM persuasion attempt, but the women do not.

Second, in line with the agentic (male) versus communal (female) assumption of the selectivity hypothesis (Meyers-Levy, 1988), message content that matches gender roles or identity should be most persuasive (especially or only when sex roles are primed). The literature in this area shows that sometimes the theory holds and sometimes it does not, although the measure of gender, gender identity, and roles varies widely.

A handful of studies shows that women may be more flexible than men in their acceptance of and response to non-sex-typed messages. Feminist scholars in the United States tend to corroborate the literature that women are more familiar with both androcentric (emphasis on masculine interests or a masculine viewpoint) and gynocentric (emphasis on feminine interests or a feminine viewpoint) messages, whereas men are less likely to process or draw inferences from gynocentric messages (Stern, 1991, 1993). Similarly, Wolin (2003) argues that women are more likely to accept advertisements and brands targeted to male segments than vice versa.

In line with this form of thinking, in an early study of sex role and advertising matching, Prakash (1992) found that men prefer an advertising appeal that demonstrates competition with others (as opposed to competition with oneself) due to their achievement motivation and desire to show mastery over others. In contrast, women are not opposed to competition advertising appeals, but they evaluate competitive appeals to self (e.g., "When competing against myself, all I need is Ting") and others (e.g., "After a day of rigorous competition against others, reach for Ting") equally well. In this study, gender identity is not measured. However, the study does not show that women were less competitive than men, but simply that the type of competitive claim does not matter for advertising persuasion.

Finally, in an innovative study, Fisher and Dube (2005) demonstrate that men's responses to stereotype-congruent or -incongruent advertisements are dependent on viewing context. That is, whereas women's responses to ads do not change across condition, men's response to messages containing stereotype-incongruent ads (featuring low agency emotions such as scared, embarrassed, warm, sentimental) vary depending on whether they watch the ad in private or in the presence of another man. When men watch in private, their indications of viewing pleasure of the ad or attitude toward the ad do not differ from those of women. Only when they watch the ads with another man (and presumably have to conform to gender-role expectations) do their ad responses differ. In addition, there is no difference with respect to private or public viewing context for high-agency emotions (stereotype congruent) for men or women.

A second set of studies examines the effectiveness of ads that appeal to the target's self-interest versus those that appeal to helping others. In line with gender-role expectations and identity suggested in the selectivity hypothesis, men should respond more favorably to help-self appeals (agentic goals) and women to help-others (caring) or help-self plus help-others appeals. Studies in this line of research, using respondents from the United States, largely support these claims. For instance, in response to public service announcements (PSAs) and advertising in alcohol messages, male adolescents respond more positively to the agentic (self-oriented) ad messages, whereas female adolescents trust and appreciate collectivistic or communal appeals more (Andsager et al., 2002).

Similarly, Brunel and Nelson (2000) reported that men respond better to a donation appeal for cancer research when the money will "help oneself" versus "oneself and others," whereas women respond better to the "help oneself and others appeal." Importantly, the authors use a measure of caring values and note that these actually mediate the influence of gender (biological sex). Thus, it is not biological sex that drives the persuasion results; rather, it is the match between the (caring) values depicted in the advertising message and those of the individual (regardless of sex) viewing the messages.

Similarly, Wang, Bristol, Mowen, and Chakraborty (2000) showed that irrespective of national culture (China, United States), men exposed to a "separated from others" appeal (e.g., "the art of being unique") indicated a higher attitude toward a fictitious watch brand than those exposed to a "connected to others" appeal (e.g., "a reminder of relationships"), and vice versa for women. Similarly to the Brunel and Nelson (2000) study reported before, the findings for gender (measured as biological sex) are mediated by another construct or explanatory variable—in this case, a measure of the "dependence" dimension of a self-construal measure. In other words, it is not biological sex, but rather the individual's self-construal or identity that is related to persuasion.

Finally, Hupfer (2006) shows that Canadian men and women respond better to message appeals for blood donation containing a help-self appeal (over a help-others appeal). However, men differ from women in that they respond better when the level of self-referencing (i.e., mental processing that links information to self-concept) is moderate rather than low across both help-self and help-others appeals. For women, the level of self-referencing relates to the type of appeal (i.e., low self-referencing for help-others ad and moderate self-referencing for help-self ad).

Thus, as a whole, the body of research shows that the selectivity model holds best for men. Historically, men are more likely to respond favorably to advertising that is congruent with their sex role or gender identity related to a competitive, "high agency" self, whereas women appear to be more flexible in their advertising response. The underlying reasons for these responses have not been thoroughly investigated. Perhaps in the United States, where most of the research has been conducted, women are allowed a greater range of gender roles, whereas men are still mainly viewed in traditional stereotypical ways. Some evidence of this claim, at least in terms of television advertising content, is supported (Paek, Nelson, & Vilela, 2011). It is encouraging that while most of the reviewed research measured gender according to biological sex, some research demonstrated that another construct (e.g., of caring values, self-construal) may be a better predictor of message response than biological sex.

Message Processing

In addition to message response, advertising persuasion depends on consumers' interpretation, judgment, and processing of communication messages (e.g., Batra & Ray, 1986; Kardes, 1988). In this stream of research, Meyers-Levy's (1989a, 1989b) selectivity hypothesis is based on the notion that women and men employ different strategies to process a communication message. She proposes that women process information more comprehensively, attempting "to assimilate all available cues," while men tend to "employ various heuristic devices that serve as surrogates for more detailed processing." Based on this model, "males rely on single, as opposed to multiple cues to make judgments" (Meyers-Levy, 1989a, p. 221).

Women as Comprehensive Processors

Women attempt to assimilate all available cues, attending equivalently to a single cue and to multiple cues. Based on U.S. data, women also devote substantial attention to detail-oriented specification cues and allow relatively equal processing to information relevant to the self and to the external world. Since their childhood, girls are raised in a more structured environment. Specifically, they have historically been conditioned to accept a more subordinate and submissive role in society than boys have been. They are encouraged to be driven by relationship-oriented communal goals (e.g., greater consideration for self, others, and their structures) (Hall, 1984), and they also tend to be more caring and nurturing. Consequently, women are typically more attentive to message cues in order to interpret them accurately.

Therefore, women are concerned with a broad and comprehensive range of cues that facilitate responsiveness to others and may be more likely to process the whole attributes of a message (Meyers-Levy, 1989a, 1989b; Meyers-Levy & Sternthal, 1991). In other words, women's comprehensiveness is expressed in their tendency to consider and reason through multiple cues. They are stimulated to generate high evaluative interpretations and express sensitivity to others and to pay attention to the particulars of relevant information when forming judgments. Women grow up engaging in a rather effortful, comprehensive, inferential, elaborative, and piecemeal analysis of the available range of information that facilitates responsiveness to others and their structures (Darley & Smith, 1995; Meyers-Levy, 1989a; Meyers-Levy & Maheswaran, 1991).

Men as Selective Processors

Men attempt to assimilate single cues. More specifically, the selectivity hypothesis predicts that if men are confronted with dual cues, they will focus on and use as a basis of response the single or salient cue that is more available. Men will only use multiple cues if such cues are conceptually singular. Thus, they often do not engage in comprehensive processing of all available information as a basis for judgment. Instead, they use single cues or cues that convergently imply a single inference. In addition, men usually focus on self-related information, which acts as a peripheral device upon which to base judgments or behaviors. They employ objective and categorical states in interpretation. They are encouraged to assume an agentic and single-minded position through selective processing of stimuli.

In contrast to females' socialization, males in the United States are encouraged to concentrate on self-concerns with low sensitivity to others. In brief, evidence suggests that males' selective mode of judgment, responsiveness, and processing are frequently driven by a reliance on cues that are highly and readily available, as well as particularly salient in the focal context. Males' processing of information requires minimal processing of understated detail in favor of highly available singular cues. Men are relatively selective in the information cues they use in interpreting and acting upon the world (Darley & Smith, 1995; Meyers-Levy, 1989a, 1989b). Based on the processing differences outlined by the selectivity model, we review selected research that examines the theoretical predictions in the areas of information search and message processing.

Information Search

Consistent with the selectivity hypothesis, we would expect that men would engage in a targeted information search that relies on heuristics, whereas women should engage in a more comprehensive search that solicits and integrates multiple sources. Some evidence in scholarly research and advertising practice conforms to these expectations. For example, Laroche, Saad, Cleveland, and Browne (2000) surveyed men and women in a large city in Canada about their Christmas shopping strategies. Their results show that the women in their sample indicated that they used a significantly greater number of information search strategies and sources when shopping for gifts as compared with men, who more frequently rely on the help of a salesperson.

A subsequent cross-cultural study soliciting information search strategies among men and women in Britain, the United States, and Canada (Cleveland, Babin, Laroche, Ward, & Bergeron, 2003) reported similar gender results across national cultures. The authors in both studies conclude that men are less comprehensive in their information search patterns and tend to rely on the "heuristics" of a salesperson's advice, whereas women search for and process information from multiple sources before making a decision. The selectivity hypothesis is cited as a theoretical explanation for their findings. Gender is measured using self-reported demographic (male or female) survey information.

More recently, however, within the context of the selectivity hypothesis, studies examine the predictive nature of biological sex versus a measure of gender identity for information search. For example, using survey methodology, Ramkissoon and Nunkoo (2010) report that gender identity (but not biological sex) is a significant predictor of how individuals search for travel-related information. Those people who score high on femininity traits engage in the most information searches (internal as well as external searches) as compared with those who score high on masculinity and show much lower information searches.

Similarly, in a broader context, Hupfer and Detlor (2006) compare the effects of sex versus gender identity (self- vs. other orientation) on individuals' web search strategies for information (e.g., health, hobbies) relevant to self or a close other. They find no differences in sex on information search strategy. Rather, the self- and other orientation is most predictive of information search strategies. Those with a predominant self-orientation (irrespective of their biological sex) indicate a lower search strategy across information types and relevance, whereas those with an other-orientation indicate more effortful search and a higher search frequency for self and others. As a whole, however, the evidence for information search strategies consistently shows that men, or those who score high on masculinity, appear to use less comprehensive information-gathering strategies when searching for product- or service-related information, and vice versa for women.

Studies in Message Processing

In addition to information search, studies explore gender differences in message processing in multiple ways. Some studies consider the audiences' attention to cues in messages (e.g., Meyers-Levy & Maheswaran, 1991; Meyers-Levy & Sternthal, 1991). Others gauge message processing by asking respondents to write down their thoughts or "cognitive responses" to a message (e.g., Brunel & Nelson, 2003; Putrevu, 2004; Vilela, 2010). The authors then code the number, content, and elaboration of those thoughts to see if cognitions vary by gender and/or help predict advertising persuasion.

The first body of literature examines the ways in which men and women attend to or use informational cues in persuasion messages to form evaluations. Although not explained according to the selectivity hypothesis, Widgery and McGaugh (1993) contrast men's and women's perceptions of the salience of various message appeals to their decisions when choosing a new vehicle. They find that among the older people in their sample, women are significantly more likely than men to indicate that several product attributes, dealership attributes, and incentives are important for their decision. In other words, more types of message cues are considered important for evaluation and decision making to women but not to men.

With respect to evaluation of brand extensions, Lau and Phau (2010) report that women were better than men at attending to or processing moderately incongruent advertisement imagery from brand extensions and then linking that information to the parent brand. In essence, women were better able to establish branding image fit and brand personality fit evaluation than men were. Their findings are consistent with previous studies (Meyers-Levy & Maheswaran, 1991; Meyers-Levy & Sternthal, 1991) reporting that gender impacts how message cues with different levels of congruity affect product evaluation. In sum, these results are in line with the predictions of the model. However, Peracchio and Tybout's (1996) study showed no evidence of processing differences among men and women when evaluating desserts; rather, differences in processing are attributed to the amount of knowledge individuals possess about the product category.

Results from another related set of studies, using various methodologies and contexts, suggest that gender-related information processing differences result in a male desire for simplicity in message content and design, whereas females prefer additional informational cues or complex messages. For example, Chamblee, Gilmore, Thomas, and Soldow (1993) analyzed the complexity of print ads in *Reader's Digest* and *Time* by calculating the type-token ratio (TTR; essentially comparing the number of separate or different words used to the total number of words used). They then related the magazine's TTR to its Starch Readership Scores (noted, associated, read most) by gender. Their results show that women are more likely than men to "read most" (elaborate) the ads across magazines, but particularly when the ads had a higher TTR (were more complex, offering more product information). The scholars explain their findings according to literature regarding gender differences in information processing

(Meyers-Levy & Sternthal, 1991). Although this study was innovative in its use of secondary research materials (i.e., Starch Readership Scores, content analysis of complexity of advertising), it did not illuminate individual-level gendered processing to particular advertisements.

Several other experimental and survey studies help fill in that gap. In an evaluation of print advertisements for a Dodge truck, men demonstrated more positive attitudes toward the ad and the brand and higher purchase intention scores than did women when the ad was simple. In contrast, women showed higher scores on these three variables when the ad was complex and informative (Putrevu, 2004). In another study using a mall survey, Phillip and Suri (2004) tested the favorability of various components of promotional e-mails. They found that e-mail information content and the visual presentation used in e-mails are likely to be evaluated differently by men and women. Mainly, their results suggested that women consider e-mails as a source of product information and evaluate the presence of links to additional sources of information more positively than do men. The authors specifically cite the selectivity hypothesis (Meyers-Levy & Maheswaran, 1991) as an explanation for their findings. Women want the opportunity to find out information, even if it means a more cluttered look.

In addition, in a strictly visual context, Tuch et al. (2010) explore the effect of web page symmetry on various measures of websites (e.g., intuitive beauty, classical and expressive aesthetic design). Their findings reveal that there is some impact of symmetry on intuitive straightforward beauty appraisals and on classical and expressive aesthetic judgments. Asymmetrically designed websites are considered to be less beautiful, receiving lower scores on the classical and expressive dimensions. Relevant to this chapter, the symmetry effect only occurs among male respondents (men showing negative responses to asymmetrically designed websites), while women are not affected by asymmetrical web pages. From a processing viewpoint, some argue that symmetry provides redundancy of visual information, making the information less complex (Chipman, 1977) and resulting in a more favorable aesthetic response (Reber, Schwarz, & Winkielman, 2004). In this way, males prefer the simpler processing view, in line with processing predictions from the selectivity hypothesis.

With respect to the value of the selectivity hypothesis in predicting actual message elaboration as measured by cognitive responses, the literature is mixed. There are studies showing no differences between women and men in generating more cognitive responses (total number of thoughts) (Putrevu, 2004; Vilela, 2010), in motivation to engage in cognitive elaboration (Petracchio & Tybout, 1996), and in preference for lexical complexity (Putrevu et al., 2004). In addition to advertising message processing, Kempf et al. (2006) examine the extent and nature of processing related to product trial information when information is lacking in the ads across two product categories (experiential: grammar checking software; nonexperiential: virus scanner). They find, as predicted and in line with the selectivity hypothesis, that women list a greater number of total cognitions (especially for the experiential product) than do men. In addition, for the nonexperiential product, women are more likely than men to notice and question the completeness of the information provided during the product trial. Overall, the authors suggest that women are more likely to engage in more comprehensive processing of information across advertising and product trial, whereas men seemingly accept the information given as a basis for product evaluation.

The body of research as a whole seems to suggest that women (but not men) favor messages or product trial experiences in which they can acquire, gather, or evaluate information more comprehensively. This general result holds true across methodology and persuasion contexts; however, most of the studies used biological sex as the measure of gender.

Some Caveats: Gender Differences Under Certain Conditions

Thus far, we have reviewed the selectivity hypothesis model and the resultant expectations for persuasion and processing. Because within the published literature scholars often seek to find gender differences, that is what is most often reported. However, an important characteristic of the selectivity hypothesis that is often not discussed is that women and men employ different strategies to process messages under certain circumstances or conditions (e.g., low/moderate involvement). Gender differences in message processing disappear if situational factors motivate men to engage in comprehensive processing. Mainly, under high-involvement conditions, gender differences in processing—with women more likely to engage in detailed elaboration of message content and men more likely to be driven by overall message themes or schemas—may not occur (Meyers-Levy, 1989a, 1989b; Meyers-Levy & Sternthal, 1991).

For example, in a within-subjects design, Brunel and Nelson (2003) found that message processing differences for help-self or help-others ads, in line with the selectivity model, were dependent on situational involvement. That is, under low situational involvement (Experiment 1: advertising evaluation was regarded as an experimental "filler task"), the value-based ad matching preferences (i.e., that men would prefer help-self and women would prefer help-others appeals) do not hold; rather, irrespective of advertising appeal, the women prefer the first ad they see, whereas the men prefer the last ad they see. These preferences are explained according to primacy or recency effects, indicative of ad processing. However, when situational involvement is high (i.e., respondents were told this was a real copy-testing situation), gender differences in processing disappear. Now, all respondents appear to exhibit primacy effects for the first ad they see (in listing thoughts). Further, men show evidence of systematic processing when the ad matches their values (help-self appeal). The authors concluded that gender differences in persuasion (value-matching gender identity) and processing are dependent on situational involvement, among other factors.

A few other studies also predict and find conditional results for men and women in line with Meyers-Levy and colleagues' findings (Meyers-Levy & Maheswaran, 1991; Meyers-Levy & Sternthal, 1991). For example, in another study conducted with Pacific Rim university students, Chang (2007) shows that the processing predictions of the selectivity hypothesis hold for women (i.e., women employ similarly elaborative processing strategies across both comparative and noncomparative advertising appeals). However, when men are encouraged to engage in elaborative processing by viewing comparative advertising appeals, they are also likely to engage in elaborative processing (but not so for noncomparative advertising). Thus, situational factors (e.g., recall task, recognition) and/or message factors (e.g., cue incongruity, comparative ad appeals; Chang, 2007) may also affect the model, as they motivate both genders to engage in detail-sensitive processing (Meyers-Levy & Maheswaran, 1991). As a whole, moving forward, the literature that tests or cites the selectivity model should consider the conditions under which gender differences emerge or do not emerge.

LIMITATIONS AND FUTURE RESEARCH

After a review of the selectivity hypothesis model and associated literature conducted on gendered message response and processing, we return to the original question (and title of this chapter): "Is the selectivity hypothesis model still relevant?" The answer to the question is a qualified "yes" and "no." In the first case, the theoretical framework offers an explanatory value for a range of studies demonstrating gender response and persuasion for over the past 20 years. As a whole, women and men in the United States (where most of the research has been conducted) often respond differently to different types of content appeals, and they look for and process information in different ways. In particular, men tend to respond according to their traditional masculine gender roles and identity in favor of agentic appeals, whereas women tend to respond well to both agentic and communal appeals.

Further, in an information search, message evaluation, and processing, women tend to look for and assimilate multiple cues, whereas men are more likely to focus on singular cues, especially when conditions do not suggest a particular mode of processing. Although there are instances where the model does not hold true, there are numerous other studies that provide empirical support for the theoretical framework, as reviewed in this chapter. However, the real difficulty in fully assessing the question is related to two primary issues: (1) The measures of gender (or gender identity, gender roles) are not consistent across studies, and (2) the explanation for why or how gender matters is often lacking.

Future research might test for (and measure) the influence of sociocultural influences on gender and on message response and persuasion. As advocated by other researchers (Palan, 2001; Wolin, 2003), studies should measure for self-reported gender as well as other measures of self-construal (Wang et. al., 2000), values (Brunel & Nelson, 2000), gender identity (Coughlin & O'Connor, 1985; Fischer & Arnold, 1990, 1994; Ramkissoon & Nunkoo, 2010), and gender roles (Fischer & Arnold, 1994; Jaffe, 1991). Although gender identity and gender roles might be slow to change in some cultures, there are also some trends in the media and advertising that encourage a wider range of gender identity and roles nowadays.

For instance, in April 2011, J. Crew released in the United States an ad that shows its president and creative director, Jenna Lyons, painting her young son's toenails with a hot pink Essie nail polish. The caption of the ad, which was e-mailed to customers to advertise free shipping, read "Lucky for me I ended up with a boy whose favorite color is pink. Toenail painting is way more fun in neon." Despite the controversy it generated, with some calling the ad "blatant propaganda celebrating transgendered children" or saying that "J. Crew is targeting a new demographic of mothers of confused boys," there is a tendency, especially in Western countries, to embrace (and accept) a facade of liberal gender or cross-gender identity politics (Macedo, 2011). Further examples include celebrity actors Angelina Jolie and Brad Pitt allowing their 4-year-old daughter, Shiloh, to dress as a tomboy—that is, not following the expected gender role behavior for her age. Therefore, measuring gender identity and gender roles solely might not be an effective tool.

Studies could also investigate or try to replicate findings in cultural contexts that promote more egalitarian gender roles and fluid gendered identities (i.e., Denmark, Sweden, Norway; Hofstede, 1980) to see if the findings reported using North American respondents hold. For example, would Scandinavian men be reticent to show emotions toward sad advertisements when watching them with other men as shown in Fisher and Dube's (2005) study among American men?

In addition to sociocultural influences, checking for biological (sex) differences with the use of new technologies might also be possible. In 1989, Meyers-Levy attributed differences in how exposure to visual/spatial/linguistic tasks may influence how men and women process messages and categorize "poor exemplar" products into product categories. She further suggested that cognitive processes are related to "differences in the genders' hemispheric organization" (p. 84)—the way that genders use the left and right brain to process information, but laments the fact that the processes could not be directly observed.

Now, 20+ years later, researchers have access to technology and tools that allow them to study brain patterns directly. Indeed, spatial-cognition perception and performance is one area where consistent results have been found for gender differences (e.g., Grön, Wunderlich, Spitzer, Tomczak, & Riepe, 2000). Results of fMRI scans showed that the navigation patterns of men and women through maze exploration (representative of spatial processing) result in different brain activation patterns (Grön et al., 2000). Would such differences in spatial processing influence the ways in which men and women respond to two- or three-dimensional design or to gaming situations where brands are often placed? For example, a study in Britain finds that males prefer business and greeting card designs that are designed by men and vice versa for women, even though respondents do not know the gender of the designer. Among other differences, the male designs are described as more three-dimensional than female designs

(Moss & Colman, 2001). Future research might examine the conditions for which sociocultural and potential biological gender differences arise in gendered responses to messages.

A second response to the question of the relevance of the theory—for advertising practice—is a qualified "No." Historically, advertising has been sold on the basis of a demographic audience such as gender. According to some scholars, gender is often used as a segmentation strategy because it is easily identifiable, accessible, measurable, and responsive to marketing mix elements and, finally, gender segments are large and profitable (Darley & Smith, 1995).

However, Nielsen and CBS recently stated that demographics such as age and sex are not relevant for measuring TV ad effectiveness. Viewer behaviors and attitudes predict consumers' purchases better than do the demographic variables. David Poltrack, CBS corporate chief research officer, revealed in a conference at the Advertising Research Foundation's *Re: Think 2011* (in March 2011) that there is a growing amount of data showing that "using demographics to target commercials is essentially invalid and a misallocation of television advertising investment" (Neff, 2011). Although this is but one example, future research might also see whether the theoretical predictions of the theory hold in advertising practice.

REFERENCES

Allison, Neil K., Linda L. Golden, Gary M. Mullet, & Donna Coogan (1980). Sex-typed product images: The effects of sex, sex role self-concept and measurement implications. In Jerry C. Olsen (Ed.), *Advances in consumer research* (Vol. 7; 604–609). Ann Arbor, MI: Association for Consumer Research.

Andsager, Julie L., Erica W. Austin, & Bruce E. Pinkleton (2002). Gender as a variable in interpretation of alcohol-related messages. *Communication Research, 29* (June), 246–270.

Angrist, Shirley S. (1969). The study of sex roles. *Journal of Social Issues, 15* (January), 215–232.

Bakan, David (1966). *The duality of human existence.* Chicago, IL: Rand McNally.

Batra, Rajeev, & Morris L. Ray (1986). Affective responses mediating acceptance of advertising. *Journal of Consumer Research, 13* (September), 234–249.

Beall, Anne E., & Robert J. Sternberg (1993). *The psychology of gender.* New York, NY: Guilford Press.

Bem, Sandra L. (1974). The measurement of psychological androgyny. *Journal of Consulting and Clinical Psychology, 42* (April), 155–162.

Bem, Sandra L. (1981a). Gender schema theory: A cognitive account of sex typing. *Psychological Review, 88* (July), 354–364.

Bem, Sandra L. (1981b). *Bem sex-role inventory.* Palo Alto, CA: Consulting Psychological Press.

Bem, Sandra L. (1993). *The lenses of gender—Transforming the debate on sexual inequality.* New Haven, CT: Yale University Press.

Brehm, Sharon S., & Jack W. Brehm (1981). *Psychological reactance: A theory of freedom and control.* New York, NY: Academic Press.

Bristor, Julia M., & Eileen Fischer (1993). Feminist thought: Implications for consumer research. *Journal of Consumer Research, 19* (March), 518–536.

Brunel, Frédéric F., & Michelle R. Nelson (2000). Explaining gendered responses to "help-self" and "help-others" charity ad appeals: The mediating role of world-views. *Journal of Advertising, 29* (Fall), 15–28.

Brunel, Frédéric F., & Michelle R. Nelson (2003). Message order effects and gender differences in advertising persuasion. *Journal of Advertising Research, 43* (September), 330–341.

Chamblee, Robert, Robert Gilmore, Gloria Thomas, & Gary Soldow (1993). When copy complexity can help ad readership. *Journal of Advertising Research, 33* (May/June), 23–28.

Chang, Chingching (2007). The relative effectiveness of comparative and noncomparative advertising—Evidence for gender differences in information-processing strategies. *Journal of Advertising, 36* (Spring), 21–35.

Chipman, Susan F. (1977). Complexity and structure in visual patterns. *Journal of Experimental Psychology: General, 106* (September), 269–301.

Chiu, Yu-Bin, Chieh-Peng Lin, & Ling-Lang Tang (2005). Gender differs: Assessing a model of online purchase intentions in e-tail services. *International Journal of Service Industry Management, 15* (May), 416–435.

Cleveland, Mark, Barry J. Babin, Michel Laroche, Philipa Ward, & Jasmin Bergeron (2003). Information search patterns for gift purchases: A cross-national examination of gender differences. *Journal of Consumer Behavior, 3* (September), 20–47.

Costa, Jeneen A. (1994). *Gender issues and consumer behavior.* London, England: Sage Publications.

Coughlin, Maureen, & P. J. O'Connor (1985). Gender role portrayals in advertising: An individual differences analysis. In Elizabeth C. Hirschman & Morris B. Holbrook (Eds.), *Advances in consumer research* (Vol. 12; pp. 238–241). Ann Arbor, MI: Association for Consumer Research.

Cross, Susan E., & Hazel R. Markus (1993). Gender in thought, belief, and action: A cognitive approach. In Anne E. Beall & Robert J. Sternberg (Eds.), *The psychology of gender* (pp. 55–98). New York, NY: Guilford Press.

Darley, William K., & Robert M. Smith (1995). Gender differences in information processing strategies: An empirical test of the selectivity model in advertising response. *Journal of Advertising, 24* (Spring), 41–56.

Deaux, Kay (1984). From individual differences to social categories: Analysis of a decade's research on gender. *American Psychologist, 39* (February), 105–116.

Deaux, Kay (1985). Sex and gender. *Annual Review of Psychology, 36,* 49–81.

Deutsch, Bob (2010). How to market to males. *Marketing Daily* (May 21), http://www.mediapost.com/publications/?fa=Articles.showArticle&art_aid=128658

Eagly, Alice H. (1987). *Sex differences in social behavior: A social-role interpretation.* Hillsdale, NJ: Lawrence Erlbaum Associates.

Eagly, Alice H., & Maureen Crowley (1986). Gender and helping behavior: A meta-analytic review of the social psychological literature. *Psychological Bulletin, 100* (November), 283–308.

Eagly, Alice H., & Wendy Wood (1991). Explaining sex differences in social behavior: A meta-analytic perspective. *Personality and Social Psychology Bulletin, 17* (June), 306–315.

Eagly, Alice H., Wendy Wood, & Amanda B. Diekman (2000). Social role theory of sex differences and similarities: A current appraisal. In Thomas Eckes & Hanns M. Trautner (Eds.), *The developmental social psychology of gender* (pp. 123–174). Mahwah, NJ: Lawrence Erlbaum Associates.

Feshbach, Norma D. (1982). Sex differences in empathy and social behavior in children. In Nancy Eisenberg (Ed.), *The development of prosocial behavior* (pp. 315–338). New York, NY: Academic Press.

Fischer, Eileen, & Stephen J. Arnold (1990). More than a labor of love: Gender roles and Christmas gift shopping. *Journal of Consumer Research, 17* (December), 333–345.

Fischer, Eileen, & Stephen J. Arnold (1994). Sex, gender identity, gender role attitudes, and consumer behavior. *Psychology & Marketing, 11* (March/April), 163–182.

Fisher, Robert J., & Laurette Dube (2005). Gender differences in responses to emotional advertising: A social desirability perspective. *Journal of Consumer Research, 31* (March), 850–858.

Fishman, Jennifer R., Janis G. Wick, & Barbara A. Koenig (1999). The use of "sex" and "gender" to define and characterize meaningful differences between men and women. In *Agenda for research on women's health for the 21st century: A report of the task force on the NIH (National Institutes of Health) women's health research agenda for the 21st century* (Vol. 2), U.S. Department of Health and Human Services, Public Health Service, National Institutes of Health, 15–20, http://sexandgendercourse.od.nih.gov/pdf/agenda_book_2.pdf

Gefen, David, & Detmar W. Straub (1997). Gender differences in the perception and use of e-mail: An extension to the technology acceptance model. *MIS Quarterly, 21* (December), 389–400.

Gentry, James W., & Mildred Doering (1977). Masculinity-femininity related to consumer choice. In Barnett A. Greenberg & Danny N. Bellenger (Eds.), *Contemporary marketing thought: 1977 educators' proceedings*. Chicago, IL: American Marketing Association, 423–427.

Gentry, James W., & Mildred Doering (1979). Sex role orientation and leisure. *Journal of Leisure Research, 11*(2), 102–111.

Gentry, James W., Mildred Doering, & Terrence V. O'Brien (1978). Masculinity and femininity factors in product perception and self-image. In Kent Hunt (Ed.), *Advances in consumer research* (Vol. 5; pp. 326–332). Ann Arbor, MI: Association for Consumer Research.

Gentry, James W., & Debra Haley (1984). Gender schema theory as a predictor of ad recall. In Thomas C. Kinnear (Ed.), *Advances in consumer research* (Vol. 11; pp. 259–264). Ann Arbor, MI: Association for Consumer Research.

Gill, Sandra, Jean Stockard, Miriam Johnson, & Suzanne Williams (1987). Measuring gender differences: The expressive dimension and critique of androgyny scales. *Sex Roles 17* (October), 375–400.

Golden, Linda L., Neil Allison, & Mona Clee (1979). The role of sex role self-concept in masculine and feminine product perceptions. In William L. Wilkie (Ed.), *Advances in consumer research* (pp. 599–605). Ann Arbor, MI: Association for Consumer Research.

Gould, Stephen J., & Barbara B. Stern (1989). Gender schema and fashion consciousness. *Psychology & Marketing, 6* (Summer), 129–145.

Gould, Stephen J., & Claudia E. Weil (1991). Gift-giving roles and gender self-concepts. *Sex Roles, 24* (May), 617–637.

Graham, Judy F., Edward J. Stendardi, Jr., Joan K. Myers, & Mark J. Graham (2002). Gender differences in investment strategies: An information processing perspective. *International Journal of Bank Marketing, 20*(1), 17–26.

Grön, Georg, Arthur P. Wunderlich, Manfred Spitzer, Reinhard Tomczak, & Matthias W. Riepe (2000). Brain activation during human navigation: Gender-different neural networks as substrate of performance. *Nature Neuroscience, 3* (April), 404–408.

Grunig, Larissa A., Elizabeth L. Toth, & Linda C. Hon (2000). Feminist values in public relations research. *Journal of Public Relations Research, 12* (January), 49–68.

Hall, Judith A. (1984). *Nonverbal sex differences: Communication accuracy and expressive style.* Baltimore, MD: Johns Hopkins University Press.

Hofstede, Geert (1980). *Culture's consequences: International differences in work related values.* London, England: Sage Publications.

Hupfer, Maureen E. (2006). Helping me, helping you: Self-referencing and gender roles in donor advertising. *Transfusion, 46* (June), 996–1005.

Hupfer, Maureen E., & Brian Detlor (2006). Gender and web information seeking: A self-concept orientation model. *Journal of the American Society for Information Science and Technology, 57* (June), 1105–1115.

Hyde, Janet S. (2004). *Half the human experience—The psychology of women* (6th ed.). Boston, MA: Houghton Mifflin Company.

Jaffe, Lynn J. (1991). Impact of positioning and sex-role identity on women's responses to advertising. *Journal of Advertising Research, 31* (June/July), 57–64.

Joubert, Charles E. (1990). Relationship among self-esteem, psychological reactance and other personality variables. *Psychological Reports, 166* (June), 1147–1151.

Kahle, Lynn R., & Pamela Homer (1985). Androgyny and midday mastication: Do real men eat quiche? In Elizabeth C. Hirschman & Morris B. Holbrook (Ed.), *Advances in consumer research* (Vol. 12; pp. 242–246). Ann Arbor, MI: Association for Consumer Research.

Kardes, F. R. (1988). Spontaneous inference processes in advertising: The effects of conclusion omission and involvement in persuasion. *Journal of Consumer Research, 15* (September), 225–233.

Kempf, DeAnna S., Russell N. Laczniak, & Robert E. Smith (2006). The effects of gender on processing advertising and product trial information. *Marketing Letters, 17* (January), 5–16.

Laroche, Michel, Gad Saad, Mark Cleveland, & Elizabeth Browne (2000). Gender differences in information search strategies for Christmas gifts. *Journal of Consumer Marketing, 17*(6), 500–524.

Lau, Kong C., & Ian Phau (2010). Impact of gender on perceptual fit evaluation for prestige brands. *Journal of Brand Management, 17* (March), 354–367.

Lenney, Ellen, Joel Gold, & Chris Browning (1983). Sex differences in self-confidence: The influence of comparison to others' ability level. *Sex Roles, 9* (September), 925–942.

Lerner, Gerda (1986). *The creation of patriarchy.* New York, NY: Oxford University Press.

Macedo, Diane (2011). J. Crew ad showing boy with pink nail polish sparks debate on gender identity. Foxnews.com (April 11), http://www.foxnews.com/us/2011/04/11/jcrew-ad-showing-boy-pink-nail-polish-sparks-debate-gender-identity/

Meyers-Levy, Joan (1988). The influence of sex roles on judgment. *Journal of Consumer Research, 14* (March), 522–530.

Meyers-Levy, Joan (1989a). Gender differences in information processing: A selectivity interpretation. In Patricia Cafferata & Alice M. Tybout (Eds.), *Cognitive and affective responses to advertising* (pp. 219–260). Canada: Lexington Books.

Meyers-Levy, Joan (1989b). Priming effects on product judgments: A hemispheric interpretation. *Journal of Consumer Research, 16* (June), 76–86.

Meyers-Levy, Joan, & Durairaj Maheswaran (1991). Exploring differences in males' and females' processing strategy. *Journal of Consumer Research, 18* (June), 63–70.

Meyers-Levy, Joan, & Brian Sternthal (1991). Gender differences in the use of message cues and judgments. *Journal of Marketing Research, 28* (February), 84–96.

Modaffari, Mary K. (2011). Advertising to women/moms—A brief history, Engage: moms. *MediaPost,* March 30, http://www.smarterfaster.com/?p=2295

Moss, Gloria, & Andrew M. Colman (2001). Choices and preferences: Experiments on gender differences. *Journal of Brand Management, 9* (November), 89–99.

Neff, Jack (2011). CBS: Viewers' age and sex shouldn't matter to marketers. *AdAge Mediaworks* (March 23), http://adage.com/article/mediaworks/cbs-viewers-age-sex-matter-marketers/149534/

Nelson, Michelle R., Frédéric F. Brunel, Magne Supphellen, & Raj Manchanda (2006). Effects of culture, gender and moral obligations on responses to charity advertising across masculine and feminine cultures. *Journal of Consumer Psychology, 16*(1), 45–56.

Paek, Hye-Jin, Michelle R. Nelson, & Alexandra M. Vilela (2011). Examination of gender-role portrayals in television advertising across seven countries. *Sex Roles, 64* (February), 192–207.

Palan, Kay M. (2001). Gender identity in consumer behavior research: A literature review and research agenda. *Academy of Marketing Science Review, 10,* 1–24.

Peracchio, Laura A., & Alice M. Tybout (1996). The moderating role of prior knowledge in schema-based product evaluation. *Journal of Consumer Research, 23* (December), 177–192.

Phillip, Marissa V., & Rajneesh Suri (2004). Impact of gender differences on the evaluation of promotional emails. *Journal of Advertising Research, 44* (December), 360–368.

Prakash, Ved (1992). Sex roles and advertising preferences. *Journal of Advertising Research, 32* (May/June), 43–52.

Putrevu, Sanjay (2004). Male and female responses to print advertisement. *Journal of Advertising, 33* (Fall), 51–62.

Putrevu, Sanjay, Joni Tan, & Kenneth R. Lord (2004). Consumer responses to complex advertisement: The moderating role of need for cognition, knowledge, and gender. *Journal of Current Issues and Research in Advertising, 26* (Spring), 9–24.

Ramkissoon, Haywantee, & Robin Nunkoo (2010). More than just biological sex differences: Examining the structural relationship between gender identity and information search behavior. *Journal of Hospitality and Tourism Research* (November 19), published online before print.

Reber, Rolf, Norbert Schwarz, & Piotr Winkielman (2004). Processing fluency and aesthetic pleasure: Is beauty in the perceiver's processing experience? *Personality and Social Psychology Review, 8* (November), 364–382.

Schmitt, Bernd H., France Leclerc, & Laurette Dube-Rioux (1988). Sex typing and consumer behavior: A test of gender schema theory. *Journal of Consumer Research, 15* (June), 122–128.

Seemann, Eric A., Walter C. Buboltz, Steve M. Jenkins, Barlow Soper, & Kevin Woller (2004). Ethnic and gender differences in psychological reactance: The importance of reactance in multicultural counseling. *Counseling Psychology Quarterly, 17* (June), 167–176.

Spence, Janet T. (1984). Masculinity, femininity, and gender-related traits: A conceptual analysis and critique of current research. *Progress in Experimental Personality Research, 13,* 1–97.

Stern, Barbara B. (1988). Sex-role self-concept measures and marketing: A research note. *Psychology & Marketing, 5* (Spring), 85–99.

Stern, Barbara B. (1991). Literary analysis of an advertisement: The commercial as soap opera. In R. H. Holman and M. Solomon (Eds.), *Advances in consumer research* (Vol. 18; pp. 164–171). Provo, UT: Association for Consumer Research.

Stern, Barbara B. (1993). Feminist literary criticism and the deconstruction of ads: A postmodern view of advertising and consumer responses. *Journal of Consumer Research, 19* (March), 556–566.

Tuch, Alexandre N., Javier A. Bargas-Avila, & Klaus Opwis (2010). Symmetry and aesthetics in website design: It's a man's business. *Computer in Human Behavior, 26* (November), 1831–1837.

Vilela, Alexandra M. (2010). *Consumer processing of cause-related marketing (CRM): The influence of gender on message evaluations.* Germany: VDM—Verlag Dr. Müller.

Vilela, Alexandra M., & Michelle R. Nelson (2006). Values: Better than sex segmentation strategy for cause-related marketing messages. Paper presented at the Annual Meeting of the International Communication Association, Dresden International Congress Centre, Dresden, Germany, June 19–23.

Wang, Cheng L., Terry Bristol, John C. Mowen, & Goutam Chakraborty (2000). Alternative models of self-construal: Dimensions of connectedness-separateness and advertising appeal to the cultural and gender-specific self. *Journal of Consumer Psychology, 9* (April), 107–115.

Widgery, Robin, & Jack McGaugh (1993). Vehicle message appeals and the new generation woman. *Journal of Advertising Research, 33* (September/October), 36–42.

Wolin, Lori D. (2003). Gender issues in advertising—An oversight synthesis of research: 1970–2002. *Journal of Advertising Research, 43* (March), 111–129.

Worchel, Stephen, & Joel Cooper (1976). *Understanding social psychology.* Homewood, IL: Dorsey Press.

WHO (World Health Organization) (2004). Gender and women's health (GWH), http://www.who.int/gender/whatisgender/en/

Wood, Julia T. (1997). *Gendered lies: Communication, gender, and culture* (2nd ed.). Belmont, CA: Wadsworth.

6

Gender and Media Literacy: Women and Men Try On Responses to Objectification in Fashion Advertising

*Jacqueline Lambiase, Tom Reichert,
Mark Adkins, and Michael S. LaTour*

INTRODUCTION

For more than two decades, Jean Kilbourne, Sut Jhally and his Media Education Foundation, and other critics have created training materials to educate people about the ways in which media producers create images, fabricate demand for consumer goods, and distort perceptions of the human body. Yet despite educational initiatives in other parts of the English-speaking world, media literacy efforts in schools have lagged in the United States (Kellner & Share, 2005). These efforts often focus on an inoculation or protectionist approach to the "disease of mainstream media" (VanMeenen, 2009; for example, see Brucks, Armstrong, & Goldberg, 1988). Academic and industry studies about the effectiveness of any style of media literacy for advertising consumption are insufficient and focus only on short-term effects or recall, rather than on actual behaviors or predictive theories (Eagle, 2007). Indeed, few systematic tests of media literacy efforts are attempted, even though at least three scholarly journals—the *Journal of Communication* in 1998, the *American Behavioral Scientist* in 2004, and *Afterimage: The Journal of Media Arts and Cultural Criticism* in 2009—have published special issues to encourage new assessment and broader outlooks.

The present qualitative study seeks to join this important conversation by adding to the small body of empirical literature on gender and advertising media literacy, which has been almost entirely quantitative in its approach. By using simple codes, along with rhetorical and theme analyses, researchers examined 145 open-ended responses to advertisements using sexually oriented appeals. Responses from a control group were compared and contrasted to responses from participants in a treatment group, which viewed a media literacy video before considering the advertisements. Working along with the participants to create meaning, this research charts the ways in which women and men evaluate these ads and whether they identify ads as sexist. In addition, evidence of sexual thoughts and evaluation of those thoughts by female and male participants are considered and coded, to determine the range of thoughts triggered by viewing sexually oriented advertisements, along with participants' feelings about those thoughts.

This study seeks to answer these research questions:

- When male and female consumers respond to advertising that utilizes sexually oriented appeals, what broad evidence of media literacy may be discerned? In other words, what does media literacy sound like, in the words of participants?
- Does exposure to a media literacy video increase the chances that participants will use vocabulary and evaluations that indicate an understanding or interpretation of objectification and sexism?
- When participants recognize sexual thoughts produced by viewing the advertisements, in what ways do they describe, interpret, and evaluate these thoughts? Are there connections between these thoughts and statements about their own media literacy?
- Do participants make connections between the texts they are analyzing and the contexts in which these advertisements are produced?

The discussion and conclusion sections of this chapter will focus more globally on how participants' responses produce categories and strategies of critical analysis that may guide future literacy projects away from a protectionist outlook and toward more predictive theories about consumer response, behavior, and learning.

REVIEW OF THE LITERATURE

In the advertising discipline, some progress has been made toward building an inventory of studies addressing media literacy. For example, one quantitative study on objectified images of women in advertising features an experiment with undergraduate students who were shown the Media Education Foundation's *Still Killing Us Softly*, in which Jean Kilbourne describes the ways that some advertising, much of it using sexual appeals, misrepresents women (Ford, LaTour, & Middleton, 1999). These researchers found that students viewing the video experienced increased levels of feminist consciousness, according to scores on the Arnott female autonomy inventory, and both male and female participants expressed enhanced sensitivity to women's roles in advertising. In addition, this study reports influencing beliefs about feminism and intentions to boycott marketers that use sexist promotion materials through use of a sex-role inventory (see Lundstrom & Sciglimpagila, 1977). In a similar study of the effects of an intervention video, Irving and Berel (2001) found that Kilbourne's *Thin Hopes*, produced by the Media Education Foundation, did not significantly affect young women's body images or internalization of the thin ideal, but did increase their skepticism toward the media.

In an earlier study, Ford and LaTour (1996) use a stratified random sample in a socioeconomically diverse SMSA to demonstrate that years of education positively influence scores on the Arnott inventory (higher levels of feminism), which in turn drive negative perceptions of sexist female roles in advertising. Those perceptions carry over to negative views of the sponsoring corporation and boycott intentions. So, it can be readily inferred from these two studies that a key part of the education process is exposure to videos and other materials that can quickly elevate sensitivity to female role portrayals.

A more recent study examines the effects of media literacy within the context of sexual objectification of women in advertising (Reichert, LaTour, Lambiase, & Adkins, 2007). The findings reveal a gender effect in which, after viewing literacy materials, women evaluate ads containing objectifying images of women much more negatively than do men. Women view the models as significantly less realistic and respond negatively to the ad, the brand, and intentions to purchase products advertised with sexualized images of women. Males, on the other hand, manifest no literacy effects. The researchers conclude that involvement may play a role; a person may be much more likely to respond to a literacy event when one is the object of discussion. In addition, male sexual arousal to the images of women could mitigate any negative evaluations of the advertising. The researchers identify the gender effect but call for additional qualitative research to explain the divergence in gender responses.

Beyond these experimental studies using media literacy components, effects research focuses on sexist, sexually oriented, and/or decorative portrayals in advertising, and these demonstrate that sexually attractive images of women have unintended effects, including short-term devaluations of one's own—and one's partner's—attractiveness (Kendrick, Gutierres, & Goldberg, 1989; Richins, 1991). Additional studies find that these images support attitudes of aggressiveness toward women (MacKay & Covell, 1997), that gendered stereotypes and gender-role expectations are triggered (Lafky, Duffy, Steinmaus, & Berkowitz, 1996; McKenzie-Mohr & Zanna, 1990), and that body image distortions occur (Harrison & Cantor, 1997; Lavine, Sweeney, & Wagner, 1999; Myers & Biocca, 1992). Sex-role socialization, studied by Signorelli (1993), may lead to limited conceptions of women, as do stereotypes (Merskin, 2004). Many factors may contribute to this socialization, but advertising images may prove to be especially powerful because they "idealize" reality while providing clues to attitudes and behavior (Pollay, 1986).

Media Literacy

Kellner and Share (2005) believe that media literacy "helps people to use media intelligently, to discriminate and evaluate media content, to critically dissect media forms, to investigate media effects and uses, and to construct alternative media" (p. 372). Other scholars echo this definition, asserting that media literacy involves developing strategies for enhancing a viewer's skill in reading, analyzing, and evaluating media (Thoman & Jolls, 2004) and putting "media programming into meaningful perspective" (Silverblatt, 2004, p. 35). Messaris (1998) emphasizes media literacy as "knowledge about how the mass media function in society," with a focus on media's "economic foundations, organizational structures, psychological effects, social consequences" and "representational conventions" (p. 70).

All of these definitions encompass text-centered and context-centered approaches to media literacy, a problem that may lead to "incoherence" when media literacy is used to develop public policy and educational strategies (Lewis & Jhally, 1998, p. 117). VanMeenen (2009) points to other problems in the way that media literacy is operationalized in educational systems by scholars who are aligned with a standpoint

> that rejects protectionist theories and the efforts to "inoculate" media consumers (especially youth) against the disease of mainstream media... Instead, they work from the assumption that much media production offers positive effects and that an informed practice of critical literacy may enhance enjoyment of this [*sic*] media. (p. 2)

Eagle (2007) urges researchers to focus on a range of advertising forms and to develop better theory in terms of recognition, perception, and behavioral effects, going well beyond inoculation theory.

Of particular interest to this chapter is an emphasis on text-centered approaches to media literacy because participants were prompted to write responses to content in specific advertisements; yet, the context proves to be important to participants as well, making rhetorical analysis of their responses an important tool to connect text with context. Analyzing consumer understanding of the visual language of advertising fits one of the major goals recommended for media scholarship and education (Messaris, 1998). In addition, participant responses that link text and context may provide important information about recognition and perception of sexually oriented appeals, a goal suggested by Eagle (2007).

Rhetorical Analysis

Beyond coding responses as favorable or unfavorable toward an advertiser, product, or advertisement itself, researchers may also use theme and rhetorical analyses to understand these reactions, which are based on viewers' interpretations of the symbol systems at work in the advertising. Many researchers encourage the use of rhetorical and narrative analyses to tease meaning from consumer reactions and consumer-produced narratives (Stern, 1990; Stern, Thompson, & Arnould, 1998). Others encourage rhetorical analysis of advertising itself, to aid in understanding how viewers may receive messages from schemes and tropes that permit multiple readings (McQuarrie & Mick, 2003; Scott, 1994). To make sense of advertising, viewers must create information to interpret messages because "schemes *push* these meanings onto the reader, where tropes *pull* them out of the reader" (McQuarrie & Mick, 2003, original emphasis, p. 200); "one and the same message must both gain attention and be persuasive" (p. 215). Through analysis of open-ended responses, this attention-getting function of advertising may be studied, along with whether or not it is persuasive, which may be measured by a negative, positive, mixed, or neutral reaction.

Rhetorician Kenneth Burke provides a basis for studying both text and context through his notion of intrinsic and extrinsic readings based on his dramatistic pentad, which encompasses act, agent, agency, scene, and purpose (1967). These intrinsic and extrinsic categories allow analysis to toggle between (a) how the narrative scene depicted in an advertisement is interpreted by an individual participant, and (b) how the text is given a broader purpose by a participant. This purpose may fit within a meaning and production system that lies far beyond the advertisement's images and text, and a fixed interpretation is usually not possible. In this way, Burke's pentad serves as an invention machine, in which "a viewer's interaction with the scene determines its message, and while viewer interpretations may be stereotyped by ad producers or agents, some viewers will resist identification with an ad's scene" (Lambiase & Reichert, 2003, p. 257). In the case of some sexually oriented images, these multiple interpretations actually rely on the broadest sort of media literacy and are deliberately embedded "to be relatively obvious to knowledgeable viewers....The message is not just about sex but also about being media-savvy and hip" (Messaris, 1997, pp. 62–63).

METHOD

We used a mixed-methods approach, first coding responses in quantitative fashion and then qualitatively applying rhetorical and theme analyses to categorize and interpret short narratives of 145 racially diverse participants. We split these participants into two groups for the study: 88 in a treatment group and 57 in a control group. In total, 66 women and 79 men participated (see Tables 6.1–6.4); all were recruited from business and communication courses at a large public university because students are viewed as an important group regarding media literacy research. The average age of these students was 23, with a racial or ethnic distribution

TABLE 6.1

Advertising Evaluation by Gender and Literacy Treatment

Valence	Females[a]		Males	
	Control (%)	Treatment (%)	Control (%)	Treatment (%)
Positive	37.0	10.3	36.7	28.6
Negative	40.7	51.3	23.3	32.7
Mixed	11.1	20.5	20.0	10.2
Neutral	11.1	17.9	20.0	26.5
Total	100	100	100	100
	($n = 27$)	($n = 39$)	($n = 30$)	($n = 49$)

Note: $n = 145$.
[a] There was a marginal relationship between responses and treatment for females ($p = .06$).

TABLE 6.2

Identification of the Ads as Sexist by Gender and Literacy Treatment[a]

Mention	Females		Males	
	Control (%)	Treatment (%)	Control (%)	Treatment (%)
Explicit	11.1	25.6	0.0	6.1
Indirect	18.5	35.9	30.0	51.1
None	70.4	38.5	70.0	38.8
Total	100	100	100	100
	($n = 27$)	($n = 39$)	($n = 30$)	($n = 49$)

Notes: $n = 145$.
[a] There was a relationship between responses and treatment for both sexes ($p < .05$).

of 72% White, 15% Hispanic, 6% African American, 5% Asian or Asian American, and 2% other. Males represented 54% of the total sample. All participants signed consent forms based on institutional research board guidelines, which promised anonymity and confidentiality; students could receive extra credit in their various courses for participating in the study.

Before viewing one of two sexually oriented advertisements, along with another control ad, participants in the treatment group were exposed to a 10-minute segment of *Dreamworlds II*, narrated by Sut Jhally and produced by the Media Education Foundation. The DVD features sexually oriented depictions of women in music videos and discusses their objectification, and the 10-minute segment included information considered by scholars to be essential to a strong media literacy curriculum, including information about the message's purpose, creator, and creative techniques (Thoman & Jolls, 2004).

TABLE 6.3

Evidence of Sexual Thoughts by Gender and Literacy Treatment

Mention	Females		Males	
	Control (%)[a]	Treatment (%)	Control (%)[a]	Treatment (%)
Explicit	14.8	20.5	40.0	36.7
Indirect	18.5	25.6	23.3	20.4
None	66.7	53.8	36.7	42.9
Total	100	100	100	100
	($n = 27$)	($n = 39$)	($n = 30$)	($n = 49$)

Note: $n = 145$.
[a] Female versus male control groups differed from each other ($p = .05$).

TABLE 6.4

Valence of Sexual Thoughts by Gender and Literacy Treatment

Valence	Females		Males	
	Control (%)[a]	Treatment (%)[a]	Control (%)[a]	Treatment (%)[a]
Positive	25.0	5.6	50.0	46.2
Negative	62.5	66.7	5.6	30.8
Mixed	0.0	0.0	5.6	7.7
Neutral	12.5	27.8	38.9	15.4
Total	100	100	100	100
	($n = 8$)	($n = 18$)	($n = 18$)	($n = 26$)

Note: $n = 70$.
[a] Female versus male control groups and treatment groups differed from each other ($p < .05$).

From a pool of nearly 20 full-page magazine advertisements featuring female models in decorative or traditional roles (Ferguson, Kreshel, & Tinkham, 1990), the two most sexually-tinged advertisements with objectified female models were selected by a group of gender studies professors and graduate students in a program unrelated to the authors' academic units. The first advertisement for a jeans company features a male model embracing a female model in a short dress, while another female model stares through a window at the couple. In the second ad for a clothing designer, two attractive, twin-like female models wearing tight and revealing clothing embrace each other.

Participants were gathered in a computer classroom in groups of 25–30 students over a 2-week period; they were randomly shown either the *Dreamworlds* video (treatment group) or a video about the Grand Canyon (control group) and then asked to take a survey rating the videos, to obscure the researchers' purpose. Students also were told they would be participating in three different studies. Next, students were asked to complete a comprehensive health-related questionnaire. After students finished the questionnaire, they were told they would participate in another study about advertising and then were shown two ads, either the jeans ad or the belts ad, along with a control ad about a minivan. In about half of the sessions, the minivan ad was shown to participants first, followed by one of the two target ads; in the other half, one of the two target ads was shown before the minivan ad, to correct for ordering effects. Each ad was shown for about 20 seconds, and then the participants were given about 2 minutes to write their reactions to the advertisements.

To begin the analysis, the researchers coded participant responses using these four categories (see Tables 6.1–6.4):

- General evaluation of the advertising (positive, negative, mixed, or neutral)
- Identification of the advertising as sexist or as objectifying women (explicit, indirect, none)
- Evidence of sexual thoughts (explicit, indirect, none)
- Evaluation of those sexual thoughts by the participant (positive, negative, mixed, neutral)

Next, responses in these groupings were categorized using rhetorical and theme analysis to determine whether and how participants commented on both the text (the ad itself) and the context (the broader cultural perspective), as well as other themes, such as using the vocabulary from the DVD about music videos to describe the images used in the clothing advertisements. The authors followed coding guidelines to ensure that saturation had occurred, in terms of discovering all possible types of themes within participants' responses (Bauer & Gaskell, 2000).

Along with participants' initial evaluations of advertisements that we coded, we have woven participants' codes, comments, and meanings into the "Findings and Discussion" section of this chapter. These participant-generated themes were first identified and then used as categories for further coding of responses. We identify each statement in the analysis as generated by a male or female participant, with a participant number, followed by the word "treatment" or "control." Most of the 145 participants provided responses containing just two or three short statements. Because we cite 45 responses from 41 participants in this chapter, we opted to forgo assigning pseudonyms to these participants, classifying them as male or female instead. We regard the narratives written by the control group members (as well as themes derived from the control group) as equal in importance to those from the treatment group.

FINDINGS AND DISCUSSION

Evaluation Coding

The initial quantitative coding by the authors of responses determined general trends across all 145 participants to build validity for the subsequent rhetorical and theme analyses of each response. A brief description of these coding results follows. Women in the treatment group who saw the *Dreamworlds* DVD rated the advertisements more negatively and saw these ads as sexist more often than women from the control group and men from both groups (see Tables 6.1 and 6.2). For men, the only difference between the treatment and control groups may be seen in Table 6.2: Men were more apt to identify the ads as sexist after the media literacy treatment [chi-square $(2, N = 79) = 7.99$, $p < .05$]. With regard to expression of sexual thoughts, men were more likely to express them compared to women in the control condition [chi-square $(2, N = 57) = 5.88$, $p = .05$], but there was no difference between men and women after viewing the treatment. However, the valence of sexual thoughts did differ between men and women for the both the control [chi-square $(3, N = 26) = 10.30$, $p < .05$] and treatment conditions [chi-square $(3, N = 44) = 11.13$, $p < .01$]. When men expressed a sexual thought, it was more likely to be positive compared to women's sexual thoughts—regardless of the literacy treatment.

Participants' Themes

Several common themes emerged in participants' responses: questions about logic and credibility; identification of sexism and objectification; expressions of anger, rejection, or sarcasm in the sexual thoughts of women; expressions of enjoyment, humor, or indignation/sarcasm in the sexual thoughts of men; awareness of media literacy concepts; and awareness of the advertising text and its context. We discuss each theme in this section, followed by examples of participant responses coded as using these themes.

Logic and Credibility

To answer the first research question—what does media literacy sound like?—we relied on theme analysis to explore the responses of women and men in both the control and treatment groups. Participants who did not accept the most obvious or dominant narratives from the ads offered many reasons why these ads did not work or did not make sense.

Two overall themes emerged: logic and credibility. The first of these covers responses that offer a logical rebuttal. Many of these rebuttals, which are often coded as negative or mixed/neutral responses in the quantitative coding, make links between text and context:

- "If they made jeans then why did the model not wear any jeans... Why does she have to be half-naked?" [female 4, treatment]
- "Is this ad saying that if I wear these jeans, I am going to get laid?" [female 20, treatment]
- "I don't see the relevance to clothing. I don't even see a relationship between the people." [female 118, treatment]
- "In fact, the girl was not wearing any jeans." [male 1, treatment]
- "The actual clothes aren't presented." [male 26, control]
- "The ad attempted to influence consumers to buy their product by making them think they would look like the people in the ad." [male 53, control]
- "Clothes? Is that what this ad is for?" [female 57, control]

In the treatment group of 39 women, more than half (20) used language containing a logical rebuttal or a rhetorical question seeking logic. There were many fewer themes of logic in the control groups, especially among women (just 5 of 27). In these first seven examples, many participants toggled between an intrinsic reading of the narrative within the ad in their comments about models and clothing (Burke's scene) and the extrinsic reality of fashion advertising, where scantily clad models are expected.

With regard to the second theme, participants questioned the advertiser's strategy by using language that revealed doubt as to the credibility of the advertised brand and the industry. One woman said that the advertiser was "trying to get into the fad—of ads that say nothing—a little too late" [female, 19, treatment]. Another woman commented that "because they have a reputation for these types of ads, it is effective only for [this advertiser's] reputation" [female 81, control].

Objectification and Sexism

This study's second research question sought to link the language of the media literacy DVD with participant responses. Participants in the treatment group, especially women, were more likely to use the vocabulary and evaluations that appear in the *Dreamworlds* DVD than those in the control groups. Because the DVD focuses on music videos, participants apply or transfer terms from that context to the print advertisements. Only one participant out of 145 refers to *Dreamworlds,* writing that "it relates back to the video" [female 133, treatment].

A few participants, both male and female, made the link to sexism through their focus on a sign that appears in the jeans advertisement, with the word "serve" on it:

- "The sign in the back, 'serve,' that somewhat upset me for I didn't like the impression that the ad was giving that a man can just serve himself a willing woman anytime he wanted." [female 3, treatment]
- "I noticed that the sign said 'serve' like the girl was serving the guy in the picture." [male 16, treatment]
- "The self serve sign in the top right corner seemed to promote free sex. I noticed that the female was sitting on the male's lap with a smile. It seemed to all be happy." [male 21, treatment]

One participant from the control group noticed the sign: "The fact that there is a sign that says 'serve' that is pointing to the man in the ad suggests that the woman will do whatever he wants if he is wearing those jeans" [male 61, control]. One of the women in the treatment group who noticed sexism expressed that she is "somewhat upset" about the "serve" sign, while a male participant in the treatment group who noticed the sign opened his narrative by saying that he "liked this ad."

In terms of the theme of objectification, vocabulary borrowed from the video and participants' own experiences with media literacy includes these phrases from the treatment group: "overly explicit material," "women as sexual objects," "same old sexual commercials," "sexist," "false assumptions," "male gaze," and "female objectification." A female in the control group had this response: "They are trying to convey the message that because she looks good in the jeans, so will you [viewer]. Fallacy of the unrepresentative sample" [female 59, control]. Many participants from the treatment and control groups also acknowledged, sometimes positively, that an advertisement worked because it "caught my attention" or "was interesting to look at."

Yet many participants voiced resistance to advertising messages. Two men in the treatment group acknowledged that "this kind of ad doesn't do much for me anymore" [male 106, treatment] and that this "sex in ads...using an old style...[is] not very interesting any more" [male 5, treatment, original ellipses], which may show signs of media literacy as well as a kind of media maturity. A woman in the control group had a similar response: "What the hell was that all about? It's somewhat cool; however, it does NOT make me want to run out and buy the product" [female 57, control].

No Sexual Thoughts or Negative Sexual Thoughts From Women

Participants used a full range of emotions, but more women did *not* express sexual thoughts than did, in terms of this study's third research question about how participants describe or evaluate sexual thoughts. Many women in both groups expressed no sexual thoughts in their narratives (54% in the treatment group; 67% in the control group; see Table 6.3). More women in the treatment group expressed sexual thoughts, either explicitly or indirectly, and these thoughts were overwhelmingly negative (see Table 6.4). Women expressed a range of emotions, including anger, rejection, and sarcasm. Examples of these emotions include:

- "Service, and a chick flung back like she is about to moan sexually. Is this ad saying that if I wear these jeans I am going to get laid?" [female 20, treatment]
- "Why would I want to look like a slut?" [female 116, treatment]

- "Whatever!!! This ad is also degrading to women...because the women are too affectionate with each other." [female 138, treatment]
- "Two girls who are that close to each other is a real turn-on to some men...Are real women like that? I DON'T THINK SO!" [female 23, treatment]

The only positively coded reflection by a female participant on an explicit sexual thought is this one: "Very sexy ad. Hot. I did not think much about jeans. Great looking models just made me think about sex and heat and being blonde. I could barely see the jeans. Intense." [female 89, control]

Humor and Enjoyment for Men

Men expressed varying emotions around and through their recorded sexual thoughts, including humor, enjoyment, indignation (rather than anger), and sarcasm. The percentage of men who did express explicit or indirect sexual thoughts (57% in the treatment and 63% in the control group) almost equals the percentage of women who did *not* express sexual thoughts. A few examples of an indignant and/or sarcastic sexual thought by males include:

- "I thought that the company must think the general public are idiots...it was purely connotated [*sic*] as sexual." [male 1, treatment]
- "They do look good in their jeans, but so what? I suppose some idiots might actually think that they'd look like that if they went out and purchased the jeans." [male 112, treatment]
- "I doubt the women come with the product." [male 132, treatment]

Humor and enjoyment were much more common emotional evaluations by men who stated sexual thoughts, as in these examples:

- "Sexy mamas come to daddy!" [male 122, treatment]
- "Makes me think about sex and beautiful women." [male 105, treatment]
- "I want to have sex with both of those girls at the same time." [male 92, control]
- "A good ad because it makes you want them." [male 37, treatment]

- "If I had the money to buy a pair of [jeans], with that woman on the advertisement, it will be an 'of course!'" [male 10, treatment]
- "Where can I meet these two women? Are they bisexual?…Tasty! ;->" [male 123, treatment]

Awareness of Media Literacy Language

Beyond expressing these thoughts on the sexual content in these advertisements, participants also made connections between these thoughts and their own media literacy. In these next examples, participants can clearly be seen "trying on" a range of media literacy language:

- "Why is it always women—they show women for men's ads and women for women's ads. What is up with that??" [male 62, treatment]
- "It shows the women as sexual objects. It portrays perfect, good-looking people wearing jeans. This ad is persuasive." [female 136, treatment]
- "That chick was hot. I did not even think about the product until the end when I was thinking why would they do this kind of ad?…I am not sure if this kind of advertising works but I sure enjoyed the ad." [male 99, treatment]

These three comments may be different or may be interpreted as weaker (especially the second and third examples) when compared to the language of the music video. Furthermore, when compared to the stronger language of responses that clearly reject this sort of advertising strategy, these examples capture media literacy as it is used by participants.

Connections Between These Advertising Texts and Larger Contexts

Using the tools of rhetorical analysis—specifically Burke's intrinsic and extrinsic delineations—the authors found that participants did toggle between assessing the advertisement and assessing a larger context in which advertisements are produced. Many participants showed a high level of sophistication through the variety of questions or comments they quickly made; many also talked about both text and context and intrinsic scene and extrinsic purpose. Rather than commenting on the advertisement itself, as instructed, many participants started their narratives with these extrinsic perspectives, which are signs of media literacy in action.

In the following six examples, all participants immediately think of the audience or consumer group viewing the advertisements:

- "This ad made me wonder if all the people who buy this brand of clothing will look this way." [male 129, treatment]
- "This ad is very appealing to males." [male 103, treatment]
- "First of all, I am assuming that the ad is for women to buy jeans and believe me, it is not going to make me run out and by [*sic*] jeans. Especially since they didn't really even show the jeans." [male 62, treatment]
- "I don't think that many people will be looking at the jeans in this ad." [female 136, control]
- "I can't relate to the age group. Effective for younger age group... advertiser is selling jeans, but sending exploitative messages to young adults." [female 137, treatment]
- "By looking at this ad I would not know what type of audience this is being aimed at unless I had previous knowledge on the company." [female 65, control]

These extrinsic evaluations are examples of resistance to the dominant narratives portrayed within the advertisements because participants jump directly to comments about a range of production, strategy, demographic, and consumption issues. All six of these readers—women and men, treatment and control group—seem firmly in charge of interpreting these advertising texts because of a "critical understanding" (Flynn & Schweickart, 1986, p. 35) that allows them to see the text in layers, in both text and context.

CONCLUSIONS

As previously stated, the purpose of this chapter is to take a global, contextual approach in assessing how themes derived from participants' responses can be used to guide future literacy projects away from the most traditional or protectionist perspectives. As the findings demonstrate, participants' reactions are much more complex than previous quantitative studies reveal. For example, many participants refuse the scene or narrative presented in the advertisement or include critical comments or extrinsic comments about the advertisement after first playing along with the intrinsic narrative. But many do not. Some participants gave responses that seemed deliberately at odds, such as the woman who described an advertisement as using women "as sexual objects" and then called the advertisement "persuasive." Equivocal responses such as this one give good evidence for many ranges of media literacy that cannot be captured by quantitative coding or surveys alone.

Overall, some participants in both treatment and control groups seemed fluent from the standpoint of media literacy, deftly handling complicated relationships among consumers, advertisers, and media with a few short sentences. While some participants interpreted the ads without complexity—"It looks like people in this ad are friends and it makes the ad more personal" [female 109, control]—many used mixed approaches for making meaning from the advertisements, and these ways of seeing again demonstrated that most of the participants possessed media literacy skills. One participant started his comments with "Damn nice looking women," but ended with "The focus is not on quality or value. The ad represents what people want to see" [male 94, control].

The simple statistics in Tables 6.1–6.4 add validity to these findings and, together, the evaluation coding and the qualitative themes deliver ample evidence about the ways that participants make meaning. These interpretations provide caution signs to advertisers about sexually-oriented appeals. Two streams of evidence support this assertion, and it is a warning that has been suggested by other studies (LaTour & Henthorne, 1994, 2003). The first evidence is that just 10% of the treatment group of female participants offered positive evaluations of these sexualized ads (see Table 6.1), and well under half of the other groups did as well. Qualitative analysis shows that many positive comments were accompanied by negative or neutral comments.

The second reason confirms what many studies suggest: that processing of sexual information interferes with other memory processes, taking focus away from brands and marketing messages (Grazer & Keesling, 1995). As one woman aptly expressed, "People in this kind of business should be more careful of what they're trying to portray because it really creates a bad impression" [female 126, treatment].

While many participants engaged in logical examination of these two fashion advertisements (especially women in the treatment group), participants also engaged in emotional responses that might be termed "literacy plus anger," "awareness plus sarcasm," and "skepticism plus humor." Again, these kinds of emotions—all coupled with an agonistic, outsider stance that is evidence of media literacy—challenge the pathways for messages to be recalled by consumers and, at worst, doom an advertisement to be resisted or ignored.

All of these judgments by participants offer implications for future research, in terms of touching upon well-developed theories that address information processing, information flow and diffusion of ideas, and social learning. Additionally, these participants' responses point to interesting studies that could be conducted on media literacy and its relationship to and reliance on emotions such as anger, curiosity, and humor. The pleasures of these texts should also be considered. How might these emotions be developed in classroom settings so that students may take the tools of media literacy—freed from protectionist pedagogies—and apply them to their own media products or to their own media consumption, in ways that are satisfying to them? How could men become more engaged in critiquing media depictions of women and vice versa?

Limitations of this study include the use of only college-aged students. In addition, there is an intended lack of correspondence between the media literacy treatment (female representation in music videos) and the awareness outcomes (reactions to advertising). Whereas the method reduced demand effects, it is possible that male respondents are unable to make contextual connections. In addition, a DVD focusing on both female and male objectification might increase men's awareness of this attention-getting strategy in advertising. Future research can address these and other challenges, including the ability to make connections between what participants say about advertising and their ultimate purchase intentions. Asking respondents to comment on sexually-oriented Internet advertising and then asking them to shop online from among brands using sexually-oriented advertising might be an experimental method to test participants' talk against their actions.

In some ways, the treatment/control dichotomy, more familiar to quantitative than to qualitative research, provides advantages and disadvantages, and most disadvantages are related to the large number of responses that need to be coded and considered through an iterative, recursive process. However, retaining responses from the control group that did not see the *Dreamworlds* DVD proved beneficial because the study could include participants who were perhaps unaware of the purpose of the research by the media literacy video.

While it makes sense to find more obvious displays of media literacy among the treatment group, texts from the control group provide important clues for making sense of and reevaluating both sets of complex responses. Using logic plus emotions such as anger and humor—while toggling attention between the intrinsic text and the extrinsic context—participants develop many of their own methods for testing, contesting, and making meaning from these sexually oriented advertisements. When a male participant writes that an advertisement "made me think more about sex than buying blue jeans" [male 64, control], a too-quick evaluation might dismiss this as a sexual thought, rather than a media-literate response. It is certainly both. In fact, this response provides as example of text and context being linked by a participant—one of the goals set by Eagle (2007) in her discussion of pushing media literacy beyond an inoculation approach.

A few female participants expressed sexual pleasure after viewing the advertisements, and these should not be dismissed too quickly as naïve or uneducated reactions. In fact, women may need encouragement to express these sexual thoughts, as well as their doubts about the ways in which advertising portrays women and men. The labels, categories, and contradictions that participant responses provide demonstrate that media literacy may be dressed in both familiar and unfamiliar clothing. While a media literacy DVD may help college students try on standpoints about sexually oriented fashion advertising, they will need time and space—in an open forum free of the protectionist agenda—to create their own indigenous fit inside and outside their mediated world.

REFERENCES

Bauer, Martin W., & George Gaskell (2000). *Qualitative researching with text, image and sound: A practical handbook.* London, England: Sage Publications.

Brucks, Merrie, Gary M. Armstrong, & Marvin E. Goldberg (1988). Children's use of cognitive defenses against television advertising: A cognitive response approach. *Journal of Consumer Research, 14* (March), 471–482.

Burke, Kenneth (1967). Dramatism. In Lee Thayer (Ed.), *Communication: Concepts and perspectives* (pp. 327–360). Washington, DC: Spartan Books.

Eagle, Lynne (2007). Commercial media literacy: What does it do, to whom—and does it matter? *Journal of Advertising, 36*(2), 101–110.

Ferguson, Jill H., Peggy J. Kreshel, & Spencer Tinkham (1990). In the pages of *Ms.*: Sex role portrayals of women in advertising. *Journal of Advertising, 19*(1), 40–51.

Ford, John B., & Michael S. LaTour (1996). Contemporary female perspectives of female role portrayals in advertising. *Journal of Current Issues and Research in Advertising, 16* (Spring), 81–95.

Ford, John B., Michael S. LaTour, & Courtney Middleton (1999). Women's studies and advertising role portrayal sensitivity: How easy is it to raise "feminist consciousness"? *Journal of Current Issues and Research in Advertising, 21* (Fall), 77–87.

Flynn, Elizabeth A., & Patrocinio P. Schweickart (1986). *Gender and reading: Essays on readers, texts, and contexts.* Baltimore, MD: The Johns Hopkins University Press.

Grazer, William F., & Garland Keesling (1995). The effect of print advertising's use of sexual themes on brand recall and purchase intention: A product-specific investigation of male responses. *Journal of Applied Business Research, 11*(3), 47–58.

Harrison, Kristen, & Joanne Cantor (1997). The relationship between media consumption and eating disorders. *Journal of Communication, 47*(1), 40–67.

Irving, Lori M., & Susan R. Berel (2001). Comparison of media-literacy programs to strengthen college women's resistance to media images. *Psychology of Women Quarterly, 25*(2), 103–111.

Kellner, Douglas, & Jeff Share (2005). Toward critical media literacy: Core concepts, debates, organizations, and policy. *Discourse: Studies in the Cultural Politics of Education, 26*(3), 369–386.

Kendrick, Douglas T., Sara E. Gutierres, & L. L. Goldberg (1989). Influence of popular erotica on judgments of strangers and mates. *Journal of Experimental Social Psychology, 25*(2), 159–167.

Lafky, Sue, Margaret Duffy, Mary Steinmaus, & Dan Berkowitz (1996). Looking through gendered lenses: Female stereotyping in advertisements and gender role expectations. *Journalism and Mass Communication Quarterly, 73*(2), 379–388.

Lambiase, Jacqueline, & Tom Reichert (2003). Promises, promises: Exploring erotic rhetoric in sexually oriented advertising. In Linda Scott & Rajeev Batra (Eds.), *Persuasive imagery: A consumer perspective* (pp. 247–266). Mahwah, NJ: Lawrence Erlbaum Associates.

LaTour, Michael S., & Tony L. Henthorne (1994). Ethical judgments of sexual appeals in print advertising. *Journal of Advertising, 23*(3), 81–90.

LaTour, Michael S., & Tony L. Henthorne (2003). Nudity and sexual appeals: Understanding the arousal process and advertising response. In Tom Reichert & Jacqueline Lambiase (Eds.), *Sex in advertising: Perspectives on the erotic appeal* (pp. 107–132). Mahwah, NJ: Lawrence Erlbaum Associates.

Lavine, Howard, Donna Sweeney, & Stephen H. Wagner (1999). Depicting women as sex objects in television advertising: Effects on body dissatisfaction. *Personality and Social Psychology Bulletin, 25* (August), 1049–1058.

Lewis, Justin, & Sut Jhally (1998). The struggle over media literacy. *Journal of Communication, 48*(1), 109–120.

Lundstrom, William, & Donald Sciglimpaglia (1977). Sex role portrayals in advertising. *Journal of Marketing, 41*(3), 72–79.

MacKay, Natalie J., & Katherine Covell (1997). The impact of women in advertisements on attitudes toward women. *Sex Roles, 36* (9/10), 573–583.

McKenzie-Mohr, Doug, & Mark P. Zanna (1990). Treating women as sexual objects: Look to the (gender schematic) male who has viewed pornography. *Personality and Social Psychology Bulletin, 16* (June), 296–308.

McQuarrie, Edward F., & David Glen Mick (2003). The contribution of semiotic and rhetorical perspectives to the explanation of visual persuasion in advertising. In Linda Scott & Rajeev Batra (Eds.), *Persuasive imagery: A consumer perspective* (pp. 191–221). Mahwah, NJ: Lawrence Erlbaum Associates.

Merskin, Deborah (2004). Reviving Lolita? A media literacy examination of sexual portrayals of girls in fashion advertising. *American Behavioral Scientist, 24* (September), 119–129.

Messaris, Paul (1997). *Visual persuasion: The role of images in advertising.* Thousand Oaks, CA: Sage Publishing.

Messaris, Paul (1998). Visual aspects of media literacy. *Journal of Communication, 48*(1), 70–80.

Myers, Philip N., & Frank A. Biocca (1992). The elastic body image: The effect of television advertising and programming on body image distortions in young women. *Journal of Communication, 42* (Summer), 108–133.

Pollay, Richard W. (1986). The distorted mirror: Reflections on the unintended consequences of advertising. *Journal of Marketing, 50* (April), 18–36.

Reichert, Tom, Michael LaTour, Jacqueline Lambiase, & Mark Adkins (2007). A test of media literacy effects and sexual objectification in advertising. *Journal of Current Issues and Research in Advertising, 29*(1), 81–92.

Richins, Marsha L. (1991). Social comparison and the idealized images of advertising. *Journal of Consumer Research, 18* (June), 71–83.

Scott, Linda M. (1994). The bridge from text to mind: Adapting reader-response theory to consumer research. *Journal of Consumer Research, 21* (December), 461–480.

Signorelli, Nancy (1993). Television, the portrayal of women, and children's attitudes. In Gordon L. Berry & Joy K. Asamen (Eds.), *Children and television: Images in a changing sociocultural world* (pp. 229–242). Newbury Park, CA: Sage Publications.

Silverblatt, Art (2004). Media as social institution. *American Behavioral Scientist, 48* (September), 35–41.

Stern, Barbara B. (1990). Literary criticism and the history of marketing thought: A new perspective on "reading" marketing theory. *Journal of the Academy of Marketing Science, 18*(4), 329–336.

Stern, Barbara, Craig J. Thompson, & Eric J. Arnould (1998). Narrative analysis of a marketing relationship: The consumer's perspective. *Psychology & Marketing, 15*(3), 195–215.

Thoman, Elizabeth, & Tessa Jolls (2004). Media literacy—A national priority for a changing world. *American Behavioral Scientist, 48* (September), 18–29.

VanMeenen, Karen (2009). Mind over matter: Modern media literacy. *Afterimage, 37*(2), 2.

Section III

Gender, Culture, and the Market

7

Viewing Gender as a Value-Creative Resource

Gokcen Coskuner-Balli and Burçak Ertimur

INTRODUCTION

Firm–consumer interactions in value creation mark the recent scholarly discussions in marketing, spanning streams of research from consumer culture theory (hereafter, CCT) to service-dominant logic (hereafter, S-D logic) and strategic marketing (Arnould & Thompson, 2005; Prahalad & Ramaswamy, 2004; Vargo & Lusch, 2004). This growing body of work emphasizes the shift away from the traditional formulation of value creation toward one of value cocreation, in which consumers play an active role in creating and determining value, as opposed to passively consuming offerings created and embedded with value solely by firms. Specifically, consumers participate in value creation by deploying their social, cultural, and physical resources and by drawing upon firm-supplied resources (Arnould, 2005; Arnould, Price, & Malshe, 2006).

For example, as consumers engage in consumption practices to attain their life projects, they may draw on firm-supplied resources such as mass-marketed brands and inscribe them with sociocultural meanings, sometimes differing from what marketers may have intended, to cocreate legitimate brands (Kates, 2004). Thus, value is cocreated through firm–consumer resource interaction, integration, and transformation (Vargo & Lusch, 2008). As consumer researchers strive to comprehend the interplay of firm and consumer resources in creating value, and as firms are advised to "co-opt consumer competence" to stay abreast within the competitive marketplace (Prahalad & Ramaswamy, 2004), we investigate how gender works as an operant resource in value cocreation practices.

While consumer researchers have long shown that products and consumption practices are gendered and are suggestive of gender (Fischer & Arnould, 1990; Schroeder & Borgerson, 1998; Thompson, 1996), a systematic analysis of the role of gender in value cocreation is lacking. Gender, along with other cultural resources, is applied in various consumption contexts and determines how consumers utilize marketer-provided resources. For instance, mothers are recruited in the viral marketing campaign for the *Twilight* movie as a result of their feminine capital and deep engagement with the brand (Schau, Muniz, & Arnould, 2009). Male members of the Porsche brand community take on the role of defending the brand's masculine image by engaging in hypermasculine behaviors (Avery, 2008). Looking at value cocreation from the lens of gender generates several important research questions: How does gender work as an operant resource in consumer–marketer collaborations of value cocreation? How do consumers deploy gender in value cocreation practices? How does gender interact with other operant and operand resources in value cocreation?

In this chapter, we draw from CCT and S-D logic research to reexamine value cocreation at the intersection of gender and consumption. We begin with an overview of the value cocreation construct and consumers' operand and operant resources. Next, we discuss how gender can be viewed as an operant resource and introduce the concept of gender capital rooted in Bourdieuan theory. Then we present our conceptual framework illustrating how gender operates as an operant resource in cocreation of value and examine different ways in which consumers perform gender in value cocreation practices. We conclude by summarizing our understanding of consumers' gender capital, deriving implications for marketers' interactions with consumers and positing applications in the areas of meaning creation and management.

BACKGROUND

Value Cocreation

The theoretical and empirical contributions of S-D logic and CCT research provide a basis for understanding the notion of value cocreation.

Essentially, value cocreation includes two nested concepts: coproduction and cocreation (Vargo & Lusch, 2006, 2008). Coproduction refers to "participation in the creation of the core offering itself." For example, consumers may design their own sneakers (e.g., Nike), write code for open-source software (e.g., Linux), and post reviews on products and services (e.g., Amazon). Cocreation of value, on the other hand, represents a higher-order concept and captures the idea that the consumer determines value in the consumption process or through use. Hence, value cocreation may occur with or without coproduction.

Value is cocreated through application and exchange of resources. S-D logic, with its theoretical foundation resting partly on resource advantage theory (Hunt, 2000) and core-competency theory (Prahalad & Hamel, 1990), distinguishes between operand and operant resources. Operand resources are those that are often physical, tangible, and static "on which an operation or act is performed," whereas operant resources are typically intangible, invisible, and dynamic resources that are capable of producing effects (Vargo & Lusch, 2004, p. 2). At the firm level, core competencies such as knowledge and skills are considered operant resources, while tangible resources such as goods and raw materials are categorized as operand resources (Hunt & Madhavaram, 2006).

Marketing traditionally focuses on operand resources (e.g., goods) and considers them as primary units of exchange. Even consumers, who are recognized as providing important inputs into exchange processes, are nevertheless viewed as operand resources to be acted upon (e.g., segmented) in the process of value creation. The shift from value creation to value cocreation, however, implies also a shift in the primacy of resources, with operant resources constituting the primary unit of exchange. Moreover, the S-D logic for marketing views consumers as operant resources and marks the importance of consumers' competencies as they engage to cocreate value. With this guiding framework, our goal is to illustrate how value is cocreated through performance and deployment of gender as an operant resource. However, we must first provide an overview of consumers' operant and operand resources in general and explain how they interact with those of firms in cocreation of value.

Consumers' operand resources consist of culturally constituted economic resources such as income, wealth, material objects, and physical spaces. Their operant resources, on the other hand, can be categorized into three groups: social (e.g., family relationships, brand communities), cultural (e.g., cultural capital, skills), and physical (e.g., emotions, physical endowments; Arnould et al., 2006). In accordance with their life cycle and changing circumstances, consumers manage different roles and pursue a variety of constantly evolving life projects (McCracken, 1987). These life projects and goals are a configuration of operant resources that influence how consumers deploy not only their operand resources, but also those of firms in value creation (Arnould et al., 2006). That is, the firm figures as one of many sources of operant resources upon which customers rely to achieve their life projects and perform their life roles.

For instance, McAlexander, Schouten, and Koenig's (2002) ethnographic research on Jeep "brandfests" shows how marketers, with the use of operand resources such as organizing activities and supplying promotional materials, can create the context in which consumer-to-consumer and consumer–firm interaction occurs and how consumers can build a community around the brand by applying their social resources. Furthermore, Jeep owners deploy their cultural operant resources in Jeep brandfests, expressing their devotion to and knowledge about the brand and cocreating meanings and associations around the brand (e.g., Jeep as a caring institution, Jeep people as family). Consumers act upon firm-produced resources to perform, recover, or even create preferred cultural schemas— some firm initiated, others customer driven. For instance, Muniz and Schau (2007) illustrate how members of the Apple Newton brand community draw on their specialized knowledge and skills to perpetuate, extend, and revitalize the brand by creating ads for it long after Apple discontinued the brand.

Consumers' use of operant resources rooted in their family, class, gender, and other communities to which they belong shapes consumer–firm interactions and, in turn, cocreation of value (Arnould, 2005). Although the value of viewing consumers as operant resources is already recognized, most uses of resource theory do not consider gender as an operant resource in any systematic fashion. For example, in their examination of collective value creation within brand communities, Schau et al. (2009) note certain communities that consist primarily of male or female members; however, they do not elaborate on whether community members distinctively deploy their gender resources and the impact on cocreated value. The motivation underlying this chapter is the idea that gender needs to be taken into account as an operant resource to conceptualize consumers' cocreative competencies fully. Toward this end, we next introduce the concept of gender capital rooted in Bourdieuan theory and discuss how gender can be viewed as an operant resource.

Gender Capital

Bourdieu's (1984) notion of capital, very much like resource theory, draws on the idea of consumers' strategic use of skills and knowledge toward a desired (social) outcome. According to Bourdieu (p. 737), individuals use various resources or capitals (i.e., economic, social, and cultural) "like the aces in a game of cards" to gain advantage in social fields. While he does not explicitly explore the relation between gender and forms of capital, his work paves the way for feminist writers (e.g., Lowell, 2000; McCall, 1992; Skeggs, 1997, 2004) to articulate on gender as a key resource in social relations. These discussions help us analyze the gendered deployment of consumers' operant resources.

In exploring how gender fits into Bourdieu's theory of social distinction, feminist sociologist Leslie McCall (1992) suggests that embodied dispositions—that is, the long-standing dispositions of the mind and body— operate as gendered cultural capital or gender capital. While Bourdieu's treatment of educational, economic, and social capital seems to be gender neutral (only considering gender as a secondary form of social classification that is "hidden" and "unofficial"), McCall points out evidence within Bourdieu's work for how gendered dispositions are utilized to accrue capital. In *Distinction*, for instance, Bourdieu (1984) acknowledges that the petite bourgeoisie women derive occupational and therefore economic profit from their charm(s) and beauty, both of which are increasingly valued in labor markets. He also notes that the type of educational capital gained will be different for boys and girls: "more often literary for girls, more scientific for boys" (p. 105).

The transference of femininity to female students in schools offers only a limited form of capital to girls. Boys, on the other hand, acquire masculine capital in educational institutions, which is then easily transferred to symbolic capital in other fields. In *Masculine Domination*, Bourdieu (2001) discusses that the gendered dispositions of women can be mobilized to mount up economic, cultural, and social capital for their families. The Kabyle women in Algeria, for example, engage in husbanding (cultural housekeeping) by displaying cultural taste and investing in social ties with kin as capital accumulation strategies for their family. While husbanding potentially reduces women to objects of capital, rather than capital-holding subjects in their own rights (Lowell, 2000), this construct nonetheless illustrates how femininity can be an important resource for families.

A number of feminist scholars extend McCall's (1992) view of gender as a form of embodied cultural capital, focusing especially on women and their employment of femininity to gain benefits in their social relations and positions. In her famous study of working-class women in England, Skeggs (1997) explores the adoption of femininity as capital. She argues that working-class women invest in respectability via elaborate reworking of their bodies, clothes, and homes as means to accrue some symbolic value to their devalued and vulnerable class position. She suggests that these women inhabit a contradictory subject position between the dominant notions of bourgeois womanhood (i.e., elegance, refinement, and controlled eroticism) and working-class femininity (i.e., common, vulgar, and sexually promiscuous) and that they take on a particular set of consumption investments to construct a respectable womanhood. Skeggs concludes that

> [Femininity as capital is] the discursive position available through gender relations that women are encouraged to inhabit. Its use will be informed by the network of social positions of class, gender, sexuality, religion, age and race which ensures that it will be taken up by (and resisted) in different ways. (p. 10)

Reay's (2004, p. 61) study on women's involvement with their children's education is an excellent example of how gendered dispositions, especially those related to emotions, vary by class. Exploring the relationship between emotional capital (i.e., "emotionally valued assets and skills, love and affection expenditure of time, attention, care and concern") and educational achievement, she posits that emotional capital is largely utilized by women. The role of motherhood involves the constant emotional labor of managing the children's education as well as the husband's needs. Working-class women, however, experience greater difficulty than middle-class women in transferring their emotional capital to educational achievement for their children. This is mostly because working-class women are "hampered by poverty, negative personal experiences of schooling, insufficient educational knowledge and lack of confidence" (p. 65). Middle-class women, on the other hand, are more accepting of their children's emotional suffering for their educational pursuit in the sense that they tend to push their children more to study, prepare for exams, and so on. Hence, emotional capital is both gendered and classed and is key to understand how contemporary educational markets work.

More recent work explores how women might use gender as a resource in the labor market. In her analysis of women's experiences within the field of paid caring work, Huppatz (2009, p. 50) distinguishes between female and feminine capital. She suggests:

> Female capital is the gender advantage that is derived from being perceived to have a female body; whereas feminine capital is the gender advantage that is derived from a disposition or skill set learned via socialization, or from simply being hailed as feminine. (p. 50)

Huppatz (2009) demonstrates that female capital indeed can help women gain employment in care work and develop a sense of sisterhood with female patients and management. The women in the study also use feminine skills and dispositions as a form of cultural capital. In a related study, Ross-Smith and Huppatz (2008) explore the role of femaleness and femininity as a form of embodied cultural capital in managerial careers. As is true in the domain of paid-care work, women in managerial positions use female capital to gain entry to the workforce, taking advantage of the equal opportunity discourse. The women's feminine experiences, such as being a mother, and their feminine dispositions (e.g., being better communicators and being detail oriented) as well as their feminine appearance and sexuality are used to gain tactical advantages in the field of management. However, both in the paid-care work and the managerial field, men enjoy advantages over women in being promoted to senior-level management positions, indicating the greater currency of masculine gender capital over feminine forms of capital. Hence, these findings indicate that femininity can only be used as a cultural resource in "tactical rather than strategical ways" (Skeggs, 1997, pp. 8–10).

While feminine forms of capital have gained more attention in feminist work, research also explores how men use masculine capital to attain economic and/or social advantage. Connell (1995) suggests that at any given time, one form of masculinity will dominate others, implying the increased currency of this form of masculinity in social fields. Indeed, her famous notion of hegemonic masculinity is "a question of how particular groups of men inhabit positions of power and wealth, and how they legitimate and reproduce the social relationships that generate their dominance" (Carrigan, Connell, & Lee, 1987, p. 92).

Referring to the notion of physical capital, Coles (2009) emphasizes the importance of the male body as a power-generating capital. He posits that men's bodies are resources, not only in their size and shape, but also in how they are used (e.g., posture, gait, gestures, speech, and so on). Hegemonic notions of masculinity epitomize bodies that are muscular, lean, and young because such bodies are associated with strength, power, discipline, health, and virility. However, the market value of different types of masculine capital is bounded by class positions and subfields. For example, the muscular, fit, and young businessman who is well dressed and groomed may represent culturally hegemonic masculinity, but it is not necessarily the dominant masculinity across all social classes, age groups, and/or ethnicities (Connell & Messerschmidt, 2005).

In summary, Bourdieuan theory and its extensions posit gender as a type of cultural capital/resource that is strategically drawn upon in maintenance and attainment of social class positions. Our review of feminists' and other social theorists' examination of contemporary gender practices provides extensive evidence for the employment of gendered dispositions to accumulate economic, social, and cultural capital. Next, we place these conceptualizations into the context of value cocreation, discussing gender as a critical dimension of consumers' operant resources and demonstrating how consumers produce and perform gender in value cocreation practices.

EMPLOYING GENDER CAPITAL IN VALUE COCREATION PRACTICES

As with Bourdieu's notion of capital and its extensions, we view gender as a form of embodied cultural capital that may be utilized as an asset in different markets (e.g., the labor market, the marriage market, the educational market). In developing our conceptual framework of the role of gender in value cocreation practices, we also make a distinction between the ways in which consumers employ gender to construct traditional versus alternative masculinities/femininities. Traditional gender performances refer to the employment of market resources to enact and furthermore reinstate dominant cultural models of masculinity and femininity. Consumers may defend the hegemonic gender meanings of brands when the opposite sex attempts to co-opt the service to support new gender ideologies (e.g., Porsche brand community members; Avery, 2008).

Alternative gender performances, on the other hand, challenge the dominant cultural models via mobilizing market resources in consumers' identity projects. For example, consumers may adopt the hypermasculine meanings around brands to create alternative femininities (e.g., female riders of Harley Davidson bikes; Martin, Schouten, & McAlexander, 2006). From the consumer's perspective, the firm is the provider of the operant and operand resources that enable both traditional and alternative performances. From the firm's perspective, the consumer is a cocreator of its services who can give his or her own meanings to firm-provided resources. In what follows, we review the extant literature to propose insights as to how gender capital produces traditional and alternative performances in four domains of value cocreation: core offerings, consumer–marketer communications, retail and "servicescapes," and economic propositions. We then discuss strategic implications of gendered capital for value cocreation, and note areas of future research. Figure 7.1 provides examples illustrative of consumers' traditional and alternative gender performances in these different domains of value cocreation.

Core Offerings

Viewing brands as socially constructed entities, many researchers demonstrate the ways in which consumers activate product and brand meanings, as well as alter or create their own meanings through consumption practices (e.g., Brown, Kozinets, & Sherry, 2003; Fournier, 1998; Holt, 1995; McCracken, 1986; Muniz & O'Guinn, 2001; Muniz & Schau, 2005). Several studies also explicitly focus on the role gender plays in brand value creation processes. We examine this stream of research, discussing how consumers perform with their gender upon brands in cocreating brand essence, personality, and meanings, and how these gender performances can be viewed as supporting, strengthening, and perpetuating the dominant gender ideology or as creating new (or distorting traditional) gender ideologies.

Deployment of Gender Capital	Domains of Value Cocreation				
		Core Offerings	Retail and Servicescapes	Consumer-Marketer Communications	Economic Propositions
Traditional		Gender stereotyping as a means to strengthen gender-appropriate meanings of offerings (Avery 2008)	Navigating and utilizing servicescapes in ways that are consistent with gender norms (Kozinets et al. 2004)	Female consumers' engagement in word-of-mouth communications (Berner 2006; Schau and Thompson 2010)	Female consumers' thrift shopping (Bardhi and Arnould 2005; Miller 1998) and male consumers' bargaining strategies (Herrman 2004)
Alternative		Employing offerings in gender-bending performances (Martin, Schouten, and McAlexander 2006)	Gender orientation/ socialization/ resistance in liminal market spaces (Kates and Belk 2001)	Participating in consumer-generated ad campaigns featuring products associated with different gender identities (Duffy 2010)	Male consumers' care-oriented thrift behavior (Coskuner-Balli and Thompson 2009)

FIGURE 7.1

Illustrated examples of consumers' traditional and alternative gender performances in value cocreation.

We know from past research that products and brands are "perceived as gendered and expressive of gender," and that such gendered meanings are socially shared and acknowledged (Martin et al., 2006, p. 173). Marketers support consumers' identity projects by creating gendered product images and brand personalities. However, consumers also perform their gender onto brands, cocreating a multitude of gendered meanings. For instance, when the car manufacturer Subaru's market research revealed a large lesbian following, the company began to tailor its advertising to appeal to the lesbian community and, in turn, cocreated a gay brand personality (Palmer, 2000). Traditional gender performances occur when consumers draw on gender-appropriate product images and brand personalities to enhance their masculinity or femininity and, in turn, reinforce the prevailing gender ideology.

Avery (2008), for example, examines consumer reactions toward the androgenization of the Porsche brand with the introduction of the Porsche Cayenne SUV. The Porsche brand has traditionally been an exclusive marker of hegemonic masculinity, supporting consumers' identities in line with the "breadwinner" and the "rebel" masculinity myths (Holt & Thompson, 2004). The launch of the Porsche Cayenne SUV, which was intentionally targeted toward women by the marketer, brought feminine identity meanings to the brand, stigmatizing existing Porsche owners. In response to this gender contamination of the brand, existing owners turned to stereotyping, attaching derogatory feminine meanings to the SUV while creating a boundary to protect the dilution of the masculine identity meanings associated with Porsche. In doing so, Porsche owners engaged in traditional gender performances whereby they limited the attractiveness of the brand for gender experimentation and supplanted as well as strengthened the brand's already existing hegemonic masculine meanings.

While consumers perform with products in ways that reflect their tacit acceptance of conventional gender identities and contribute to the reproduction of traditional gender identities, they also engage in alternative gender performances that challenge and/or differentially articulate dominant gender ideologies. For example, in their study on consumer acculturation, Üstüner and Holt (2007) examine the identity projects that poor Turkish women pursue after migrating from a rural village into a large modern city. Their findings reveal interesting differences on the gendering between first- and second-generation women's (i.e., mothers and daughters) identity projects. For instance, the mothers adopt modern technological products in ways that strip them from their normative uses and carefully select few city commodities to enter into their lives. In doing so, they improve upon the comfort of their ancestral village while maintaining the ideals of village women and cocreate a counterhegemonic gender ideology that the authors refer to as "the modern village woman." The daughters, in contrast, perform with brands associated with the Western lifestyle of successful and fashionable upper middle-class Turkish women in an attempt to align themselves with the dominant gender ideology.

Similarly, Sandikci and Ger's (2010) study on Islamic veiling in Turkey illustrates how gender interacts with other forms of cultural capital, such as occupation and education, in transforming a stigmatized practice into a fashionable one for many women. In the past two decades, forms of veiling have changed from a small scarf that women traditionally used to cover their heads in a casual manner (i.e., *basortusu*) to a more vigilant covering with a large scarf that covers the head as well as the neck and shoulders and is worn with a long and loose overcoat (i.e., *tesettur*). Examining how the meanings of veiling change as forms change, the study depicts the construction of different styles of femininity. In particular, through coproducing (i.e., crafting, personalizing, and aestheticizing), the head scarf and veiling, women seek an asexual femininity in contrast to the modern, oversexualized style of femininity and thus create a modern yet religious, feminine yet wholesome consumer identity.

While marketers often target masculine products to appeal to males and feminine products to appeal to females, gendered products can be embraced by either sex. Alternative gender performances also occur in contexts of gender-bending consumption, where consumers co-opt "consumption practices, products, and brands of the opposite gender to support new gender ideologies" (Avery, 2008, p. 2). For example, in their discussion of American masculine ideologies, Holt and Thompson (2004) divert attention to how male consumers selectively embrace goods and activities associated with feminine domains (e.g., sewing, relationship-oriented "chick" flicks)—not to construct themselves as feminine, but rather to rebel against prominent masculinities and to create alternative masculinities.

Similarly, Martin et al. (2006) examine factors that drive women to participate in the male-dominated subculture of Harley Davidson owners. There is no question that gender and specifically hypermasculine values mark subcultural capital (i.e., power) in the Harley Davidson community. The idea that women can be competent bike riders and can even assume leadership positions in the bike subculture creates a gender paradox and clashes with the traditional association between men and riding. Given the gendered nature of the biker subculture, one may expect women riders to be highly masculine.

On the contrary, the findings reveal that women riders co-opt only certain hypermasculine aspects of motorcycling while maintaining their femininity. They are attracted to this subculture because it empowers them and allows them to broaden and often break with their traditional feminine roles (e.g., being a mother). Their riding values and styles, however, are different from those of men. While they resist certain hypermasculine aspects of motorcycling such as disobeying traffic rules, they redefine other aspects, such as customizing their helmets with stickers that emphasize gender equality. Hence, these women riders engage in alternative performances, transgressing gender stereotypes and adding a multitude of meanings to this originally hypermasculine subculture.

Another prominent example of the use of gender as an operant resource in the form of alternative performances is demonstrated in Kates's (2002, 2004) work focusing on the gay men's community. In his examination of this subculture, Kates (2002) tells how consumer goods help gay men navigate the tensions between appearing gay enough while avoiding a stigmatized heterosexual stereotype. In line with the oppositional character of subcultures, gay men are often comfortable with using stereotypically feminine products, liberating them from traditional gender conventions. As they construct playful gender identities via such practices, they also redefine symbolic gendered meanings of products.

More specific to cocreation of brands, Kates (2004) explores the processes through which brands develop legitimate social fit with the gay community's shared norms. His findings reveal that gay men confer legitimacy on brands by evaluating the socially approved deeds that brands accomplish for the gay community and hold brands accountable for actions that affect their community. Overall, the study depicts how consumers, although constrained by institutionalized meaning to some extent, can exercise some control over brands by continuously negotiating gender-related meanings such as homophobia and gay friendliness. In another words, gay men's deployment of their gender influences how they use brands and firms' other operand resources in creating preferred cultural schemas.

Prior literature pays less attention to the gendered nature of coproduction than that of cocreation. An exception is Gelber (2000), who examines domestic masculinity (i.e., taking over jobs previously done by professionals) in the realm of do-it-yourself (DIY) activities. Adopting a historical perspective, he traces the emergence of DIY practices and how they came to be dominated by men. He argues that, for men, "the use of traditional male skills contributes to a sense of domestic masculinity" (p. 77) and that these coproductive activities enable them to partake in family activities while maintaining and enhancing their masculinity.

Interestingly, while DIY continues to be a legitimate arena for men to engage in traditional gender performances and in turn sustain prevailing gender roles, marketers today are increasingly targeting females due to their progressively broader involvement in DIY practices (Watson & Shove, 2009). Such focus on females is supported by evidence suggesting that women are expressing an increasing interest in coproduction (e.g., through customizing clothing; Campbell, 2005). As consumer–firm collaborations in coproduction of offerings emerge as alternatives to firm-based production (O'Hern & Rindfleish, 2010), how consumers deploy their gender capital in new product development becomes a fruitful area of future research with implications for innovation processes.

Retail and Servicescapes

While retail settings are central in scholarly discussions in marketing, studies are traditionally interested in the efficiency of product placement and distribution decisions such as differences between brick-and-mortar stores and online retailing, whether to engage in direct sales, or the effects of store atmospherics on consumer decision making. A recent culturally-oriented body of research explores consumers' experiences and identity performances in retail settings (Arnould, 2005; Borghini et al., 2009; Haytko & Baker, 2004; Kozinets et al., 2004; Tuncay & Otnes, 2008). In this body of work, retailers are conceptualized as institutions that offer desirable resources for consumers' identity projects (Arnould, 2005). Accordingly, firms bundle a series of value propositions through the retail space that are then selectively integrated to consumers' lives through their patronage in these settings. These firm-proposed cultural resources are oftentimes employed in enactments of gender performances.

CCT work that explores gender performances in retail spaces mostly documents how firm resources are used to reproduce traditional gender roles, norms, and expectations. From this theoretical point of view, consumption practices and performances in various retail settings tend to perpetuate prevailing gender norms (Borghini et al., 2009; Haytko & Baker, 2004). For example, Kozinets et al. (2004) conclude that the themed retailer ESPN Zone is a masculine play space that "reproduces particular gender roles and relations, providing multiple cues for appropriate gendered behavior" (p. 157). In a similar theoretical spirit, American Girl Place hosts a gamut of interactions between three generations of women that creates emotional and historical ties for all female generations in a family (i.e., grandmother, mother, and daughter). For mothers, the dolls are symbols of shields protecting their daughters from the current culture that involves less traditional practices. In addition, the store atmosphere and brand experience provide added value, contributing to the bonding and bridging of family ties.

Regarding masculine identities, studies describe gender role transcendence, with men increasingly shopping for fashion and grooming products as well as frequenting feminine and domestic retail settings, while also underlining the dominance of hegemonic cultural discourses in male shopping behavior. In their study, Otnes and McGrath (2001) refute three stereotypes regarding male shopping behavior. In contrast to the commonly held assumptions about how and why men shop, their study documents that men rarely engage in "grab and go" strategies, do not necessarily whine and complain about shopping or wait passively, and frequent "feminine" venues and develop expertise in feminine product categories or domestic arenas. However, the authors link male consumers' shopping to a traditional identity value of achievement: While men engage in feminine activities, their shopping in these settings is motivated by their desire to achieve professional, financial, and sexual success in their lives. Because men's retail experiences are oriented by demonstrating expertise and control, they suggest that retailers should offer resources that enhance men's self-esteem and sense of power.

Similarly, Tuncay and Otnes's (2008) study on urban male consumers finds that while these consumers express a desire to shop for grooming and fashion products, their servicescape experiences are characterized by their fear of being labeled as homosexual and/or feminine. The authors posit that the hegemonic notions of masculinity such as avoiding being perceived as gay and shopping for achievement color the experiences and motivations of male shoppers. Based on these studies, "retailscapes" can be seen as resources to be integrated into traditional performances of masculinity.

There is limited work documenting consumers' gender-bending practices in the servicescapes. Kates and Belk's (2001) work on gay parades notes the importance of liminal market spaces for more alternative identity performances. They suggest that consumers use Lesbian and Gay Pride Day (LGPD) to carve out an alternative cultural space for their sexual identity. LGPD challenges the mainstream notions of sexuality and family. The authors suggest that "LGPD may be interpreted as a collective form of consumer resistances: a manner of constructing alternative meanings and social worlds alongside those of the dominant heterosexual mainstream through the use of products" (p. 403). The festive and liminal space of the festival provides resources to resist mainstream gender norms.

On a similar note, Coskuner-Balli and Thompson (2009) discuss the yearly stay-at-home dad (SAHD) convention as a liminal space where fathers become oriented to alternative forms of masculinity. At this convention, men share advice and information regarding household products and other forms of domestic knowledge—such as how to style their daughters' hair—that have been culturally coded as feminine knowledge and are largely foreign to their own gender socialization. From this standpoint, the convention functions as a kind of remedial servicescape, where men can acquire new forms of gendered cultural capital, and stands in contrast to commercial servicescapes that cater more commonly to men. While the latter reinforce traditional gender roles and men's identity association with nondomesticated spheres of interests, such as in the case of ESPN Zone (Kozinets et al., 2004), remedial servicescapes facilitate alternative gender performances, as in the case of the SAHD convention.

Kozinets's (2002) work on the Burning Man festival also highlights the role of physical space in alternative performances. This hypercommunity is able to create strong, caring, sharing, social ties and positions itself at a distance from the marketplace. Through its temporariness and dynamism, the community maintains its authenticity and evades co-opting the alternative meaning system. Future research is needed to explore gender-bending performances in retail settings and to theorize consumers' development of alternative gender capital through their interactions with service settings. For example, as male consumers are increasingly involved in body grooming and fashion practices, household activities, and daddy boot camps, their experiences in female-oriented servicescapes such as manicure/pedicure spas, parenting classes, grocery stores, and children's gyms could offer insights as to how men employ these service settings in their identity projects.

Consumer–Marketer Communications

Advertising and word-of-mouth marketing (WOMM) constitute the major communication tools that firms use to position their offerings in the marketplace and to inform, persuade, and remind consumers. In this section, we discuss the recent developments in advertising and WOMM theory and practice, which suggest that both communications tools increasingly involve dialogue and interaction between consumers and marketers. We also examine the role that gender capital plays in this cocreative communication world.

Advertisements are complex, culturally constituted artifacts that convey cultural values and meanings (McCracken, 1987). Researchers draw attention to the social character of advertising, examining the portrayal of gender identities and roles in ads and revealing the part that advertising plays in constructing, maintaining, and representing gender (Schroeder & Borgerson, 1998). In invoking gender identity, advertisements often rely on stereotyped images of masculinity and femininity. Such representations convey, form, and perpetuate conceptions of gender norms in society that in turn guide social behavior. They also produce market segments such as the "new man" and the "homemaker" (Gentry & Harrison, 2010). While advertising content has traditionally been under the control of marketers, a novel form of cocreative practice—namely, consumer-generated advertising (CGA)—is revolutionizing the advertising landscape by eroding the separation between ad producers and consumers and allowing consumers to shape representations in advertising (Berthon, Pitt, & Campbell, 2008; Muniz & Schau, 2007).

CGA involves ordinary consumers creating ads for various market offerings. In the past few years, companies such as General Motors, PepsiCo-Doritos, Heinz, and Unilever have invited consumers to create ads for their products and aired the winning ads during events such as the Super Bowl and the Oscars (Petrecca, 2007). While such initiatives are representative of "crowdsourcing" (Howe, 2006), consumers also use their own resources to create ads without any support from companies and post them on video-sharing sites such as YouTube. Regardless of whether CGA is solicited or unsolicited by companies, it represents a role reversal, with consumers rather than advertisers creating ads for products. In conjunction with participating in the generation of the ad (i.e., coproduction), consumers also create their own meanings (i.e., cocreation of value).

So, how does gender capital play a role in this new world of advertising where consumers create and broadcast ads? To address this question, we draw on the potential of CGA to shape advertising representations of masculinity and femininity and explore how gender capital may influence the types of CGAs that are created and, in turn, the meanings other consumers may derive from these ads.

Prior research reveals gender differences in consumer responses to advertising that pertain but are not limited to ad appeals, ad cues, and role portrayal (Wolin, 2003). Such studies provide justification for the rationale behind segmentation and targeting as the building blocks of advertising strategy: Targeted ads are presumably more effective because, by definition, they have been tailored to fit the preferences of particular consumer segments. For example, by drawing on knowledge about gay consumers, companies such as IKEA and AT&T are able to tailor their promotion efforts to these groups of individuals and are in turn deemed to be very successful (C. Miller, 1994). Thus, the implication for marketers is that they should design ads differently based on the gender makeup of the targeted consumer groups.

The case of CGA, however, directs marketers' attention to *consumers as designers* of ads. An example is Unilever's Dove Supreme Cream Oil Body Wash Ad Contest in 2007, which invited "real women" to create ads for Dove's line of body cleansers. This CGA campaign was part of a larger feminist agenda of Dove (i.e., Dove Campaign for Real Beauty) that encouraged featuring real women instead of models in ads in light of its mission "to make women feel more beautiful every day by challenging today's stereotypical view of beauty and inspiring women to take great care of themselves" (*PR Newswires*, 2007).

At the outset, this campaign represents a shift away from women as consumers to women as producers. Via this coproductive effort, women are expected to perform alternative gender performances that challenge the traditional discourses of beauty associated with hegemonic feminine norms. It is not clear, however, how many ads were actually created by women, even though the contest called for "real women" to participate with Dove executives, emphasizing that the ads were to be created and chosen by real women. In truth, both women and men voted and commented on the contest entries, and these inputs were used by Dove to narrow the ads down to five finalists (Duffy, 2010). Therefore, it is also not transparent who was making the role-portrayal decisions in this particular campaign.

This example raises three main issues worthy of further exploration regarding the role that gender capital plays in the cocreative practice of CGA. The first issue is how consumers' involvement in ad creation can affect gender portrayals in advertising. Gendered communications are often criticized for creating gender bias. In their critique of advertising's role in supporting and perpetuating traditional gender norms, Gentry and Harrison (2010), for instance, show how masculine role representations in advertising are out of touch with reality. Consumers are moving targets (e.g., homemakers become career woman) and, as gender roles change, marketers are advised to alter their advertising accordingly (Barry, Gilly, & Doran, 1985). Viewed in this light, CGA is a promising cocreative practice that, by allowing consumers to decide on the content of ads, can address these critiques of advertising regarding stereotyped and status quo gender role portrayals. Toward this end, research is needed to examine similarities and differences among ads created by males versus those created by females, with particular attention to how consumers deploy their gender capital in creating ads for traditionally gendered products.

The second issue pertains to the gender capital of consumers who may participate in CGA campaigns. Instead of engaging in research to determine guidelines as to how to design ads tailored for each gender, CGA implies that companies have to attract consumers with varying amounts and kinds of gender capital to create ads for their products (i.e., co-opting gender capital). Research shows that cocreators who participate in CGA campaigns are motivated by the possibility of career enhancement (Berthon et al., 2008). These cocreators may not be in the target market for the featured product or be experts in that product category. Instead, they may possess creative personalities and may rely on their general knowledge in producing ads.

These possibilities imply that male (female) consumers may create ads for feminine (masculine) products and therefore indicate a greater potential for cocreators to perform their gender capital in alternative ways in creating ads. Coupled with this issue of whether CGA participants possess the gender capital necessary for successful creation of ads, whether ordinary consumers would have the knowledge and expertise in creating ads reflective of gender differences also deserves examination. For example, in Dove's CGA campaign, although the contest rules prevented professional filmmakers from participating, half of the contestants reported having degrees or experiences in film or web design. In fact, Dove's criteria for judging the ads were based on originality, creativity, and adherence to the creative assignment and excluded any criteria related to gender (Duffy, 2010).

The third issue pertains to other consumers' responses to CGA, as the relationship between the content of ads and consumers' reactions is not static and easily predictable. Consumers actively construct as well as distort meanings; they are "the final arbitrators of advertising meanings" (Mick & Buhl, 1992, p. 318). Marketers hope that their intended meanings in fact match consumers' actualized meanings. Grier and Brumbaugh (1999), for example, study the differences in the ways in which target and nontarget consumers derive meanings from ads. Their findings indicate that consumers' interpretations of ads not only depend on their individual experiences, but are also influenced by shared cultural and subcultural perceptions. Future research should focus on how gender capital may influence the meanings consumers derive from ads.

As with the changing landscape of advertising, WOMM—that is, "the intentional influencing of consumer-to-consumer communications by marketing professionals"—has recently been transformed, largely due to the development of and capabilities offered by the Internet (Kozinets, de Valck, Wojnicki, & Wilner, 2010, p. 71). While extant research examines how marketers employ social media to engineer WOMM and how cultural and communal interests and norms shape coproduction of marketing messages and meanings, a gender-based analysis of these communications has not been systematically performed (for an exception, see Schau & Thompson, 2010).

Evidence from the marketplace, however, suggests that companies' efforts to engage consumers by seeding them with new, gendered offerings to generate WOMM involves careful co-opting of consumers' gender capital. Procter and Gamble (P&G) is a great example of a company that aggressively embraces WOMM. Its Tremor Program, which recruits women to test and share their experiences of a variety of products, is founded on the premise that women are more likely to engage in WOM due to their gender roles (Berner, 2006; Feick & Price, 1987). By co-opting their gender capital in traditional ways, P&G encourages women to talk about feminine products, reach out to their social networks, and provide feedback to the company. Future research that examines the interaction between consumers' communication strategies and their gender capital will be valuable for marketers as they leverage consumers' resources in WOMM campaigns.

Economic Propositions

Price has mostly been conceptualized and studied from an economic point of view in marketing and consumer behavior studies. Economic resources, however, can be tightly related to "identity projects that are organized around long-standing cultural schemas associated with frugality, thriftiness, value for money, or perhaps even perceived thinking costs" (Arnould, 2005, p. 91). While some research exists on frugality, frugal lifestyles (Lastovicka, Bettencourt, Shaw-Hughner, & Kuntze, 1999), deal proneness (Lichtenstein, Netemeyer, & Burton 1995), and coupon proneness (Bagozzi, Baumgartner, & Yi, 1992), there is very little work on how gender, economic resources (thrift, frugality) and identity projects interact.

While thrift behavior is oftentimes practiced in retail settings, employment of thrift in gender performances calls for a separate discussion. We are interested in articulating how economic propositions are employed in consumers' identity projects rather than the physical and social interactions in a retail setting. Furthermore, some thrift-oriented behaviors and practices, such as searching for coupons, sharing them with others, and doing repair work at home, often take place outside retail and servicescapes.

So far, research that explores the relation between economic resources and gender documents the enactment of traditional gender roles. In *A Theory of Shopping,* D. Miller (1998) suggests an interesting link between gender and thrift. Focusing on female homemakers' provisional shopping at London supermarkets, he proposes that for these women, thrift is a moral act through which they can demonstrate their love to their family. Using the metaphor of sacrifice, he argues that women devote their time and labor for their family and that thrift acts as a sacrificial rite. Bardhi and Arnould (2005, p. 6) observe similar findings within the context of thrift-store shopping in the United States. Their informants, who are primarily female homemakers, engage in thrift shopping for themselves as well as for their loved ones. In their shopping trips, female thrift-store shoppers screen and search for items that their family and friends might need. The authors report that the shoppers rely on a "mental calendar of household celebrations and events and the different consumption needs that arise as a consequence" and they shop year round for the people in their social network.

In related research, Price, Feick, and Guskey-Federouch (1988) explore female consumers' couponing behaviors, reporting that the most identifiable demographic characteristic of this segment of consumers—the market mavens—is their gender. Their findings suggest that besides getting a thrill from getting good deals, an integral part of the market maven identity involves enhancing social relationships in one's network. The market mavens are not just knowledgeable about markets, but are involved in telling others about products, places to shop, sales, and so on—an insight used by marketers such as P&G. For female market mavens, grocery shopping and coupon clipping are social events in which they participate with their friends and family. Furthermore, market mavens give coupons to those in their immediate networks and even feel it is somehow their duty to provide coupons to others. While the couponing behaviors of male consumers remain an area rich for exploration, research on male consumer shopping underlines hypermasculine motives behind men's search for deals in the marketplace (Otnes & McGrath, 2001). In their ethnographic study of male consumers' shopping behaviors, the authors conclude that men shop to win and that they hunt for bargains as a way of beating the market.

Work on bargaining in garage sales also supports this finding. Herrmann (2004) suggests that men bargain more than women at garage sales and links this finding to the cultural norms related to masculinity and femininity. Whereas it is expected for men to be aggressive in negotiation, women are often embarrassed or shy in such contexts. Accordingly, Otnes and McGrath (2001) suggest that retailers should take the motives of winning and being in control into consideration when devising couponing strategies. They argue:

> Because men tend to enjoy bargaining, it seems advisable that retailers allow their male customers to emerge from any negotiations feeling like winners. Salespeople could be trained to help male customers feel they have "struck a hard bargain" or they are forces to be reckoned with in the marketplace. (p. 133)

We do not doubt that such strategies can strike a chord with male audiences who enact traditional gender roles. However, we think that female consumers' couponing behavior can be as much driven by beating market motivations as men's and that men's couponing and/or thrift behavior can be oriented by care (see also Coskuner-Balli & Thompson, 2009). Much more research needs to be conducted on linkages between gender and couponing practices across product categories. Furthermore, how men and women develop skills as well as cultural resources for thrift shopping and couponing and use thrift to create and perform alternative gender identities deserves further study. As firms increasingly engage consumers in pricing decisions, how gender operates on price and value perceptions in auctions, secondary markets (e.g., craigslist), and other consumption settings where consumers create their own prices (e.g., digital album sales) is an area ripe for unpacking.

DISCUSSION

In line with the recent call for research on the connections among the set of roles consumers enact in their everyday lives, their deployment of operant resources, and traditional marketing variables (Arnould, 2007), we focus on the mobilization of consumers' gendered resources in four primary venues of consumer–firm interaction: core offerings, retail and servicescapes, consumer–marketer communications, and economic propositions. Our discussion identifies gender as an embodied cultural–capital resource that is central to understanding consumers' motivations for and competencies in value cocreation. Several important theoretical and empirical implications emerge from our examination of how gender operates in value cocreative practices.

Interaction of Gender Capital and Operant/Operand Resources

One key implication of integrating gender in the analysis of value cocreation practices is that it reveals how consumers' gender capital interacts with their operant as well as operand resources. While the feminist literature has recently started to explore the interactions between gender and other forms of capital (educational, social, and economic), consumer research that examines these relationships is scarce. Arnould and colleagues' (2006, p. 91) categorization of consumers' resources into social (e.g., family relationships, brand communities), cultural (e.g., cultural capital, skills), and physical (e.g., emotions, physical endowments) resources parallel the forms of capital identified by Bourdieu. They posit that these resources are integrated to "cocreate value through patterns of experiences and meaning embedded in the cultural life-worlds of consumers." Our framework brings to light gender as a key component of consumers' cultural life-worlds and hence the processes of value cocreation that have remained largely hidden until now.

Gender is important not only as a cultural resource in and of itself, but also as an operant resource that interacts with consumers' other operant and operand resources. For example, gender is closely linked to consumers' social resources. Prior research suggests that women are more relation oriented than men and undertake the majority of the husbanding and emotional work (Bourdieu, 2001; Reay, 2004), which correspondingly informs their consumption practices such as gift shopping (Fischer & Arnould, 1990), brand relationships (Fournier, 1998), and care-oriented shopping (Thompson, 1996). Future research should explore how men's gender capital is transferred to social resources for their families and how women's gender capital is mobilized as a social resource outside the domestic sphere of their homes, such as in their brand communities.

Consumers' physical resources (physical endowments and emotions) are also gendered. Female and male bodies are often constructed around hegemonic cultural ideals (Connell, 1995). Consumers, however, can also challenge the dominant norms of femininity and masculinity through adopting alternative fashion and grooming practices (Kates, 2002; Sandikci & Ger, 2010). Marketers need to be aware of these consumer actions and tendencies as their offerings engage consumers' physical resources. While consumers' physical endowments receive more attention from consumer researchers, consumer emotions as operant resources are almost completely neglected. As the importance of emotions in new service economies is increasingly noted (Illouz, 1997), we believe that the notion of emotional capital has the potential to open new doors in research on value cocreation.

Moreover, gender capital also interacts with consumers' operand resources. Commuri and Gentry's (2005) study of women as chief wage earners demonstrates this case in point, as they find the distribution of household resources closely linked to alleviating the threat to the bread-winner role of husbands. In most families where women earn more than their husbands, couples pool their resources together to blur income differences. The authors note that "the wife sacrifices any recognition that she is the principal economic actor in the household, and the husband is willing to retain that distinction" (p. 192) and suggest future research to explore the role of gender orientations in pooling of economic resources.

Other scholars document the gendered nature of consumer poverty that is more commonly experienced by female consumers than by males (Caterall & Maclaran, 2002). Indeed, women's increasing involvement in sales of cosmetics and cleaning products in developing countries showcases an interesting collaboration between poor women and multinational corporations operating in these countries. In their study of Avon's recruitment of women in South Africa, for instance, Dolan and Scott (2009) view these partnerships as a win–win situation. Avon capitalizes on women's gender capital and social networks to distribute its cosmetics and women, in turn, are able to transfer their gender capital to the financial well-being and empowerment of their communities.

Social and Managerial Implications of Gender Performances in Value Cocreation

In addition to revealing how gender interacts with consumers' other operant and operand resources, our framework also outlines the deployment of gender in traditional and alternative performances in various value cocreative practices. While we identify the implications of consumers' differential performance of gender for meaning generation and point out future research directions throughout our discussion, managerial and social policy implications of how gender capital produces traditional and alternative performances in the various domains of value cocreation also deserve attention.

In the S-D logic and CCT literature, consumers are conceptualized as active agents who are energetically involved in value-creation processes rather than just paying for their tickets and silently watching the show. S-D logic further emphasizes the joint application of operant resources among firms and consumers to create value for the customer (Vargo & Lusch, 2006). While these discussions acknowledge consumer agency and firms' roles as offering solutions to consumers, they mainly focus on the managerial implications of value cocreation partnerships. Consumers are viewed as operant resources that, if categorized and segmented correctly, can be co-opted successfully into firms' operations (Prahalad & Ramaswamy, 2004). There is no doubt that understanding consumers' traditional competencies and co-opting them accordingly will benefit companies. Already, emerging market practices showcase how firms are engaging consumers' gender capital (e.g., P&G using housewives to generate WOMM or Dove recruiting women to create CGA).

However, we suggest that marketers also need to think more about social implications of segmenting consumers on the basis of their traditional gender capital. For example, while women's use of feminine capital in value cocreation practices tends to reproduce traditional gender roles, it seems that it can also generate tactical advantages for them as they transfer their feminine capital into economic and social capitals (e.g., female Avon representatives). Furthermore, our framework points out that consumer–marketer relationships are not limited to the deployment of gender capital in traditional performances and that consumers and marketers can collaborate to cocreate alternative gender roles and meanings. In this latter type of collaboration, consumer resources are not allocated prior to firm–consumer interaction, but rather are emergent through their interaction with firm-provided resources.

This insight suggests that consumers can also discover their gender dispositions and skills through experimentation, as they perform their gender in the marketplace. Rather than just co-opting consumers' traditional competencies, firms can help consumers with gender-bending consumption, legitimization of new gender roles, and with acquiring new resources, skills, and capital for their new gender roles.

The marketing activities of firms have been criticized, probably rightfully so at times, for reinstating traditional gender roles. Historical analyses of advertising repeatedly suggest that men and women are portrayed in stereotypical ways (Gentry & Harrison, 2010). In *Never Done,* Strasser (1982) highlights the role of advertisers and home economists in the process of creating women as consumers and proposes that mass marketing and distribution introduced buying things as a new task and a new pastime for women. While women are often confined to the role of a housewife preoccupied with consumption, men are viewed as responsible breadwinners or independent rebels

(Friedan, 2001; Gentry & Harrison, 2010; Holt & Thompson, 2004). We hope our focus on traditional as well as alternative gender performances helps to view gender as more than a stereotypical and stand-alone social category that marketers condition and constrain as they market *with* consumers.

SUMMARY

The goal of our chapter is to uncover the ways in which gender works as an operant resource in value cocreation practices. Toward this end, we integrate the feminist literature on gender capital, the work in CCT on gender and consumption, and the value cocreation discussions in S-D logic. The feminist literature guided us in envisioning gender as an embodied form of cultural capital that interacts with consumers' operant and operand resources. The CCT studies aided us in formulating consumers' mobilization of gender in traditional and alternative performances. The S-D logic framework assisted us in outlining the different domains and types of firm–consumer collaborations in value cocreation processes. Via this particular amalgamation, we address the three-way relationship between gender, consumption, and production that is often overlooked by consumer researchers but is key for understanding consumers' value-creative competencies, as well as for theorizing firm–consumer resource integration in the cocreation of value.

REFERENCES

Arnould, Eric J. (2005). Animating the big middle. *Journal of Retailing, 81*(2), 89–96.

Arnould, Eric J. (2007). Service-dominant logic and consumer culture theory: Natural allies in an emerging paradigm. In Russell W. Belk & John F. Sherry, Jr. (Eds.), *Consumer culture theory: Research in consumer behavior* (Vol. 11; pp. 57–78). New York, NY: Elsevier.

Arnould, Eric J., Linda L. Price, & Avinash Malshe (2006). Toward a cultural resource-based theory of the consumer. In Robert F. Lusch & Stephen L. Vargo (Eds.), *The service-dominant logic of marketing: Dialog, debate, and directions* (pp. 91–104). Armonk, NY: M. E. Sharpe.

Arnould, Eric J., & Craig J. Thompson (2005). Consumer culture theory (CCT): Twenty years of research. *Journal of Consumer Research, 31* (March), 868–883.

Avery, Jill (2008). *Defending the markers of hegemonic masculinity: Consumer resistance to gender-bending brand extensions* (Working Paper). Boston, MA: Simmons School of Management.

Bagozzi, Richard P., Hans Baumgartner, & Youjae Yi (1992). State versus action orientation and the theory of reasoned action: An application to coupon usage. *Journal of Consumer Research, 18* (March), 505–518.

Bardhi, Fleura, & Eric J. Arnould (2005). Thrift shopping: Combining utilitarian thrift and hedonic treat benefits. *Journal of Consumer Behavior, 4*(4), 1–11.

Barry, Thomas E., Mary C. Gilly, & Lindley E. Doran (1985). Advertising to women with different career orientations. *Journal of Advertising Research, 25*(2), 26–34.

Berner, Robert (2006). I sold it through the grapevine. *BusinessWeek,* May 29, http://www.businessweek.com/magazine/content/06_22/b3986060.htm

Berthon, Pierre R., Leyland Pitt, & Colin Campbell (2008). Ad lib: When customers create the ad. *California Management Review, 50*(4), 6–30.

Borghini, Stefania, Nina Diamond, Robert V. Kozinets, Mary Ann McGrath, Albert M. Muniz, Jr., & John F. Sherry Jr. (2009). Why are themed brandstores so powerful? Retail brand ideology at American Girl Place. *Journal of Retailing, 85*(3), 363–375.

Bourdieu, Pierre (1984). *Distinction: A social critique of the judgment of taste.* London, England: Routledge and Kegan Paul.

Bourdieu, Pierre (2001). *Masculine domination.* Stanford, CA: Polity Press.

Brown, Stephen, Robert V. Kozinets, & John F. Sherry Jr. (2003). Teaching old brands new tricks: Retro branding and the revival of brand meaning. *Journal of Marketing, 67* (July), 19–33.

Campbell, Colin (2005). The craft consumer: Culture, craft and consumption in a postmodern society. *Journal of Consumer Culture, 5*(1), 23–42.

Carrigan, Tim, Bob Connell, & John Lee (1987). Toward a new sociology of masculinity. In H. Brod (Ed.), *The making of masculinities: The new men's studies.* Boston, MA: Allen & Unwin.

Caterall, Miriam, & Pauline Maclaran (2002). Gender perspectives in consumer behavior: An overview and future directions. *The Marketing Review, 2,* 405–425.

Coles, Tony (2009). Negotiating the field of masculinity: The production and reproduction of multiple dominant masculinities. *Men and Masculinities, 12,* 30–44.

Commuri, Suraj, & James W. Gentry (2005). Resource allocation in households with women as chief wage earners. *Journal of Consumer Research, 32* (September), 185–195.

Connell, R. W. (1995). *Masculinities: Knowledge, power and social change.* Berkeley, CA: University of California Press.

Connell, R. W., & James Messerschmidt (2005). Hegemonic masculinity: Rethinking the concept. *Gender & Society, 19* (December), 829–859.

Coskuner-Balli, Gokcen, & Craig J. Thompson (2009). Legitimating an emergent social identity through marketplace performances. In Ann L. McGill & Sharon Shavitt (Eds.), *Advances of consumer research* (Vol. 36; pp. 135–138). Duluth, MN: Association for Consumer Research.

Dolan, Catherine, & Linda Scott (2009). Lipstick evangelism: Avon trading circles and gender empowerment in South Africa. *Gender and Development, 17* (July), 203–218.

Duffy, Brooke Erin (2010). Empowerment through endorsement? Polysemic meaning in Dove's user-generated advertising. *Communication, Culture & Critique, 3,* 26–43.

Feick, Lawrence F., & Linda L. Price (1987). The market maven: A diffuser of marketplace information. *Journal of Marketing, 51* (January), 83–97.

Fischer, Eileen, & Stephen Arnould (1990). More than a labor of love: Gender roles and Christmas gift shopping. *Journal of Consumer Research, 17* (December), 333–345.

Fournier, Susan (1998). Consumers and their brands: Developing relationship theory in consumer research. *Journal of Consumer Research, 24*(4), 343–373.

Friedan, Betty (2001). *The feminine mystique.* New York, NY: W. W. Norton (original 1963).

Gelber, S. (2000). Do-it-yourself: Constructing, repairing, and maintaining masculinity. In Jennifer Scanlon (Ed.), *The gender and consumer culture reader* (pp. 70–93). New York, NY: NYU Press.

Gentry, James W., & Robert L. Harrison (2010). Is advertising a barrier to male movement toward gender change? *Marketing Theory, 10*(1), 74–96.

Grier, Sonya A., & Anne M. Brumbaugh (1999). Noticing cultural differences: Ad meanings created by target and non-target markets. *Journal of Advertising, 28*(1), 79–93.

Haytko, Diana L., & Julie Baker (2004). It's all at the mall: Exploring adolescent girls' experiences. *Journal of Retailing, 80* (January), 67–83.

Herrmann, Gretchen M. (2004). Haggling spoken here: Gender, class, and style in US garage sale bargaining. *Journal of Popular Culture, 38*(1), 55–81.

Holt, Douglas B. (1995). How consumers consume: A typology of consumption practices. *Journal of Consumer Research, 22* (June), 1–16.

Holt, Douglas B., & Craig J. Thompson (2004). Man-of-action heroes: The pursuit of heroic masculinity in everyday consumption. *Journal of Consumer Research, 31*(2), 425–440.

Howe, Jeff (2006). The rise of crowdsourcing. *Wired Magazine, 14*(6), http://www.wired.com/wired/archive/14.06/crowds.html

Hunt, Shelby D. (2000). *A general theory of competition: Resources, competences, productivity, economic growth.* Thousand Oaks, CA: Sage Publications.

Hunt, Shelby D., & Sreedhar Madhavaram (2006). The service dominant logic of marketing: Theoretical foundations, pedagogy and resource-advantage theory. In Robert F. Lusch & Stephen L. Vargo (Eds.), *The service-dominant logic of marketing: Dialog, debate, and directions* (pp. 67–84). Armonk, NY: M. E. Sharpe.

Huppatz, Kate (2009). Reworking Bourdieu's "capital": Feminine and female capitals in the field of paid caring work. *Sociology, 43,* 45–66.

Illouz, Eva (1997). *Consuming the romantic utopia: Love and the cultural contradictions of capitalism.* Berkeley, CA: University of California Press.

Kates, Steven M. (2002). The protean quality of subcultural consumption: An ethnographic account of gay consumers. *Journal of Consumer Research, 29* (December), 383–399.

Kates, Steven M. (2004). The dynamics of brand legitimacy: An interpretive study in the gay men's community. *Journal of Consumer Research, 31* (September), 455–464.

Kates, Steven M., & Russell W. Belk (2001). The meanings of Lesbian and Gay Pride Day: Resistance through consumption and resistance to consumption. *Journal of Contemporary Ethnography, 30,* 392–429.

Kozinets, Robert V. (2002). Can consumers escape the market?: Emancipatory illuminations from Burning Man. *Journal of Consumer Research, 29* (June), 20–38.

Kozinets, Robert V., Kristine de Valck, Andrea C. Wojnicki, & Sarah J. S. Wilner (2010). Understanding word-of-mouth marketing in online communities. *Journal of Marketing, 74* (March), 71–89.

Kozinets, Robert V., John F. Sherry Jr., Diana Storm, Adam D. Duhachek, Krittinee Nuttavuthisit, & Benet DeBerry-Spence (2004). Being in the zone: Staging retail theater at ESPN Zone Chicago. *Journal of Contemporary Ethnography, 30,* 465–510.

Lastovicka, John L., Lance A. Bettencourt, Renee Shaw-Hughner, & Ronald J. Kuntze (1999). Lifestyle of the tight and frugal: Theory and measurement. *Journal of Consumer Research, 26* (June), 85–98.

Lichtenstein, David R., Richard G. Netemeyer, & Scott Burton (1995). Assessing the domain specificity of deal proneness: A field study. *Journal of Consumer Research, 22* (December), 314–326.

Lowell, Terry (2000). Thinking feminism with and against Bourdieu. *Feminist Theory, 1*(1), 11–32.

Martin, Diane M., John W. Schouten, & James H. McAlexander (2006). Claiming the throttle: Multiple femininities in a hyper-masculine subculture. *Consumption, Markets and Culture, 9*(3), 171–205.

McAlexander, James H., John W. Schouten, & Harold F. Koenig (2002). Building brand community. *Journal of Marketing, 66* (January), 38–54.

McCall, Leslie (1992). Does gender fit? Bourdieu, feminism, and conceptions of social order. *Theory and Society, 21,* 837–867.

McCracken, Grant (1986). Culture and consumption: A theoretical account of the structure and movement of the cultural meaning of consumer goods. *Journal of Consumer Research, 13* (June), 71–84.

McCracken, Grant (1987). Advertising: Meaning or information. In Melanie Wallendorf & Paul Anderson (Eds.), *Advances in consumer research* (Vol. 14; pp. 121–124). Provo, UT: Association for Consumer Research.

Mick, David Glen, & Claus Buhl (1992). A meaning-based model of advertising. *Journal of Consumer Research, 19* (December), 317–338.

Miller, Cyndee (1994). Top marketers take bolder approach in targeting gays. *Marketing News, 28* (July 4), 1–2.

Miller, Daniel (1998). *A theory of shopping.* Ithaca, NY: Cornell University Press.

Muniz, Albert M., & Thomas C. O'Guinn (2001). Brand community. *Journal of Consumer Research, 27* (March), 412–432.

Muniz, Albert M., & Hope J. Schau (2005). Religiosity in the abandoned Apple Newton brand community. *Journal of Consumer Research, 31* (March), 737–747.

Muniz, Albert M., & Hope J. Schau (2007). Vigilante marketing and consumer created communications. *Journal of Advertising, 36*(3), 35–50.

O'Hern, Matthew S., & Aric Rindfleish (2010). Consumer co-creation: A typology and research agenda. In Naresh K. Malhotra (Ed.), *Review of Marketing Research* (pp. 84–106). Bingley, England: Emerald Group Publishing Limited.

Otnes, Cele C., & Mary Ann McGrath (2001). Perceptions and realities of male shopping behavior. *Journal of Retailing, 77* (Spring), 111–137.

Palmer, Kimberly S. (2000). Gay consumers in the driver's seat: Subaru's new ad campaign is among those signaling to homosexual buyers. *The Washington Post,* July 4, http://www.pouxcompany.com/interior/pdfs/wp_070400.pdf

Petrecca, Laura (2007). At Cannes: Madison Avenue wants you! *USA Today,* June 20, http://www.usatoday.com/money/advertising/2007-06-20-cannes-cover-usat_N.htm

PR Newswires (2007). Real woman creates new Dove TV commercial, February 26, http://www.prnewswires.com

Prahalad, C. K., & Gary Hamel (1990). The core competence of the corporation. *Harvard Business Review, 68* (May–June), 79–91.

Prahalad, C. K., & Venkatram Ramaswamy (2004). *The future of competition: Co-creating unique value with customers.* Boston, MA: Harvard Business School Press.

Price, Linda L., Lawrence F. Feick, & Audrey Guskey-Federouch (1988). Couponing behaviors of the market maven: Profile of a super couponer. In Michael J. Houston (Ed.), *Advances in Consumer research* (Vol. 15; pp. 354–359). Provo, UT: Association for Consumer Research.

Reay, Diane (2004). Gendering Bourdieu's concepts of capitals? Emotional capital, women and social class. In Lisa Adkins & Beverley Skeggs (Eds.), *Feminism after Bourdieu*. Malden, MA: Blackwell Publishing.

Ross-Smith, Anne, & Kate Huppatz (2008). *Management, women and gender capital* (UTS: School of Management Working Paper No. 2008/4).

Sandikci, Özlem, & Güliz Ger (2010). Veiling in style: How does a stigmatized practice become fashionable? *Journal of Consumer Research, 37* (June), 15–36.

Schau, Hope, J., Albert M. Muniz, & Eric J. Arnould (2009). How brand community practices create value. *Journal of Marketing, 73*(September), 30–51.

Schau, Hope J., & Katherine Thompson (2010). Betwixt and between: Liminality and feminism in the *Twilight* brand community. In Margaret C. Campbell, Jeff Inman, & Rik Pieters (Eds.), *Advances in consumer research* (Vol. 37). Duluth, MN: Association for Consumer Research.

Schroeder, Jonathan E., & Janet L. Borgerson (1998). Marketing images of gender: A visual analysis. *Consumption, Markets, and Culture, 2*(2), 161–201.

Skeggs, Beverley (1997). *Formations of class and gender: Becoming respectable*. London, England: Sage Publications.

Skeggs, Beverley (2004). Context and background: Pierre Bourdieu's analysis of class, gender and sexuality. In Lisa Adkins & Beverley Skeggs (Eds.), *Feminism after Bourdieu*. Malden, MA: Blackwell Publishing.

Strasser, Susan (1982). *Never done: A history of American housework*. New York, NY: Pantheon.

Thompson, Craig J. (1996). Caring consumers: Gendered consumption meanings and the juggling lifestyle. *Journal of Consumer Research, 22* (March), 388–407.

Tuncay, Linda, & Cele C. Otnes (2008). The use of persuasion management strategies by identity-vulnerable consumers: The case of urban heterosexual male shoppers. *Journal of Retailing, 4* (December), 487–499.

Üstüner, Tuba, & Douglas B. Holt (2007). Dominated consumer acculturation: The social construction of poor migrant women's consumer identity projects in a Turkish squatter. *Journal of Consumer Research, 34* (June), 41–56.

Vargo, Steve L., & Robert F. Lusch (2004). Evolving to a new dominant logic for marketing. *Journal of Marketing, 68* (January), 1–17.

Vargo, Steve L., & Robert F. Lusch (2006). Service-dominant logic: Reactions, reflections, and refinements. *Marketing Theory, 6* (September), 281–288.

Vargo, Steve L., & Robert F. Lusch (2008). Service-dominant logic: Continuing the evolution. *Journal of the Academy of Marketing Science, 36*, 1–10.

Watson, Matthew, & Elizabeth Shove (2009). Product, competence, project and practice. *Journal of Consumer Culture, 8*(1), 69–89.

Wolin, Lori D. (2003). Gender issues in advertising—An oversight synthesis of research: 1970–2002. *Journal of Advertising Research, 43*(1), 111–129.

8

Lived Consumer Bodies: Narcissism, Bodily Discourse, and Women's Pursuit of the Body Beautiful

Helen Woodruffe-Burton and Katie Ireland

INTRODUCTION

The body has received academic attention over the years and Vaknin (2006), among others, has demonstrated how our daily lives are becoming a mirage of images that result in a total preoccupation with image management and self-enhancement. This phenomenon is not overlooked by marketers; products and services relevant to body image issues can be seen to have profound influences on consumers. Marketing plays a role in consumers' perceptions of body image and underpins aspects of the cultural ideology of the body that underlies consumers' sense of an ideal or more desirable body. This bodily discourse is manifested through advertising (Thompson & Hirschman, 1995), media images, and product symbolism, for example, as well as through social interaction.

At the same time, conditions of postmodernity, while purporting to offer the postmodern consumer freedom to choose from a wide range of cultural narratives and identities, may be seen as an optimistic theoretical construction far removed from freedom in the self-understanding expressed by consumers (Thompson & Hirschman, 1995). Indeed, conditions of postmodernity can give rise to uncertainty about the self and may even undermine self-concept (Kernis & Goldman, 2003). The existing literature on the political, symbolic, and public aspects of the body is reviewed here because these aspects are particularly pronounced in the context of body image and cultural ideology of the body.

The literature on narcissism (the work of Lasch, 1979, in particular) offers a useful theoretical framework for understanding individuals' struggle for identity and the suffering associated with the postmodern condition in the twenty-first century. Moreover, taking the view that consumption itself is embodied (Falk, 1994) and that consumers' performative enactment of identity "must occur through the body" (Saren, 2007, p. 344), this chapter argues that bodily manifestations of self are inevitably gendered both politically and culturally. Theoretical advancement within this area of consumer research therefore rests on our understanding of gender in consumers' lived experience of consumption. Underpinned by the theoretical and conceptual explorations described before, a study of women who are self-professed "gym addicts" has been undertaken to explore contemporary women's lived experience of body maintenance and body image. The findings are examined through the lens of gender, academic perspectives on the body, and narcissism.

NARCISSISM AND SELF

Since Lasch's 1979 work on narcissism, the subject has continued to enjoy the attention of academics internationally. An examination of recent publications illustrates that the role of narcissism in the context of self-esteem (e.g., Campbell et al., 2007; McGregor et al.; Trzesniewski et al., 2008), impulsivity (Vazire & Funder, 2006), and celebrity worship (Ashe et al., 2005) occupies the minds of researchers in psychology and elsewhere. Studies of narcissism in applied contexts such as the study of leadership (e.g., Judge et al., 2006; King, 2007) and company strategy and performance (Chatterjee & Hambrick, 2007) highlight the more wide-ranging nature of the concept. The sexual politics of narcissism come under scrutiny in contemporary feminist discourse (Tyler, 2005). A new book, *The Narcissism Epidemic: Living in the Age of Entitlement* (Twenge & Campbell, 2009), claims that 10% of Americans in their 20s suffer from narcissistic personality disorder fueled by, among other factors, the emphasis placed on self-esteem and self-promotion by the media and Internet social networking.

Narcissism and Society

Lasch notes that, in its pathological form, narcissism originates as a defense against feelings of helpless dependency in early life that, he suggests, is prolonged through modern society into adult life. He presents his ideas that individuals in Western society have been struggling with "the void within" in the postwar era. Cushman (1990, p. 604) speaks of the "empty self" and proposes that this "inner emptiness" is expressed in many ways within our culture: low self-esteem (the absence of a sense of personal worth), values confusion (the absence of a sense of personal convictions), eating disorders (the compulsion to fill the emptiness with food or to embody the emptiness by refusing food), and drug abuse (the compulsion to fill the emptiness with chemically induced emotional experience of "receiving" something from the world). It may also take the form of an absence of personal meaning.

Lasch (1979) also considers that society itself is, to an extent, narcissistic and that people with narcissistic personalities play a conspicuous part in contemporary life, often rising to positions of eminence and thriving on the adulation of the masses. These celebrities set the tone of both private and public life, according to Lasch, because the machinery of celebrity fails to distinguish between the public and the private realm. Success in such conditions is nothing more than a narcissistic fantasy that does not stem from accomplishment but instead is based on uncritical adoration—a narcissistic fantasy of celebrity based on nothing more tenuous than celebrity itself (Lasch, 1979).

Giddens (1991) notes that while there are other sources giving rise to narcissism, especially within personality development, narcissism is a prime type of behavior pathology associated with commodifying influences (referring to Lasch's 1979 thesis). In the context of consumerism, commodification promotes appearance as the prime arbiter of value and sees self-development above all in terms of display; thus, narcissistic traits are likely to become prominent. Lasch (1979) simply suggests that narcissism appears to represent the best way of coping with the tensions and anxieties of modern life and therefore prevailing social conditions tend to bring out narcissistic traits present, in varying degrees, in everyone.

The Narcissistic Personality

Fromm (1964) has used the term narcissism fairly loosely to cover all forms of vanity, self-obsession, parochialism, and fanaticism. However, Lasch (1979) argues that Fromm neglects to recognize Sennett's (1977) contention that narcissism has more in common with self-hatred than with self-admiration and is simply a defense against aggressive impulses. Lasch also identifies links between narcissistic personalities and certain characteristics of contemporary culture, including fear of old age and death and changing or deteriorating relations between men and women. He goes on to assert that critics are using narcissism as a loose synonym for selfishness and a mere metaphor for the state of mind in that the world appears as a mirror of the self (Lasch, 1980).

Unlike many other borderline conditions in psychology, narcissism is considered the least severe because it allows continuation, often quite successfully, of everyday life, and sufferers are less likely to lose control and harm themselves (Capps, 1993). However, it is important to recognize that within the clinical perspective, there are different types of narcissism. Lasch (1979) offers comprehensive discussion of the various types: primary, secondary, and pathological. These detail the journey from the newborn infant at the center of his or her own universe to the adult narcissist continuously striving for this position. In short, Lasch describes the modern narcissist as someone who expertly manages the impressions he or she gives to others, someone who craves admiration but has contempt for those who give it, someone who seeks emotional experiences to fill the inner void, or someone who is terrified of ageing and death (Lasch, 1979).

Lowen (1983) provides an extensive summary of narcissistic personality characteristics that includes grandiosity and extreme self-centeredness. A further key characteristic, according to Lowen, is the remarkable absence of interest in and empathy for others, particularly in light of the fact that narcissists constantly seek the approval and admiration of others. Seemingly a personality of contradictions, on the one hand, the narcissist has an overinflated sense of self-importance, accomplishments, and talents and the expectation that his or her "specialness" should be noticed. The narcissist often overestimates the extent to which he or she is attractive or intelligent and is overly optimistic about academic performance (Sedikides & Brewer, 2001).

On the other hand, the narcissist frequently experiences feelings of unworthiness (American Psychiatric Association [APA], 1987) and, in pursuing goals of "unlimited success, power, brilliance, beauty or ideal love" (APA, p. 350), experiences overwhelming envy of those perceived to be more successful than himself or herself. Thus, the pursuit of goals is imbued with a pleasureless quality and marked by an ambition that cannot be satisfied. The result is fragile self-esteem, a preoccupation with performance relative to others, and a need for constant attention and admiration (APA, p. 350).

ACADEMIC PERSPECTIVES ON THE BODY

In addition to the bodily discourse that surrounds and confronts individuals, the body has received vast academic attention from many perspectives over the years and this is pertinent in any exploration into narcissism. It is featured heavily in a variety of both ancient and present art forms and remains the subject of great attention in even the most primitive of cultures (Dutton, 1995). As mentioned previously, the body and embodied consumer behavior are the focus of a great deal of marketing activity.

The Political Body

According to Bordo (1993), our bodies are forced to learn their own limits and the appropriate ways in which they are supposed to behave according to gender, race, and class. Whitley (2001) proposes that the cultural gender belief system includes such factors as stereotypes about men and women and attitudes toward appropriate roles for the sexes. Craik (1994) suggests that if sex is determined by biology, then gender "is learned and acquired as a set of social trainings about how female bodies behave" (p. 43).

Butler (1990) asserts that gender is encoded via the repeated stylization of the body and of action within a rigid frame; Sharp (1996) notes that gendered identity takes on its apparently "natural" presence through the repeated performance of gender norms. Thus, the body is at once both enabling and restricting—something we have as well as something we are. Importantly, this becomes increasingly significant for women for whom life is centered around the body through beautification and reproduction

(Bordo, 1993). It is so important, in fact, that such prescribed standards of beauty determine almost all aspects of a woman's body, defining and limiting physical appearance.

Other writers contend that notions of gender and body are difficult to disentangle and claims are made that, while theorizing of gender rests to a large degree on social structures, there exists an argument for replacing concepts of gender with the concept of "lived body" (Young, 2005, p. 9). Maternal bodies (particularly *pregnant* maternal bodies) are also the subject of substantial attention in the literature in a range of fields (Hopfl & Hornby Atkinson, 2000; Tyler, 2000), further underlining the embodied (and political) nature of gender in terms of women's lived experience.

From a cultural perspective, Oliver (2001) refers to the historical and philosophical mind/body dualism found in Dewey's work (1922) that has created a space within our culture where human beings, women in particular, become disembodied and objectified in ways that are debilitating (Oliver, 2001). Women's magazines are a key site for depictions of the self, beauty, and culturally mediated feminine ideals centered on a thin body (see, for example, Duke, 2002; Frith, Ping, & Cheng, 2005; Stevens, Maclaren, & Brown, 2003), emphasizing the extent to which the endless struggle of body enhancement and maintenance is particularly pertinent in women's culture. Women's bodies are used as a means of regulating behavior (Bordo, 1989; Foucault, 1977, 1985; Oliver, 2001; Shilling, 1993; Sparkes, 1996, 1997; Wright, 2000), supporting the feminist critiques that argue that women face oppression through the acculturation of their bodies (Bloom & Munro, 1995).

Consistent with the justifications and explanations of narcissism, Oliver (2001) accepts that girls are continuously bombarded with messages about their bodies. The result is that the body is transformed into a site for political struggles in line with Wolf's (1990) statement that "the more legal and material hindrances women have broken down, the more strictly and heavily and cruelly images of female beauty have come to rest upon them" (p. 1). Fifteen years on, Tyler (2005) defines a state of "negative narcissism" (p. 30) where women can be acutely conscious of the way that cultural ideals of femininity have a negative effect on their own self-esteem and yet still seem to feel compelled to conform to those ideals in order to allay fears of failure. Aptly, Tyler points out, "Hence the dictum, no beauty without pain" (p. 30).

The Symbolic Body

Evidently, the importance of the body appears to be based firmly upon the messages imbued within a certain appearance. This subject has been extensively recognized by symbolic interactionists (Becker, 1963; Blumer, 1969; Goffman, 1959/1990), who believe that the body is a symbol of individual status ("what you are") and individual consumption power ("what you have"). For example, as discussed by Bordo (1993), muscles that were previously symbolic of race and class are today rather more indicative of character. A muscled body formerly represented masculine power and was associated with manual labor and proletarian status, as well as racial meaning (Bordo, 1993), as Frueh (2001, p. 82) notes, "as if bodily bigness that is firm to hard can only be male." However, today the interpretation is somewhat different; muscles are glamorized and sexualized, now symbolizing having the correct attitude and managing one's self and one's life (Bordo, 1993). Similarly, being thin represents a triumph of discipline and willpower over the body and the thin body (that can be described as the "nonbody") is associated with "absolute purity, hyperintellectuality and transcendence of the flesh" (Bordo, p. 148).

Consistent with the association of a thin body equating to a capable mind is the research that draws parallels between anorexia, body building, and compulsive exercise. Studies support that sufferers are often perfectionists and high achievers with a need for control. For example, Bordo (1993) notes that the current craze for long-distance running and fasting is largely a phenomenon of "young upwardly mobile professionals" (p. 153). Thus, the evidence suggests that culture features heavily in what is deemed appropriate and desirable with regard to appearance for women. This is reflected in society's evolving dictations of the appropriate weight. Previously, bulging stomachs were a status symbol necessary for businessmen in the mid-nineteenth century; today, substantial weight is only acceptable as long as it is tightly managed. The size and shape of the body have come to symbolize the emotional, moral, or spiritual status of the individual and to operate as a marker of personal internal order—or, indeed, disorder (Bordo, 1993).

Commensurate with this notion, Brace-Govan (2002) extends her discourse of the body to include the term "bodywork." This concept is broader than simply adorning, embellishing, or training the body (which she refers to as the body's physicality) to include the body's motility. Thus, she recognizes the importance of movement and gesture in understanding ourselves and each other. Combining physicality and bodywork recognizes that the body is active and embodied; therefore, it is both a vehicle for communication and self-creation (Brace-Govan, 2004). Significantly, regardless of the current body style "must-have," if an individual is not fortunate (or driven) enough to create it (i.e., has a "normal" body), then she consequently becomes classified as unattractive (Bartky, 1988; Bordo, 1990; Coward, 1985; Martin, 1987; Spitzack, 1990; Wolf, 1990). The fact is that people cannot be in the world without bodies (Bartky, 1988; Brace-Govan, 2004; Grosz, 1994); humans cannot be "unbodied." This means that the symbolic meanings conveyed by bodies are emphasized and bodily characteristics such as demeanor, presentation, look, size, and physicality are "automatically and deeply perceived and read like a text at an automatic and deep level of perception" (Brace-Govan, 2004, p. 404).

Public and Private Bodies: The Body as a Class System

It is well recognized that Western women have a turbulent relationship with their bodies (Brampton, 2006). For example, Bordo (1990) argues that women grow up despising the idealized female form because it resembles that of a young boy: wide shoulders, narrow hips, and tight muscles. These issues are further aggravated by our inability to keep the body private. Facing a number of prescribed standards of beauty, the body remains a public domain for judgment and ridicule. Even when the body can retain some of its privacy behind the closed doors of our own bedrooms, many women continue to undress in the dark or back out of rooms to avoid showing any cellulite (Johnson, 2006). However, such behavior is of little surprise when one considers the culture within in which we live. Dutton (1995) even goes so far as to suggest that the class system has evolved. Previously, class was determined by profession and social status and signifiers of social class included the size of someone's car and home. Today, it is body size that determines an individual's relative position within society. Dutton (1995) describes this as facing fierce and widely accepted "body bigotry" (p. 177).

Clear connections between the body and narcissism can be found particularly when the implications of a symbolic association attached to the body are considered in relation to objectification. Davis, Dionne, and Shuster (2001) talk of the prevalence of self-objectification of women.

Similarly, Roth and Baslow (2004) refer to the daily toil of dieting, exercising, shaving, and doing hair and makeup to prime one's own object. Subsequently, Guthrie and Castelnuovo (1994) advise caution that these routines can be internalized and become central within the formation of self-identity and self-image. This is particularly salient for "attractive" women, who place greater emphasis on their appearance than do their less attractive counterparts because they are more likely to be judged on their outward appearance and are therefore more likely to self-objectify (Davis, Dionne, & Shuster, 2001).

Significantly, women are not only taught to be insecure by culture, engaged constantly in physical improvement, but also taught how to see bodies (Bordo, 1993). Tied into this argument and extremely relevant to the narcissistic personality is constant evaluation (e.g., by the male gaze) and objectification (e.g., media presentation of bodies and body parts) of women. It is argued that the combination of these two causes women, particularly young women, to internalize this external view of themselves in a process of self-objectification (Fredrickson & Roberts, 1997). This process whereby sole evaluation is based on appearance can produce highly negative consequences, including greater appearance anxiety, body shame, and disordered eating (Fredrickson, 1998).

However, referring to a purely "male" gaze is inadequate because it ignores the multiplicity of meanings that can be read into every cultural act and practice and the various power plays within them (Bordo, 1993). Similarly, according to Johnson (2006), men neither care nor really notice if women put on weight. In contemporary society, women are arguably their own biggest critics and as such this piercing gaze often spreads to include other women and their respective failings. This is consistent with Bordo's view that individuals are taught how to see bodies.

As such, we arrive at another interpretation of the "gaze" (Berger, 1972; Mulvey, 1984). This is the idea that women, subjected to the evaluation of others, are tempted to use their looks to gain approval. However, as mentioned, first, this can be extremely disempowering and, second (and arguably of greater concern to the narcissist), although women can control every aspect of their appearance and the image that they portray almost down to minute detail, society's "gaze" implies that any meanings and interpretations are determined by discursive texts outside women's control (Smith, 1990, p. 182). If looking to defend the narcissist, it could be argued that women, themselves objects who constantly face society's gaze, cannot escape the impact of the prescriptive nature of our culture regarding feminine appearance (Brace-Govan, 2002). However, the situation will simply rise in prominence while women continue to reproduce the images and messages surrounding them.

GYM BODIES—THE STUDY

A study was designed to understand contemporary women's lived experience of body maintenance and body image and their motivations for going to the gym in light of their feelings about their bodies. The research also explores the enactment of narcissism in relation to the pursuit of the body beautiful. A purposive sampling approach was used to recruit women to participate in the study through "word of mouth" and social networks. This helped ensure that the (small) sample would be information rich (Patton, 1990) and would consist of women for whom the research was relevant (Glaser & Strauss, 1967) in terms of their own self-identification as gym addicts. The group, though small, was quite diverse in nature; the key common ground for participation were predicated solely upon their self-identified gym "addiction." It should be pointed out that no attempts were made to assess levels of addiction (using addiction scales, for example); rather, the women's self-expressed (and therefore subjective) self-description as gym addicts was considered justification for their inclusion in the study. The women who took part are described in Table 8.1 (all names have been changed to provide anonymity).

Data collection methods included phenomenological interviews to form small-scale, in-depth case studies (five in total), combined with

TABLE 8.1

Research Participants

Respondent	Age	Ethnicity	Occupation	Family
Anne	49	White British	Housewife	Husband/two children
Suzie	40	Indian British	Medical doctor	Partner/three children
Sarah	21	White British	Graduate student	Single/no children
Michelle	40	Jamaican British	Civil servant	Partner/two children
Laura	26	White British	Retail assistant	Single/no children

direct observation, participation, and reflexivity. The primary research was conducted by one of the authors (the gym addict one!) adopting an autobiographical/biographical approach (Birch, 1998) in which she sometimes shared her own experiences as part of the dialogue with the women who participated, as well as telling her own story in a parallel manner to that of the other case studies (recording these experiences in the form of a diary).

The interviews were transcribed and then, alongside the reflexive diary, the interpretive process was shared by the two researchers in an iterative cycle; both researchers read the transcripts independently several times and identified broad thematic categories and then worked together in an effort to refine the emergent themes. Utilizing a part-to-whole process, the researchers aimed to develop a deep understanding of the individual women's experiences as depicted within each separate transcribed narrative account, while also noting the commonalities of experiences and individual differences across transcripts (Thompson & Hirschman, 1995), following a hermeneutic process (Hirschman, 1992; Thompson, Pollio, & Locander, 1994). The conceptual model and analysis and discussion of the findings presented in this chapter represent the culmination of this process.

FINDINGS

A number of themes emerged from the research that helped address the research questions articulated earlier. They are presented here.

The Role of (Going to) the Gym: Feeling Good, Losing Self, Flow

First, the centrality of the gym within these women's lives was key in this study. (Going to) the gym clearly plays an important role in these women's lives that goes way beyond the mere provision of exercise facilities and equipment. In fact, it plays multiple roles and satisfies individual needs, as the following excerpts show. Michelle, for example explicitly describes the feel-good factor from the gym:

It physically feels like I'm walking on air. You can physically feel the difference in how you…well, I feel the difference in how I walk: very light footed and I just feel very spongy and I'm bouncing and I'm…that's the rush.

Going to the gym can also be a coping mechanism, as Sarah recalls:

Like the other day, my boyfriend was really annoying me and it was making me so cross, so I went to the gym and I deliberately thought about him, about all his crappy behavior. Like, think about it really hard you know, and at the same time pushing it really hard to try and work out through my body all the anger and stress. I'm not sure it always works but I've had plenty of practice! [laughs]

For Ann, the escape that the gym can offer is hugely important:

A lot of the time, because you have the headphones on, you just get kind of lost in it, don't you? I quite like losing myself, actually, because I can make my mind go completely blank and just get engrossed in rubbish TV that I would never normally watch, you know [laughs] and I just find I can switch off and sometimes that's quite good.

This "escape from self" reflects Baumeister's (1991, 1995) view that, under certain circumstances, people find self-awareness to be aversive and will try to escape from it. They accomplish this most commonly by restricting their attention to an extremely narrow focus on the here and now, "thereby reducing self to mere body, experience to mere sensation and action to mere muscle movement" (Baumeister, 1995, p. 84). The following diary extract echoes a similar theme about the gym representing an escape from external pressures and worries:

When I went [to the gym] I wouldn't say it made me feel good but it stopped me feeling bad about myself. The gym became really important to me. I was really unhappy out there [working abroad] and it was the only place I felt OK…the only place that I felt things were going OK. It was essential for me to go, a weight has been lifted. I needed the release; I needed the gym on so many levels.

These accounts of feelings about going to the gym also reflect Csikzentmihalyi's (1988) notion of flow as intense involvement, deep concentration, clarity of goals and feedback, loss of a sense of time, lack of self-consciousness, and transcendence of a sense of self—leading to an autotelic (that is, intrinsically rewarding) experience that can further our understanding of the nature and importance of the role of the gym in "addicted" gym goers' lives. Other research has linked flow with esteem and the experiences of working mothers (Wells, 1998) and with existential consumption (Woodruffe-Burton & Eccles, 2005), as well as using flow to explore people's experiences of extremely challenging or technically demanding activities such as mountain climbing (Csikzentmihalyi, 1988). There are clear parallels between aspects of flow and aspects of narcissism that support the development of the theoretical framework we are proposing.

The Need to Boost Confidence and Self-Esteem

Second, the desire to boost confidence and self-esteem is another key theme emerging from the study. Indeed, it comes across very powerfully, as these accounts illustrate. Laura says:

> I feel much more confident after I've been to the gym. Especially, you know, in the summer when I'm tanned and slim and I go and have a good work-out. My times are good; I know my body looks good and I feel great—happy and healthy and full of energy.

This quote highlights the significant link between appearance and self-esteem (Johns & Johns, 2000). Within contemporary society the importance of exercise, diet, and weight loss is increasingly associated with enhancing appearance rather than performance. As with the narcissist (Maccoby, 1976), however, this boost to self-esteem may only be felt if a certain level of performance is achieved, as Susie describes:

> When my times are good I felt great, really alive and healthy. Physically, I feel great, really fresh and ready to go. But more than that, I feel lifted psychologically—like I can go on and achieve in other areas. It sets me up for the day, ready to go.

The existence of negative and enduring past experiences can also drive the need to boost self-esteem, as Michelle shows:

I've always been conscious of how I've looked, so from a very young age it's been hard because I used to get bullied at primary school 'cause obviously the last year of primary school, I was 5 feet, 9 inches, with thick glasses. The boys used to run and jump on me 'cause I was a mountain. I think that's probably why. Right, I've got that mentality; I'll do whatever I have to do, what I want. I don't like hurting like that but if exercise gives me the rush, it improves my self-esteem, it makes me happy, so that's what I'll do.

Similarly, Sarah states, "I think I've got to the age now where I recognize that I have this being good enough complex, you know. It's from the bullying I'm sure, but that doesn't stop me from being caught under that spell again." Here, respondents hint at feelings of inadequacy or being singled out and made to feel uncomfortable for being different. The gym for these consumers appears to represent not only a means to enhance self-confidence but also a barrier, a protection mechanism that deflects negative thoughts from within and from others.

Fear of Failure, Fear of Becoming Unattractive, Not Valued, Horrid, and Fat

Research has shown that an attractive body is a valuable personal attribute, facilitating success in social, romantic, and economic endeavors (Berscheid, Hatfield, Walster, & Bohrnstedt, 1973; Brislin & Lewis, 1968; Davis, 2001; Hatfield & Sprecher, 1986), so it can be easy to make a link between looking good (as a result of going to the gym) and increased self-esteem. However, it may be that fear of failure; of becoming fat, undesirable—unattractive even—is a more powerful driver for this activity than the desire to boost self-esteem. Again, these are aspects of narcissism adding further weight to the development of our theoretical model. Perhaps going some way to explain these fears is this telling comment from Ann, which exemplifies the public body in terms of the scrutiny of female bodies by the male gaze, in this case that of her husband:

I suppose in some ways I keep slim for him [her husband] as well, you know what I mean? Because he's very critical of big women and I think, "Oh, I'd better not get big then" [laughs]. And I'm sure he'd be very accepting if I did, that that was happening, especially as we get older and things. But if he sees someone who's a big woman or she's got chunky legs, he says, "Oh she shouldn't wear that; she's too big to wear that" or "She shouldn't wear a skirt as short as that. She's got the wrong type of clothes." And things like that.

Being unable to attend the gym for some reason is the cause of significant anxiety and irritation, both in terms of annoyance at being prevented from attending and in terms of self-hatred (Horney, 1950) and fear of what might happen if attendance continues to be curtailed. Sarah says:

> I just feel horrid, like sluggish and fat. I just don't feel good. But it's not so much the days when I haven't exercised; it's more thinking about not being able to go, or when I plan to and then something gets in the way. So, like say I'm injured—and I mean really injured, like I really know I can't go—that's different. Then I just feel crap, flabby, useless, sluggish. Like not go-getting and capable like normal. But it's more when people start to make plans that interfere, when I'm perfectly capable of going. I feel panic; my breathing gets short; I just feel very unsettled. People laugh at me because I'm so obsessive about it. I won't stay overnight if I can help it. I'd rather go home so I know that I'm there ready to carry on with my exercise regime as normal in the morning. Even if I have to work out later, it makes me edgy and agitated. My worst fear is waking up too late [because] that means I haven't got time to go before work. Even talking about it makes me feel a little uneasy. I know it's irrational but it really does fill me with horror. I won't interrupt my routine for anyone—boyfriend, sister, best friend. Exercise comes first.

Fear of failure seems to be heightened among these women. As discussed by Maccoby (1976), existing in the back of the narcissist's mind is the fear that she will be associated with the losers. This fear may contribute to the fact that, for these consumers, the gym appears to hold an unusually fierce significance. For example, consider this further comment from Sarah about not being able to go to the gym:

> Yeah, you know, it's almost like I don't feel like me when I don't go in, like my world is slowly unraveling, like I'm not in control anymore…to be honest I'm not sure I could cope [without the gym]. I mean I know it sounds silly but fitness is my life; it holds everything together; it's who I am. If I didn't do it, I don't know who I'd be anymore.

Here, Sarah is describing the level to which she is prepared to force herself to go to the gym:

It was crazy! I was working solidly when I was in the house, which was hardly ever. I was doing loads of exercise anyway, but I still didn't feel I could stop going to the gym. So I still got up at six every morning and went to the gym or went running for over an hour…most of the time I felt crappy at the gym and it was a real struggle, but I was always glad I went afterwards.

Narcissistic Space: Mirrors, Reflections From Every Angle, Personal and Public Gaze

The gym itself can be represented as a narcissistic space with mirrors on every available wall so that gym users are able to see their bodies from every angle—as can all the other people in the gym, illustrating how the gym effectively bridges the divide between the public and the private body. Importantly, within this environment, it appears to be acceptable and even expected that, in certain areas of the gym, the body is studied and scrutinized closely and publicly. Sarah says:

I wouldn't say all the time, but I definitely go through periods of feeling fat. It's funny: One day I can feel really skinny and then the next I can feel as big as a house. Certainly the mirrors don't help. I mean I like to check out my form, especially when I'm doing weights to make sure I'm doing it properly so that I don't hurt my back or anything. But then it seems sometimes that all I'm doing is looking in the mirror. And each time I do, I find something else that I really don't like. Um, I guess at least that helps to motivate me to pedal that bit harder [laughs].

Furthermore, the fact that the gym is socially acceptable would be highly significant for the narcissist. Laura states, "Oh, definitely, I think people are envious of my body and definitely my ability to find the motivation to go back to the gym day after day. Not envious enough to get off their backsides and do it themselves though!" Significantly, the issue of what should be the perfect shape (muscular or slender) for women was expressed by these "addictive" gym consumers and their notions of what is acceptable reflect both political and symbolic bodily discourse:

Sarah: I kind of feel like I burn more calories at the gym and therefore I should go there [instead of running]. But now I keep messing
about with what I'm doing 'cause I'm thinking runners are always
slim, right? So maybe I should be doing more running, and then my
muscles might get a little bit smaller too.

Interviewer: Why do you want your muscles to get smaller?

Sarah: Well, I like them, 'cause at least I don't have bingo wings
[laughs], but I guess I just feel a bit manly. I mean they aren't feminine. I know I'm not massive or anything, but I would like to be a
little more delicate.

Similarly, Laura says:

Yeah, a few people have said to me, "Ooh! You're getting a bit big now, looking a bit strong." But I've heard that if you have more muscles, then you
burn more calories, have a quicker metabolism even [when] you're resting,
so I am getting quite into my weights. It is a worry, though. I want to tone
but I am really careful that I don't let myself get any bigger.

Self-Hatred: Disgust, Dissatisfaction With Self

Sennett (1977) contends that narcissism has more in common with self-
hatred than self-admiration. Indeed, self-hatred (Horney, 1950) comes
through here as a strong driver for some of the women who took part in
the study. According to Sarah:

It's an awful feeling. I hate it. It's almost like I want to be outside of my
body. I am so disgusted with myself and I hate myself, so I want to punish
myself by working even harder in the gym. I don't think that being anything less than way above average is acceptable and therefore it bothers me
immensely when I fall into this state. It doesn't help that I wear very little
in the gym. I wear little shorts and a top and, although I feel much more
comfortable when I'm not showing off my flesh, it's just too hot to wear
anything else. And I hate being hot. Basically, when I'm feeling fat I just
want to get straight out of there and hide. If I could make myself invisible,
then I would.

Sarah goes on to say:

> To be honest, it doesn't really have much to do with the workout itself, but rather how I feel in myself. So if I'm feeling fat, then I often feel very uncomfortable in the gym and I can't wait for the workout to be over.

Both these comments clearly articulate a preference for being invisible and thus immune to any form of gaze as they describe fiercely negative feelings when they are subjected or subject themselves to it. O'Mahoney (2006) argues that image is almost irrelevant to how good one feels about one's body; instead, it rests upon how one feels inside. For instance, Michelle explains:

> Well, it's not about anyone else; it's just about how I feel about me—that's what it's about. Because I have people that go, "Oh, you don't look 40 and, um, you're in really good nick; there's nothing spare on you." But it's meaningless.

DISCUSSION

It is clear that many aspects of these women's gym behaviors can be compared to other concepts explored in consumer research as discussed in the preceding section. However, it is the authors' contention here that narcissism provides the most useful theoretical lens through which to examine this particular form of consumer behavior. Likening gym consumption to Belk, Ger, and Askegaard's (2003) studies on desire provides a greater understanding of women's behavior: a state of enjoyable discomfort (Campbell, 1987), affirming, energizing, and invigorating, yet addictive and destructive. Consistent with the narcissistic personality, Belk et al. (2003) contend that we all desire to desire, readily imagining a better life and certainly a better body. Notably, it is desire's association with hope that allows the desire to be formed and subsequently pursued until fulfilled, displaying parallels with the insatiable, lifelong pursuit of self-creation for the narcissist. Davis and Cowles (1991), among others, identify the issue that may explain obsessive consumption of the gym: namely, the increased pressure for women to look thin and attractive, a thinness that is often at a level unachievable by healthy means.

As a means of self-management, going to the gym offers positive benefits in the form of admiration and approval as opposed to sympathy, disgust, or even pity that is frequently the response to other methods of obtaining and maintaining the "ideal" body, such as dieting, gastric band surgery, or other cosmetic surgery procedures. These negative emotions would appear to be deemed undesirable to the narcissist as they are not in keeping with the "perfect" image. Therefore, the gym becomes the most acceptable and beneficial choice of body management. According to previous research, body alterations represent a lifelong quest for even those women who demonstrate minimal narcissistic tendencies.

For example, Dworkin (1974) calls body alterations continuous and repetitive, vital to the economy, the major substance of male–female differentiation, and the most immediate physical and psychological reality of being a woman. According to Dworkin, the average woman spends vast amounts of money, time, and energy beautifying herself. Therefore, it arguably follows that the "addictive" gym consumer would often spend nearly *all* her time improving herself, dipping into the most depleted of energy sources just to follow her regime rigidly.

In order to obtain the idealized slim body (Garner & Garfinkel, 1980; Horvath, 1979; Wiggins, Wiggins, & Conger, 1968), dieting and exercise have become a national preoccupation (Bordo, 1993). Importantly, some argue that the ideal "fit" body represents a hybrid as it includes the feminine look (in dress) and yet also the feminist image (strong and muscular) (Kenen, 1987). The personal dilemmas of the women as to what their perfect body shapes should be are illustrated in the research. For women, there is said to be a very thin line between achieving the new slender, masculine body ideal that emerged as the result of an increase in women athletes; the gaunt, waiflike figure of a few years previously; and the overtly masculine forms of the female body builders. Hargreaves (1994) notes that this new ideal requires even greater discipline; it is argued that thinness has been exchanged for "tautness and containment" (p. 161), where a smooth line and firm appearance is prized over thinness per se and any wrinkles or saggy areas that might spoil it are to be avoided at all cost.

As discussed, through the gaze of others (increasingly, women) and immersion in desirable images via the media, individuals tend to self-objectify (Davis, Katzman, & Kirsh, 1999). According to the literature, this is particularly salient for the narcissist, who sees himself or herself not only as an object, but also a lifelong project of continuous management and improvement (Lasch, 1979). Women found to report higher levels of self-objectification concurrently reported reduced body satisfaction, body esteem, and self-esteem (Strelan, Mehaffey, & Tiggemann, 2003). Here is another example of the gendered nature of body image (Dworkin, 1974; Hargreaves, 1994) that reinforces the idea that understanding of self and identity within consumer research is fundamentally gendered. Consumer behavior research must acknowledge the underlying gendered nature of self and identity in the lived consumer body—for example, by explicitly examining behavior through the lens of gender.

CONCLUDING COMMENTS

Rather than confirming the extremely negative associations with regard to narcissism, narcissistic-type gym consumption appears to be employed both constructively and positively as a coping mechanism, as illustrated by the experiences of the women who took part in this research. Thus, this study demonstrates support for previous research that shares this notion from a number of perspectives including the narcissistic literature (Lasch, 1979; Sennett, 1977), the sociology of sport literature (Blumenthal, Otoole, & Chang, 1984; Yates, Leehey, & Shisslak, 1983), and the addictive consumption literature (Eccles, 2002). In this instance, the ability to cope stems from a means of forming and presenting an "appropriate" identity that may facilitate an improvement in self-esteem. Accordingly, narcissistic-type gym consumption can be associated with greater positive connotations. It can be used effectively and productively by women to make sense of and control their lives in much the same way that shopping addiction (Eccles, 2002) and retail therapy (Woodruffe, 1997) are used. Indeed, with concern about rising levels of obesity in the United States and the UK in particular, gym "addiction" could be lauded as a positive endeavor and one to be encouraged.

While the continual project of identity construction in terms of the idealized feminine body is well established and prescribed both culturally and politically, it should be noted that there now exists an emerging stream of research into the effect on men of media representations of idealized (male) body images (Aubrey & Taylor, 2009; Pompper, Soto, & Lauren, 2007; Chapter 4 in this volume). Pompper et al. (2007) contend that, while there exists a developing theory of magazines as standard bearers for the ideal woman, this may be modified to suggest that magazines also set standards for the ideal man that their research suggests fuels males' ambivalence toward their bodies.

Aubrey and Taylor's work (2009) investigating the effects of "lad" magazines on male body self-consciousness and appearance anxiety would appear to support this contention. Body image and bodily objectification are held to be gender issues and examination of these emerging streams of research and theoretical developments and, in particular, of the differences (such as may exist) between men's and women's engagement with this mediated bodily discourse and its concomitant effects may well challenge prevailing cultural gender belief systems.

Within this chapter, the authors have argued for a model of consumer behavior in relation to body image that is posited on the understanding that consumers are themselves embodied (Falk, 1994; Turner, 1984) and that identity must occur through the body (Saren, 2007).

In order to research embodied consumers, it is necessary to accept the role of gender as both cultural identity (Butler, 1990; Craik, 1994) and cultural ideology (Thompson & Hirschman, 1995). It is acknowledged that "gender" and "body" are difficult to disentangle as gender theorizing rests to a large degree on social structures that do not account fully for the concept of body in terms of the embodied (and political) nature of gender with regard to women's lived experience. Thus, there have been calls within the social sciences for a concept of the lived female body (Gattrell, 2007; Young, 2005). From the point of view of this research, an alternative perspective necessary to understand consumer behavior and body image and the concept of the lived consumer body is proposed.

This concept of the lived consumer body cannot be examined satisfactorily without acknowledging that bodies are political, symbolic, and both public and private; that the body can be limiting and restricting for women; that it is both a public domain for evaluation (e.g., by the male gaze) and objectification (e.g., media presentation of bodies and body parts) and a private domain for self-objectification, even self-hatred; and that class-bound messages are imbued in appearance. Further research is envisaged in the future in order to examine more closely politically and symbolically embodied/disembodied lived consumer bodies in order more deeply to understand self-concept and identity through the theoretical framework of gender, bodily discourse, and narcissism.

REFERENCES

American Psychiatric Association (APA) (1987). *Diagnostic and Statistical Manual of Mental Disorders*, 3rd ed. Washington, DC. 349–51.

Ashe, Diane D., John Maltby & Lynn E. McCutcheon (2005). Are celebrity-worshippers more prone to narcissism? A brief report. *North American Journal of Psychology*, 7, June-July, 239–246.

Aubrey, Jennifer S., & Laramie D. Taylor (2009). The role of lad magazines in priming men's chronic and temporary appearance-related schemata: An investigation of longitudinal and experimental findings. *Human Communication Research, 35* (January), 28–58.

Bartky, Sandra L. (1988). Foucault, femininity and the modernization of patriarchal power. In Irene Diamond & Lee Quinby (Eds.), *Feminism and Foucault: Reflections on resistance* (pp. 61–86). Boston, MA: Northeastern University Press.

Baumeister, Roy F. (1991). *Meanings of life*. New York: Guilford Press.

Baumeister, Roy F. (1995). Self and identity: An introduction. In Abraham Tesser (Ed.), *Advanced social psychology* (pp. 51–98). New York, NY: McGraw–Hill.

Becker, Howard (1963). *Outsiders: Studies in the sociology of deviance*. New York, NY: Free Press.

Belk, Russell W., Guliz Ger, & Soren Askegaard (2003). The fire of desire: A multisited inquiry into consumer passion. *Journal of Consumer Research, 30* (December), 326–351.

Berger, John (1972): Ways of seeing. London: BBC/Harmondsworth: Penguin.

Berscheid, Ellen, Elaine Hatfield, G. William Walster, & George W. Bohrnstedt (1973). The happy American body: A survey report. *Psychology Today, 7* (November), 119–131.

Birch, Maxine (1998). Re/constructing research narratives: Self and sociological identity in alternative settings. In Rosalind Edwards and Jane Ribbens (eds), *Feminist dilemmas in qualitative research*. USA and London: Sage 171–185.

Bloom, Leslie R., & Petra Munro (1995). Conflicts of selves: Nonunitary subjectivity in women administrators' life history narratives. In J. Amos Hatch & Richard Wisniewski (Eds.), *Life history and narrative*. Washington, DC: Falmer Press.

Blumenthal, James A., Leslie C. Otoole, & Jonathon L. Chang (1984). Is running an analogue of anorexia nervosa? *Journal of the American Medical Association, 252* (July), 520–523.

Blumer, Herbert (1969). *Symbolic interactionism; perspective and method*. New York, NY: Prentice Hall.

Bordo, Susan (1989). The body and the reproduction of feminity: A feminist appropriation of Foucault. In Alison M. Jaggar and Susan Bordo (Eds.), *Gender/body/knowledge: Feminist constructions of being and knowing* (pp. 165–184). New Brunswick, NJ: Rutgers University Press.

Bordo, Susan (1990). Reading the slender body. In Mary Jacobus, Evelyn Fox Keller, & Sally Shuttleworth (Eds.), *Body politics: Women and the discourse of science* (pp. 83–112). New York, NY: Routledge.

Bordo, Susan (1993). *Unbearable weight: Feminism, Western culture, and the body.* Berkley, CA: University of California Press.

Brace-Govan, Jan (2002). Looking at bodywork, women and three physical activities. *Journal of Sport & Social Issues, 26* (November), 403–420.

Brace-Govan, Jan (2004). Weighty matters: control of women's access to physical strength. *The Sociological Review, 52* (November), 503–531.

Brampton, Sally (2006). Is your body messing with your mind? *Easy Living Magazine* (January), 76.

Brislin, Richard W., & Steven A. Lewis (1968). Dating and physical attractiveness: A replication. *Psychological Reports, 22* (June), 976–984.

Butler, Judith (1990). *Gender trouble: Feminism and the subversion of identity.* New York, NY: Routledge.

Campbell, Colin (1987). *The Romantic ethic and the spirit of modern consumerism.* London, England: Blackwell.

Campbell, W. Keith, Jennifer K. Bosson, Thomas W. Goheen, Chad E. Lakey, & Michael H. Kernis (2007). Do narcissists dislike themselves "Deep Down Inside"? *Psychological Science ,18* (March), 227–229.

Capps, Donald (1993). *The depleted self, sin in a narcissistic age.* Minneapolis, MN: Ausberg Fortress.

Chatterjee, Arijit., and Donald Hambrick (2007). It's all about me: narcissistic CEOs and their effects on company strategy and performance. *Administrative Science Quarterly, 52* (September), 351–386.

Coward, Rosalind (1985). *Female desires: How they are bought sought and packaged.* New York, NY: Grove Weidenfeld.

Craik, Jennifer (1994). *The face of fashion: Cultural studies in fashion.* London, England: Routledge.

Csikzentmihalyi, Mihalyi (1988). The flow experience and human psychology. In Mihalyi Csikzentmihalyi & Isabella S. Csikzentmihalyi (Eds.), *Optimal experience* (pp. 3–35). New York, NY: Cambridge University Press.

Cushman, Philip (1990). Why the self is empty. *American Psychologist, 45* (May), 599–611.

Davis, Caroline (2001). Addiction and the eating disorders. *Psychiatric Times, 43*: 59–63.

Davis, Caroline, & Michael Cowles (1991). Body image and exercise: A study of the relationships and comparisons between physically active men and women. *Sex Roles: A Journal of Research, 25* (January), 33–44.

Davis, Caroline, Michelle Dionne, & Barbara Shuster (2001). Physical and psychological correlates of appearance orientation. *Personality and Individual Differences, 30* (January), 21–30.

Davis, Caroline, Debra K. Katzman, & Cynthia Kirsh (1999). Compulsive physical activity in adolescents with anorexia nervosa: A psychobehavioral spiral of pathology. *Journal of Nervous & Mental Disease, 187*, 6 (June), 336–342.

Dewey, John (1922/1983). *Human nature and conduct.* Carbondale, IL: Southern Illinois University Press.

Duke, Lisa (2002). Get real! Cultural relevance and resistance to the mediated feminine ideal. *Psychology & Marketing, 19* (February), 211–233.

Dutton, Kenneth R. (1995). *The perfectible body: The Western ideal of physical development.* London, England: Cassell.

Dworkin, Andrea (1974). *Woman-hating* (pp. 113–114). New York, NY: Dutton (emphasis in the original)

Eccles, Susan M. (2002). The lived experiences of women as addictive consumers. *Journal of Research for Consumers, 4,* 11–23.

Falk, Pasi (1994). *The consuming body.* London, England: Sage Publications

Foucault, Michel (1977). L'oeil du pouvoir. In Michelle Perrot (Ed.), *Le panoptique* (pp. 7–31). Paris, France: Pierre Belfond.

Foucault, Michel (1985). *The history of sexuality: Vol. 2. The use of pleasure.* New York, NY: Random House.

Fredrickson, Barbara L. (1998). What good are positive emotions? *Review of General Psychology,* Vol 2(3), (September), 300–331.

Fredrickson, Barbara L., & Tami-Ann Roberts (1997). Objectification theory: Toward understanding women's lived experiences and mental health risks. *Psychology of Women Quarterly, 21* (July), 173–206.

Frith, Katherine, Shaw Ping, & Hong Cheng (2005). The construction of beauty: A cross-cultural analysis of women's magazine advertising. *Journal of Communication, 55* (March), 56–70.

Fromm, Eric (1964). *The heart of man: Its genius for good and evil.* New York, NY: Harper and Row.

Frueh, Joanna (2001). *Monster/beauty: Building the body of love.* Berkeley, CA: University of California Press.

Garner, David M., & Paul E. Garfinkel (1980). Socio-cultural factors in the development of anorexia nervosa. *Psychological Medicine, 10* (November), 647–656.

Gattrell, Caroline (2007). A fractional commitment? Part-time work and the maternal body. *International Journal of Human Resource Management, 18*(3) 462–475.

Giddens, Anthony (1991). *Modernity and self-identity: Self and society in the late modern age.* Cambridge, UK: Polity Press.

Glaser, Barney G., & Anselm L. Strauss (1967). *The discovery of grounded theory: Strategies for qualitative research.* London, England: Weidenfeld and Nicolson.

Goffman, Erving (1990). *The presentation of self in everyday life.* Harmondsworth, England: Penguin (original work published 1959).

Grosz, Elizabeth A. (1994). *Volatile bodies. Toward a corporeal feminism.* St. Leonards, NSW, Australia: Allen & Unwin.

Guthrie, Sharon R., & Shirley Castelnuovo (1994). The significance of body image in psychosocial development and in embodying feminist perspectives. In Margaret Costa & Sharon Guthrie (Eds.), *Women and sport: Interdisciplinary perspectives* (pp. 307–322). Champaign, IL: Human Kinetics.

Hargreaves, Jennifer (1994). *Sporting females.* London, England: Routledge.

Hatfield, Elaine, & Susan Sprecher (1986). *Mirror, mirror... The importance of looks in everyday life.* Albany, NY: State University of New York Press.

Hirschman, Elizabeth (1992). The consciousness of addiction: Toward a general theory of compulsive consumption, *Journal of Consumer Research, 19* (September), 155–179.

Hopfl, Heather, & Pat Hornby Atkinson (2000). The future of women's careers. In Audrey Collin & Richard Anthony Young (Eds.), *The future of career* (pp. 130–143). Cambridge, England: Cambridge University Press.

Horney, Karen (1950). *Neurosis and human growth.* New York: Norton.

Horvath, Theodore (1979). Correlates of physical beauty in men and women. *Social Behavior and Personality, 7*(2), 145–151.

Jennings, Eugene E. (1971). *Routes to the executive suite.* New York, NY: McGraw–Hill.

Johns, David P., & Jennifer S. Johns (2000). Surveillance, subjectivism and technologies of power, analysis of the discursive practice of high-performance sport. *International Review for the Sociology of Sport, 35* (June), 219–234.

Johnson, Rachel (2006). You lookin' at me? *Easy Living Magazine,* January, 92.

Judge, Timothy A., Jeffery A. LePine, & Bruce L. Rich (2006). Loving yourself abundantly: Relationship of the narcissistic personality to self- and other perceptions of workplace deviance, leadership, and task and contextual performance. *Journal of Applied Psychology, 91* (July) 762–776.

Kenen, Regina H. (1987). Double messages: Double images: Physical fitness, self concepts and women's exercise classes. *Journal of Physical Education, Recreation and Dance, 58* (August), 76–79.

Kernis, Michael H. & Brian M. Goldman (2003). Stability and variability in self concept and self esteem. In Mark R. Leary (Ed.), *Handbook of self and identity,* 106–127. New York, NY: Guilford Press.

King, Granville III (2007). Narcissism and effective crisis management: A review of potential problems and pitfalls. *Journal of Contingencies and Crisis Management, 15* (December), 183–193.

Lasch, Christopher (1979). *The culture of narcissism: American life in an age of diminishing expectations.* New York, NY: Warner Books.

Lasch, Christopher (1980). The culture of narcissism. *Bulletin of The Menninger Clinic, 44* (September), 426–440.

Lowen, Alexander (1983). *Narcissism: Denial of the true self.* New York, NY: Macmillan.

Maccoby, Eleanor E. 1976. Sex Differentiation During Childhood. *Catalog of Selected Documents in Psychology, 6* (August), 97.

Martin, Emily (1987). *The woman in the body: Cultural analysis of reproduction.* Boston, MA: Beacon Press.

McGregor, Ian, Paul R. Nail, Denise C. Marigold, & So-Jin Kang (2005). Defensive pride and consensus: Strength in imaginary numbers. *Journal of Personality and Social Psychology, 89* (December), 978–996.

Mulvey, Laura (1984). Visual pleasure and narrative cinema in *Art after modernism.* Ed. Brian Wallis. New York, 361–373. Reprinted from Screen, Vol. 16(3), (Autumn) 1975, 6–18.

Oliver, Kimberley L. (2001). Images of the body from popular culture: Engaging adolescent girls in critical inquiry. *Sport, Education and Society, 6* (March), 143–164.

O'Mahoney, Ellie (2006). It's Your Body! *Good housekeeping magazine,* (July), 16–26.

Patton, Michael Q. (1990). *Qualitative evaluation and research methods.* London, England: Sage Publications.

Plummer, Olena K., & Young O. Koh (1987). Effect of "aerobics" on self-concepts of college women. *Perceptual and Motor Skills, 65* (August), 271–275.

Pompper, Donnalyn, Jorge Soto, & Piel Lauren (2007). Male body image and magazine standards: Considering dimensions of age and ethnicity. *Journalism & Mass Communication Quarterly, 84* (Autumn), 525.

Roth, Amanda, & Susan Baslow (2004). Femininity, sports, and feminism: Developing a theory of physical liberation. *Journal of Sport and Social Issues, 28* (August), 245–265.

Saren, Michael (2007). To have is to be? A critique of self-creation through consumption. *Marketing Review, 7* (December), 343–354.

Sedikides, Constantine, & Marilynn B. Brewer (2001). *Individual set relational set collective set.* Philadelphia, PA: Psychology Press.

Sennett, Richard (1977). *The fall of public man* (p. 324). New York, NY: Knopf.

Sharp, Joanne P. (1996). Gendering nationhood: A feminist engagement with national identity. In Nancy Duncan (Ed.), *Bodyspace: Destabilizing geographies of gender and sexuality* (pp. 97–108). London, England: Routledge.

Shilling, Chris (1993). *The body and social theory.* London, England: Sage Publications.

Smith, Dorothy (1990). *Texts, facts, and femininity: Exploring the relations of ruling.* London, England: Routledge.

Sparkes, Andrew. C. (1996). The fatal flaw: A narrative of the fragile body-self. *Qualitative Inquiry, 2*, December, 463–294.

Sparkes, Andrew C. (1997). Reflections on the socially constructed physical self. In Kenneth R. Fox (Ed.), *The physical self: From motivation to well-being* (pp. 83–110). Champaign, IL: Human Kinetics Press.

Spitzack, Carole (1990). *Confessing excess: Women and the politics of body reduction.* Albany, NY: State University of New York Press.

Stevens, Lorna, Pauline Maclaren, & Stephen Brown (2003). *Red* time is me time: Advertising, ambivalence, and women's magazines. *Journal of Advertising, 32* (Spring), 35–45.

Strelan, Peter, Sarah J. Mehaffey, & Marika Tiggemann (2003). Self-objectification and esteem in young women: The mediating role of reasons for exercise. *Sex Roles: A Journal of Research, 48* (1/2), 89–95.

Thompson, Craig J., & Elizabeth Hirschman (1995). Understanding the socialized body: A poststructuralist analysis of consumers' self-conceptions, body images and self-care practices. *Journal of Consumer Research, 22* (September), 139–153.

Thompson, Craig J., & Howard R. Pollio, & William B. Locander (1994). The spoken and the unspoken: A hermeneutic approach to understanding the cultural viewpoints that underlie consumers' expressed meanings. *Journal of Consumer Research, 21* (December), 432–453.

Trzesniewski, Kali H., M. Brent Donnellan, & Richard W. Robins (2008). Is "Generation Me" really more narcissistic than previous generations? *Journal of Personality, 76* (August), 903–918.

Turner, Bryan (1984). *The body and society.* Oxford, England: Basil Blackwell.

Twenge, Jean M., & W. Keith Campbell (2009). *The narcissism epidemic: Living in the age of entitlement.* New York, NY: Free Press.

Tyler, Imogen (2000). Reframing pregnant embodiment. In Sara Ahmed, Jane Kilby, Celia Lury, Maureen McNeil, & Beverley Skeggs (Eds.), *Transformations: Thinking through feminism* (pp. 288–301). London, England: Routledge.

Tyler, Imogen (2005). Who put the me in feminism? The sexual politics of narcissism. *Feminist Theory, 6* (April), 25–44.

Vaknin, Sam (2006). *Malignant self love, narcissism revisited.* Prague, Czech Republic: Narcissus Publications.

Vazire, Simine & David C. Funder (2006). Impulsivity and the self-defeating behavior of narcissists. *Personality and Social Psychology Review, 10* (May) 154–165.

Wells, Anne J. (1988). Self-esteem and optimal experience. Optimal experience: Psychological studies of flow in consciousness. In Mihaly Csikszentmihalyi and Isabella S. Csikszentmihalyi (Eds), *Optimal experience: Psychological studies of flow in consciousness*, (pp. 327–341). New York, NY, US: Cambridge University Press.

Whitley, Bernard E., Jr. (2001). Gender role variables and attitudes towards homosexuality—Statistical data included. *Sex Roles: A Journal of Research, 45* (December), 691–721.

Wiggins, Jerry S., Nancy Wiggins, & Judith C. Conger (1968). Correlates of heterosexual somatic preference, *Personal and Social Psychology, 10* (September), 82–90.

Wolf, Naomi (1990). *The beauty myth*. London, England: Vintage.

Woodruffe, Helen R. (1997). Compensatory consumption: Why do women go shopping when they're fed up? and other stories. *Marketing Intelligence and Planning, 15*(7), 325–334.

Woodruffe-Burton, Helen R., & Susan M. Eccles (2005). Be/longings: Consumption and flow. *European Advances in Consumer Research, 7*, 471–476.

Wright, Jan (2000). Bodies, meanings and movement: A comparison of the language of a physical education lesson and a Feldenkrais movement class. *Sport, Education, & Society, 5* (March), 35–51.

Yates, Alayne, Kevin Leehey, & Catherine Shisslak (1983). Running—An analogue of anorexia? *New England Journal of Medicine, 308* (February), 251–255.

Young, Iris M. (2005). *On female body experience: Throwing like a girl and other essays*. Oxford, England: Oxford University Press.

9

Escalated Expectations and Expanded Gender Roles: Women's Gift-Giving Rituals for and Resistance to Valentine's Day Events

Angeline G. Close

INTRODUCTION

"Valentine's Day is far too materialistically driven. I think that the focus needs to be on spending time together, not money on each other!" [female, single]. As this informant strongly feels, Valentine's Day is a marketed holiday event that should be about spending time, not money. Instead, many of the day's events entail a focus on gift-exchange rituals and often lavish evenings or weekends away. Gift-exchange rituals during special occasions and holidays are reflective of the marketplace and gender roles with close tie-ins with contemporary society, culture, and relationships. Holiday events such as Christmas (e.g., Belk, 1987) and Thanksgiving (Wallendorf & Arnould, 1991) offer an important lens to understand consumer behavior. Those studies provide us knowledge of rituals, materialism, and social/ romantic interactions. An important event for personal relationships, retailing, and marketing is Valentine's Day, which is, for one, a consumption context that hosts a vast potential for contributing knowledge on consumer rituals, gift exchange, motivations, and gender roles.

In this chapter, I focus on women's gift exchange—namely, gift-giving— in the romantic context of a holiday event—Valentine's Day. It is an especially valuable context for studying consumption phenomena for several reasons. For one, it is a holiday where gender roles are highlighted along with women's ritual performance, common to many holidays and special events in the United States. For instance, the allure of the white wedding draws many women (and their fiancés) to help direct, plan, stage, and enact a lavish wedding (Otnes & Pleck, 2003). Second, such social exchange rituals are embedded in romantic discourses of dating and marriage—an aspect of consumption that may shape much marketplace behavior and that lends itself to much knowledge seeking. Third, the religious connotation of Valentine's Day is minimized in the modern marketplace. Where other U.S. gift-laden holidays (e.g., Christmas, Easter) may involve a cultural divide between secular and religious themes, Valentine's Day is more neutral. Despite these attributes, this event remains relatively underexplored as a consumption context.

Collectively, U.S. retail sales for Valentine's Day totaled $16.9 billion for 2011 (National Retail Federation, 2011), granting this event substantial economic significance. Based on an ongoing survey of Valentine's Day intentions and practices from the National Retail Federation, a majority (58%) of consumers in the United States plan on celebrating Valentine's Day and spending an average of $116. Gift-giving among love interests remains the prominent market exchange ritual. In 2011, couples spent an average of $69 (of the $116) on gifts for their significant other or spouse. The National Retail Federation's ongoing study of Valentine's Day also provides evidence that U.S. consumers share common gift traditions; these include cards (52%), candy (48%), flowers (34%), jewelry (17%), and clothing (14%). Other traditions are experiential. For instance, many share an evening out (35%). These traditional gifts and experiences are marketed as a social exchange to foster togetherness, love, and romance; however, commercial, economic, and psychological aspects are at work.

Because this day is largely considered a female day in the United States and women are a growing subset of gift-givers (compared to their more traditional role of gift recipients), my chapter focuses on women's gift-exchange rituals. Otnes, Ruth, and Milbourne (1994) contributed insights on male behavior and perceptions of Valentine's Day, and this chapter will serve as a way to illuminate the differences between the genders and the times in these areas. Whereas Ruth, Otnes, and Brunel (1999) focus on the gift recipient's perceptions of the existing relationship, the gift, the ritual context, and emotional reactions converge to impact relationship realignment. Here, I also include a focus on the gift-giving experiences. Further, I seek to expand insights on social exchange theory into the Valentine's Day holiday context by addressing two research questions:

- What are women's defining gender roles and key motivations to participate in gift exchange for Valentine's Day?
- What aspects of the holiday's traditions do women resist and why?

To address these questions, I employ complementary qualitative methods. This chapter is organized as follows. First, I discuss the contextual and conceptual foundations—namely, in the areas of rituals, gifts, materialism, culture, roles, and self-gifts. Then, I provide the methods and data analysis. Next, I present findings to the research questions and deploy these findings to extend social exchange theory in the areas of rituals and gift exchange. Gift exchange is also a social exchange, so social exchange theory is deployed in order to help explain the findings for the two research questions. Finally, I discuss implications for theory and practice, limitations, and avenues for future scholarly research.

CONTEXTUAL AND CONCEPTUAL FOUNDATIONS

Rituals

Valentine's Day is an event laden with rituals. Defined, a ritual is an "expressive, symbolic activity constructed of multiple behaviors that occur in a fixed, episodic sequence, and that tend to be repeated over time" (Rook, 1985, p. 252). Rituals are scripted and performed formally, seriously, and with inner intensity (Rook, 1985). The transformative, symbolic effects of rituals are bracketed from mundane life (Tetreault & Kleine, 1990). Rituals are akin to maintaining and modifying systems of society, knowledge, and nature and are enacted in events marking a change of status such as marriage or a transition through cycles (Tetreault & Kleine, 1990). A ritual coagulates content and structural components of both everyday and extraordinary experiences. Here, I focus on the extraordinary experience that occurs annually in February. Consumers are guided by rituals and tied by cultural ideology, which may be seen in expressions of either praise or discontent.

Each holiday market has distinct rituals—for instance, sharing a turkey dinner on Thanksgiving, gathering around a Christmas tree to exchange gifts, or trick-or-treating on Halloween. On Valentine's Day, rituals are often embedded in sexual or romantic discourse and include card- and gift-giving exchanges that are market prescribed (Close & Zinkhan, 2006). These rituals may be opposed in the marketplace, lending to market resistance (Close & Zinkhan, 2007, 2009). Valentine's Day also serves as a context to develop knowledge on theories of the social component of gift exchange (Belk, 1976; Belk, 1978; Otnes, Lowrey, & Kim, 1993; Sprott, 1997), buyer behavior and purchase intention (Netemeyer, Andrews, & Durvasula, 1993), male behavior (Otnes et al., 1994; Polonsky, Brito, Pinto, & Higgs-Kleyn, 2001), and power (Rugimbana, Donahay, Neal, & Polonsky, 2003). The female mind-set, perceived gender roles, and any related resistance have yet to be fully understood.

Gifts and Obligation, Altruism, Romantic Love

Valentine's Day is embedded in a distinct romantic discourse. Based on interviews with college-aged males in Australia, Polonsky et al. (2001) find three motives that drive gift-giving: obligation, altruism, and romantic love. Interestingly, obligation is the strongest motive and, among young Australian men, even dominates the love-based motivations. The most salient motivation for gift-giving on Valentine's Day is related to the length of the relationship; obligation lessens and altruism and love develop over the course of the relationship (Polonsky et al., 2001).

Gift-giving is an expression of agapic love (Belk & Coon, 1993). Agapic expressiveness is necessary for understanding gift-giving and perhaps for understanding consumer behavior in general (Belk & Coon, 1993). Although most Valentine's Day advertising emphasizes romantic love, there are different types of love. First, romantic love entails affiliation, dependency, physical attraction, exclusiveness, and idealization (Critelli, Myers, & Loos, 1986). However, conjugal love between friends—especially women—may also be a growing part of this holiday. Conjugal love is associated with strong trust, friendship, acceptance, respect, sharing, intimate knowledge, and sacrifice (Critelli et al., 1986).

On the one hand, love can be genuine love, which is an expression of optimal functioning surrounded by intimacy without roles or masks (Fromm, 1956). On the other hand, Valentine's Day may arouse pseudolove—characterized by passiveness and neurotic dependency (e.g., the need to be in a romantic relationship on Valentine's Day). Genuine love is not created or sustained because of externalities (e.g., rituals or market-suggested scripts; Fromm, 1956). That said, genuine love cannot be created or sustained with materialistic gestures.

Culture and Gift-Giving

In some cultures, families, and family-like contexts, reciprocity is discouraged and there is less need to build relationships through gift-giving. For instance, consumer behavior for Valentine's Day in Israel (Dalakas & Shoham, 2010) has strong gender role viewpoints in the country that are at times reinforced through the holiday. A gender-role attitude of egalitarianism (i.e., being equal in gift exchange) could predict gift-giving behaviors; yet social norms about gift-giving may override the impact of egalitarianism attitudes on gift-giving in Israel. Advertisers and marketing managers can gain from creating, nurturing, and marketing ritualistic gift-giving exchanges (Dalakas & Shoham, 2010).

In Asian cultures, family, self-measure, and self-fulfillment are key aspects of gift-giving. Further, reciprocity is not expected and is somewhat discouraged (Joy, 2001). For Valentine's Day in many Asian cultures, the gift-giving is only performed by women (a separate holiday, White Day, reverses the gender roles). Yet, in the United States, Valentine's Day is a female-oriented day, where the woman is generally courted and showered with attention and gifts. Specifically, Japan (see Minowa, Khomenko, & Belk, 2001) has witnessed social changes in gift-giving rituals for this event. Various levels of intimacy in gift relationships manifest via cultural rules such as reciprocity, sentiment, and face (Joy, 2001). This culture is further reinforced by mass media, which depict ads of happy women receiving roses and jewelry.

Roles and Holiday Gift-Giving

Valentine's Day is a holiday that may differ from or reverse the critical female gift-giving and ritual performance responsibility that is common to most other holidays. Overall, while holiday shopping may be a "labor of love" to some, it is widely construed as a part of the female gender role (Fischer & Arnold, 1990, p. 333). For instance, during Christmas, women are more involved than men in shopping and gift-giving rituals; men are likely to be more involved if they hold egalitarian gender-role attitudes (Fischer & Arnold, 1990).

Besides gender roles, other roles influence holiday gift-giving. Using interpretive techniques, Otnes, Lowrey, & Kim (1993) find meaning underlying Christmas shoppers' casting of gift recipients as easy or difficult to shop for. Gift-givers seek to express social roles through the gift exchange. Specifically, there are six key roles that gift-givers express to different recipients: pleaser, provider, compensator, socializer, acknowledger, and avoider. These roles are assumed alone or in combination.

METHODS

I employed complementary qualitative methods in order to acquire a deep understanding of this emotionally charged topic. For an exploratory understanding, I conducted a focus group with six college-aged women. The focus group enabled me to observe social dynamics. In this study, I also focused on women's diaries and on an online analysis. Table 9.1 summarizes the methods, sample sizes, informants, and focus.

TABLE 9.1

Methods

Method (sample size)	Informants	Focus
Focus group (*n* = 6)	College students Females Ages 18–22 In a dating relationship	Exploratory To gain a social perspective
Diaries (*n* = 149)	Males and females Ages 18–47 Various relationship status	Cultural rituals, gender roles, enjoyment factor, retail associations, and comparison to other holidays
Online diaries/postings (*n* = 47)[a]	Posters to e-diaries and boards during Valentine's Day	Naturalistic consumer thought of holiday meaning and materialism

[a] Web posting date documented; sources include diaryland.com, opendiary.com, mydiary.org, diarist. net, mydeardiary.com.

Recruitment and Participants

I recruited informants for the off-line study via newspaper ads in the main newspaper in a midsized southeastern town. In addition, other informants were recruited in one of three undergraduate courses in exchange for extra credit. The online data were collected from various online diary websites and thus no recruitment was involved. Considering each data collection method, informants ranged in age from 18 to 62; however, the vast majority were college aged. In addition, I documented the informant's romantic relationship status. I left romantic relationship status as an open-ended question, and most informants wrote in "single," "dating," "dating exclusively," "married," or "divorced." Most discussed or wrote about a person of the opposite sex and, for privacy reasons, I left it up to the informant to volunteer to specify a homosexual relationship.

Data Collection Procedures

Diaries

During the few days before and after Valentine's Day, 149 informants wrote diary entries. This less intrusive method leads to richer data, and, due to the intimate nature, informants may feel more comfortable writing about their romantically related rituals (or lack thereof) versus discussing them with a researcher. Informants wrote about their attitudes and documented their experiences—both positive and negative—with the holiday. They were asked to include the following topics in their entries: holiday culture, gender roles, commercial aspects, and enjoyment factor.

To gather a sense of whether or not their attitudes and behaviors were specific to Valentine's Day, I then asked informants to write how their attitudes and behaviors concerning this holiday compared to those for other holidays. For this data collection method, the majority of the data was from the student sample, and the age ranged from 18 to 67 (median = 24). A relatively even distribution of men and women (slightly more females) participated; however, the females tended to write more. Because the women are of interest for this chapter, I focus on the women's perceptions.

Online Postings

To reach a broader sample (in terms of age and geography), I collected online diary-type entries or postings on various websites. I searched for e-diary entries or electronic postings on days before, on, and immediately after the holiday (to be consistent with the off-line method). While online posters often do not give their name, they often share a screen name. Their sex, age range, and relationship status are often embedded in their stories, and I report such if this information is available.

This method, especially, provided rich, less censored sentiments and emotionally charged experiences. Importantly, those who share their experiences online do so from their inner desire and passion. Because the focus of this aspect of the data collection was not to study a specific site's online community, this method was not considered a netnography. Rather, the purpose here was to supplement and enrich the off-line method, to add breadth to the sample, and to overcome any social-desirability bias in a more traditional approach.

Analysis and Theme Development

Data were analyzed and interpreted according to the protocol for phenomenology suggested by Moustakas (1994). Moving back and forth between the individual entries and transcripts and the entire set of data, I identified significant meaning statements from the informants' lived experiences. These statements were combined into meaning units (Creswell, 1998) with an accompanying description and identifying quotes to allow for elaboration of each unit. Finally, I developed an interpretive description for each meaning unit as it related to the specific research questions and the overall story of Valentine's Day rituals. I iteratively analyzed the data based on the objectives, theories, and themes identified in the literature. Via axial, open, and selective coding, I grouped similar findings and observations into categories of meaning. This contributed toward revealing emergent patterns (Wolcott, 1990). In the process, new themes became apparent. I reviewed subsequent data interpretations until saturation.

Validity and Reliability

I used suggested approaches (Spiggle, 1994) to ensure validity and reliability. I used multiple methods to depict an overall, holistic understanding of the objectives as suggested by Creswell (1998). I triangulated the data in several ways to gain a full phenomenological understanding (Moustakas, 1994). For instance, I collected data in electronic environments in addition to the off-line environment. I considered multiple theories along with the findings. I bracketed introspective notes. I followed up with informants and presented at seminars, to scholars in multiple disciplines, and executives in related industries for feedback.

―――――――

FINDINGS

I return to the research questions: What are women's defining gender roles and key motivations to participate in gift exchange for Valentine's Day? What aspects of the holiday traditions do women resist and why? In the next section, I discuss how these findings can extend aspects of social exchange theory in the context of gift exchange. Overall, some key findings and themes are shown as they compare to males' perceptions of Valentine's Day from a prior study by Otnes et al. (1994) in Table 9.2. The main themes of interest relating to the research questions are discussed in detail: (1) women's defining gender roles to participate in gift exchange, and (2) women's resisted aspects of gift exchange in the context of Valentine's Day.

Gender Roles and Gift Exchange

Development of Gender Roles

Valentine's Day, like other holidays, is governed by cultural roles (Dalakas & Shoham, 2010), family roles (Green et al., 1983), and gender roles (Fischer & Arnold, 1990) that may motivate behavior during this annual event. Whereas informants reference Super Bowl Sunday as "a man's day," many women discussed Valentine's Day as their day—a female day. Gender roles build from a lifetime of experiences surrounding the holiday. Informants reference childhood as a time that primes their gender role behavior on this holiday:

TABLE 9.2

Key Findings: Male and Female Perceptions of Valentine's Day

Domain	Males' Perception of Valentine's Day[a]	Females' Perception of Valentine's Day[b]
Perceived purpose of holiday event	To show care/affection Obligation Response to a commercial holiday	To show care/affection To be recognized in all roles in their life (as mother, girlfriend, wife) Social exchange To develop closeness and intimacy Commercialization of love and romance
Likeable aspects	Gift receipt (tangible and intangible) Self gifts Sex/intimacy Socializing with other single friends Affective state	Queen for a day Virtual Valentines to other females Continuation of the childlike behaviors of candy and card exchange Opportunity to recognize other females
Disliked aspects	Lack of significant other (i.e., inability to participate) Lack of gift/attention from significant other Pressure of giving Costs of gift-giving	Role exhaustion Pressure of sex Mass marketization Escalating expectations Exclusion
Purpose of gifts/cards	Show caring for significant other Show love/affection Fulfill obligation Altruism Express feelings Function	Show caring for many loved ones (romantic and other) Terminal gift syndrome may result from gift exchange for the sake of it To make up for perceived shortcomings
Reason for nonparticipation	Lack of romantic partner Lack of adequate resources Too commercial a holiday	Exclusion (perceived) Ambivalence Market resistance

[a] Otnes, Ruth, and Milbourne, 1994. *Advances in Consumer Research, 21,* 159–164.

[b] Close, A. G. In print.

> The Valentine's [Day] that I was aiming for yesterday was inspired by being around the Olsen[1] house when I was younger. So, I put up a couple streamers and bought six balloons for the kids. They loved it. We talked about Valentine's Day all day. I did not accomplish everything that I was going for, but I did bake a cake from scratch. I feel like I missed the lover part—I did not do a card and I fell asleep on the couch. I will make up for it in the next couple of days. But, I did cook dinner and he was happy with that. His card to me was precious. I really have some making up to do. [F, married, online]

This woman's gender role for this event is broad—from recognizing the kids with balloons for the holiday, to decorating the home, baking, cooking dinner, and sex. Still, it is interesting that even though she baked a cake (from scratch), she appears to feel guilty about skipping out on the traditional romantic ritual of giving her husband a card and for falling asleep on the couch—perhaps in lieu of giving her husband sex for the event. Despite all that she did do, she still feels like she has to make it up to her husband. Recall that, traditionally, this is the woman's day to be courted. This finding suggests that for some women, there is a perceived obligation to return the favor after being recognized and thanked on this female day. How could these perceived gender roles develop?

During childhood, traditions of cards, candy, and exchanges of affection are often gender neutral and egalitarian; both young boys and girls celebrate the holiday (minus the romantic rituals) and expect to receive recognition from their peers (Close & Zinkhan, 2007, 2009). Note that young children recognize their peers of the same sex and of the opposite sex during traditional childhood valentine exchange. These behaviors learned and rituals established at an early age appear to contribute to the perceived gender roles of girls and women by recognizing both men and women alike. The informant cited earlier feels it is her role to recognize her children. This is in stark contrast to most heterosexual men, who do not traditionally exchange cards or gifts with other men (Close & Zinkhan, 2007, 2009).

Thus, perceived roles change from the boyhood egalitarian Valentine exchange to the perceived roles that many men have for this holiday. Women, however, appear to maintain the gender role of recognizing loved ones, beyond romantic partners, on Valentine's Day regardless of gender. Women receive cards and send small gifts to girlfriends, mothers, grandmothers, sisters, and, to a lesser extent, colleagues and neighbors. These gender-based expectations and behaviors evolve over the course of a lifetime, and roles develop along with the person as she matures into womanhood and motherhood.

Coexisting and Updating Gender Roles

Many women look forward to a day to give and receive special attention. Women perceive that their roles are synergistic with men as they perceive that males have a role to "woo" or romance with gifts and women have the role to reciprocate:

> Males are expected to give their partner gifts and presents because they don't want to get in trouble. This is…because they want to give the gifts or because they love the person. Women love the idea of romance so they usually have high expectations and give good gifts to their partner in return. The idea of the holiday traditions is great—take a day to celebrate your love with the person that you are with. But, unfortunately, this has become the idea that you have to spend a lot of money and give gifts or look like you really don't care about the person. [F, 23, engaged, diary]

Thus, this informant feels the need to give gifts so that it does not appear that she does not care about her boyfriend. She feels the need to spend money to help establish her relationship. She notes the traditional male gift-giver role in the United States, but she and other women still share the role of the gift-giver. While men overwhelmingly spend more for this day (National Retail Federation, 2011), I found over the multiyear inquiry that women are spending significant time, thought, and money for this event. This leads to cocreation and updating of gender roles. For women, these roles are expanding: Women are both princesses and workers for Valentine's Day.

Escalating Lavishness

Due in part to the coexistence of men and women as gift-givers, I find that gifts and their lavishness are escalating among some women who celebrate the holiday. Instead of one person planning and giving, both members of an exchange dyad perceive their role as a giver. As a way for both to give lavishly, some women share extraordinary lavishness that expands

Valentine's Day into "Valentine's Weekend." For example, one newly engaged woman documents her quite lavish weekend:

> My fiancé and I knew that we would not be able to spend much time together on Valentine's Day, so we decided to have a "Valentine's Day weekend." So, on Friday we rented sappy movies and cooked dinner together. Then, on Saturday we went out to dinner. On Sunday, we made some chocolate fondue with fruit. Every day, he gave me a small gift. On Friday, he gave me a gift certificate to go get my nails done. On Saturday, he gave me a candle specially made with a picture of us on it as well as a poem. On Sunday, he gave me a heart-shaped fondue pot (complete with the chocolate fondue and fruit that he served). Then, on Monday, the "real" Valentine's Day, he sent me a dozen red roses to my work. He also came and picked me up from work to take me to a nice lunch. [F, 23, engaged, diary]

In this story, themes of escalating lavishness are apparent as the woman receives a gift or experience each day leading up to Valentine's Day, where she received a dozen roses. It is of note that she is engaged without children, so her gender role is not that of a mother as was the previous informant's. As a fiancé and young woman, she notes her role more exclusively as to be courted with lavishness. Lavishness is expected to escalate within a "Valentine's Day weekend" as the previous informant terms it. Furthermore, some young women who have been in a relatively long-term dating relationship expect lavishness to escalate from year to year. Some women, as indicated in the next quote, perceive that the male's gender role is to plan or create a day that is more lavish each year: "Each Valentine's Day I can't wait to see what fun/exciting thing Terrance has in store for us. We have been together 4.5 years and this will be our 5th V-day. He has outdone himself every year" [F, 23, dating, diary].

The escalating lavishness causes excitement as this woman looks forward to Valentine's Day each year, in part because her boyfriend has outdone himself each of the 4+ years of their courtship. She appears to take on more of a "princess role," as she does not mention what she does for her boyfriend or anyone else. It may be due to her age and lack of other prominent roles (e.g., mother or colleague). While this young woman takes on more of the "princess role" to be courted single-handedly for the event at this stage of her life, other women do not like the gendering of the holiday and how women are catered to. The following single woman believes that the holiday is not supposed to be gendered:

> I don't celebrate Valentine's Day. I realize that it is a holiday and it is meant to
> be celebrated. It was not meant to be gendered, but society has turned it that
> way. If someone opts not to celebrate or doesn't like the holiday, then that
> is their own decision. Women shouldn't be catered to. [F, 21, single, diary]

Because of her belief that Valentine's Day should not be gendered and
that women should not be catered to, she opts out of celebrating the day.
This is especially interesting in light of how marketing and advertising
often position Valentine's Day as the one day that highlights and embraces
femininity and womanhood. As this woman evidences, perhaps not all
women embrace the day because they feel that society has unnecessar-
ily gendered this holiday. While she resists on a gender viewpoint, other
women find that the event fosters closeness and/or intimacy.

Developing Closeness and Intimacy

While men feel the purpose of Valentine's Day is to show care and affection (Otnes et al., 1994), women perceive another of their roles is to
develop closeness or intimacy. Women use gifts, both material and sexual,
to show that they care about the recipient and to foster feelings of intimacy. Further, their gift and the gesture itself are thought to share their
emotions, such as love, in order to create a bond. However, other women
do not expect that the gift itself communicates their feelings, as a married
woman notes:

> I went out to dinner with my husband…again. We also went to a movie.
> We took in some dancing at the restaurant. Most people are set in their
> ways of giving…For some people outside of a steady relationship, it may be
> a gender-neutral holiday. I think that Valentine's Day simply offers a day to
> express love to a special someone. [F, 44, married, diary]

Her gender role for this event is also defined by her role as a wife.
This woman, like others, gives in part to instill closeness but also in
part because her rituals have become habitual. Note that she went out
to dinner "again." In what sounds like a nice gesture and evening out,
her husband has become set in his ways of recognizing the holiday. She
seems to get past the routine and understand that the meaning of the
holiday is to show love and affection. Her gender role is that of a wife

and to enact a romantic evening and share a two-way expression of love. While such gender roles are embraced, other aspects of the holiday lean toward resistance.

Aspects of Women's Resistance to Gift Exchange for Valentine's Day

The second research question focuses more on the dark side (Sherry, McGrath, & Levy 1983)—aspects of women's resistance to gift exchange for the event. I find that more women than one may expect resist some aspects of gift exchange for Valentine's Day. The main themes are exclusion, commercialization of love and romance, materialism, and obligation.

Exclusion

If Valentine's Day is a party, many women, especially singles, feel uninvited or have uninvited themselves intentionally. In turn, some ritualistically give an anticelebration:

> We have had this great anti-VD party every year. This is the sixth one (entitled "666" of course). I have been responsible for the more bizarre decorations. This year, I am skewering a fluffy white VD bear with a sword and spraying it generously with fake blood. What a good time. [F, single, online]

Yet, people in a relationship have been single at some point, and they can remember years when they felt left out. Thus, both single and attached informants resist the exclusion that this holiday brings: "When I am in a relationship, I like Valentine's Day. When I'm not in a relationship, I don't like the holiday because I feel left out. I am the only single in my group" [F, 21, single, diary].

While she feels exclusion because she is the only single girl among her girlfriends, another young woman goes so far as to suggest she may become depressed if she were to be single during the event:

> This year, I like Valentine's Day, mostly because I am attached. I am sure, especially being a girl, that I would not enjoy it as much if I were single. I might even get depressed if I did not have anyone during Valentine's Day." [F, 21, dating, diary]

Both women agree that relationship status influences their experiences. Informants who are in a nontraditional relationship or separated do not feel included to a certain extent, while singles tend to feel the most excluded. This single informant feels excluded, and she creates a time to compare herself to others:

> I hate Valentine's Day! It's that one day of the year that singles out the single. The ones who have someone to be with have nothing to worry about—they just curl up with their loved one and feed each other chocolates. Or, say someone broke up with you on V-Day and you haven't gotten over it. Maybe your true love died and you guys always spent Valentine's together, and you have to spend it alone. Or, maybe you have to watch all the beautiful people going out and having a good time thinking no one will ever love you, or you will never have anyone to cuddle with. It is a horrible holiday if you have no one to be with. Now, more than ever, you are realizing that, because now it's not just that you are alone, it's that you are alone on Valentine's Day! [F, single, online]

This woman then explains her habit of breaking up with each of her boyfriends just before Valentine's Day. Although she does not have to give a gift to someone after a breakup, she does temporarily wish that she was still in the relationship in order to be included in the day. To confound this, she feels excluded from gift exchange rituals. She does not give gifts to her family because she feels that they already have someone to celebrate the holiday with:

> It's been this way for the last 3 years or more. I break up with my boyfriend just a few months before the BIG love day. Then, I sit and wish I had [him] to love or to love me. But I do not, and now I know this for sure! I am alone. Right now my sisters are out with someone they love or just like, at *least* a fling. Even my mom has a boyfriend and I do not! And my twin, she has a boy while I do not! [F, single, online]

As this woman's passionate story illustrates, exclusion is dynamic. At one time, she gave gifts and felt included. However, following her breakups, she felt isolated and excluded with no partner with whom to spend the holiday or with whom to exchange gifts or romance. Following social exchange theory, exclusion (assuming that she does not choose exclusion) is associated with power loss (Skvoretz & Willer, 1993). Even though she initiated the breakup, she may feel powerless as she sits at home wishing she had someone to love on this day.

On the one hand, her exclusion may be gratifying and positive (i.e., if it is self-imposed). Note that she broke up with each of her boyfriends prior to Valentine's Day for the last 3 years. She may willingly want to stay in and avoid the lovers in the marketplace and turn off the TV, radio, Internet sites, and social media pages to suppress the influx of romantic posts and ads that may remind her that she feels romantically isolated. I refer to this exclusion as *internal exclusion* because it is self-imposed and can have some empowering attributes.

On the other hand, exclusion may be a confidence-reducing, negative force (i.e., if it is imposed by external forces). I refer to this as *external exclusion* because the perceived exclusion is imposed by external forces. For example, a woman may want to participate in Valentine's Day events, yet feel excluded because they are for couples. External exclusion may also occur when a service provider books up for the holiday (e.g., denies a couple seating for dinner or a hotel room or denies a woman a spa service). Interestingly, for some resistant consumers, external exclusion could also have positive outcomes (e.g., relief when denied dinner reservations on February 14 because they were going out of guilt). Senses of exclusion are tied into the commercialization of love and romance.

Commercialization of Love and Romance

I find that many women do not feel it necessary to set aside one prescribed day for love and relationships. Instead, they prefer to express their feelings and give or receive on a day of their own choosing. For instance, some women feel that giving gifts and spending excess money for this holiday are unnecessary to maintain a healthy relationship, as this married woman states: "I have never really understood the point of Valentine's Day. I don't think that I dislike it, it just does not really seem like anything special. I think my husband just considers himself lucky (no gifts!)" [F, 38, married, diary].

This woman feels ambivalent about the event. Consumer ambivalence is the "simultaneous or sequential experience of multiple emotional states, as a result of the interaction between internal factors and external objects, people, institutions, and/or cultural phenomena in market-oriented contexts that can have direct and/or indirect ramifications on pre-purchase, purchase, post-purchase attitudes and behavior" (Otnes, Lowrey, &

Shrum, 1997, p. 82). Her ambivalence leads her to opt out of gift exchange because she does not think the market-prescribed event is special. A second motivation to opt out is that she lets her husband off the hook from the traditional male role of gift-giver.

While this particular woman is ambivalent, other women share that they really do like and appreciate the *meaning* of the holiday. However, these women react to the marketplace's suggestions of *when* to show their love. As one woman writes, love or intimacy should not be reserved like a dinner reservation. "Yes, they [traditions] are okay, but I feel that we should demonstrate love all year long, not just on one particular day. It might be done out of compulsion, not motivated from the heart" [F, 33, dating, diary]. She feels that the holiday compulsion compromises sincerity. Likewise, she does not want an external source to dictate when to exhibit affection. However, some women enact the rituals because they assume that their partner enjoys them or because aspects of materialism are enjoyable.

Materialism

Many women feel that the meaning is overshadowed by gifts. Materialism theories provide guidance for understanding gift-giving rituals. Terminal materialism is consumption for the mere sake of consumption (Csikszentmihalyi & Rochberg-Halton, 1981). Extending this concept, I propose the term *terminal gift-giving* to explain the phenomenon where a gift is given for the mere sake of it, with little or no thought to any associated deeper meaning (e.g., love). For instance, one gives a box of chocolates simply because of the perceived need to give a gift. The day is great, but the material aspect is not, according to some women. As one woman feels:

> The idea of the holiday event is great—take a day to celebrate your love with the person that you are with. But, unfortunately, this has become the idea that you have to spend lots of money and give material gifts or it seems like you just don't care. [F, 23, engaged, diary]

Another young woman (coincidentally, also engaged) suggests that retailers should not put such a big focus on Valentine's Day because it places a material focus on the day, making her uncomfortable. She explains:

> Retailers should continue their daily business that is not strictly focused on Valentine's Day so that it (the shopping experience) is not strictly focused on Valentine's Day materialism. Then, people who don't like V-Day don't feel pressured to buy the V-Day products. [F, 22, engaged, diary]

Gift exchange, in some cases, is a means without an end. Many women, especially those in established relationships, agree that time together and shared experiences are more valuable than material gifts (e.g., roses). Yet, still, many women feel obligated to give gifts to their partner for this holiday. Thus, the material exchange is a perceived obligation for some for this event.

Obligation

In addition to giving to show care and instill closeness, women also feel obligated to do so, to an extent. This finding supports past research (Otnes et al., 1994). Informants feel an obligation to their partner, and that it is encouraged via marketing (e.g., in terms of promotional messages that support specific gifts or activities). Yet, women feel financial obligations for more of the nontangible or supplementary items—often including a night out, wine, a card, and babysitting service:

> We feel expected to give our partner gifts and presents because [we] don't want to get in trouble—instead of because [we] want to or because [we] love the person. Women love the idea of romance, so we usually have high expectations to receive gifts as well. Sometimes, we feel the need to give good gifts in return. [F, 23, engaged, diary]

Another woman clarifies her point:

> It just seems like if you are dating someone you just have to do something. It is really just like any other day, just with a card and a title. Just a day to make people show love that usually do not…but you should show love every day. [F, 20, dating, diary]

This woman does not like to have to do things that "you have to do." By acknowledging the day as a normal day "with a card and title," she frees herself from perceived obligations. Instead, she regains power by modifying traditional rituals (e.g., giving a card to her boyfriend on a random day instead of the holiday). Some informants express negative attitudes about traditional gift exchange. Many of these informants are ambivalent about the tradition and are noncompliant with enacting a market-prescribed exchange during a suggested time. However, some modify the tradition, gaining power in the exchange and feeling content and even proud that they resisted obligation.

Obligation is associated with negative attitudes toward marketers and retailers. During this time, informants feel subordinate in the exchange (i.e., less powerful than marketers or retailers). This state may be intensified by the *planned procrastination* common to holiday shopping. I define *planned procrastination* as having a plan to wait until the last moment to perform an action—having intentions to put it off. Some informants plan to wait until the last minute to make a dinner reservation, find a babysitter, or pick up wine and a heart-shaped box of chocolates. Sometimes, waiting until the last minute to fulfill perceived obligations intensifies at the final purchasing moments prior to the holiday. This intensity sparks guilt while retailers' gift stock decreases, and it subsequently leads the consumer to intensified spending. It may be in the retailers' best interests to remind consumers of their upcoming obligations, yet it is in the consumers' best interests to resist the ads if they are prone to plan procrastination or have anxiety. While anxiety and higher expenditures feed the resistance cycle, women often feel obligated to enact their multifaceted roles.

Resistance Behaviors

In Figure 9.1, I clarify women's resistance behaviors across two dimensions: overt versus covert and financially versus nonfinancially motivated. This classification brings up some interesting points. It shows that most women's resistance behaviors are both overt and nonfinancially motivated. Some behaviors have potential financial implications, but the primary motivations are not financial. For these behaviors, resistance is not primarily due to the monetary expenses associated with the holiday. Many informants do not mind spending the money; however, they resist the obligations associated with how they should celebrate the day and when to spend.

Overt resistance behaviors are not secret or disguised. Often, overt resistance includes sharing and spreading resistance attitudes with others. Examples of word-of-mouth resistance include posting to antiholiday websites or relabeling the holiday (e.g., V.D.—otherwise an abbreviation

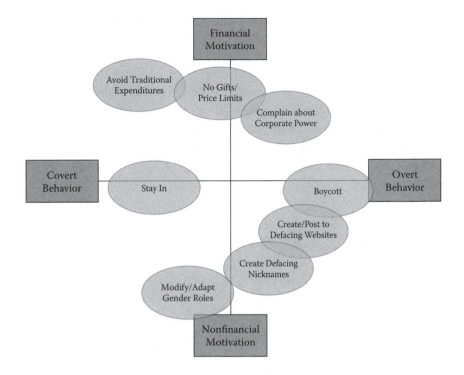

FIGURE 9.1

Females' covert and overt market resistance due to perceived exclusion, commercialization of romance, materialism, and/or obligation.

for venereal disease—or Singles Awareness Day [SAD]) when speaking with others—especially other resistant individuals. Some women are so resistant that they go out of their way to sabotage others' enjoyment. For example, one woman ate the chocolates and pulled apart the roses that were sent to her roommate. She felt empowered (but guilty) about her act of resistance.

Other times, resistance behaviors are covert (e.g., staying in and ignoring the holiday) and may be disguised as apathy or laziness. Some women have tenacious attitudes against traditions, but they quietly choose to ignore the day and surrounding hype. While staying in could be one way to save money, most of the financially motivated, covert behaviors include avoiding giving traditional gifts. While some women enjoy a more simplified version (e.g., cooking at home), they nonetheless find themselves resisting some aspect of prescribed behaviors.

Within the realm of Valentine's Day, a segment of consumers challenge prescribed traditions. Some consumers take direct action to change the way the market traditions are celebrated and practiced. Other consumers resist prepackaged solutions that marketers have developed. Specific situational factors, sociocultural factors, and common conditions influence these evolving behaviors (see Figure 9.1). I find that Valentine's Day arouses strong attitudes from women, which may trigger market resistance. Resistance is a part of larger power struggles among business, culture, and consumers.

CONTRIBUTIONS TO THEORY

Exchange and Social Exchange Theory

Key Exchange Concepts and Assumptions

Exchange theory entails four key concepts, each with assumptions (Molm, 2001). First, exchange entails actors. Exchange actors are individuals or groups. Second, exchange entails resources, or the currency of exchange. When given to the recipient, this exchange resource is termed a cost; when received, it is termed an outcome. Exchange resources are either intangible or tangible and may be gifts (of focus here). A third component of exchange theory is exchange structures—dependent relationships that support the exchange. Last, exchange processes are the interactions necessary to conduct an exchange. They are negotiated or reciprocal, and may lead to an exchange relationship, incurring a series of exchanges among actors (Molm, 2001).

Social Exchange Theory

Rooted in exchange theory, social exchange theory (Emerson, 1976; Thibault & Kelly, 1952) more specifically guides these research questions. Social exchange theory differs from classical microeconomic theories of exchange in that microeconomic theories assume that exchanges take place between strangers, while social exchange theory assumes that longer term relationships are of interest (Molm, 2001). Social exchange theory states that the exchange of social and material resources (e.g., gifts) is a fundamental form of human interaction (Emerson, 1976). Social exchange theory also holds that power relationships guide interaction patterns among people. In turn, any imbalance of power results in efforts to achieve balance in exchange relations (Emerson, 1976). I find this in the example of women giving gifts, even to themselves, on a day on which, traditionally, women are the gift recipients, in order to maintain balance to the gift ritual.

The roots of social exchange expand the assumptions of utilitarian economics to include the cultural and structural aspects of anthropology, behavioral psychology, and sociology (Molm, 2001). An underlying assumption of social exchange theory is that people seek to maximize rewards and minimize costs; they then base the chances of developing a relationship with someone (e.g., the gift recipient) on the perceived possible outcomes (Emerson, 1976). When these outcomes are perceived to be greater, people tend to give more and foster a closer relationship with another person (Thibault & Kelly, 1952). Other assumptions are that people act in their own interests (Thibault & Kelly, 1952) and seek to extract a profit from interactions (Emerson, 1976). This is interesting to consider in the context of love-based relationships that we have seen.

The assumption that people seek profit and avoid loss with each interaction in life is consistent with psychology studies (e.g., Freud) that show that people tend to avoid pain and seek pleasure. In considering social exchange theory from a psychology perspective, people reenact fears or their childhood with each new life situation (e.g., first date after a divorce). Biological desires and the potential for fear are innate from birth and develop (and are developed by) experiences. Specific biological desires include the needs to admire and be admired, have independence, and for power, aggressiveness/revenge, safety, and comfort. Specific biological fears include abandonment/exclusion, attack, and power loss. These fears may bring a tendency for an anxious or fearful person to revert to earlier stages of life (e.g., childhood, singlehood). Despite any temporary reversion, people desire to mature, become a whole adult, and lead a full life—often with a romantic partner. This may explain some of the findings of exclusion.

Gifts as Social Exchange

I find that gifts are largely a social exchange in the context of Valentine's Day. Despite being criticized as a concept outside the Kotlerian sphere of marketing theory (Belk & Coon, 1993; Firat, 1984, Hirschman, 1986), the marketing as an exchange analogy remains the crux of the gifting literature in marketing. People have a fundamental impulse to display, share, and bestow via gift exchange (Malinowski, 1961). Following Weiner (1992), gift exchange is a search of permanence in a social world that is constantly changing. Mauss (1924) views gift-giving as a moral obligation and prototypical contract; however, there is a semiotic significance of gift exchange behaviors (Joy, 2001), especially during holidays or special events.

I consider the findings in light of three perspectives on gift exchange for a holistic understanding. Brought into the context of female's Valentine exchange, I suggest another dimension: *gifting as solidification*. The findings here strongly show that females give gifts to solidify their gender roles in the relationship or family, as well as to solidify the state of their romantic relationship. In other cases, the resistance to giving a gift or partaking in gift exchange is an attempt to solidify the strength of one's relationship or marriage to show that material possession exchange is not needed.

DISCUSSION

Valentine's Day is a holiday and an event that may appear light spirited for females; yet, the emotions revealed online and off-line and consumer behavior decisions for many females in the United States can be quite complex. My multimethod research uncovers themes that contribute to an understanding of female consumer behavior, expanded gender roles, and gift-exchange rituals in the context of Valentine's Day. Extending prior conceptual discussions, findings suggest that females have escalating expectations (from themselves as well as loved ones). Despite this being a day where some women feel that they are a "queen for a day," other females share some less desirable feelings and emotions related to Valentine's Day events. Some, even women happily in a romantic relationship, feel a degree of exclusion on the holiday. Other women feel the holiday is laden with materialism and terminal gift syndrome and obligations, and they have a surprisingly low need for enacting traditional Valentine exchange traditions.

Women perceive a broader gender role that transcends that of just recognizing their romantic interest. Women feel responsibility and obligation to recognize their female loved ones: mothers, sisters, daughters, grandmothers, girlfriends (especially single girlfriends), and even their pets. Women have often been givers—even on this day on which women traditionally receive. The day has broadened for women and there is a shift in the sphere of exchange and consumption from the traditional marketplace to the virtual marketplace and/or the home. Women rely on the Internet and online platforms to discuss their roles and to help carry them out (e.g., via "e-tail" purchases and by sending virtual valentines). Such escalation of the day and related gender roles may lead to market ambivalence or resistance.

Examples of perceived gender roles include the female as giving intimately and as a more active gift-giver to a love interest and beyond on Valentine's Day. For instance, while women spend significantly less money than men on average (National Retail Federation, 2011), they spend time and effort to be sexual and intimate or by physically creating objects (e.g., a virtual valentine or a homemade certificate for a back rub). Many women think through this day, stress over this day, and have anxiety about the holiday's events. Often, women see their role as to overcome mass-commercialized love and romance and find something more meaningful— such as a family bond. In part perhaps to revalue the role of the woman as a sexual being on this holiday, some women convert the holiday from a celebration of sexual intimacy to a celebration of familial love. By realigning gender roles on this holiday and giving more, these women seek more meaning and enjoyment, as expected by social exchange theory.

It is also of note that some women have a desire for revenge—to balance out past suffering or exclusion by allowing others to suffer similarly or be excluded. Most women have felt excluded, lonely, or abandoned on a special day such as Valentine's Day, and perhaps this is one reason for participating in more inclusive (i.e., for those in a romantic relationship) holiday rituals as an adult. In this sense, acting as the dominant person (e.g., gift-giver) in an exchange dyad is a way to instill emotional security and power. Most informants, however, are simply ambivalent to their gender roles for this holiday event.

Ambivalence About Market Traditions

Ambivalence refers to uncertainty, hesitancy, or indecisiveness as to which course or tradition to follow. Resistance entails a feeling of ambivalence, which often includes opposing attitudes that coexist (Arkowitz, 2002).

Interestingly, I find that consumers have opposing attitudes and behaviors that commingle. While their attitudes are often either antitradition (e.g., "boycott the card market!") or protradition ("I welcome the card exchange traditions"), sometimes their behaviors are in opposition to these attitudes. For example, some consumers say they love the holiday and its traditions. However, they make sure to avoid mass-marketed products and the traditional marketplace. Some consumers loathe the holiday and its traditions. Nonetheless, they purchase heart-shaped boxes of chocolate, lingerie, and expensive restaurant meals on February 14. Some informants act on their resistant attitudes. It is a day where many feel that commercialism nullifies sincere romance.

Informants experience opposing attitudes and behaviors during this holiday in other ways. Some consumers dislike aspects of the holiday (e.g., perceived obligation, exclusion, unfulfilled expectations). With respect to cognition, some consumers are not certain about the meaning of the holiday's traditions, or they do not believe in the authenticity of the holiday. As shown previously, some believe that Hallmark invented the holiday for profit-seeking purposes.

Despite their attitudinal resistance, many consumers behaviorally conform to some aspects of the holiday traditions. I offer several explanations why negative attitudes surrounding the holiday traditions often coexist with conforming to these traditions:

- Some women feel strongly that their significant other expects the traditional exchange—namely, sex. They feel that their loved ones will be let down if they do not receive intimacy along with a Hallmark card, chocolates, roses, a night out, and lingerie.
- There may be an underlying insecurity that store-bought, mass-marketed products are superior to any idea or gift that is created by an individual.
- Some women believe that they are alone in their resistance to the traditional exchanges, so they experience considerable pressure to conform—intimately or via market-constructed norms.
- Some women feel that, because more work is involved with resisting traditions, it is easier to give in and buy the traditional items and act out traditional experiences in the marketplace and home.

Overall, this mismatch of attitudes and behaviors creates ambivalence.

That said, power (the power to resist or indulge) is an essential aspect of social exchange theory. Many times, a power imbalance leads the less empowered party to resist. Informants view marketing, retailing, culture, and society as dominant parties during this holiday. This may further perpetuate feelings of ambivalence. Obligation is another source of consumer subordination during this holiday. Recall that many informants purchase and exchange gifts, in part, because their partner (or other dominant powers such as the marketplace) deems it necessary. Perceived obligation may negatively transfer to marketers, advertisers, and retailers who promote and sell such "obliged" gifts. Consumers' feelings of subordination are intense within a short time period. This experience is heightened due to planned procrastinations.

Limitations and Directions for Future Research

Most informants focused on heterosexual relationships. One direction for future research is to examine, in detail, other kinds of relationships. Other limitations include restricted demographic focus. For example, children were not directly included in this study. Thus, they are an important group for future studies on resistance to marketed events and early memories.

My framework serves as a base for scholars to continue making theoretical contributions. I suggest extensions in two areas: cross-cultural and marketing communications. Cross-cultural differences in gender roles are a key difference in the celebration of this holiday across the globe. Thompson and Arsel (2004) explain some American consumers' anticorporate experiences of globalization. On the one hand, traditional American practices (associated with Valentine's Day) are becoming further commercialized and exported. On the other hand, there are movements in some cultures to block the spread of an American-style Valentine's Day. Key questions for scholarly research include

- What is the meaning behind gift exchanges in other cultures?
- What are their gender roles associated with the holiday?
- To what extent are these global consumption rituals adopted or resisted? Why?

Addressing such questions to continue this research can help scholars and theorists understand consumer behavior for special events, such as Valentine's Day, that are market driven and becoming more global. Valentine's Day is a consumption context that hosts a vast potential for contributing knowledge on consumer rituals, gift exchange, motivations, and gender roles, as evidenced by the focus on women in this study.

NOTE

1. Pseudonyms are used throughout for informant anonymity. When available, I note gender, age, and romantic status.

REFERENCES

Arkowitz, Hal (2002). Toward an integrative perspective on resistance to change. *Journal of Clinical Psychology, 58* (February), 219–227.

Belk, Russell W. (1976). It's the thought that counts: A signed digraph analysis of gift-giving., *Journal of Consumer Research, 3* (December), 155–162.

Belk, Russell W. (1987). A child's Christmas in America: Santa Claus as deity. Consumption as religion. *Journal of American Culture, 10* (Spring), 87–100.

Belk, Russell W. (1988). Possessions and the extended self. *Journal of Consumer Research, 15* (September), 139–157.

Belk, Russell W. (2001). Materialism and you. *Journal of Research for Consumers, 1* (May), 17.

Belk, Russell W., and Gregory S. Coon (1993). Gift giving as agapic love: An alternative to the exchange paradigm based on dating experiences. *Journal of Consumer Research, 20* (December), 393–417.

Close, Angeline G., & George M. Zinkhan (2006). A holiday loved and loathed: A consumer perspective of Valentine's Day. In Linda Price & Cornelia Peshman (Eds.), *Advances in consumer research* (Vol. 33; pp. 356–365). Valdosta, GA: Association for Consumer Research.

Close, Angeline G., & George M. Zinkhan (2007). Consumer experiences and market resistance: An extension of resistance theories. In Gavan Fitzimmons & Vicky Morwitz (Eds.) *Advances in consumer research* (Vol. 34; pp. 256–262). Valdosta, GA: Association for Consumer Research.

Close, Angeline G., & George M. Zinkhan (2009). Market resistance and Valentine's Day events. *Journal of Business Research, 62*(2), 200–207.

Creswell, John W. (1998). *Qualitative inquiry and research design: Choosing among five traditions.* London, England: Sage Publications.

Critelli, Joseph W., Emilie J. Myers, & Victor E. Loos (1986). The components of love: Romantic attraction and sex role orientation. *Journal of Personality, 84* (June), 354–371.

Csikszentmihalyi, Mihaly, & Eugene Rochberg-Halton (1981). *The meaning of things: Domestic symbols and the self.* New York, NY: Cambridge University Press.

Dalakas, Vassilis, & Aviv Shoham (2010). Gender-role views and gift-giving behaviors in Israel. *Journal of Consumer Marketing, 27*(4), 381–389.

Emerson, Richard M. (1976). Social exchange theory. *Annual Review of Sociology, 2*, 335–362.

Firat, A. Fuat (1984). Marketing science: Issues concerning the scientific method and the philosophy of science. In Paul F. Anderson & Michael J. Ryan (Eds.), *Scientific method in marketing: AMA winter educators' conference proceedings.* (22–25). Chicago, IL: American Marketing Association.

Fischer, Eileen, & Stephen J. Arnold (1990). More than a labor of love: Gender roles and Christmas gift shopping. *Journal of Consumer Research, 17* (December), 333–345.

Fromm, Elliott (1956). *The art of loving.* New York, NY: Bantam.

Green, Robert T., Jean-Paul Leonardi, Jean-Louis Chandon, Isabella C. M. Cunningham, Bronis Verhage, & Alain Strazzieri (1983). Societal development and family purchasing roles: A cross-national study. *Journal of Consumer Research, 9*(4), 436–442.

Hirschman, Elizabeth C. (1986). Humanistic inquiry in marketing research: Philosophy, method, and criteria. *Journal of Marketing Research, 23* (August), 237–249.

Joy, Annamma (2001). Gift giving in Hong Kong and the continuum of social ties. *Journal of Consumer Research, 28* (September), 239–256.

Malinowski, Bronislaw (1961). *Dynamics of culture change: An inquiry into race relations in Africa.* New Haven, CT: Yale University Press.

Mauss, Marcel (1924). *The gift: The form and reason for exchange in archaic community.* New York, NY: W. W. Norton.

Minowa, Yuko, Olga Khomenko, & Russell W. Belk (2011). Social change and gendered gift-giving rituals: A historical analysis of Valentine's Day in Japan. *Journal of Macromarketing, 31* (March), 44–56.

Molm, Linda D. (2001). *Theories of social exchange and exchange networks.* London, England: Sage Publications.

Moustakas, Clark (1994). *Phenomenological research methods.* Thousand Oaks, CA: Sage Publications.

National Retail Federation (2011). National Retail Federation Valentine's Day consumer intentions and actions survey. http://www.nrf.com/modules.php?name=News&op=viewlive&sp_id=1075

Netemeyer, Richard G., J. Craig Andrews, & Srinivas Durvasula (1993). A comparison of three behavioral intention models: The case of Valentine's Day gift-giving. *Advances in Consumer Research, 20,* 135–141.

Otnes, Cele, Tina M. Lowrey, & Young Chan Kim (1993). Gift selection for easy and difficult recipients: A social roles interpretation. *Journal of Consumer Research, 20* (September), 229–244.

Otnes, Cele, Tina M. Lowrey, & L. J. Shrum (1997). Toward an understanding of consumer ambivalence. *Journal of Consumer Research, 24* (June), 80–93.

Otnes, Cele, & Elizabeth Pleck (2003). *Cinderella dreams: The allure of the lavish wedding.* Berkeley, CA: University of California Press.

Otnes, Cele, Julie A. Ruth, & Constance C. Milbourne (1994). The pleasure and pain of being close: Men's mixed feelings about participation in Valentine's Day Gift Exchange. *Advances in Consumer Research, 21,* 159–164.

Polonsky, Michael, Pedro Quelhas Brito, Jorge Pinto, & Nicola Higgs-Kleyn (2001). Consumer ethics in the European Union: A comparison of northern and southern views. *Journal of Business Ethics, 31* (May), 117–130.

Rook, Dennis (1985). The ritual dimension of consumer behavior. *Journal of Consumer Research, 12* (December), 251–264.

Rugimbana, Robert, Brett Donahay, Christopher Neal, & Michael J. Polonsky (2003). The role of social power relations in gift giving on Valentine's Day. *Journal of Consumer Behavior, 3* (September), 63–73.

Ruth, Julie A., Cele C. Otnes, & Frederic F. Brunel (1999). Gift receipt and the reformulation of interpersonal relationships. *Journal of Consumer Research, 25* (March), 385–402.

Sherry, John F., Mary Ann McGrath, & Sidney J. Levy (1993). The dark side of the gift. *Journal of Business Research, 28* (November), 225–244.

Skvoretz, John, & David Willer (1993). Exclusion and power: A test of four theories of power in exchange networks. *American Sociological Review, 58* (December), 801–818.

Spiggle, Susan (1994). Analysis and interpretation of qualitative data in consumer research. *Journal of Consumer Research, 21* (December), 491–503.

Sprott, David E. (1997). Gift giving: A research anthology. *Journal of Marketing Research, 34* (November), 541–542.

Tetreault, Mary A. Stanfield, & Robert E. Kleine, III (1990). Ritual, ritualized behavior, and habit: Refinements and extensions of the consumption ritual construct. *Advances in Consumer Research, 17,* 31–38.

Thibault, John W., & Harold H. Kelley (1952). *The social psychology of groups.* New York, NY: John Wiley & Sons.

Thompson, Craig, & Zeynep Arsel (2004). The Starbucks brandscape and consumers' (anticorporate) experiences of globalization. *Journal of Consumer Research, 31* (December), 631–642.

Wallendorf, Melanie, & Eric Arnould (1991). "We gather together": Consumption rituals of Thanksgiving Day. *Journal of Consumer Research, 18* (March), 13–31.

Weiner, Annette B. (1992). *Inalienable possessions: The paradox of keeping-while-giving.* Berkeley, CA: University of California Press.

Wolcott, Harry F. (1990). *Writing up qualitative research.* Newbury Park, CA: Sage Publications.

Section IV

Masculine Discourses

10

Masculinity and Fashion

Jacob Ostberg

INTRODUCTION

Wearing the right socks used to be easy—at least for the average Joe in the Western world during the last couple of decades. The selection of socks was essentially a nonissue. This was not always the case: Throughout history the male fashion dictates surrounding socks have varied considerably. Just consider the sixteenth century, when brightly colored hose were in vogue to emphasize the sexiness of the male leg (Laver, 1995) or the end of the 1940s when "fancy hose" accounted for 60% of all men's sock purchases (Flusser, 2002). But from the 1950s onward, "the synthetic one-size-fits-all sock engaged the practical side of the American man's brain, and soon everyone's *plat du jour* was a choice between black, navy, and brown stretch socks" (Flusser, 2002, p. 181).

American men were not the only ones faced with the monochrome sock selection because stores across the Western world offered little else than a range of ankle socks in subdued colors, from dark gray to black, and the only choices to be made had to do with finding the correct size and the appropriate quality. Tricky enough, for sure, but still relatively easy compared to the cacophony of colors, models, and materials available in the women's section. Things became slightly more complicated when white sport socks were introduced. All of a sudden these nice, comfortable socks were available at a good price but still, according to the style police, one was not supposed to wear them at any occasion.

This is when things started to get complicated, but also interesting. The white-sport-sock/subdued-color-formal-sock duality opened up a simplistic space for playing games of distinction. The dichotomous sock universe became a safe playground for men wanting to show their distinction. "Everyone" with the slightest interest in sartorial matters—that is, matters relating to clothes, especially the finer types of tailored clothes—knew that wearing white sport socks with a suit or formal slacks was in bad taste. Pointing fingers to the ones who did was an easy way for men to bond over their common sartorial *fingerspitzengefühl*. Mythical figures—such as men wearing white sport socks with sandals—representing archetypal bad taste were also invented to reinforce this simple sartorial principle. The traditional heuristic was thus the following: dark socks = good; white socks = bad.

Nothing lasts forever, however, and even this beautiful, simple world of unambiguous sock categories had to come to an end. As so often is the case in sartorial matters, it appears, when something takes on the character of dogma, merely following conventions holds little meaning. Basic semiotic theory informs us that meaning is created by difference (see, for example, Hall, 1997), and in their quest to create meaning, men aspiring to stand out started to challenge the convention of dark and white socks. Quite simply, they started to behave differently. When "the new man" saw the light of day in the 1980s (Mort, 1996), the simple dichotomous world of socks started to vanish.

These tendencies became even more accentuated around the turn of the century as the so-called metrosexual man made his way into the public consciousness (Simpson, 2002). Suddenly even Average Joes were supposed to be comfortable playing around with colors, thus supposedly connecting with their feminine side (yes, this is indeed a problematic notion; I return to it later). As time moved on, merely choosing dark socks to stick to conventions was no longer a sign of refinement, but a sign of insecurity. Sophistication had turned to anxiousness in a heartbeat. The new man-influenced heuristic that substituted for the old one looked something like this: dark socks = boring; colored socks = fresh; white socks = not even on the map.

At this time, men started playing around with colored socks and the creativity of matching was abundant. Initially, suggestions for the insecure ranged from picking up on colors that were otherwise represented in the clothes, such as this advice from a style guide book: "If colored socks make you insecure you should quite simply stick to the monochromatic. Otherwise one adjusts the socks' dominant color to the color of the t-shirt, the shirt or the pullover" (Engel, 2004, p. 79). But soon the advice turned bolder and bolder. One of Sweden's most popular fashion bloggers even suggested that one could (and perhaps should—style advice has a way of working like that) match one's socks with the color of one's bike (Enckell, May 11, 2009). Everyone was indeed going bananas. A veritable sock anarchy was in place; anything but white or dark socks was fine and the only rule to follow was to follow no rules.

Again, by the simple semiotic process of differentiation, wearing wildly colored socks suddenly became a less meaningful activity. Because style and fashion is a game of distinctions, those aspiring to carve out their own stylistic niche had to come up with something new. Perhaps the time was ripe for the renaissance of the white sock? Well, there was still a great deal of hesitancy as illustrated by the reaction to influential fashion blogger Scott Schuman's (aka the sartorialist) blog post (http://thesartorialist. blogspot.com, March 11, 2009). It featured a picture of a stylish gentleman in his late 50s to early 60s sitting at a café table in Paris looking dapper in a dark suit, light blue shirt, dark bow tie, and—here is the big surprise—casual footwear influenced by tennis shoes and WHITE SOCKS. The sartorially inclined readers of the blog reacted the way they had been trained: white socks = bad taste. The commentator field was rapidly filled with statements about this man not possibly being stylish because he was wearing white socks. The fact that he was wearing tennis shoes with his dark suit seemed less problematic; the socks caught the attention.

A bold few, however, had spotted this possibility to carve out a unique identity space by advocating or using white socks. An example occurred when an influential fashion blogger in Stockholm (Herrbloggen, February 28, 2008) posted an old picture taken in 1946 featuring Robert F. Kennedy and a group of his Harvard friends sitting on a set of stairs casually sporting grey flannel suits, black leather shoes, and beautiful, thick, white sport socks. The blogger made a snide remark about all the people out there being afraid to wear white socks. According to the blogger, shying away from white socks was a sign of insecurity because men of real confidence can handle the white sock—that is, the new white sock, not any old sport sock. Sure enough, it was not long before one of the more influential Stockholm socialites was photographed at a restaurant sporting—what else—a nice pair of thick, white sport socks (Stureplan.se, May 12, 2008).

We see here a sudden shift in the semiotic landscape of socks. Wearing white sport socks starts having the same connotations that colored socks used to have: that is, breaking conventions and signaling that the wearer is a man with panache. Sure enough, the mainstream publications followed suit and declared colored socks to be so-last-year. For example, *King,* Sweden's largest men's fashion magazine, placed colored socks on its list of the 10 worst fashion faux pas in the spring of 2009. What we witness here is a veritable sock semiotic meltdown: The new white socks are the new colored socks; the dark socks are also the new colored socks; the colored socks are the new (old) white socks; the old white socks are still the old white socks.

So why should we care about socks, you might rightfully ask? The sock example is intended to introduce the types of discourses and the underlying status games that are constantly at play in the area of masculinity and fashion. While socks might seem trivial, verging on the silly, they offer the potential to illustrate how the norms of male fashion are socially and culturally constructed. The sock example, on a very basic level, illustrates how the available choices at each point in time and in each location present themselves as self-evident. Our freedom to choose is thus always circumscribed by the available discourses of how to consume (Murray, 2002; Thompson & Haytko, 1997). The sock example illustrates how these discourses are made available and negotiated in the public sphere.

One of the purposes of this chapter is to look at the discursive strategies utilized by the traditional elite to strengthen their sense of masculinity in light of a new and allegedly feminized mainstream consumption ethos. The way that changing gender ideologies in our consumer society ripple through the social classes and affect the groups that, according to their own mythology, are not easily influenced by consumer fads and fashions is thereby put in focus. Throughout this chapter, I will suggest that seemingly trivial activities, such as discussions of sock color, are micropolitical acts that reinforce power structures and make class and status positions visible.

I first introduce some historical and theoretical starting points to the discussion of masculinity and fashion. I then provide a discussion of relevant studies concerning masculinity and fashion within the marketing field. Next, I provide an empirical illustration of masculinity and fashion wherein I use the sock example, as well as complementary material, to show how consumers, the market system, and popular culture negotiate over fashion meanings and constantly create borders that delineate acceptable behaviors from unacceptable ones.

LITERATURE REVIEW: A BRIEF
INTRODUCTION TO MEN'S FASHION

Although sartorial customs have changed over time in Europe and elsewhere, such as the imperial courts of China and Japan, fashion as we understand it can hardly be said to have existed prior to the beginnings of mercantile capitalism in medieval Europe (Wilson, 1985/2003). It was then, during the court life in the fourteenth century, that changes in dress started showing the dynamics and the speed of change necessary to talk about fashion. At that time, clothing styles became much more elaborated and the silhouettes changed from various body parts being displayed in tightly fitting garments to others being exaggerated through creative use of fabric and other materials. Both men and women were equally engaged in following fashion, as can easily be noted for those visiting an art museum displaying historical portraits where changes in styles can be noted almost from decade to decade (for an overview of historical changes in dress, see Laver, 1995).

At first, fashion changed slowly—perhaps slowly enough for the people not to notice that they were doing anything other than dressing the only way available to them. The faster paces of change—change that was fast enough for garments that were not worn out to be disposed of—came about during the eighteenth century in what Campbell (2007, p. 23) calls "the modern Western fashion pattern." This had to do with the developments of modernity at the time of the industrial revolution, a time characterized by such phenomena as mass production, rapid transport systems, and greater mobility. Together with the birth of mass media, these led to a speeding up of life and experience, the early signs of democracy, the rise of an organized industrial proletariat and the bourgeoisie, and changes in the relationships between men and women (Wilson, 1985/2003). Due to these large shifts in how societies were organized, individuals came in contact with people, ideas, and styles that would never have crossed their paths of life before.

These developments eventually led to the questioning of the taken-for-granted nature of things, of whether it was indeed possible to change one's life course through hard work and, not to be forgotten, particular detail to sartorial matters. Whereas the earliest fashion behaviors largely concerned court life across Europe, subsequently an increasing number of

strata in society came to engage with and be affected by fashion developments. Toward the end of the nineteenth century, virtually all classes in
society were, to varying degrees, involved in fashion. When fashion thus
spread across the social classes and when class and wealth no longer necessarily coincided, it became increasingly hard to figure out where in the
stratified society a particular individual belonged.

When the first traces of changes in fashion started appearing, during
the Middle Ages, they created anxieties among the royalty and the aristocracy, who were afraid that people would dress above their social standing. To offset this tension, the higher strata in society installed so-called
sumptuary laws that forbade the common people from wearing certain
garments and colors and put limitations on the number of buttons, the
amount of fabric or the type of fabric that was allowed (Laver, 1995).

These laws thus created a cat-and-mouse game where the elite tried to.
stay ahead of the common man—a game that we can still detect today,
as I illustrate later in this chapter. During periods of time, exceptionally
complicated sumptuary laws trying to control those who found loopholes
and managed to display wealth and success in ways threatening to those
in power were in place. For example, the fashion of slashing (i.e., having
slashes in the outer fabric of a garment so that the lining becomes visible) during the Elizabethan era is sometimes attributed to rich merchants
wanting to display colors that were not permitted for their outer garments.

The Emergence of Modern Men's Fashion

Today, when we enter a clothing store—unless it is a very progressive or
even avant-garde store—the most fundamental distinction is that between
the men's and the women's sections. The division of clothes into gendered
categories presents itself as natural to us. As an example, the iconic signs
for male and female public lavatories feature the symbol of a skirt as the
metonym for women and a bifurcated garment as the metonym for men
(cf. Entwistle, 2000, p. 141). This distinction is, as Wilson (1985/2003) contends, not at all the most fundamental distinction in dress, although today
we many times take it for granted.

From a historical perspective, for example, the distinction between the
draped and the sewn is far more fundamental (Wilson, 1985/2003, p. 17).
It was, in fact, not until the eighteenth century that gender difference in
dress began to be of overriding importance. The practice of wearing suits

started to develop during this time out of the everyday dress of the land-owning aristocracy and gentry. Their everyday riding clothes of woolen cloth in quiet colors slowly evolved into the conventional day dress of the modern urban man. Thitherto men of means had dressed themselves in more extravagant cloth such as brocade, lace, and velvet. When men thus started to wear the early predecessors of the modern suit, it was a fundamental change in male apparel—a change many times described as the "great masculine renunciation" (McNeil & Karaminas, 2009). This term implies that from this day (i.e., the decades following the French Revolution), men gave up all pretensions to beauty and dressed for function alone.

This is not true, however, as aptly described by Wilson (1985/2003, p. 29), who suggests that this "cliché of fashion history obscures a more complex reality." But the myth of the great masculine renunciation persists among dress historians and as a folk theory of how men "naturally" dress. Ever since the 1930s, when dress historian Flügel launched the term, there have been repeated attempts to overturn this supposed aesthetic hegemony (Bourke, 1996). A more moderate view of the developments of men's fashions suggests that men now display beauty in a rather different way, emphasizing fit and cut rather than more ostentatious displays. As the very rich literature on the historical but increasingly mythical figure of "the dandy" has shown (e.g., Baudelaire, 1863/2010; Walden, 2002), the move toward more formalized and monochrome stylistic expressions in no way excluded the expressions of both sexual and other distinctions.

The New Man?

Recently, it has been proposed that we see a "new hegemonic masculinity" (Patterson & Elliott, 2002, p. 241) that includes a feminization of masculinity and invites men from all social positions to partake in the carnival of consumption in ways previously reserved predominantly for female consumers (Edwards, 2009; Schroeder & Zwick, 2004). One of the consequences of this change in mainstream masculinity is that the traditional elite is challenged in its role as tastemaker *par excellence* (cf. Bourdieu, 1984; Osgerby, 2001). The advent of popular-culture outlets for new gender ideologies—a trend that got off to a mainstream start with the TV show *Queer Eye for the Straight Guy*, self-help books such as *The Metrosexual Guide to Style,* and the abundant availability of men's lifestyle magazines and, increasingly, web-based blogs—makes the cultural capital previously reserved for the higher social classes available to the masses.

Consequently, the legacy of the traditional elite is challenged. Style is always about making distinctions, about defining whether certain consumption objects and consumption practices should be deemed stylish or not. There is nothing natural about these distinctions; they are socioculturally constituted constructions that tend to reify a particular status system (Baudrillard, 1996). Hence, the groups who claim the right to define these categories are in a position of power. When the consumption codes of men from social groups that have historically paid particular attention to appearance have become popularized—and, according to their own judgments, indeed, vulgarized—the power struggle over definitions of what is stylish comes into strong relief.

Past research shows that consumption practices play a dominant role in constructing, maintaining, and making comprehensible human identity, including gender identity (Bourdieu, 2001; Miller, 1987). Most gender research in the consumer research field, however, focuses largely on feminist issues. Over the years, many studies have investigated the impact of consumerism on women and femininity, leaving men's experiences with consumption and consumerism relatively unexplored (Swiencicki, 1998). While mainstream consumer research is criticized for taking an implicit masculine starting point (Bristor & Fischer, 1993), less attention is directed at how masculinity actually gets produced in everyday life. Notable exceptions are a few studies that profile male consumers and discuss how traditional masculinities are expressed and reproduced through consumption (Belk & Costa, 1998; Holt & Thompson, 2004; Schouten & McAlexander, 1995).

In recent years, a few studies have started to focus on how masculine identities are forged in the marketplace, a traditionally feminized arena for identity construction. In their study of male shoppers, Otnes and McGrath (2001) investigate male consumers' motivations, while Kates (2002) reports on how gay men's consumption differentiates them from "vulgar" heterosexual men. Researchers also investigate how heterosexual urban male shoppers of fashion and grooming goods use various strategies to refine their conceptualizations of heterosexual masculinity (Tuncay & Otnes, 2008). Patterson and Elliott (2002) study how the increasing visualization of male bodies in advertising and the media makes the negotiation and renegotiation of male identities all the more possible, and they suggest that the male gaze has been inverted.

Schroeder and Zwick (2004) question this position. They suggest instead an expansion of the male gaze and analysis of the male body as a discursive "effect" created at the intersection of consumption and several marketing discourses such as advertising, market segmentation, and visual communication. Ostberg (2010) follows up on their work and illustrates how in subtle and not so subtle ways, advertising, media, and popular culture coconstruct a taken-for-granted view of phallic masculinity. He argues that males are caught in a discursive cross fire, potentially made to feel anxious about their anxiousness and embarrassed about their embarrassment. While insightful, these studies do not articulate how gender identities are created or how they are enacted through consumption.

Holt and Thompson (2004) address this topic more directly and discuss how men construct their masculinity through everyday consumption. They situate American working-class men as caught in a struggle between two traditional roles: the breadwinner and the rebel. This dialectical tension is resolved by the emergence of a new type of masculinity entitled "the man-of-action hero." This figure handles the potential lack of manliness in, for example, household chores, by recasting them as masculine power games. A real man, for example, does not just take out the trash. Instead, he invents a system so that he can take out the trash in a super-efficient manner and be the best trash handler in the neighborhood. Such introductions of competitiveness symbolically transform stereotypical female activities into masculine endeavors.

The tension between the rebel and the breadwinner is not, however, the only tension putting stress on the modern man. Another important but not well-theorized tension resides between the more traditionally masculine consumer roles that focus on rationality and usability and the more feminized consumer roles that focus on appearance. Contemporary male consumers, especially in the younger age groups, must negotiate these seemingly contradictory roles in their everyday consumption to construct an appropriately suave male consumer identity. Tuncay (2005) theorizes that contemporary heterosexual male consumers need to find a balance between conforming to gender roles while still expressing individuality and between caring too much about appearance (and thus running the risk of appearing homosexual) and expressing sufficient levels of heterosexuality.

Rinallo (2007) puts forth a similar argument and shows that between the polar opposites of effeminacy and sloppiness, there is a "safe zone" where heterosexual men can safely experiment with consumption activities and objects. On either side of this "safe zone" lies a "danger zone." If a man shows no care of self, he will suffer negative social consequences, and if a man is too careful with his appearance, he will be viewed as effeminate.

This insecurity among male consumers is connected to an increasingly popular conception that something has happened to the traditional masculine consumer role. The last couple of decades we have repeatedly heard rallying cries about some "new masculinity" overtaking some older, primitive, or perhaps even natural masculinity (Edwards, 2009). This discussion has been especially true in the realms of clothing and fashion. In the 1980s, men's lifestyle magazines wrote about and companies tried to sell products and services to the "new man" (Mort, 1996). This creature was subsequently shuffled off the stage by the "new lad" in the 1990s (MacKinnon, 2003), only to be replaced, quickly but forcefully, by the so-called metrosexual in the first years of the new millennium (Simpson, 2002).

One should be careful, however, to take the outcries about new masculinities at face value and think that there has been some substantial change to masculinity in the last couple of decades that is qualitatively different from previous changes. Rather, it is more feasible to regard these new conceptualizations as coproductions of a media and marketing system in which there is constant pressure to define new target groups in order to sell both advertising space and new products (Mort, 2009). After all, the idea that something allegedly new constantly has to overtake something allegedly old lies at the heart of the contemporary fashion marketing system (Kawamura, 2005).

The last wave of "new masculinity" to hit the stage was the metrosexual, a concoction of journalist Mark Simpson and the market research agency Euro RSCG (see Rinallo, 2007, for a good description of the birth of the metrosexual). While the metrosexual might not be as radically new as the hype suggested, one peculiarity sets the metrosexual movement apart from other changes. Consumers became reflexively aware of this marketized way of "being a man" and masses of people (including Arnold Schwarzenegger [Dowd, 2003] and the entire cast of *South Park* [season 7, episode 8]) wanted to self-assign to this new, popular, and apparently attractive market segment. As pointed out by Cova, Kozinets, and Shankar (2007), consumers are not naïve about living in a commercialized world where marketers place them in segments in order to market lifestyle products and brands to them; instead

> ...like Madonna, they are commercial-material boys and girls. They know the game plan; they read the playbooks; they know the strategy. Conscious of a partial manipulation, they decide to what extent they will be manipulated and they manipulate too. (p. 8)

The metrosexual should thus be regarded more as a special case of market reflexivity than a substantially new way of being a man. Regardless of this distinction, the explicit market reflexivity among groups of consumers that did not previously pay careful attention to their appearance has altered the power relations among those competing to define what is stylish and fashionable and what is not.

EMPIRICAL CASE: SPEAKING OF SOCKS

I will now return to the sock example in the introduction and use various types of data to discuss how men's style and fashion are negotiated in consumer society. Discussing a particular location of data collection is tricky in today's consumer culture, which is characterized by global interlinkages where the local constantly intersects with the global. Consumers inevitably are exposed to media, as well as people, from various parts of the world. Clothing and fashion are played out in a local setting, where people meet each other and see what they wear, react to it, and use it for classifications. But this all happens against a global backdrop, where global style authorities, such as those readily available on the Internet, set the standard.

The study accounted for in this chapter takes Stockholm, the capital of Sweden, as its departure but then follows the various style authorities that are recurrently referenced. For example, the Swedish fashion bloggers recurrently refer to the main global fashion magazines, blogs, and books and do not constrain themselves to the particular geographic locality. Stockholm is a particular location to study men's fashion for a number of reasons. First, Sweden and Stockholm in particular have managed to produce a number of clothing brands in the last few years—such as

ACNE, Cheap Monday, Fifth Avenue Shoe Repair, Filippa K, Hope, and Whyred—that have made it onto the international market, prompting the Swedes to talk about "the Swedish fashion wonder" (Falk, 2011).

This attribution is perhaps slightly blown out of proportion; however, the fact that these Swedish brands have made it onto the international fashion scene—being represented at hotspots such as Colette in Paris and Opening Ceremony in Los Angeles—gives the Stockholm fashionistas a heightened confidence. This visibility is further valorized with the mention of Stockholm on influential blogger Scott Schuman's list of cities that he recurrently visits and whose styles he hails: "One of the reasons I keep going back to Stockholm is because they are very good at taking classic shapes and shrinking, stretching, or pulling them into a new play on proportion" (The Sartorialist, March 17, 2009). This notation might indeed seem trivial, but fashion is a game of confidence and these types of affirmations do seem to play a large role. The end result is that the Stockholm fashion crowd is convinced that Stockholm has a unique sense of fashion and style that is surmounted by only the hippest of the hip.

One group that has to grapple with Stockholm's newly won status as a fashion center is those aspiring to be connected to the traditional elite in Sweden. The members of the aristocracy or traditional elite traditionally express their masculine identities through knowledge of sartorial types and practices of refined consumption and thus set themselves apart from the masses by appearing to be more inherently stylish. Now that fashion has become a pastime for the masses and sartorial codes are made available to anyone willing to listen, the traditional elite must partake even more actively in the game of distinctions.

The term *traditional elite* that I use in this chapter merits a brief comment due to the particularities of the Swedish class system. Swedish politics across the range of (moderate) left to (moderate) right have shared the goal over the last century to create a society characterized by relative economic equality. The result is that differences in economic capital between different groups are rather small and that self-understanding in Sweden is that there are no classes. While large differences in cultural and social capital still exist—for example, there is still a book of noble families even though they no longer have special privileges—the belief in possible movement between different social positions is strong (Ostberg, 2007; Western & Wright, 1994). Hence, groups try to connect themselves to the traditional elite even though they might not have any historical ties.

For the purpose of this chapter it is beside the point whether they are indeed old aristocrats. The interesting issue is that there is a rather large group in Stockholm that affiliates itself with some sort of faux aristocracy, claiming lineage to the old aristocratic families. Throughout this chapter, I will refer to this group as the traditional elite even though it should be forcefully stated that the link it holds to the aristocracy or traditional elite is far from a given.

METHOD

In order to illustrate how the fashion distinctions are socially and culturally constructed, I employ the methodological procedures of discourse analysis (Elliott, 1996). Discourse is seen here as a system of statements that constructs an object, supports institutions, reproduces power relations, and has ideological effects (Parker, 1990). Language is thus the site where the social world is constructed, replete with contradiction, paradox, and contest. In the field of marketing and consumer research, discourse analysis is used to show how texts—such as guide books, advertising, and material from consumer groups—offer ideal interpretive positions and how authoritarian voices in society (i.e., the ones whose discourses get noticed and thus reproduced) privilege and marginalize various modes of understanding (e.g., Caruana, Crane, & Fitchett 2008; Fischer, 2000; Ostberg, 2010; Thompson, 2004).

In conducting the analysis, I use a number of different types of texts where normative discourses of style and fashion are produced and negotiated: fashion or style blogs including comments to the blog posts, self-help style guides, magazines, and online and print advertising. These sources are neither coherent nor exhaustive. There are plenty of other potential sources, such as films, TV series, and novels, where normative accounts about the issue occur. My goal was not to produce an exhaustive account of all the instances where style or fashion discourses get produced and negotiated. Rather, as suggested by Elliott (1996, p. 66), I sought to find variations in linguistic patterning. The material I analyze in this chapter thus should not be viewed as a sample trying to represent a larger source of material accurately. Rather, the material is typical, illuminating, and deemed noteworthy, important, and interesting (cf. Schroeder & Borgerson, 1998, p. 164; Schroeder & Zwick, 2004, p. 23).

I collected the material over a 3-year period. During this time, I browsed various data sources for occurrences of materials that in one way or the other dealt with the topic of defining what should be deemed stylish and fashionable. The material thus collected was examined holistically and analyzed in order to find prominent features of how stylistic prescriptions are negotiated. The discursive strategies utilized by the traditional elite to strengthen their sense of masculinity became prominent during the analysis of the data. After this initial analysis, I engaged in iterative movement between the empirical examples and relevant theoretical accounts that deal with consumer culture and fashion, as well as masculinity and gender more broadly. Finally, I chose prominent examples from the empirical material to be represented in this chapter. As Elliott (1996) suggests, the analysis involved two closely related phases of a search for patterns in the data and the hypothesizing of functions and effects.

The patterns found function as interpretive repertoires (i.e., recurrently used systems of meaning that potentially can be used by individuals in making sense of the world). In line with the argument put forth by Fischer (2000), I am attempting to show "the discourses that intentionally or otherwise have found their way into or been marginalized in these texts, in order to understand some of the implications for both consumer research and those who [are faced with these texts]" (p. 288). There are, as will be illustrated below, different and contrasting sets of interpretive repertoires constantly negotiating what should be deemed stylish and fashionable. The functions and effects of these available interpretive repertoires, both for individual consumers and for consumer culture, are not available for direct study using this methodological approach. Rather, again as suggested by Elliott (1996), I hypothesize the functions at the end of the chapter, where the political implications of these hegemonic approaches to masculinity and fashion are discussed.

Constructing the Traditional Elite

In the beginning of this chapter, I gave an introduction to the recent sock semiotic meltdown whereby the fairly stable rules of what socks to wear were challenged and overturned. Socks, it should be said, might not be of paramount importance to the well-being of humankind (even though

TABLE 10.1

The Fashion Inclinations of Traditional Elite and Mainstream Consumers:
A Binary System

Traditional Elite	Mainstream Consumers
Style	Fashion
Being	Appearing
Permanence	Change
Original	Copycat
Confidence	Anxiety
Intrinsic style compass	Extrinsic style compass
Influenced by tradition	Influenced by media and popular culture

Swedish brand Happy Socks [http://www.happysocks.com/us/] does seem
to claim connections to happiness). Nevertheless, the battle over who has
the right to define what socks are a pertinent part of *real* men's outfits
illustrates the way in which style and fashion are negotiated—negotiations
that in turn reflect and reinforce status hierarchies and the connected
identity games more broadly.

It is through employing various discursive strategies that define legitimate and illegitimate ways of approaching sartorial matters that status
hierarchies are kept in place. The use of binary oppositions (see Table 10.1)
is a key feature in the construction of the discursive strategies aimed to
distinguish between the consumption behaviors of the insiders (in this
case, the traditional elite) and the outsiders (in this case, the group con-
cocted as the mainstream consumers). By constructing clear dichotomies,
the incoherent and ever changing "consumptionscape" (Ger & Belk, 1996)
is portrayed as neatly ordered and graspable.

At the core of this binary system lies the distinction between *style* and
fashion whereby style is constructed as something emanating from within
that comes with the mother's milk and fashion as something that people
follow anxiously in an attempt to fit in. This distinction is not novel; variations of the "you have style, but you merely follow fashion" mythology are
abundant and many times mirrored in catchy one-liners by great fashion
icons, such as the quote typically attributed to the late Yves Saint Laurent:
"Fashions fade, style is eternal." These mythologies are reinforced by the
traditional elite by constructing the behaviors of ordinary men as copycat
strategies—explicit and crude emulation set apart from its own behaviors
that are instead constructed as "natural" and given.

One of the magazines geared toward the broad gamut of ordinary, working-class men, *Slitz*, recently published a guide to how "ordinary men" could gain access to the privileged domains of the upper class (*Slitz*, June 2008). This style guide with "six versions of Player styles" promised that the ones following the guide should be able to "infiltrate the upper class and enjoy the free champagne." This is a very explicit example of how the cultural codes of the upper class are dispersed to the masses.

Whether we are dealing with "the real upper class" or whether the ones mimicking the styles are really thinking they will change is beside the point. The point is that the cultural codes of a specific subculture that draws its identity from an association with the aristocracy are being dispersed to a large group of consumers who previously had neither access to nor interest in this type of knowledge. This dissemination creates new arenas for identity construction for the previously relatively disinterested men. More importantly, at least from the perspective of this chapter, this spread of the cultural codes forces the consumers who identify themselves with the old aristocracy to sharpen their consumption game in order to set themselves apart from the vulgar masses.

A key feature of those aspiring to be part of the old aristocracy is that they claim to subscribe to an eternal style outside the realms of fashion. In order to degrade the style tips from the fashion magazines, they point toward the futility in even trying to view it as a *style*. The classic aristocratic style is not about what you wear; it is about what you *are*. One of the official tastemakers of the Stockholm scene, Roland-Philippe Kretzschmar, who was at the time the fashion editor of the web page "*Stureplan: La publication glamoreuse, superfashion et tres exclusif,*" immediately reacted to the previously mentioned fashion spread in *Slitz* by simply publishing a copy of it on his blog and commenting, "OK, this is just too much." Immediately, the readers of Kretzschmar's blog could comment and reinforce how refined they were and how distant they were from the simple readers of *Slitz*:

> Haha! Amazingly funny. Brilliant! The Brothers[1] stores in the countryside are going to have a great summer.
> Hehe! The fashion spread looks like an Ellos[2] catalogue.
> Amazing! *C'est tout le contraire[3] du savoir-vivre...n'est-ce pas?*

By thus degrading the ambition of the copycats and making fun not only of the styles but also of the retail outlets, the members of the faux aristocratic subculture draw symbolic boundaries between their own expressions and the ones of the imitators. Furthermore, the use of French expressions that we see in the subtitle of the web page Stureplan and in the preceding comment is a blunt way to signal sophistication. In light of the vague suggestions among the members of this subculture of a link to the old aristocracy in Sweden, one could interpret the use of this foreign language as a little nod toward the use of French as the official language of the royalty during the Baroque era. To be fluent in French is still clearly a symbol of high cultural capital, something that supposedly sets the members of this subculture apart from the common people. The fact that posters many times get it wrong, as the fluent speaker will notice in the subtitle of the web page Stureplan, is yet another sign that it is more a question of posing with the cultural capital than actually possessing it.

Consumers striving to come across as the traditional elite thus utilize a number of strategies to demonstrate that they are different from the "common" consumers occupying the same spaces. Simmel (1904/1957) detects the basic means of doing when he examines the social processes of emulation in general and fashion in particular. He claims that two antagonistic forces, which mutually limit each other, influence the individual and the public minds: the tendencies of generalization and specialization or, in other terms of expression, adaptation, and differentiation. The former "gives rest to the soul" whereas the latter permits a freedom to "move from example to example" (Simmel, 1904/1957, p. 542). This dualism is, according to Simmel, represented *socially* through social adaptation and differentiation, where fashion satisfies both those needs through *imitation* and *demarcation*. *Imitation* works in favor of social adaptation, transfers responsibility of choice onto others, and is therefore in a sense passive. The tendency of *demarcation,* on the other hand, is satisfied through a constant change of content—not the least through the division between social classes.

The crux of the matter is that the other groups—those with which one is trying to associate and those from which one is trying to disassociate—know the rules of the game far too well. Today's consumers are reflexively aware of the games of association and disassociation constantly taking place. Ever since Veblen's (1899/1934) studies at the turn of the last century, it has been customary to conceptualize the diffusion of style and fashion as a matter of trickle down. In essence, the styles of the upper classes are slowly adopted by the groups who are immediately below in social status, which are in turn mimicked by the groups under them in social status, and so forth. Even though the trickle-down model of diffusion is widely used to explain various fashion phenomena, it has been harshly criticized over the last couple of decades (Campbell, 1995). The claim is that the trickle-down idea rests on a view of society as rigidly structured in social classes. Because our late-modern society no longer has the same stable characteristic as the society upon which Veblen built his model, the model is obsolete (Slater, 1997). Of course, Veblen's own period was also far from stable and it was precisely that flux that intrigued him. Or the claim is that the sophisticated consumers of today are far too smart merely to be "aping one's betters."

Several authors have tried to launch other conceptualizations, such as trickle-up or trickle-across, to account for the idea that styles are many times taken from the lower classes (if we still claim to have those classes) and adopted by the higher classes. The popularity of styles such as baggy jeans and trucker hats is given as evidence that styles may trickle up just as much as they trickle down. Such reasoning, however, shows a disregard for the inherent power structures available in fashion. For someone in good economic standing to appropriate a style from someone less privileged has little to do with consumers anxiously striving upward in the status system (Ulver-Sneistrup & Ostberg, 2007).

I will, however, note Corrigan (1997), who suggests that it is not so much a matter of trickle down as it is a matter of chase and flight. The status system might indeed look different today, and there may be several different status systems existing in parallel at each given time. But still, within the different status systems there is a constant struggle over symbolic capital and those in lower rank are chasing and mimicking others with higher social standing. The latter then must flee in order to keep their edge, and so it goes. The case of the faux aristocracy in the Stockholm scene is a brilliant illustration of this pattern, especially because the group is actively trying to rebuild the traditional status system that the critiques of emulation theory claim is no longer in place.

I now present two brief empirical themes that illustrate how the traditional elite sets itself apart from the supposedly common and vulgar masses. First, its members view themselves as defenders of timeless stability; second, they are connecting to an imagined elite of global players.

Defenders of Timeless Stability: The Retrosexuals

The first characteristic of the traditional elite's consumption is that its members do not regard themselves as representing something new or as following contemporary trends. Instead, they construct themselves as defenders of stability and provide a timeless, classic (and classy) masculinity as an alternative to all the currently available fast-moving consumer fads. The dichotomy constructed is one of an eternal or classic style based on a fixed stance toward clothing versus an anxious following of fashion in order to conform.

Those taking on the identity of the traditional elite are characterized more by conservatism and a willingness to uphold—what they perceive to be—traditional values, than the more rebellious traits usually upheld by similar youth constellations (cf. Hall & Jefferson, 1976; Hebdige, 1979). Instead of manifesting their identity by rebelling against the parent generation, they act in a rebellious fashion by trying to resurrect conservative values of an imagined past. They are thus escaping the temporality of contemporary, faddish consumption, of which they would regard the new feminized masculine consumption as a prime example, by attaching themselves to a timeless ethos of style.

In the online communities, references are many times made to how the traditional elite do things with style, whereas others—particularly the new elite—lack the ability, both economically and culturally, to be stylish. One principal way for them to distinguish their consumption from that of the new elite is to frame the latter's consumption behaviors as overly conscious or even girlish (cf. Rinallo, 2007); if one *really* has style, one rarely has to show it in the explicit way utilized by the new elite. The traditional elite here resorts to the use of subtle signals, a strategy common for those possessing high cultural capital in order to communicate to others "in the know" (Berger & Ward, 2010). One of the official tastemakers in Stockholm, the aforementioned Roland-Philippe Kretzschmar, strongly suggests that when it comes to style, just buying a fancy outfit will not suffice: One needs some depth and history in one's closet; one need to be a "retrosexual":

> It is not until you have 7 suits, 7 pairs of shoes and 21 shirts…, that you can start experimenting with jeans, t-shirts, slacks, sneakers and jackets. You are smart, so you never go for fashion-fashion, but for the timeless classics. Call it preppy, call it carefree, call it retrosexual…

The oh-so-stylish Mr. Kretzschmar continues by drawing lines between those who have understood what style is and others that are just anxiously following the lead of whoever is portrayed as the fashion guru of the day:

> the retrosexual man, when it comes to appearance, is a man who is strategic, long-term, and smart. It's all about investing in one's lifelong success, not about day trading with one's appearance. It's about being confidently relaxed in oneself and not about being a fashion-poof who dances to Tom Ford's pipe. It's about Ralph Lauren but not Karl Lagerfeld, Adrian Brody but not Kevin Federline, Bernard Arnault but not Donald Trump. It's about men with class, finesse, and natural panache.

In this way, the traditional elite expresses that it does not *need* brands and fashion to show that it is stylish. Instead, this quality seems to be almost inherent to who it is. The crux of the matter is that the traditional elite wants to at least imagine that this comes naturally to it, while it might be hard for onlookers to know who is just posing and who was born that way. Despite calls to staying true to the eternal codes of style rather than following the whims of fashion, what is stylish at every given point of time is constantly changing. Distinguishing the exclusive classic style from the marketized version available to the masses is becoming increasingly hard.

Returning once again to the sock example, it is evident how various authorities aim at giving advice to those trying to fit in—advice that they claim is giving the reader access to a marketized set of secret codes:

> In the fashion world there are rules that are not in an encyclopedia. They still deserve at least as much attention. One of these unspoken rules deals with the sock that snuggly clasps the man's leg. One should keep the following in mind: the sock should be long enough for the man's hairy calves not to show either when he stands or sits, because that would disrupt the manifestation of a perfect appearance. (Engel, 2004, p. 45)

Roetzel (1999, p. 186) gives almost identical advice where the horror of having a man's naked and hairy, or even furry, legs showing is further reinforced.

The authors of these style guides here reinforce the idea that there are rules that some men just intrinsically know, whereas other men have to study in order to gain access to the set of conventions. When the rules are thus dispersed to the mainstream, it becomes important for those claiming lineage to the traditional elite to emphasize that style is not about following rules, but rather is about having a special sense, a sense with which some are born and some are not. The fashion blogger Olof Enckell resorts to the metaphor of art to show that one needs special talents to be able to play these games: "There is more to learn about the art of choosing the right socks than one might think. And yes, you can wear other socks than black without coming across as a clown" (Enckell, posted March 6, 2007). Believing in one's sense of just knowing what works and what does not is tricky, especially considering the historical connections drawn between caring for one's appearance and femininity. Men are frequently reminded that they might not have the sense to understand what works, that they might "run into trouble," as illustrated by the following excerpt from a style guide:

> Monochromatic [socks] are easiest to combine. With patterned exemplars things instantly gets more complicated, since the pattern has to harmonize with the rest of the attire. Those who run into trouble with different color and pattern combinations should therefore better be safe than sorry and choose monochromatic socks (Engel, 2004, p. 45)

Being anxious about making sartorial choices is not an entirely masculine condition, however, as suggested by Miller (2004) in the aptly named book chapter, "The Little Black Dress Is the Solution, but What Is the Problem?" Miller suggests that in a world where we are taught that we are judged on our ability to choose correctly, choosing black becomes one of the few safe choices. It is essentially a nonchoice. But making nonchoices is also something that feeds into the identity building—in this case as a missed chance to show distinction. Traditional style authority Flusser (2002) suggests the following:

> While appropriate for formal wear and practically obligatory for those swathed head to toe in regulation black, black hose should be avoided at other times. "Hose noir" transforms the ankle into a black hole, diminishing that which it could beautify. (p. 173)

Another illustration of the cat-and-mouse game of fashion and style can be given by the Spanish company Zara, which introduced a new line of suits a few years ago catering to the stylish gentleman. One of the features was that the cuffs could be unbuttoned, traditionally a sign that the jacket was made by a tailor. The traditional elite used to wear one button unbuttoned to signal subtly to the likeminded that they were wearing an expensive jacket. On the Zara suits there was a little tag explaining this behavior to the prospective buyers and thus giving away the secret code. When these codes are spread to the masses, the traditional elite has to adapt. The following quote, taken from a web page catering to the ones more interested in classic style than fashion (A Suitable Wardrobe, posted January 25, 2008) illustrates how the traditional elite has to vulgarize its old behaviors in order to stay one step ahead of the crowd:

> When struck by the urge to undo a jacket sleeve button, walk quickly to a large public men's room. Unbutton and roll up your sleeves and wash your hands. Then dry your hands and button the sleeves again. You'll demonstrate that your sleeve buttons work to many men without embarrassing yourself and after a few repetitions the urges will cease.

Connecting to a Timeless Global Elite

Another common denominator for what is deemed stylish—and thus a suitable blueprint for the construction of masculinity—is that it should be connected to that in which other, imagined groups of similar consumers around the world are engaging and always have engaged. In this way, the traditional elite tries to escape the spatial and temporal restrictions of its present consumption by attaching itself to an imagined community of global cosmopolitans. Again, we see an active construction of a dichotomy: on the one hand, consumption behaviors that are not limited to the here and now of the Stockholm scene and, on the other hand, behaviors that are cast as pathetic attempts to gain status and respect in the short run. A mythology is thus constructed in which the vulgar masses are competing for recognition whereas the ones constructing themselves as the global elite are merely "being" rather than "appearing."

It might be difficult by merely looking at a person to judge if he or she is anxiously following fashion advice dispersed in the mainstream media or if someone is but the last reincarnation in a lineage of stylistic superiority. Thus, these distinctions need to be made clear through discourse. One way to do so is to claim superior knowledge of why certain garments are worn in certain ways, such as the example with the picture of Robert F. Kennedy wearing white socks in the introduction. Someone knowledgeable about this picture is not just wearing white socks; he is wearing white socks *like* Kennedy. It might look the same, but it has different meanings. Socks, as I have tried to argue here, is one area where insecurities about what and what not to do are apparent. Therefore, it is not strange to see that style authorities—such as Scott Schuman, aka *The Sartorialist*—get the following types of questions:

> One of the most asked questions to style experts is "Should my socks match my shoes or my pants?" The answer you get may depend on where you live. The Americans advice [*sic*] matching socks to your pants. The Italians seem to contrast with both shoes and pants. The English, always the eccentrics, wear maroon socks with everything! I have a photo to defend this point… (posted July 28, 2006)

While the answer is, I suppose, a tongue-in-cheek remark, it nevertheless illustrates the type of knowledge important in the traditional elite circles: that customs are not the same everywhere and that you can get away with virtually anything as long as you know why you are doing it. By fabricating an image of global soul mates as their points of reference rather than the upward-striving new elitists, they manage to downplay the similarities between their respective consumption behaviors. The trick is to frame others' behaviors as vulgar and one's own as sophisticated.

One more ostentatious behavior that has been used in such a manner lately by the younger members of the traditional elite is the spraying of champagne, an activity that perhaps could come across as always unsophisticated. But no, apparently it all depends on *how* you do it. If you spray it for effect to get as much attention as possible, you are not getting it right; you have to adopt the right blasé attitude to make it look like it is just something that needs to be done.

Again, the fashionable web page Stureplan shows how it should be done by alluding to the really stylish people in faraway places with this description followed by a dozen pictures of people pouring champagne into the pool at the nightclub Les Caves du Roy in St Tropez: "What do the real players look like in St. Tropez, New York or Shanghai? Yes, you guessed it—like real men, not like overgrown teenagers." This is followed by a text describing how vulgar it is to spray champagne ostentatiously: to do so makes one come across as an attention-anxious teenager dying for the world to pay attention. To be stylish, in the right cosmopolitan manner, one should just turn the bottle upside down and casually let the liquid glide from the ($100) bottle at its own pace.

DISCUSSION

Throughout this chapter I discuss how connections between masculinity and fashion get negotiated in particular social circles, in a particular location, at a particular time. Why, one might ask, do I not address the more universalistic traits of men's relationships to fashion? The simple answer is that there are no universalistic principles guiding how men approach fashion. There are always dominant ideas of how men should be, or hegemonic masculinities (Connell & Messerschmidt, 2005), but these ideas do not reflect the human, or masculine, nature. Ever since the great masculine renunciation, the idea that men are naturally disinterested in appearance has been dominant, and attempts to overturn this hegemony have been viewed with skepticism (McNeil & Karaminas 2009). Rather than looking for the universalistic approach to masculinities and fashion, we should acknowledge that fashion and identity are always performed in particular locations where the underlying sociohistoric background and the underlying status games need to be taken into consideration. In this chapter I try to show one place where such negotiations take place. Other locations would expose different types of masculinities being negotiated in different ways.

Still, there are commonalities in how men approach the issue of fashion in contemporary consumer culture, due in large part to the relative homogeneity of retail outlets, brands, and style authorities. For example, caring too much about one's appearance or merely trying to dress to look beautiful seems to be constructed as something potentially dangerous for one's masculinity; indeed, it is constructed as effeminate (Rinallo, 2007; Tuncay, 2005). To offset the possibility of coming across as effeminate, traditional masculinities foreground traits such as knowledge and rationality (cf. Holt & Thompson, 2004): Real men do not just dress to look pretty; instead, they gather knowledge and become style experts, referencing authorities in distant locations and times. This knowledge further must be embodied; that is, it must seem as if there are no alternative ways of approaching sartorial matters. If one comes across as someone who is actively posing, the cultural capital loses its value (Bourdieu, 1984).

In this symbolic struggle, the individuals who claim lineage to the aristocracy or traditional elite constantly use various discursive strategies to distinguish between their consumption behaviors and those of others. In particular, the others whom they claim to be unsuccessfully trying to emulate their classic and classy styles are the vulgar masses. An important part of these discursive strategies is to downplay the visual similarities between the originals and the copies, in order instead to point to some underlying philosophy of consumption that sets the one group apart from the other. The originals construct their style as immanent; they strive to come across as born to perform, as if there were no alternative ways of *being*. The copies, on the other hand, are always trying too hard. It does not matter whether they are in fact using the same objects or engaging in the same behaviors; they just do not have the right laissez-faire stance toward their consumption and will never, in the eyes of the traditional elite, get it right.

The active construction of dichotomies of what is hot and what is not is thus an important part of the discursive strategies. One of the more prominent dichotomies constructed is that of the actual group that claims lineage to some idea of an aristocracy or traditional elite, on the one hand, and that of the vulgar masses on the other. This can be considered as a metadichotomy because the construction of all the other dichotomies is contingent on its successful construction. The lineage to the aristocracy or traditional elite is, at least in most cases, far from natural. Instead, the people with whom they are claiming (at least stylistic) kinship are better regarded as a fantasy, as a made-up image of an imagined spatiotemporally secluded other.

They are thus mimicking an abstract idea of the perfect aristocrat rather than some real person; they are a simulacrum of aristocracy (cf. Baudrillard, 1994). Campbell (2007) suggests that "the basic motivation of consumers can be regarded as the desire to experience in reality those pleasurable dramas that they have already enjoyed in their imagination" (p. 24) and that consumption thus has to do with bringing into material form the daydreams that we have. From this perspective, the symbolic game of the traditional elite should perhaps be viewed as an attempt to resurrect an idealized image of a lost class society in which the traditional elite had a natural position of power.

NOTES

1. Brothers is a chain of midrange fashion stores in Sweden.
2. Ellos is one of Sweden's largest mail-order catalogues.
3. A little while later another person commented that "*contraire* is the feminine form…" and instantly someone else got a chance to show his or her refinement.

REFERENCES

Baudelaire, Charles (1863/2010). *Painter of modern life.* London, UK: Penguin Books Ltd.

Baudrillard, Jean (1994). *Simulacra and simulation.* Ann Arbor, MI: The University of Michigan Press.

Baudrillard, Jean (1996). *The system of objects.* London, UK: Verso.

Belk, Russell W., & Janeen A. Costa (1998). The mountain man myth: A contemporary consuming fantasy. *Journal of Consumer Research, 25* (December), 218–240.

Berger, Jonah, & Morgan Ward (2010). Subtle signals of inconspicuous consumption. *Journal of Consumer Research, 37* (December), 555–569.

Bourdieu, Pierre (1984). *Distinction: A social critique of the judgment of taste.* Cambridge, MA: Harvard University Press.

Bourdieu, Pierre (2001). *Masculine domination.* Oxford, UK: Polity.

Bourke, Joanna (1996). The great male renunciation: Men's dress reform in inter-war Britain. *Journal of Design History, 9*(1), 23–33.

Bristor, Julia M., & Eileen Fischer (1993). Feminist thought: Implications for consumer research. *Journal of Consumer Research, 19* (March), 518–536.

Campbell, Colin (1995). Conspicuous confusion? A critique of Veblen's theory of conspicuous consumption. *Sociological Theory, 13*(1), 37–47.

Campbell, Colin (2007). Fashion and identity. In A. M. Gonzáles & L. Bovone (Eds.), *Fashion and identity: A multidisciplinary approach* (pp. 23–38). New York, NY: Social Trends Institute.

Caruana, Robert, Andrew Crane, & James A. Fitchett (2008). Paradoxes of consumer independence: A critical discourse analysis of the independent traveler. *Marketing Theory, 8*(3), 253–272.

Connell, Robert W., & James W. Messerschmidt (2005). Hegemonic masculinity: Rethinking the concept. *Gender & Society, 19*(6), 829–859.

Corrigan, Peter (1997). *The sociology of consumption.* London, UK: Sage.

Cova, Bernard, Robert V. Kozinets, & Avi Shankar (2007). Tribes, Inc.: The new world of tribalism. In B. Cova, R. V. Kozinets, & A. Shankar (Eds.), *Consumer tribes* (pp. 3–26). Oxford, UK: Elsevier/Butterworth-Heinemann.

Dowd, Maureen (2003). Is Arnold Schwarzenegger metrosexual? *International Herald Tribune,* September 26, 2003.

Edwards, Tim (2009). Consuming masculinities: Style, content and men's magazines. In P. McNeil & V. Karaminas (Eds.), *The men's fashion reader* (pp. 462–471). Oxford, UK: Berg Publishers.

Elliott, Richard (1996). Discourse analysis: Exploring action, function and conflict in social texts. *Marketing Intelligence & Planning, 14*(6), 65–68.

Enckell, Olof (2009). http://www.manolo.se

Engel, Birgit (2004). *Mannen Och Modet—Från Morgon Till Kväll*. Berlin, Germany: Feierabend Verlag OHG.

Entwistle, Joanne (2000). *The fashioned body: Fashion, dress, and modern social theory*. Cambridge, UK: Polity.

Falk, Karin (2011). *Det Svenska Modeundret*. Stockholm, Sweden: Norstedts.

Fischer, Eileen (2000). Consuming contemporaneous discourses: A postmodern analysis of food advertisements targeted toward women. In S. Hoch & R. Meyer (Eds.), *Advances in consumer research* (pp. 288–294). Provo, UT: Association for Consumer Research.

Flusser, Alan (2002). *Dressing the man: Mastering the art of permanent fashion*. New York, NY: HarperCollins.

Ger, Güliz, & Russell W. Belk (1996). I'd like to buy the world a Coke: Consumptionscapes of the "less affluent world." *Journal of Consumer Policy, 19*, 271–304.

Hall, Stuart (1997). The work of representation. In S. Hall & M. Keynes (Eds.), *Representation: Cultural representations and signifying practices* (pp. 13–74). Buckingham, UK: Open University Press.

Hall, Stuart, & Tony Jefferson (Eds.) (1976). *Resistance through rituals: Youth subcultures in post-war Britain*. London, UK: Hutchinson.

Hebdige, Dick (1979). *Subculture: The meaning of style*. London, UK: Methuen & Co. Ltd.

Herrbloggen (2008). http://blogg.stureplan.se/herrbloggen

Holt, Douglas B., & Craig J. Thompson (2004). Man-of-action heroes: The pursuit of heroic masculinity in everyday consumption. *Journal of Consumer Research, 31* (September), 425–440.

Kates, Steven M. (2002). The protean quality of subcultural consumption: An ethnographic account of gay consumers. *Journal of Consumer Research, 29* (December), 383–399.

Kawamura, Yuniya (2005). *Fashion-ology: An introduction to fashion studies*. New York, NY: Berg Publishers.

Laver, James (1995). *Costume and fashion: A concise history*. London, UK: Thames & Hudson.

MacKinnon, Kenneth (2003). *Representing men: Maleness and masculinity in the media*. London, UK: Arnold.

McNeil, Peter, & Vicki Karaminas (2009). Introduction: The field of men's fashion. In P. McNeil & V. Karaminas (Eds.), *The men's fashion reader* (pp. 1–14). Oxford, UK: Berg Publishers.

Miller, Daniel (1987). *Material culture and mass consumption*. London, UK: Blackwell Publishers.

Miller, Daniel (2004). The little black dress is the solution, but what is the problem? In K. M. Ekström & H. Brembeck (Eds.), *Elusive consumption* (pp. 113–127). Oxford, UK: Berg.

Mort, Frank (1996). *Cultures of consumption: Masculinities and social space in late twentieth-century Britain*. London, UK: Routledge.

Mort, Frank (2009). New men and new markets. In P. McNeil & V. Karaminas (Eds.), *The men's fashion reader* (pp. 454–461). Oxford, UK: Berg Publishers.

Murray, Jeff B. (2002). The politics of consumption: A re-inquiry on Thompson and Haytko's (1997) "Speaking of fashion." *Journal of Consumer Research, 29* (December), 427–440.

Osgerby, Bill (2001). *Playboys in paradise: Masculinity, youth and leisure-style in modern America*. New York, NY: Berg.

Ostberg, Jacob (2007). The linking value of subcultural capital: Constructing the Stockholm brat enclave. In B. Cova, R. V. Kozinets, & A. Shankar (Eds.), *Consumer tribes* (pp. 93–106). Oxford, UK: Elsevier/Butterworth-Heinemann.

Ostberg, Jacob (2010). Thou shalt sport a banana in thy pocket: Gendered body size ideals in advertising and popular culture. *Marketing Theory, 10*(1), 45–73.

Otnes, Cele, & Mary A. McGrath (2001). Perceptions and realities of male shopping behavior. *Journal of Retailing, 77*(1), 111–137.

Parker, Ian (1990). Discourse: Definitions and contradictions. *Philosophical Psychology, 3*(2/3), 189–204.

Patterson, Maurice, & Richard Elliott (2002). Negotiating masculinities: Advertising and the inversion of the male gaze. *Consumption, Markets and Culture, 5*(3), 231–246.

Rinallo, Diego (2007). Metro/fashion/tribes of men: Negotiating the boundaries of men's legitimate consumption. In B. Cova, R. V. Kozinets, & A. Shankar (Eds.), *Consumer tribes* (pp. 76–92). Oxford, UK: Elsevier/Butterworth-Heinemann.

Roetzel, Bernhard (1999). *Gentlemannen: Handbok i det klassiska herrmodet.* Köln, Germany: Könemann Verlagsgesellschaft mbH.

Schouten, John W., & James H. McAlexander (1995). Subcultures of consumption: An ethnography of the new bikers. *Journal of Consumer Research, 22* (June), 43–61.

Schroeder, Jonathan E., & Janet L. Borgerson (1998). Marketing images of gender: A visual analysis. *Consumption, Markets and Culture, 2*(2), 161–201.

Schroeder, Jonathan E., & Detlev Zwick (2004). Mirrors of masculinity: Representation and identity in advertising images. *Consumption, Markets and Culture, 7*(1), 21–52.

Schuman, Scott (2011). The sartorialist. http://thesartorialist.blogspot.com/

Simmel, Georg (1904/1957). Fashion. *American Journal of Sociology, 62*(6), 541–558.

Simpson, Mark (2002). Meet the metrosexual. http://www.salon.com/

Slater, Don (1997). *Consumer culture and modernity.* Cambridge, UK: Polity Press.

Stureplan.se (2008). Stureplan: La publication glamoreuse, superfashion et tres exclusif, http://www.stureplan.se/

Suitable Wardrobe, A (2008). A suitable wardrobe: Will's thoughts on dressing with style. http://asuitablewardrobe.dynend.com

Swiencicki, Mark A. (1998). Consuming brotherhood: Men's culture, style and recreation as consumer culture, 1880–1930. *Journal of Social History, 31*(4), 773.

Thompson, Craig J. (2004). Marketplace mythology and discourses of power. *Journal of Consumer Research, 31* (June), 162–180.

Thompson, Craig J., & Diana L. Haytko (1997). Speaking of fashion: Consumers' uses of fashion discourses and the appropriation of countervailing cultural meanings. *Journal of Consumer Research, 24* (June), 15–42.

Tuncay, Linda (2005). *How male consumers construct and negotiate their identities in the marketplace: Three essays.* Dissertation, University of Illinois.

Tuncay, Linda, & Cele C. Otnes (2008). The use of persuasion management strategies by identity-vulnerable consumers: The case of heterosexual male shoppers. *Journal of Retailing, 84* (December), 487–499.

Ulver-Sneistrup, Sofia, & Jacob Ostberg (2007). Revisiting emulation theory: An empirical illustration of consumers' status-aspirational approaches in home aesthetics. In S. Borghini, M. A. McGrath, & C. Otnes (Eds.), *European advances in consumer research* (pp. 451–458). Duluth, MN: Association for Consumer Research.

Veblen, Thorstein (1899/1934). *The theory of the leisure class.* New York, NY: Modern Library.

Walden, George (2002). *Who is a dandy?* London, UK: Gibson Square Books.

Western, Mark, & Erik O. Wright (1994). The permeability of class boundaries to intergenerational mobility among men in the United States, Canada, Norway and Sweden. *American Sociological Review, 59*(4), 606–629.

Wilson, Elizabeth (1985/2003). *Adorned in dreams: Fashion and modernity* (Rev. and updated ed.). London, UK: I. B. Taurus & Co Ltd.

11

The Rise of 草食系男子 (Soushokukei Danshi) Masculinity and Consumption in Contemporary Japan

Steven Chen

INTRODUCTION

> Today, Igarashi has a new identity (and plenty of company among young Japanese men) as one of the *soushoku[kei] danshi*—literally translated, "grass-eating boys." Named for their lack of interest in sex and their preference for quieter, less competitive lives, Japan's "herbivores" are provoking a national debate about how the country's economic stagnation since the early 1990s has altered men's behavior. (Harney, 2009)

In *Soushoku Danshi Sedai Heisei Danshi Zukan* (*Handbook of Man in the Heisei Period*), Maki Fukasawa (2009) coins the term *soushokukei danshi* ("grass-eating type men" or "herbivore men") to describe heterosexual Japanese men who lack ambition, engage in feminine consumption practices, and shirk relationships with the opposite sex. Typically young men between the ages of 20 and 34, soushokukei danshi are less status conscious than men from previous generations; rather than pursue corporate careers, they prefer lower paying, less demanding jobs. A key marker of soushokukei danshi is their feminized consumption practices, which include shopping, beautification practices, and fine dining. Rather than pursue relationships with women, they prefer being alone playing video games and surfing the Internet. As a result of their consumption practices, the popular media labels them "girly men" or "ladylike."

Soushokukei danshi are not social deviants, but rather an emergent form of Japanese masculinity. In Japan, aggressive masculinities embodied by the salaryman and *nikushokukei danshi* ("meat-eating type men" or "carnivore men") represent masculine ideals, but a shift in masculine values is under way (Dasgupta, 2009). According to a 2009 study conducted by M1 F1 Soken, a marketing research firm, 60% of unmarried Japanese men between the ages of 20 and 34 identify themselves as soushokukei danshi. The finding that many Japanese men associate themselves with "feminized" masculinity is notable in a society that was once considered the most masculine in the world (Hofstede, 2001).

SOUSHOKUKEI DANSHI CONSUMPTION PRACTICES

Soushokukei danshi consumption practices echo those of Western metrosexuals (Rinallo, 2007; Simpson, 2002; Tuncay, 2006; Tuncay & Otnes, 2008b). They are fashion conscious and sport ensembles that are considered feminine by Japanese society, such as tight pants with long flowing shirts. They are also concerned with their body and engage in beautification practices such as slimming treatments, day spas, facials, and eyebrow grooming practices (Miller, 2003). Other consumption practices include shopping, taking leisurely walks, and eating fine desserts. In everyday parlance, soushokukei danshi consumption is feminine because beautification and shopping are activities that are traditionally gendered female (Davis, 2003; Otnes & McGrath, 2001; Roberts, 1998).

Soushokukei danshi exhibit a weak career orientation. Many contemporary Japanese men reject traditional masculine ideals of elite education, high income, and physical stature (Roberson & Suzuki, 2003). Rather than pursuing upward social mobility through an intense work ethic, they prefer comfortable lifestyles, which allow time for hedonic pursuits. Aphorisms like "life is short" and "doing okay is okay" drive their life philosophies. But there is a trade-off. To maximize their leisure time, many soushokukei danshi select jobs with lower salaries.

Soushokukei danshi are heterosexual men, but are purportedly uninterested in relationships with the opposite sex (Fukasawa, 2009). However, soushokukei danshi's inability to sustain long-term, sexual relationships is more likely a result of their low income than their purported lack of interest in sex. Spa!, a Japanese marketing firm, surveyed men between the ages of 25 and 39 who earned less than 2 million yen (roughly $24,000) a year, a benchmark for classifying the "working poor," and found that 65% of men in this bracket are discontent with their sex lives, 19.3% have given up on sex, and 20% are still virgins. The video game company Konami finds that 20% of men surveyed expressed interest in dating a female video game character. There are now a variety of love simulation games, such as Love Plus, which allow players to date video game avatars.

SCHOLARLY IMPORTANCE OF SOUSHOKUKEI DANSHI

The purpose of this chapter is to identify the cultural factors that gave rise to soushokukei danshi masculinity in contemporary Japan and to understand how soushokukei danshi masculinity structures and is structured by consumption practices. There are several important reasons to understand soushokukei danshi consumption practices.

First, it is necessary to question the framing of soushokukei danshi as "feminine," "ladylike," or "girly men." The media emphasizes the sensational and deviant aspects of soushokukei danshi consumption practices (e.g., that these men wear skirts and bras, and carry purses). Such critiques are largely ahistorical and ignore the shifts in Japanese masculinity brought about by changes in the economy, society, and gender relations.

Second, soushokukei danshi lifestyle and consumption practices are of central importance for Japanese public policy. Soushokukei danshi's lack of interest in committed relationships and low levels of income embodies two of Japan's biggest problems. Japan is one of the world's oldest populations. By 2050, there will be an enormous retired population (65 years and older)—estimated at 40% of the population—that cannot be sustained by the pension taxes of the working adult population. Working adults need to produce children to offset the aging population, but soushokukei danshi's lifestyle choices are stymieing this effort.

The need for population inflation is so dire that the Japanese government is offering families 13,000 yen ($150) a month per child to stimulate growth. In 2010, the popular music celebrity Gackt held an exclusive concert for male fans to bolster men's spirit, "especially for women." Under the umbrella theme, "the way of the man," he rallied the audience against soushokukei danshi masculinity through aggressive rock songs and messages that encouraged male sexuality. Additionally, soushokukei danshi possess relatively low levels of disposable income. It is a challenge for Japanese marketers to stimulate Japan's stagnant economy when a significant portion of men is thrifty in its spending.

Finally, soushokukei danshi provide an opportunity to study masculine consumption outside the Western context (Kjeldgaard & Nielsen, 2010; Thompson & Holt, 2004). Existing research examines how articulations of masculinities based on aggression, competition, and ruggedness pattern men's consumption practices (Belk & Costa, 1998; Ging, 2005; Holt & Thompson, 2004; Schouten & McAlexander, 1995; Schroeder & Zwick, 2004). Consumption practices that deviate from the realm of masculine power and privilege are framed as "revitalizing retreats" from intense masculine competition, or "gender tourism" (Thompson & Holt, 2004). However, soushokukei danshi consumption practices are not necessarily structured by competition, and their "feminine" pursuits are not consistent with gender tourism.

METHODOLOGY

To study the rise of soushokukei danshi, I reviewed a variety of secondary sources. Data were collected from four sources:

- I gathered census data from the English-language website for the *toukeikyoku,* the Statistics Bureau of Japan. These provided longitudinal data on the Japanese population, economy, and labor force. (All statistics presented in the findings are from the Statistics Bureau of Japan unless otherwise noted).
- Historical texts provide the cultural context behind the shifts in masculinity between the postwar years to the current era. I consulted scholarly books on contemporary Japanese history that summarize important cultural and economic events in twentieth century Japan (Allinson, 1998; Duus, 1998; Gordon, 2008; Tipton, 2008). Additionally, books on gender elucidate the link between Japanese public policy and masculine production (Garon, 1997) and the role

of women in coproducing Japanese masculinity (Hidaka, 2010; Holloway, 2010; Okano, 2009).

• I selected 47 popular press articles through a stratified random sampling process. I used three key phrases—"Japanese masculinity," "Japanese economy," and "Japanese population"—as filters in search engines to cull an initial set of articles. Subsequently, quota sampling was used to select articles based on their publication dates (e.g., 2005 and later) and their relevance to the research agenda.

• I analyzed popular media texts based on their relevance to soushokukei danshi production and reinforcement. I selected mainstream comics, TV shows, films, self-improvement manuals, and magazines published between 2007 and 2011.

Using data from the popular press articles and popular media culture offers two advantages: the ability to draw representations of consumption practices as they were depicted at the time and depiction of an understanding of shared social meanings of consumption practices (Golder, 2000; Henry, 2010; Humphreys, 2010).

Interpretive, hermeneutical analysis was the main mode of data analysis (Arnold & Fischer, 1994; Thompson, Locander, & Pollio, 1989). I began analysis with close readings of materials to identify major themes related to Japanese masculinity and consumption practices. Subsequently, parts-to-whole analysis was used to compare themes with the census data and literature on Japanese history and gender. Through an iterative, back-and-forth process, I refined four themes germane to soushokukei danshi masculinity.

FINDINGS

Shifts in Japan's Economic Climate Structure Masculine Values

Gender discourses are produced in state and institutional life as much as they are in interpersonal transactions (Connell, 1993). Thus, an investigation into soushokukei danshi masculinity and consumption starts with a historic analysis of postwar Japan. The Japanese government has a history of structuring family and gender roles that advance the state's capitalist agendas (Bishop, 2005; Garon, 1997). For instance, Japan's Meiji regime

(1868–1912) initiated modernization projects as a means of strengthening Japan against Western colonial powers (Karlin, 2002). The empire prescribed discourses of gender and sexuality that encouraged men to become productive laborers and soldiers and women to become good wives and mothers (Sievers, 1983). These gender prescriptions trickled down from government to social institutions, including the military, law, education, and popular media culture (Dasgupta, 2003).

The following passages will document the economic and social policies that patterned hegemonic masculine values in postwar Japan in two periods: 1955–1989 and 1990 to the current day. These dates correlate to two distinct periods in twentieth century Japanese history: the "economic miracle" and the "bursting of the bubble" (aka the "lost decade"), respectively.

1955–1989: The Economic Miracle

The postwar rise of Japan into one of the largest industrial economies in the world after being humbled in defeat is often referred to as the "economic miracle" or "economic bubble." According to one perspective, the strategic policies of the postwar Japanese government made economic growth possible (Duus, 1998; Gordon, 2008). First, the end to prewar protectionism meant that Japan no longer faced tariffs and other barriers to export and was able to obtain raw materials for production. Second, a political consensus for economic growth became a national agenda. This commitment to growth led to the formation of the Economic Planning Agency, which managed economic decision making for Japan.

Third, the lifting of protectionist policies allowed industrialists to invest in raw materials such as oil, chemical fertilizer, plastics, machine tools, and artificial fibers. Industrialists believed that as income rose, so too would demand for consumer goods developed using these raw materials, and they were correct. The fourth factor was demand for ordinary lifestyle goods, catalyzed by Japanese citizens' exposure to Western consumption culture. Since the wartime period, the public was starved of ordinary consumer goods. Finally, the combination of the Japanese work ethic and compulsive savings habits created a pool of disposable income that allowed for big-ticket purchases and laid the groundwork for economic expansion.

Another perspective downplays the role of the state in guiding the economy toward success and focuses on prewar industrialization, postwar international developments, and luck as the major contributing factors (Tipton,

2008, p. 179). Investment in heavy industry during the 1930s and continuous expansion during wartime encouraged developments that aided in postwar growth, such as product standardization, subcontracting, and seniority-based wages. The Korean War and Vietnam War were described as "gifts from the gods" because they provided demand for Japanese products, which sustained growth through the 1960s and beyond.

Regardless of which perspective is believed, Japan's economy witnessed expansive growth over the next 20 years. By the mid-1970s, it was clear to the rest of the world that Japan had achieved the status of an economic and political superpower. Growth continued into the 1980s, but in the 1990s, the economic climate changed.

1990–Today: The Bursting of the Bubble and the Population Problem

Encouraged by the prosperous economic times of the 1980s, the Japanese government, corporations, and individuals channeled their monies into domestic holdings and overseas investments (Allinson, 1998). These investments were financed with low-interest bank loans, which were easy to obtain from banks. Many of these loans were channeled into highly speculative land and real estate purchases within Japan. Wide-scale speculative investments resulted in inflated real estate prices. For example, prices in prestigious parts of Tokyo fetched the equivalent of $93,000 per square foot. Economists feared the instability of inflated real estate and stock prices, a fact that was realized in the mid-1990s when corporations and individuals could not pay back their bank loans. To curb speculative investing, the Japanese government decided to raise interest rates.

In 1990, the economic bubble suddenly burst when the Bank of Japan raised interest rates (Duus, 1998). As credit tightened, the stock market collapsed, ushering in a prolonged economic slowdown. The trickle-down effects were immediate. Consumer spending and capitalist investment dwindled. Corporations stopped hiring and new university graduates scrambled to find work. Meanwhile, Japan's Asian neighbors (especially China) were reaping the benefits of foreign investment and enjoying economic miracles of their own. These events gave rise to the *Heisei* recession, which continues to this very day.

Japan's shrinking population, aging population, and "working poor" contributed to sustained economic slowdown. The Japanese population has been decreasing in the past three decades, and it is projected to decrease each year until 2050 (Statistics Bureau, Ministry of Internal Affairs and Communications, Japan, 2010, 2011). As of 2010, Japan's population stands at 127.5 million, after contracting by 123,000 people in 2009, the most in its history.

A decrease in fertility rates (i.e., children per family) is the main contributor to population shrinkage. Government figures for 2010 show that the fertility rate for Japan is 1.37, up from the historical low of 1.25 in 2005. In dense, metropolitan centers such as Tokyo, where the cost of living is high, the average is 1.09 children per family. These statistics place Japan as the nation with the lowest fertility rate in the world. The reasons for the low birth rate are many, but one factor is the rising maternal age (age of a woman when she has the first child) of Japanese women, which increased from 25.6 years in 1970 to 29.7 in 2010.

With the advent of modern medicine and health care, the Japanese population is growing older and living longer. The life expectancy of 79.59 years for men and 86.44 years for women represents record highs. About 22.7% (29.01 million) of the Japanese population is 65 years and older. This percentage of elderly is the highest in the world. There are 1.7 times more aged people than children (0–14 years old), who comprise 13.3% (17.01 million) of the population. The ratio of the dependent population is 56.5%, which means that there are more dependents (aged and children) than there are working adults.

Compounding the economic problem is the issue of the "working poor." Of Japanese adults between the ages of 20 and 64, 23% are classified as working poor, meaning that they earn less than two million yen (roughly $24,000) a year. Only 3.5% of men between the ages of 20 and 34 make more than the average household income of six million yen (roughly $72,000) a year. The unemployment rate is 5.1%, the highest since 1995. Additionally, the growth of temporary employment agencies allows corporations to pay laborers without benefits. Of those employed, 33.7% are "nonregular staff" (e.g., temporary or part-time workers), the highest since 1991. In Tokyo, 58% of laborers are short-term laborers, with an average monthly salary of 110,000 yen (roughly $1,300), and there is 17% unemployment. These figures show that the eligible tax-paying adult population is shrinking.

The combination of the growing senior population, decreasing fertility rates, and rising numbers of "working poor" has long-term consequences for the Japanese economy. By 2050, about 40% of the population will enter retirement age. The health of the retirement system (and overall economy) depends on the pension taxes of the working adult population. However, only 61.5% of the overall labor force paid pension taxes in 2009. Individuals did not pay because they were "working poor," or they chose to invest their money through other channels. Furthermore, the decreasing fertility rate means that there will be fewer working adults to support the growing aging population. The need to bolster the working adult population of the next generation is so dire that government programs are offering incentives to produce more children, including paying families 13,000 yen (roughly $150) per child per month, eliminating daycare waiting lists, and increasing after-school programs to offload the pressures of parenting.

Rejection of Salaryman Masculinity by the *Shinjinrui* ("New Breed") and the Formation of Soushokukei Danshi Masculinity

Against Japan's twentieth century socioeconomic background emerged two opposing masculine discourses. The salaryman discourse was a valorized form of masculinity in line with the economic boom between the 1950s and 1970s. As the bubble economy collapsed in the 1990s, sentiments of the salaryman changed, and soushokukei danshi emerged as a reflexive masculine discourse adopted by the *shinjinrui,* the "new generation."

Salaryman Masculinity

Dasgupta (2003) describes the salaryman as follows:

> ...a salaried white-collar male employee of private sector organizations, typically characterized by such features as lifetime employment, seniority-based salary indexing and promotions, and a generally paternalistic concern for the employee on the part of the company in return for steady, diligent loyalty to the organization. (p. 119)

Salarymen are not limited to corporate men; they can include any man who embodies the archetypal roles of heterosexual father and breadwinner (Connell & Messerschmidt, 2005; Hidaka, 2010). Interpersonal superiority, power (especially over women), and possessiveness are traditional measures of salarymen (Ito, 1993). Emphasis on these values resulted in a high score (95 of 100) on Hofstede's (2001) scale of masculinity, composed of similar measures of control, assertiveness, and success. According to

Hofstede's study, Japan is the most masculine culture in the world (the United States scored 62 out of 100 points).

Salaryman masculinity came into prominence in the postwar era, but some historians see it as an extension of prewar masculine discourses that emerged when Japan evolved from a feudal state to a modernized, capitalist nation. According to scholars, the salaryman's duty and loyalty to and self-sacrifice for the corporation evoke virtues found in the Bushido code of the samurai elite during the feudal Tokugawa period (1600–1868) (Dasgupta, 2000). The Meiji period (1868–1912) and the Taishō and early Shōwa interwar periods (1912–1940s) saw a continuance of vigorous, militaristic masculinities embodied by loyalty to the state, imperialism, and primitivism (Karlin, 2002). Japan's defeat in World War II and the resulting economic boom in the postwar decades invalidated militaristic masculinities and promoted salarymen to the position of masculine ideal (Dasgupta, 2003). For their loyalty, intense work ethic, and self-sacrifice, salarymen were dubbed "corporate warriors" (Dasgupta, 2003).

During the boom years between the 1950s and 1960s, the salaryman represented the ideal lifestyle of the Japanese middle class, and the industrial spirit of the Japanese people (Dasgupta, 2000; Vogel, 1963/1971). Salarymen were the embodiment of the national commitment to economic growth and represented higher education. They worked long hours, sacrificed personal leisure, and provided for their families and country. To Japanese people of the time, the salaryman represented a "bright new life" (Vogel, 1963/1971, p. 9), and young men aspired to be salarymen, while women sought to marry them (Mathews, 2003).

Fall of the Salaryman

The burst of the economic bubble in the 1990s and the resulting two-decade Hesei recession saw a shift of the salaryman from masculine ideal to a "figure of ridicule" (Dasgupta, 2003, p. 128). The uncertainty and loss of national confidence wrought by economic decline invalidated salaryman masculinity and brought attention to masculine expectations (Dasgupta, 2009). The recession stripped salarymen of "their 'three treasures' of lifetime employment, seniority system of promotion and company unionism" (Roberson & Suzuki, 2003, p. 9). As a result, Japanese salarymen experienced a crisis of masculinity embodied by loss of authority, loss of seduction, and loss of genius (Roberson & Suzuki, 2003). As the salaryman's mode of life was questioned, a plurality of masculinities signified by "funky" youth cultures emerged (Dasgupta, 2009, p. 80).

The critique of the salaryman figure is captured in latter twentieth century popular media. In the postwar years, popular literature, such as magazines, self-improvement manuals, and *manga* (comics), educated young men how to perform salaryman masculinity through work and body practices (Dasgupta, 2003). While prescriptions of salaryman masculinity continue to the current day, the 1990s saw a shift in representation, as television shows, comic books, and novellas began to portray the salaryman as a weak, insipid, rank-and-file employee who is never home and ineffective in carrying out social functions beyond work (Allinson, 1998, pp. 184–187; Dasgupta, 2003). Yet despite its compromised status, other scholars emphasize that salaryman masculinity is still the prevailing ideal in Japan: "omniscient" and "unchanging" (Hidaka, 2010, p. 164).

The Shinjinruï and the Emergence of Soushokukei Danshi Values

By the millennium, the salaryman's social power, privilege, and fierce work orientation were supplanted by new masculine ideals. In a study involving three generations of men, Hidaka (2010) found that "Cohort 3," the young men of the shinjinrui, exhibited declining loyalties to the firm and frequently questioned workplace demands. Instead, these men had a willingness to forfeit their jobs to attend to familial duties, such as child rearing.

Historians outline two characteristics of the shinjinrui that laid the foundation for soushokukei danshi masculinity. The first is the only-child effect. Unlike their parents, who came from larger families, the new generation came from smaller, child-centered households. The average Japanese family in the 1960s and 1970s had fewer than two children, meaning that many children grew up without siblings. The downsizing of the Japanese family reached a historical low in 2005, when the average was only 1.25 children per family (Statistics Bureau, Ministry of Internal Affairs and Communications, Japan, 2010). This experience made the new generation more self-centered than previous generations with a weaker sense of social responsibility (Herbig & Borstorff, 1995). In the workplace, this selfishness brought a marked decline in loyalty to the firm and less willingness to make sacrifices for it (Hidaka, 2010). For the shinjinrui, work is not an end in itself, but rather a means to personal fulfillment. Fueled by the only-child effect, the shinjinrui live not by an ethic of scarcity, but rather by one of acquisition.

Second, the shinjinrui grew up in the postbubble era when the salaryman's good life was no longer attainable (Fukasawa, 2009). The average monthly income of men age 20–34 who have regular employment is 260,900 yen (roughly $3,280) (Statistics Bureau, Ministry of Internal Affairs and Communications, Japan, 2011). About 40% of Japanese men work in nonstaff positions with no job security. Many of today's young Japanese men could not attain the big-ticket purchases (e.g., cars, houses, vacations), lifestyles, and social relationships associated with salarymen. Consequently, they developed a resigned perspective toward work and turned to fashion consciousness and other forms of low-cost, hedonic consumption because it was "the only ego-booster left for them" (Otake, 2009).

Soushokukei Danshi Masculinity Is Cocreated With Japanese Women

Women of the shinjinrui rejected salarymen based on observations of their parents' marriages, which they considered to be unhappy and miserable (Hidaka, 2010). By the 1990s, the heroic status of the salaryman was vanquished in the female imagination. In its place was a critical picture depicted as follows:

> A workaholic who toils long hours for Mitsubishi or Sony or some other large corporation, goes out drinking with his fellow workers or clients after work and plays golf with them on weekends, and rarely spends much time at home with his wife and children, much less do[es] anything around the house, such as cleaning or changing diapers. (Fujimura-Fanselow & Kameda, 1995, p. 229)

Contemporary Japanese women still want to marry but increasingly seek romantic love and a husband who can be a partner and companion with shared interests (Jolivet, 1997; Roberson & Suzuki, 2003). In contrast to previous generations of women who desired salaryman husbands that embodied the three "highs" of education, income, and physical stature, many of today's Japanese women seek men who embody the *san shi* (3 Cs) of comfortable income, communication, and cooperation with housework and child care (Mathews, 2003). Additionally, women look for men who are passionate, fulfill the role of father, and provide emotional support (Holloway, 2010). These values are consistent across various age segments of Japanese women. Young Japanese women in their late teens to early 20s are interested in men for *asobi* (play); meanwhile, older Japanese women cite *ikoguchi* (comfort), how well the husbands relate to their background and upbringing, and the ability to manage relationships within the family effectively as key motivators for marriage (Okano, 2009, p. 266).

In summary, soushokukei danshi's rejection of intense corporate careers and focus on family values and hedonic pursuits are partially motivated by the need to meet the needs of modern Japanese women.

Popular Media Culture Produces and Reinforces Soushokukei Danshi Masculinity

Popular media culture offers insights into the shared meanings surrounding gender practices in Japanese mainstream society. Many scholars of Japanese masculinity use popular media culture to investigate Japanese masculinity (Dasgupta, 2003; Roberson, 2005; Wood, 2006). The rejection of salaryman masculinity and the emergence of soushokukei danshi values are prevalent themes depicted in manga, *anime* (animated cartoons), television programs, film, popular novels, magazines, and video games.

One of the most influential forms of popular media culture is manga, which is read by Japanese men and women of different age categories. Successful manga are often translated into animation, live television dramas, and movies. Through multimedia exposure, manga properties obtain an even wider audience than in print form alone. Three manga properties that exhibit themes of masculinity—particularly the negotiation between traditional aggressive masculinities and sensitive soushokukei danshi masculinity—are *Detroit Metal City, Otomen,* and *Bakuman*.

Detroit Metal City is a popular manga by Wakasugi Kiminori. The story revolves around Soichi Negishi, a sweet, timid, and well-mannered young man who has a penchant for Swedish pop music, boutique shopping, culinary experiences, and photography. Soichi moves to Tokyo to pursue his dream of becoming a pop musician and singing romantic love ballads. Instead, he encounters greater success posing as the demonic Lord Johannes Krauser II, singing profanity-laced songs for the death metal band Detroit Metal City, or DMC. He dislikes the role, but has a talent for composing songs about death and debauchery. Soichi has to reconcile both aspects of his life—the soushokukei danshi who enjoys the finer things in life and the hypermasculine, profane Lord Krauser II—when he pursues his love interest, Aikawa, who disapproves of Soichi's dark inclinations. In 2008, *Detroit Metal City* was made into a 12-episode anime series, a live action movie, and an accompanying metal soundtrack. Future plans include a video game for the Nintendo DS.

Otomen is a continuing *shojo manga* (girls' comic) by Aya Kanno. Launched in 2007, the story features Asuka Masamune, a *bishnonen* (pretty boy) who is also the coolest, manliest guy in high school. Asuka is good at judo and karate and is the top kendo fighter in the world. Below the masculine exterior lies Asuka's secret: The things that he really loves are sweets, shojo manga, sewing, and cooking. He shamefully hides this part of his life from everyone to maintain his cool image, which points to the stigma of soushokukei danshi masculinity. But he risks exposing his feminine interests to impress a girl named Ryo Miyakozuka. Like *Detroit Metal City*, the story sees Asuka attempting to court Ryo while juggling his masculine and feminine pursuits. A live-action *Otomen* television series debuted in 2009.

Bakuman, by Tsugimi Ohba and Takeshi Obata, is about two intelligent middle-school boys, Mashiro and Takagi, who shirk higher education and corporate careers to pursue their dream of creating manga. In order to make time for comic production, both boys repeatedly skip class and exert only cursory efforts on homework assignments. To maintain acceptable grades, they apply to second-tiered high schools, where they only have to compete with the lesser students. Different from *Detroit Metal City* and *Otomen*, the narrative in *Bakuman* focuses on masculine work expectations (vs. feminized practices). The negotiation between corporate careers and hedonic pursuits is depicted as Mashiro and Takagi struggle between satisfying parental expectations and pursuing childhood dreams.

Manga are not the only site of masculine productions. Equally influential are popular novels and magazines, which prescribe body practices, work practices, and grooming practices consistent with hegemonic masculinity (Miller, 2005). For example, soushokukei danshi's perceived inability to attain sexual relationships has led to the publication of self-improvement manuals that help men get girls. One popular title is "*30-sai no Hoken Taiiku*" ("Health and Physical Education for 30-Year-Old Men"), a series of lifestyle manuals intended for men over 30 who have little to no experience with women. Chapters in the volumes include topics on how to look at girls, how to ask for a date, how to declare love, appropriate ways to be a boyfriend, how to get a girl to sleep in one's bed, and sexual techniques. The first volume of the book was published in 2008. In 2010, the book series was adapted into manga format, and an anime series debuted in spring 2011.

Contemporaneously, numerous fashion magazines act as style guides to help men attain and master the aesthetic and body practices that women find attractive. On the one hand, style magazines such as *Dual Suit* and *Men's Ex* endorse the corporate aesthetics of successful salarymen (Dasgupta, 2003). On the other hand, magazines targeting men in their 20s and 30s, such as *Popeye, Men's Nonno, Men's Joker,* and *Choki,* prescribe soushokukei danshi consumption practices that could be perceived as feminine by Japanese culture. The April 2011 issue of *Popeye* features young male models with floppy hairdos, adorned in ensembles that bear descriptive names such as "skirt on shorts," "A-line silhouette," and "double bag and hair band." A style-guide insert helps readers cobble together their own ensembles based on color ways and patterns. A lengthy food section directs readers to distinctive dining establishments that serve specialty ramen, sweets and desserts, and cocktails. In total, these style magazines promote a set of feminized body practices and social practices that demarcate followers from the salaryman's corporate aesthetic.

Issues of masculinity have crept into the narratives of digital gaming. In 2011, game developer Atlus released *Catherine* for the PlayStation3 and Xbox 360. The game stars Vincent Brooks, a 32-year-old salaryman. He is contemplating marriage with his girlfriend of 5 years, Katherine, who recently told him she is pregnant. As he sits at the empty bar, a beautiful and mysterious girl named Catherine approaches him. The two spend a night together at Vincent's apartment. After their tryst, Vincent begins having nightmares, which he believes to be connected to a series of bizarre deaths in his neighborhood, where young men mysteriously die in their sleep with a look of terror on their faces. Intermingled with the horror story are themes of modern masculinity, which one video game critic describes as "a bloke going through a whole checklist of male anxieties like marriage, sexual terror, fear of women, fear of sex, fatherhood as emasculation, the loss of control over one's life...[I]t's all very Freudian" (Adi Tantimedh, www.bleedingcool.com).

In closing, manga and style magazines establish a feminized, corporeal aesthetic that is visibly distinct from salarymen. Additionally, popular media culture shows that relationships with the opposite sex are a priority for Japanese men and that feminized body practices and social practices are, in fact, a strategy to win the affections of the opposite sex.

Summary of Findings

The findings indicate that soushokukei danshi masculinity emerged as a counterpoint to salaryman masculinity. In the postwar decades, the salaryman was a heroic ideal that embodied the industrial spirit and reinvigoration of Japan. The state agenda to increase productivity promoted a masculine identity that was synonymous with self-sacrifice to one's career. As a result, the shinjinrui, the new generation, grew up without a present father, and the wives of salarymen raised families without a present husband. The collapse of the economic bubble in the 1990s invalidated the salaryman's way of life and the role of men in society came under close scrutiny.

The men of the new generation did not want to become like their absentee salaryman fathers. The rejection of salaryman masculinity was so pronounced that men of the new generation constructed a feminized body whose physical appearance and practices marked a distinct departure from those of salarymen. Based on their observations of their parents' unhappy marriages, women of the new generation sought emotionally supportive, cooperative husbands. To meet the demands of women, Japanese men reshaped a "softer" masculinity centered on family values, comfortable lives, and hedonic pursuits.

Soushokukei danshi's focus on family values and hedonic pursuits has a trade-off. By choosing comfortable jobs over intense corporate careers, soushokukei danshi are also choosing to live with less income. As a result, some Japanese men are unable to support a relationship financially. The situation is an ironic one. To meet the demands of contemporary women, men choose comfortable career paths that allow time to be spent with their partners and families. However, the trade-off results in lower incomes (vs. corporate salarymen), and some men can barely afford to date, much less sustain families. Even today, many Japanese women choose husbands who can assume the role of breadwinner (Hidaka, 2010). This trade-off is a popular theme concretized in popular media.

Finally, soushokukei danshi masculinity is an identity that is structured by marketers of popular culture. Marketers produce TV shows, celebrity personalities, comics, movies, and magazines that prescribe body practices, work practices, and other consumption practices that may be considered feminine by Japanese society. At the same time, these practices are considered cool, fashionable, and even desirable to the opposite sex. Young men pattern themselves after these representations, thereby reifying soushokukei danshi as a hegemonic, although stigmatized, form of masculinity.

DISCUSSION

This work is evocative of previous research on masculine consumption practices. By looking at soushokukei danshi masculinity in light of economic change, social change, and gender relations, significant new findings emerge. Next, I comment on each of the findings in terms of how it intersects with popular culture and existing research.

Demystifying Popular Notions of Soushokukei Danshi

The findings in this study negate two popular myths about soushokukei danshi: that they are trying to be like women and that they are uninterested in sex.

First, articles in the media frame the consumption practices of soushokukei danshi as "girly," "ladylike," and "less manly." In many cultures, shopping, fashion, and beauty practices are consumption activities traditionally attributed to women (Otnes & McGrath, 2001; Roberts, 1998). However, soushokukei danshi are not at all trying to be like women. On the contrary, their feminine pursuits in fashion, beautification, and other social activities may be part of an overall strategy to win the affections of women. The findings show that soushokukei danshi consumption practices are subsumed within a masculine identity. This strategy is evident in comics, television, and film such as *Otomen* and *Detroit Metal City*, where male protagonists abandon aggressive masculinities and adopt feminized practices to impress girls. Additionally, style magazines such as *Men's Joker* and *Popeye* teach young men how to gain attention from the opposite sex through feminized fashion and aesthetic practices.

Past research shows that heterosexual male consumers are increasingly concerned with being objects of "aesthetic and sexual appraisal" (Miller, 2003, p. 37; also see Tuncay & Otnes, 2008a). Male consumers negotiate strategies to navigate and push the boundaries of aesthetic consumption without violating their heterosexual identities (Tuncay & Otnes, 2008a). Specific to Japanese men, Miller (2003) shows that men's eyebrow grooming practices are motivated by the admiration and approval of women: "It was a girlfriend who first taught him how to do it" (p. 37). The findings in this study support past researchers' assertions that women structure men's feminized body practices. Not limited to body practices, this study also outlines women's influence on Japanese men's attitudes toward work and family.

Second, the findings reject the notion that soushokukei danshi are not interested in sex and committed relationships. The reason why some Japanese men are unsuccessful in sustaining relationships with women may be economic in nature. A large portion of Japanese men between the ages of 20 and 34 is classified as "working poor," meaning that they earn less than 2 million yen ($24,000) a year. Even though young men want relationships, they may not be able to afford and sustain one. While women seek men who can provide emotional support and *ikoguchi* (comfort) (Holloway, 2010; Jolivet, 1997; Mathews, 2003; Okano, 2009), traditional breadwinner masculinities still loom large and influence women's choice in a husband (Hidaka, 2010).

Theories of Japanese Masculinity

Scholars take different approaches to theorizing Japanese masculinities (Roberson & Suzuki, 2003). Some researchers examine the role of women in shaping Japanese masculinities (Jolivet, 1997; Mathews, 2003). Others investigate the role of historical Japanese masculinities in shaping contemporary masculinities (Dasgupta, 2000; Karlin, 2002). Yet others attribute masculine productions to the state and economy (Garon, 1997; Sievers, 1983). Finally, others investigate the role of popular media culture in shaping masculinities (Dasgupta, 2003; Miller, 2005; Wood, 2006). This study integrates these perspectives to explain the rise of soushokukei danshi masculinity.

Soushokukei danshi masculinity is reflexively cocreated with women. The historical analysis shows that contemporary Japanese women select men who display communicative, partner-like qualities, as opposed to salarymen, who are always at work (Jolivet, 1997; Okano, 2009). Additionally, Japanese women's desires with respect to the male body are reflected in media representations of male idols with slim figures and high-fashion acumen (Miller, 2003). The *bishonen* aesthetic found in Japanese comic books, characterized by handsome, effeminate male figures, embodies a rejection of the hypermasculine muscular body aesthetic by female comic artists and readers (Wood, 2006). Consequently, young Japanese men mold lifestyles and bodies to match the qualities desired by women. The findings provide evidence that men do not exclusively produce masculinity, underlining the importance of dislocating notions that assume a homology of men with masculinity (Connell, 2005; Cornwall & Lindisfarne, 1994; di Leonardo, 1991; Sedgewick, 1995).

Soushokukei danshi masculinity is a counterpoint to traditional salaryman masculinity. Men of the shinjinrui do not want to be like their workaholic fathers. They are skeptical of the salaryman lifestyle and prefer comfortable lives centered on family and hedonic pursuits. The differentiation extends beyond attitudes toward work. Japanese men develop a feminized body that is distinguished from the salaryman. By adopting male beauty practices and gender-ambiguous fashion, soushokukei danshi achieve three objectives: (1) challenging salaryman masculinity, (2) attracting women who appreciate the feminized aesthetic, and (3) transgressing oppressive gender norms (Iida, 2005).

However, a countervailing dialogue that critiques the laissez-faire lifestyle of soushokukei danshi must be acknowledged. Many young Japanese men are spoiled, only-children who have low career ambitions and incomes, but yet are driven by an ethic of materialistic consumption (Fukusawa, 2009). Ironically, this critique of soushokukei danshi mirrors the critique of salarymen in the early twentieth century. In the Taisho and Showa interwar periods, salarymen embodied the "new Japanese male." On the one hand, they were celebrated as the embodiment of a modernized and industrialized Japan and the paragon of the rising middle-class culture. On the other hand, salarymen were seen as symbols of nonchalance, materialism, and debauchery (Karlin, 2002; Roden, 1990).

Much has been written about how Japan's national agendas prescribed gender roles for men and women. In the early and mid-twentieth century, state directives encouraged men to work hard and save substantial portions of their income (Garon, 1997). The role of women in the early Japanese model of capitalism was to provide a temporary, peripheral labor force until marriage and, subsequently, to transition to domestic labor and care for children (Bishop, 2005). To a certain extent, the "heterosexual complementarity" of man/public and woman/private continues to the current day (Hidaka, 2010). But these gender roles are being broken down, blended, and transgressed. By rejecting the traditional role of salarymen, soushokukei danshi expand traditional expectations of men beyond the state-sponsored model of masculinity.

Finally, popular media culture prescribes body practices, work practices, and other consumption behaviors apropos to hegemonic masculinity. In the past, comics, television shows, and fashion magazines taught Japanese men how to achieve the ideal look and feel of corporate masculinity (Dasgupta, 2003). Today, corporate aesthetics are still endorsed, but mainstream culture is also inundated with a plurality of feminine, cool, and funky masculine aesthetics (Dasgupta, 2009).

Implications for Masculine Consumption Research

The past decade has witnessed continuous scholarly interest in masculinity and consumption. Existing research is diverse and focuses on how men express masculine values through shopping behaviors (Otnes & McGrath, 2001; Rinallo, 2007; Tuncay & Otnes, 2008a, 2008b), how brands and products express masculine attributes (Holt, 2006; Roberson, 2005), and media articulations of masculinity (Ging, 2005; Holt & Thompson, 2004; Schroeder & Zwick, 2004). Much of the existing work is situated in a Western context. An investigation into soushokukei danshi addresses the call to focus on populations outside the Western context (Thompson & Holt, 2004) and provides insights for several theoretical concepts in masculine consumption research: the crisis of masculinity, phallic consumption, gender tourism, body capital, and gender transgression.

In the United States, widespread job routinization, obsolescence in the face of postindustrial technologies, and the rise of women in the early twentieth century resulted in a "crisis of masculinity," characterized by feelings of emasculation, ineffectiveness, and loss of status (Holt & Thompson, 2004; Kimmel, 1996). American men compensate for their lost status and bolster their masculinity through symbolic consumption and engaging in rugged activities (Belk & Costa, 1998; Schouten & McAlexander, 1995). Holt and Thompson (2004) call this the "compensatory consumption thesis." British historians elaborate a similar discourse of masculine anxiety and insecurity for contemporaneous British men (Greenfield, O'Connell, & Reid, 1999). Soushokukei danshi is sometimes understood as a "crisis of masculinity" of Japan, where men's feminized practices are symptomatic of stripped economic power, materialism, and moral breakdown (Fukasawa, 2009).

Holt and Thompson (2004) reject the compensatory consumption thesis on the basis that it is a theory built from spectacular and infrequent consumption (e.g., a one-time motorcycle purchase, infrequent treks into the mountains). Focusing on everyday consumption, they find that American men achieve masculinity "through the act of achieving—through the tenacious work required to climb the socioeconomic ladder to a position of status" (p. 427). In Japan, this model of "phallic consumption" (Thompson & Holt, 2004) may explain the motivations and behaviors of salarymen. However, the collapse of the Japanese economy in the 1990s invalidated the salaryman lifestyle (Fujimura-Fanselow & Kameda, 1995). Soushokukei danshi do not become men through status achievements, but rather by focusing on family values and hedonic pursuits.

The findings suggest that soushokukei danshi's feminized consumption practices are contained within a masculine identity. Framing soushokukei danshi consumption as a "revitalizing retreat" or "gender tour," where men engage in female pursuits as a temporary refuge from intense social competition (Moore, 1988; Thompson & Holt, 2004), is not entirely accurate. Instead, soushokukei danshi masculinity is a full-time, feminized identity that helps men differentiate themselves from salarymen and, through a set of consumption practices, attract the opposite sex (Miller, 2003; Tuncay & Otnes, 2008a).

Another important theme in this study is that the body is an important vessel for capital accumulations. In contemporary Japan, the salaryman is a cultural dope (Dasgupta, 2003), gender-ambiguous fashion styles are in vogue (Miller, 2003), and women appreciate the feminized appearance of men (Miller, 2003; Wood, 2006). Holliday and Cairnie's (2007) idea of "body capital" is useful in explaining soushokukei danshi's body practices. Holliday and Cairnie find that male aesthetic surgery is a means to gain capital in a range of different fields such as careers, relationships, and sexuality. In similar fashion, effeminate aesthetics distinguish soushokukei danshi from other men, especially the salaryman.

Finally, soushokukei danshi adopt feminized consumption practices to transgress hegemonic masculinity. This finding evokes research on spectacular sites of consumption. Like Gothic and gay consumers, soushokukei danshi is a lifestyle and identity that allows Japanese men to overturn or transgress the dominant status quo through gender play (Goulding & Saren, 2009; Kates, 2002).

CONCLUSION AND LIMITATIONS

By examining economic change, social change, and shifts in gender relations in Japan, this research finds that soushokukei danshi's practices are subsumed within a framework that is undoubtedly masculine. Their feminized body practices and consumption activities are parts of an overall strategy to win the affections of women. The media frames soushokukei danshi as men who are trying to be "like women" and uninterested in sexual relationships with women. However, I present evidence that this is not the case.

These findings hold a level of optimism for Japanese public policy. Soushokukei danshi—a generation of men who seemingly do not want to reproduce, work, and spend—is a genuine concern for the Japanese government, which seeks to curb population decline, bolster its retirement system, and spur on its economy through consumption. The findings in this study indicate that this concern is misdirected. Soushokukei danshi are not running from sexual relationships; in fact, it is a masculine discourse customized to meet the demands of today's Japanese women. However, many young men are working poor, pay little to no pension taxes, and, as a result, are compounding the aging population problem.

The Japanese government could reevaluate how it plans to reconstruct masculinity to mobilize its population and spur economic growth. In the past, the government promoted salaryman masculinity, a discourse synonymous with productivity and loyalty to firm and country (Garon, 1997). One solution might be to reorient the nationally endorsed masculinity from one of work productivity to one of home productivity (e.g., focusing on family values and procreation). The government can continue and expand on extant initiatives such as offering monetary incentives for children and initiating programs to help parents raise children. To bolster the economy, marketers could create new opportunities by developing products and services that capitalize on the aesthetic needs of men (Miller, 2003). In recognition of the immense aging population, marketers could develop opportunities in creating products and services that target the elderly, such as assisted living services.

There are two notable limitations to this study:

- Feminized aesthetics characterize the trendy, hip look of the current of fashion cycle. Contemporary Japanese men's fashions comprise youthful ensembles that feature feminized characteristics, such as skinny-leg jeans, pastel colors, boat-neck T-shirts, and jeweled sequins. There is a possibility that the feminized aesthetics of soushokukei danshi may have more to do with movements in fashion than with gender and sexuality. This idea supports Coad's (2008) assertion that metrosexuality is a fashion cycle—the modern incarnation of the eighteenth century dandy, or the hegemonic man who shares a propensity to wear fancy clothes. Future research could further investigate the intersection of fashion cycles and gender construction.
- This study lacks an emic perspective of soushokukei danshi masculinity. Primary data could further augment the findings and conclusions in this chapter.

Overall, soushokukei danshi masculinity represents an exciting site to explore issues in masculinity, gender, culture, and consumption. Opportunities for future investigations abound.

REFERENCES

Allinson, Gary D. (1998). *Japan's postwar history.* New York, NY: Cornell Paperbacks.

Arnold, Stephen, & Eileen Fischer (1994). Hermeneutics and consumer research. *Journal of Consumer Research, 21* (June), 55–70.

Belk, Russell W., & Janeen Arnold Costa (1998). The mountain man myth: A contemporary consuming fantasy. *Journal of Consumer Research, 25* (December), 218–240.

Bishop, Beverly (2005). *Globalization and women in the Japanese Workforce.* London, England: RoutledgeCurzon.

Coad, David (2008). *The metrosexual: Gender, sexuality and sport.* Albany, NY: SUNY Press.

Connell, R. W. (1993). The big picture: Masculinities in recent world history. *Theory and Society, 22*(5), 597–623.

Connell, R. W. (2000). *The men and the boys.* Berkeley, CA: University of California Press.

Connell, R. W. (2005). *Masculinities* (2nd ed.). Berkeley, CA: University of California Press.

Connell, R. W., & James W. Messerschmidt (2005). Hegemonic masculinity: Rethinking the concept. *Gender and Society, 19*(6), 829–859.

Cornwall, Andrea, & Nancy Lidisfarne (1994). *Dislocating masculinity: Comparative ethnographies.* New York, NY: Routledge.

Dasgupta, Rohit (2000). Performing masculinities? The "salaryman" at work and play. *Japanese Studies, 20*(2), 189–200.

Dasgupta, Rohit (2003). Creating corporate warriors: The "salaryman" and masculinity in Japan. In Kam Louie & Morris Low (Eds.), *Asian masculinities: The meaning and practice of manhood in China and Japan* (pp. 118–134). New York, NY: RoutledgeCurzon.

Dasgupta, Rohit (2009). The "lost decade" of the 1990s and shifting masculinities in Japan. *Culture, Society and Masculinity, 1*(1), 79–95.

Davis, Kathy (2003). *Dubious equalities and embodied differences: Cultural studies on cosmetic surgery.* Lanham, MD: Rowan and Littlefield.

di Leonardo, Micaela (1991). Introduction: Gender, culture and political economy: Feminist anthropology in historical perspective. In Micaela di Leonardo (Ed.), *Gender at the crossroads of knowledge in the postmodern era.* Berkeley, CA: University of California Press.

Duus, Peter (1998). *Modern Japan.* New York, NY: Houghton Mifflin.

Fujimura-Fanselow, Kumiko, & Atsuko Kameda (1995). *Japanese women: New feminist perspectives on the past, present and future.* New York, NY: Feminist Press.

Fukasawa, Maki (2009). *Soushoku Danshi Sedai Heisei Danshi Zukan (Handbook of man in the Heisei period).* Tokyo, Japan: Kobunsha.

Garon, Sheldon (1997). *Molding Japanese minds: The state in everyday life.* Princeton, NJ: Princeton University Press.

Ging, Debbie (2005). A "manual on masculinity"? The consumption and use of mediated images of masculinity among teenage boys in Ireland. *Irish Journal of Sociology, 14*(2), 29–52.

Golder, Peter N. (2000). Historical methods in marketing research with new evidence on long-term market share stability. *Journal of Marketing Research, 37*(2), 156–173.

Gordon, Andrew (2008). *A modern history of Japan: From Tokugawa times to present* (2nd ed.). London, England: Oxford University Press.

Goulding, Christina, & Michael Saren (2009). Performing identity: An analysis of gender expressions at the Whitby Goth festival. *Consumption Markets and Culture, 12*(1), 27–46.

Greenfield, Jill, Sean O'Connell, & Chris Reid (1999). Fashioning masculinity: Men only, consumption and the development of marketing in the 1930s. *Twentieth Century British History, 10*(4), 457–476.

Harney, Alexandra (2009). The herbivore's dilemma: Japan panics about the rise of "grass-eating men," who shun sex, don't spend money and like taking walks. *Slate,* http://www.slate.com/id/2220535/ (June 15).

Henry, Paul C. (2010). How mainstream consumers think about consumer rights and responsibilities. *Journal of Consumer Culture, 37*(4), 670–687.

Herbig, Paul A., & Pat Borstorff (1995). Japan's Shinjinrui: The new breed. *International Journal of Social Economics, 22*(12), 49–65.

Hidaka, Tomoko (2010). *Salaryman masculinity: Continuity and change in hegemonic masculinity in Japan.* Leiden, the Netherlands: Koninklijke Brill LV.

Hofstede, Geertz (2001). *Culture's consequences: Comparing values, behaviors, institutions and organizations across nations* (2nd ed.). Thousand Oaks, CA: Sage Publications.

Holliday, Ruth, & Allie Cairnie (2007). Man made plastic: An alternative account of aesthetic surgery. *Journal of Consumer Culture, 7*(1), 57–78.

Holloway, Susan D. (2010). *Women and family in contemporary Japan.* Cambridge, England: Cambridge University Press.

Holt, Douglas B. (2006). Jack Daniel's America: Iconic brands as ideological parasites and proselytizers. *Journal of Consumer Culture, 6*(3), 355–377.

Holt, Douglas B., & Craig J. Thompson (2004). Man-of-action heroes: The pursuit of heroic masculinity in everyday consumption. *Journal of Consumer Research, 31* (September), 425–440.

Humphreys, Ashlee (2010). Semiotic structure and the legitimization of consumption practices: The case of casino gambling. *Journal of Consumer Research, 37* (October), 490–510.

Iida, Yumiko (2005). Beyond the feminization of masculinity: Transforming patriarchy with the feminine in contemporary Japanese youth culture. *Inter-Asia Cultural Studies, 6*(1), 56–74.

Ito, K. (1993). *Otoko Rashisi no Yukue: Dansei-Bunka no Bunkashakaigaku (The direction of manliness: The cultural sociology of male culture).* Tokyo, Japan: Sin'yosha.

Jolivet, Muriel (1997). *Japan: The childless society?* New York, NY: Routledge.

Kanng, A. (2007). *Otomen* (1–10). Tokyo: Hakushensha, Inc.

Karlin, Jason G. (2002). The gender of nationalism: Competing masculinities in Meiji Japan. *Journal of Japanese Studies, 28*(1), 41–77.

Kates, Stephen M. (2002). The protean quality of subcultural consumption: An ethnographic account of gay consumers. *Journal of Consumer Research, 29* (December), 383–399.

Kimmel, Michael (1996). *Manhood in America.* New York, NY: Free Press.

Kjeldgaard, Dannie, & Kaj Storgaard Nielsen (2010). Glocal gender identities in market places of transition: Marianismo and the consumption of the Telenovela Rebelde. *Marketing Theory, 10*(1), 29–44.

Mathews, Gordon (2003). Ikigai and masculinity in today's Japan. In James E. Roberson & Nobue Suzuki (Eds.), *Men and masculinities in contemporary Japan* (pp. 109–125). New York, NY: Routledge.

Miller, Laura (2003). Male beauty work in Japan. In James E. Roberson & Nobue Suzuki (Eds.), *Men and masculinities in contemporary Japan: Dislocating the salaryman doxa* (pp. 37–58). New York, NY: Routledge.

Miller, Laura (2005). There's more than manga: Popular nonfiction books and magazines. In Jennifer Robertson (Ed.), *Companion to the anthropology of Japan.* Hoboken, NJ: Blackwell Publishers.

Moore, Suzanne (1988). "Getting a bit of the other": The pimps of postmodernism. In Rowena Chapman & Jonathan Rutherford (Eds.), *Male order: Unwrapping masculinity* (pp. 165–192). London, England: Lawrence and Wishart.

Ohba, T., & T. Obata (2008). *Bakuman* (1–8). Tokyo: Shuisha, Inc.

Okano, Kaori H. (2009). *Young women in Japan: Transitions to adulthood.* London, England: Routledge.

Otake, Tomoko (2009). Blurring the boundaries: As the future facing Japan's young people changes fast, so too are traditional gender identities. *The Japan Times Online,* http://search.japantimes.co.jp/cgi-bin/fl20090510x1.html (May 10).

Otnes, Cele C., & Mary A. McGrath (2001). Perceptions and realities of male shopping behavior. *Journal of Retailing, 77,* 111–137.

Rinallo, Diego (2007). Metro/fashion/tribes of men: Negotiating the boundaries of men's legitimate consumption. In Bernard Cova, Robert V. Kozinets, & Avi Shankar (Eds.), *Consumer tribes* (pp. 76–92). Oxford, England: Butterworth-Heinemann, Elsevier.

Roberson, James E. (2005). Fight!! Ippatsu!!! "Genki" energy drinks and the marketing of masculine ideology in Japan. *Men and Masculinities, 7*(4), 365–384.

Roberson, James E., & Nobue Suzuki (2003). Introduction. In *Men and masculinities in contemporary Japan: Dislocating the salaryman doxa* (pp. 1–19). New York, NY: Routledge.

Roberts, Mary Louise (1998). Gender, consumption, and commodity culture. *American Historical Review, 103*(3), 817–844.

Roden, Donald (1990). Taisho culture and the problem of gender ambivalence. In J. Thomas Rimer (Ed.), *Culture and identity: Japanese intellectuals during the interwar years* (pp. 37–55). Princeton, NJ: Princeton University Press.

Schouten, John W., & James H. Alexander (1995). Subcultures of consumption: An ethnography of the new bikers. *Journal of Consumer Research, 22* (June), 43–61.

Schroeder, Jonathan E., & Detlev Zwick (2004). Mirrors of masculinity: Representation and identity in advertising images. *Consumption, Markets and Culture, 7*(1), 21–52.

Sedgewick, Eve K. (1995). Gosh, Boy George, you must be awfully secure in your masculinity! In Maurice Berger (Ed.), *Constructing masculinity*. New York, NY: Routledge.

Sievers, Sharon L. (1983). *Flowers in salt: The beginnings of feminist consciousness in modern Japan*. Stanford, CA: Stanford University Press.

Simpson, Mark (2002). Meet the metrosexual. http://www.dir.salon.com/ent/feature/2002/07/22/metrosexual

Statistics Bureau, Ministry of Internal Affairs and Communications, Japan (2010). *Statistical handbook of Japan*. http://www.stat.go.jp/english/data/handbook/index.htm

Statistics Bureau, Ministry of Internal Affairs and Communications, Japan (2011). *Japan statistical yearbook 2011*. http://www.stat.go.jp/english/data/nenkan/index.htm

Thompson, Craig J., & Douglas B. Holt (2004). How do men grab the phallus? Gender tourism in everyday consumption. *Journal of Consumer Culture, 4*(3), 313–338.

Thompson, Craig J., William Locander, & Howard Pollio (1989). Putting consumer experience back into consumer research: The philosophy and method of existential-phenomenology. *Journal of Consumer Research, 16* (September), 139–154.

Tipton, Elise K. (2008). *Modern Japan: A social and political history* (2nd ed.). London, England: Routledge.

Tuncay, Linda (2006). Conceptualizations of masculinity among a "new" breed of male consumers. In Lorna Stevens & Janet Borgerson (Eds.), *Gender and consumer behavior* (Vol. 8; pp. 312–327). Edinburgh, Scotland: Association for Consumer Research.

Tuncay, Linda, & Cele C. Otnes (2008a). The use of persuasion management strategies by identity vulnerable consumers: The case of heterosexual male shoppers. *Journal of Retailing, 84* (December), 487–499.

Tuncay, Linda, & Cele C. Otnes (2008b). Exploring the link between masculinity and consumption. In Tina M. Lowrey (Ed.), *Brick and mortar shopping in the 21st century*. New York, NY: Lawrence Erlbaum Associates.

Vogel, Ezra F. (1971/1963). *Japan's new middle class: The salary man and his family in a Tokyo suburb* (2nd ed.). Berkeley, CA: University of California Press.

Wakasugi, K. (2005). *Detroit Metal City* (1–10). Tokyo: Hakushensha, Inc.

Wood, Andrea (2006). "Straight" women, queer texts: Boy-love manga and the rise of a global counterpublic. *Women's Studies Quarterly, 34*(1/2), 394–414.

12

Masculinity, Intimacy, and Consumption

Nacima Ourahmoune

INTRODUCTION

Male lingerie is a new product category for men that appeared around the turn of the century. It refers to stylish male underwear that explicitly borrows the codes of women's lingerie. The simple semantic shift from using the term "underwear" to the popularization of the term "men's lingerie" and its appropriation by media and advertising discourse seem to be an interesting indicator of the evolution of male consumption associated with the body and intimacy. The brand HOM became the market leader because of its innovation in product design. It was the first company to use the word "lingerie" for men, creating a new range of products that competitors soon started to emulate. A new product category, men's fine underwear, was born.

This new range consists of soft-fabric boxer shorts, briefs, underpants, and thongs, echoing women's lingerie (fishnet stockings, lace or silk). The see-through fabrics, the shininess, or even the crystal stones the logo is made of reinforce the "precious" touch. Daring colors like gold or silver contrast strongly with traditional codes. The cut also changed: tightly fitting or low-waist cuts are particularly figure flattering. These new products constitute a complete break with the standard codes of the male underwear sector and of the brand itself. Most of the sales are made via websites as consumption of men's lingeie is still considered a dubious behavior, but department stores register great success, with brands like HOM claiming the largest corner. For instance, the thong for men became the bestseller of the underwear corner in the main men's department store in Paris during Christmas 2005 and 2006. Moreover, the female lingerie segment grew by 0.4% versus 6% for the male underwear segment in 2009. For the past 6 years, men's lingerie has grown by double digits each year (15% to 20%; XERFI, 2010).

It is now accepted that consumption enables people in everyday life to assign meaning through praxis, through the manipulation of products (e.g., Baudrillard, 1979; Belk, 1988; de Certeau, 1984). The role played by consumption and products pertaining to intimate practices has been only minimally investigated, especially when it concerns male intimacy. In fact, these two worlds—"intimacy" and "masculinity"—are traditionally conceived as antinomical. However, a large spectrum of products ranging from candles to lingerie or other erotic goods offers the researcher a rich field for understanding the complexity of intimate consumption and/or intimacy. This part of consumption culture has been recognized as a particularly significant facet of contemporary life, even though it has not been adequately studied (Evans, 2003). While, at a theoretical level, erotic consumption helps recharacterize the democratization of intimacy (Giddens, 1992) and the aestheticism of everyday life (Featherstone, 1991, 2000; Firat, Sherry, & Venkatesh, 1995; Maffesoli, 1990), it also indicates the need to explore the process in detail so as to understand the relationship of consumers to these products.

In this chapter I shall examine male representations of intimacy—a traditionally female stronghold—through this new form of consumption. Indeed, gender roles are undergoing major sociocultural changes that impact the market and consumption. More specifically, although male consumption is largely ignored in consumer research, it is now attracting growing interest. I wish to contribute to this research dynamic by introducing considerations of privacy into the understanding of male consumer behavior.

In the first part of the chapter, I examine the sociohistorical sedimentation of gender differences and their impact on the public/private divide. In particular, the notion of intimacy will be clarified and then recontextualized in relation to changing male identity, a shift that now has implications for the study of consumer behavior. In the second part, I present and discuss the findings of a qualitative study based on phenomenological interviews with 21 men regarding the consumption of male lingerie. Specifically, I will elaborate the findings about such consumption in relation to interactions within the heterosexual couple. While the commonly accepted idea points to the role of the female partner as dominant in this new form of consumption, men's lived experiences of this behavior have not been investigated in depth. Finally, I conclude by presenting the dimensions in relation to the concept of intimacy revealed in this study of male consumption.

GENDER AND THE MALE–FEMALE COUPLE

With variants, the male–female opposition is an anthropological constant. The great majority of societies incorporate it into the basic array of their classification instruments and into their cosmogony: *cosmos* (universe) and *genos* (generation), the part of mythology explaining the origins of the world and mankind (Levi-Strauss, 2002). A central component of taxonomies for comprehending all aspects of everyday life thus finds an originary principle in the sexual and bodily difference between men and women reexpressed in the male–female couple with its strongly hierarchical connotations.

In his work carried out in Kabylia, Algeria, in the late 1950s, Bourdieu (1998) provides one of the most comprehensive illustrations of such a taxonomy. In particular, and based on many field observations, Bourdieu suggests how the categories of male and female function as symbolic operators producing norms and meaning in every aspect of Kabyle life. Social space is divided into male and female areas. Work and ordinary activities such as consumption are gendered. Men are associated with characteristically hot, strong food (spices, salt, roasts), tools that settle disputes and spill blood (guns, sickles), the symbols of light and of domination (eagle), the central role of the nose as the symbol of holding one's head high, looking one straight in the face, and presence. Women are associated with soft, bland, boiled food, concealment (secrecy, darkness, witchcraft, the jackal), and closeness to the world of domesticated animals (cowshed).

Also, an interesting element is the existence of areas and moments of social life where the male–female opposition is blurred: the still weakly sexual status of the child or that of the old man whose virility is on the wane. In these so-called "borderline" states situated at the margins (Roman *limes*), where the opposition becomes hazy and at risk, rituals are

TABLE 12.1

Gender Oppositions

Male	Female
Dry	Moist
Above	Below
Outside	Inside
Straight	Crooked
Open	Closed
Dominant	Dominated
High	Low

Sources: Adapted from Bourdieu, Pierre (1998). *La Domination Masculine,* Paris, France: Editions du Seuil; Héritier, Françoise (1986). *Masculin/Féminin, La Pensée de la Différence,* Paris, France: Odile Jacob.

enacted to avert the threat of chaos and confusion that would occur if the binary symbols and role assignments of male and female were no longer to be defined clearly.

By combining the cosmogonies outlined by Bourdieu (1993) with Françoise Héritier's (1986) analysis of "the differential valences of the sexes," we can condense, in a simplified table, the most basic symbolic associations of male and female in Western societies (Table 12.1).

More specifically, within a historical perspective, the origins of the gendered division of labor can be traced to the Industrial Revolution, which for the first time in human history separated the place of production from the place of reproduction. In preindustrial society, it is evident that labor and household work occurred within the same area of socialization—the family—in which production and consumption merged. Whether in agriculture or craft work, at that time all or nearly all women worked. Although their activities were clearly distinct, men and women worked together on the various tasks that made up day-to-day economic life.

The division between productive work and reproductive work finds its symbolic legitimacy in the modern opposition between the domestic sphere and the public sphere, the bourgeois version of the old opposition between nature and culture. Within this perspective, the emergence of female wage earners, however necessary for satisfying growing productivity needs, comes up against the new bourgeois model of the family, which gives men responsibility for production and the monopoly of public space. In contrast, women are the guarantors of reproduction and the proper functioning of private space. They are thus set up as the guardians of a male bourgeois morality that takes a dim view of their emancipation from the family sphere, which is viewed as a threat to the general equilibrium of society.

The fact that women find employment outside the home is for them a bid for independence, but it also involves a transfer of dependence to a new male figure: the boss. Moreover, as noted by François de Singly (2001), the model of the housewife arises precisely with the bourgeoisie, which draws its inspiration from the aristocratic model: The passive woman will thus symbolically occupy the place of the aristocratic woman in bourgeois society. For men, whose honor requires that they be active in all respects, having a wife at home implies that they have the means to support someone who, in a way, does nothing. Women's paid work therefore involves a lengthy struggle against an original paradox, insofar as it is an economic necessity but is not easily accepted by the dominant morality of a system whose economy is nonetheless based largely on work.

Industrial society turned this separation of gender roles into a complementarity between the sexes that was essential for the proper functioning of society as a whole. This complementarity was justified as part of the natural order, thereby establishing differentiated normative systems for men's and women's work and, in particular, permanently anchoring these stereotypes in collective representations. From then on, men's incursion into private or intimate space became a form of social anomie.

INTIMACY

Intimacy strongly takes us back to the notion of interiority. The difference between the two is simply one of degree because intimate (*intimus*) is the superlative—that which is most inside—and interior is the comparative. Interiority refers to the "within"—what lies in the space comprised by the limits of a house or the body. The polysemy of the term returns us to the homology between the domestic interior and a person's innards. Furthermore, the terms "interior" and "intestines" share a common etymology: both are derived from the Latin preposition *intus,* meaning "within." The notion of interiority thus refers, through the awareness that the person has of his or her capacity to withdraw into himself or herself, to the subject's relationship with the outside world.

The interior is what is withdrawn from outside and suggests the individual's feeling about and awareness of himself and his own way of living. Between the inner me and the world lie the limits of my body, my skin—hence, the importance of working on appearances. Finally, intimacy, implying withdrawal, is also suggestive of the return to oneself or to one's inner circle, individuality, consciousness, and self-discovery. The intimate introduces the subject to an interiority in relation to the self, to the intimacy of being that Emmanuel Levinas (1986) refers to as "dwelling" (*recueillement*).

In Anglo-Saxon psychology, intimacy is understood rather differently. In particular, domestic intimacy transmitted through the concept of privacy is defined by Harold Proshansky (1973), Irwin Altman (1975), and Stokols and Shumaker (1981) in a multidimensional way: Privacy is a regulatory process of opening and closing in relation to the outside world and of withdrawal into oneself. It is also a call for respect by the social body of the domestic domain. And, lastly, it is the acute awareness of the legitimacy of an individual inner space that must always be defended against the intrusions of this same social body. Thus, emphasis is placed on the dynamic aspect of the demand for privacy and, indeed, on the legal manifestations of this demand. Significantly, the concept of intimacy, in the French use of the term, focuses more on the protection of an interiority, that of consciousness *of,* and of the return to oneself (Schwarz, 1990).

In fact, intimacy and privacy are often interchangeable. The boundary between the two is often blurred and hard to define, unlike the difference between public and private, which has a historically and socially mobile boundary, but is traditionally defined by the opposition society/individual (Berlant, 2000). The private refers as much to intimacy and secrecy, to ownership and possession, as it does to a realm that the actor can appropriate (Schwartz, 1990, pp. 19–34). Intimacy is both simply a particular aspect of the private and something more profound. It does not exist *per se* in the sense that it has no independent reality.

Expressed differently according to its territories (Neuburger, 2000) and cases (Simmel, 1908), intimacy is possible only in relation to something else. This linkage reveals two poles, between which intimacy oscillates, that involve both secrecy and authenticity (Bawin & Dandurand, 2003). Intimacy is part of a social game whose players alternate between protection and unveiling (Laé & Proth, 2002) in their interaction with public spaces. The boundary between these two spaces becomes porous (Castelain-Meunier, 2005), even insignificant (Tisseron, 2001).

But although the market and consumption invade all aspects of people's lives, including their private lives, intimacy has been little conceptualized in consumer research (Amy-Chinn, Jantzen, & Østergaard, 2006). It is interesting to note that a collective work on consumption and gender titled *Gender and Consumption: Domestic Cultures and the Commercialisation of Everyday Life* (Casey & Martens, 2006) refers only to women's consumer experience. In addition, the editors justified this focus by the fact that because this sociological book concerned only domestic consumption, "it was inevitable that female consumers would be central" (p. 3). In fact, the role of men in understanding the dynamics of intimacy in a consumption context is nowhere addressed. This absence strengthens Latin criticisms about the conflation of gender studies with women's studies and the sidelining of the whole question of male ideology (and consumption) (La Cecla, 2002; Welzer-Lang, 2004).

CONTEMPORARY MASCULINITIES AND INTIMACY

Male intimacy is based on camaraderie and the spirit of sacrifice and courage, whereas female intimacy is based on feelings and their expression. This strictly cultural difference is rooted in Western civilization and entails that men may only express their emotions within a heterosexual relationship (Dulac, 2003). It follows that the best friends of men are women and that they allow themselves to express themselves freely only with their wife or partner. Confined to the heterosexual couple, intimacy reinforces the stereotypes of the self-controlled, courageous man and the woman with a preference for emotional bonds.

Parsons and Bales wrote in the 1950s that men are driven by their activism and women by their feelings, but Dulac (2003) confirms that this view has not disappeared. This fact leads men to have their partner as the only person with whom they share their deepest feelings and secrets. Fear of intimacy contributes to men's isolation and loneliness. In the "house of men" (Mead, 1963) and in the process of construction of masculinity, men learn not to be women. In so doing, they learn to be *impenetrable:* impenetrable by their own feelings and those of others, leading to a renouncement of empathy, and impenetrable sexually, expressed by the obligation to be heterosexual and the channeling of their desires in this direction. Men's bodies thus constructed must as a result be *hard,* both symbolically and physically. Yet the body is organically endowed with affective states, with physical and psychological drives.

Male socialization, however, is completely oriented to the expulsion of cathexis: drive toward the outside material world and toward women and expulsion of anything that might appear feminine in them. This opposition necessarily leads to a conflict between power and individual men. The fact that the body never accepts total submission probably helps to explain why men, even though they remain dominant because they are socialized to be so, are irreducible to the model of hegemonic masculinity and why there are virtually as many masculinities as there are bodies.

But it would be futile to look for a psychological and an *a fortiori* biological explanation of the variety of masculinities. This variety is primarily the outcome of social relations, and bodily dispositions, however intimate, are always shaped in return by society and history. For Pascale Molinier (2004), male domination is precisely constituted by the social censoring of female experience, and this censoring is implemented within the very framework of men's socialization. The economic organization of the relations of production, as I pointed out earlier, requires the availability of very variable bodies depending on the position each man occupies in the domain of production. It is therefore a matter of taking into account, in any analysis of masculinities, what each masculinity owes to the degree of investment of bodies in the productive system and to the social differences that underlie them.

In 1995, Kaufmann suggested that the relations between men and women can only be properly understood by taking account of the distinction between public and private. In Kaufmann's view, the male role has varied very little in the private sphere, whereas it has undergone major changes in the public domain, where women have made significant progress (Kimmel & Tissier-Desbordes, 2000). A number of recent French publications recognize significant changes as regards the dialectic of men and privacy (Castelain-Meunier, 2005; Hefez, 2007; Welzer-Lang, 2004).

Castelain-Meunier (2005) carries out a large-scale qualitative study comparing men's discourses in the 1980s (Castelain-Meunier, 1988) to those of the early 2000s. In relation to the "first generation of feminism," she notes "a metamorphosis of masculinity" in men's relations in private, a growing and sincere involvement in the "psycho-couple," and a preeminent interest in the self and the body. She writes that "there is expression of a new fluidity of the borders between the public and the private" (p. 78) or "men concerned with the quality of their intimacy, and the sharing of love and pleasure" (p. 88). This assertion contrasts with the discourse of the cohort of men in the 1980s, who were more concerned with social norms, when they agreed (which was not always the case) to address the question of intimacy. Castelain-Meunier (2005) mentions in particular how the younger generation places great emphasis on dialogue within the couple, the search for reciprocity in intimate relationships, and the absence of constraints.

The dynamics of male intimacy is also very much the concern of the sociologist Welzer-Lang (2004), whose work over some 20 years has assessed masculinity in France, with an emphasis on men's behavior in the domestic sphere, on the one hand, and men's evolving sexuality on the other. He concludes, too, that there is a profound renegotiation of intimacy between men and women. For example, one reason for the decline in the recourse to street prostitution is because seduction by the body and appearance has become an essential part of the sexual process. He mentions that men's expectations as regards intimacy have changed:

> There's plenty of evidence that men not only want to be caressed and cuddled, but over their entire body....Previously reduced to a single dimension..., the man's body, alongside changes in men's relations with women, is opening up to other forms of imagination, other territories. (p. 247)

In another area of the social sciences, this rediscovery of intimacy and of the relation to the male body is also elaborated by the psychoanalyst Hefez (2007) on the basis of his 30 years of professional practice. He describes how male representations and men's view of intimacy have changed:

> Men today are discovering that they have a heart. They are entering an emotional and sensorial world that has hitherto been denied them, and this is disrupting their psychology...[M]en go further educationally and are better paid than women. But in the realm of intimacy, they are very confused. (p. 12)

The author adds that men are opening up to this new affective dimension through physical contact such as giving their baby a bath or changing the baby's diapers. In this way men can experience their body without any predatory sexual intent, liberating new emotional fields that were previously confined to women. Hefez (2007) notes that these young men are less pressured to prove their masculinity during adolescence. This younger generation of men is subject to less pressure in relation to virility compared to men still raised in cultures, particularly Latin cultures, where the separation of gender roles is still rigid and where men are required always to prove their masculinity (p. 77). Similar observations are made by La Cecla (2002), de Singly (2001), Welzer-Lang (2004), and Castelain-Meunier (2005).

Indeed, according to the Italian anthropologist La Cecla (2002), men's and women's behavior is clearly determined by the degree of individual interiorization of the gender cultural roles that prevail in the society in which they live. Masculinity is very much a cultural construction by which men are trained at an early age to demonstrate their masculinity under the suspicious gaze of society. Depending on the choices they make and the signals they emit, they are placed on a continuum running from tough guy to effeminate male. Masculinity implies a notion of performance, "the obligation to prove it" (p. 54), because the biological evidence is never sufficient. By contrast, for a woman, the biological potential to reproduce and give birth straightaway makes her fully feminine.

The author also argues that men have a feeling of "physical shame in regard to their body" (p. 56) and a personal and very masculine need to redefine their own corporeality. Consequently, men have an uneasy relationship with intimacy. More specifically, the individual male body (as opposed to the collective body, amid other men) is reduced to a "virtual sex" (La Cecla, 2002, p. 58). It does not exist in itself. In the Lacanian view (see Lacan's *The Signification of the Phallus*, 1958, for a discussion of this point) or that of Malossi (2000), any manifestation, demonstration, display, or visibility of the male body immediately places it in the realm of femininity. Also, the recent flood of advertisements and products involving the male body as an object challenges our understanding of this deconstruction of the gaze, gender, and intimacy and, ultimately, disrupts the codes of consumption.

MASCULINITIES AND CONSUMPTION

One of the most significant features of masculinity in recent decades is the increasing participation of men in consumption (Mort, 1988), going from a role as producers to one as consumers (Schroeder & Zwick, 2004). Our discipline is currently working in particular to decode the phenomenon by studying the meaning of new advertisements (Elliott & Elliott, 2005; Oswald & Ourahmoune, 2006; Ourahmoune & Nyeck, 2008; Patterson & Elliott, 2002; Schroeder & Zwick, 2004) offering alternative conceptions of the male body that could be described, to use Maffesoli's term, as "the cosmeticized body." Yet, "men in general are rarely studied as consumers" (Tuncay & Otnes, 2008a, p. 6). Indeed, the study of men's relationship to products—particularly in relation to the appearance market that is strongly and rapidly re-forming—entails processes, rituals, and meanings that remain opaque because they have been studied so seldom in our field (Kimmel & Tissier-Desbordes, 2000). Some previous research has, however, paved the way for the study of male consumers.

Otnes and McGrath (2001) identify the existence of male customers who enjoy shopping and consuming products traditionally described as feminine. Thus, the authors in a way deconstruct the myth of a radical difference in buying behavior between men and women. In another area, Schroeder and McDonagh (2005) explain the traditional male fascination with technology in terms of the acquisition of sensual pleasure through this form of consumption. In so doing, they help supersede this stereotype, a complex phenomenon with many contours. Furthermore, Holt and Thompson (2004) show the existence of nonstereotypical male consumer behavior in studying the American ideology of hegemonic masculinity. For example, one respondent brings feminine values up to date by rejecting participation in so-called manly sports and other macho behavior, and breaking away from the breadwinner model.

Moreover, a number of studies explore the expression of men's consumption in traditionally male areas such as the world of sport (Sherry, 1998) and ESPN Zone (Sherry et al., 2004), the mountain man myth of the American West (Belk & Costa, 1998), river rafting (Arnould & Price, 1993), Star Trek fans (Kozinets, 2001), the world of bikers (Schouten & McAlexander, 1995), and the hip-hop subculture (Damien Arthur, 2006). The "enclaves of masculinity" (Caru, Cova, & Tissier-Desbordes, 2004; La

Cecla, 2002) have evidently not disappeared from the concerns of consumer-behavior researchers.

Indeed, very little research decodes male consumption in the cultural spaces shared by men and women (Dano, Roux, & Nyeck, 2003; Kimmel & Tissier-Desbordes, 1999; Tuncay, 2006; Tuncay & Otnes, 2008b), despite the "blurred" dimension of gender (Kacen, 2000) and its societal recomposition. Single fathers raising children, young women adopting men's binge drinking habits, and young men with a passion for fashion are some examples that illustrate the need to understand gender in relation to emerging, and indeed anomic, consumption behavior.

In this respect, research on men and appearance-related products is particularly relevant for understanding how "gender trouble" affects the market and consumption. Kimmel and Tissier-Desbordes (1999) address this question and pave the way to conceptualizing masculinity through this type of consumption. They note, however, that their informants claim such consumption does not play a major part in their lives because male beauty practices are not yet socially embedded. They add that products viewed as masculine by their interviewees are often those that could be described as external, or associated with the public rather than the private domain. The authors highlight the "social fears" that can inhibit this type of consumption. These in particular are conceptualized by Rinallo (2007), in his comparison of heterosexual and homosexual fashion consumers, as an ongoing negotiation between "safe zones" and "dangerous zones" and echo the idea of the *limit* that I evoke investigating men's lingerie consumers (Ourahmoune, 2009).

Also, Tuncay (2005) examines how male consumers experience tensions as they consume fashion and grooming products. Two tensions in particular include heterosexuality versus appearing homosexual and individuality versus conformity (to gender norms). To combat this tension, men diligently monitor their boundaries of "acceptable" heterosexual, masculine behavior and engage in "masking," defined as actions that consumers take to hide or deemphasize the consumption behavior they display to others. It is clear that social norms weigh upon male consumption of finery and that these call for deeper conceptual and managerial study.

On the other hand, the consumption of adornment as a marker of masculine identity indicating the level of ideal masculinity that is sought is an idea discussed in the literature. According to Eastman, Fredenberger, Campbell, and Calvert (1997), men tend to be more materialistic than women and to give great importance to products as vectors of social prestige, particularly through wearing visible symbols such as fashion products and watches. This tendency reflects the instrumental and public sphere orientation associated with traditional views of masculinity (Laqueur, 1992; Vigarello, 2004). This logic also applies to men who wear cosmetics: the study by Dano et al. (2003) reveals that some male consumers justify their use of beauty treatments by the requirements of professional performance—in short, to look young and dynamic and shine socially. However, Tuncay (2006) mentions the growing emphasis on consumption associated with the body and the importance of romantic relationships among her interviewees.

In this context, this research wishes to help theorize men's relationships to adornment products and to add to the limited literature concerned with the entry of men into new product categories associated with women's culture. However, unlike the previously cited research, my perspective chooses to focus in particular on the relationship to products rendered "invisible" in the social sphere, as it concerns the private use of lingerie and underwear for men. In so doing, I intend to introduce the notion of intimacy for understanding the male consumer, a notion that runs through the recent sociological literature on changing masculinity, but that remains relatively absent from our field. Moreover, treating the relationship to these products in terms of the rites and representations involved in this consumption will lead us to consider aspects of men's socialization around these products, an area that remains largely underinvestigated.

METHOD

This chapter stems from a wider study of male private consumption and therefore limits the spectrum to consumers' views of the place and significance of this consumption in the context of interactions within heterosexual couples. I generated textual data from 21 phenomenological interviews with male consumers. I recruited all the correspondents from "among people I know or among people that could introduce me to people they know" (Bourdieu, 1993, p. 907). The option of going through a third party offered anonymity and allowed entry into the informants' private lives, in the hope that they would confide on a subject generally considered taboo.

The 21 men interviewed were varied in terms of age, sexual orientation, and careers (students, working people, retirees, managers, professionals). The primary selection criterion was participation in the consumption of male lingerie (for 12 men). However, in order to achieve "qualitative diversity" (Schwarz, 1990, p. 41), I also interviewed other men (homosexuals, young adults, elderly men) who were *not* consumers of lingerie.

These phenomenological interviews place the emphasis on first-person narrative and natural conversation (Thompson, Locander, & Pollio, 1989). The analysis follows the recommendations of Spiggle (1994), Thompson and Haytko (1997), Thompson et al. (1989), Thompson and Pollio (1994), and Wallendorf and Belk (1989). I conducted individual interviews with informants at times when they were fully available so as to foster a climate of trust (Fournier, 1998). They took place variously in Paris, Marseilles, and Aix-en-Provence and lasted between 1 and 2 hours. The interviews were recorded and transcribed, and informants were always offered the opportunity to read the transcripts. Seven of them agreed to discuss the results in 2009, thus increasing the validity of the study.

FINDINGS AND DISCUSSION

Women were naturally mentioned in many respects by the informants. Before addressing more specifically their representations of the interactions of couples around the use of male lingerie, I want to clarify the role of women in relation to their entry into and involvement in this atypical consumption.

Men Speaking of Women's Roles as Initiator in Intimacy-Related Consumption

According to my informants, the role of initiator clearly falls to the woman; narratives of discovery of the product through the partner and rituals of joint purchases were often offered. The fact of having an intimate relationship with someone who cared about their appearance gave rise to the wish among some informants to try out new practices:

> It was my girlfriends who initially prompted the move from basic boxers from Carrefour to nicer, fancier things....If I hadn't met women who encouraged me, I would still be buying those basic boxers from Carrefour...I happened to have girlfriends who would say, "Why not try this model?" or would buy me them as presents. (Pascal, 28, heterosexual)

Learning in the field of male appearances involves a female presence. Throughout the interviews, I noticed that my informants' constructions of appearances were often carried out with the help of women (mother, partner, female friend) because of their expertise and culture in relation to appearances, in contrast with the lack of a male tradition in this area. Indeed, in male discourse, women are viewed as the official and traditional bearers of aesthetic knowledge, and their advice, as experts in fashion, is taken by these men:

> I talk about how to wash delicate underwear with girls...because they're used to doing it, and so I don't make the mistake of ruining a pair of boxers which cost me a fortune in the washing machine! (Pierre, 23, heterosexual)

> [With my girlfriends] we often talk about skin creams, masks, you know, beauty products!...With [them], I can discuss cosmetics...and lingerie too—everything! There are really no holds barred...and that way we can have real conversations. (Sébastien, 33, heterosexual)

Most informants who engage in these practices thus seem to integrate themselves into an aesthetic network composed mainly of women. Within it there develops a specific sociability on the exchange of aesthetic information and advice on beauty—an exchange that is essential because it is intimate and allows the creation of new social bonds between men and women. This interaction with women in the construction of masculine appearance may also be seen through the partner's prescriber role:

> I think that women can really show the way when it comes to your look, and to trying out new stuff, whether it be underwear like thongs or cosmetics...for example, my sister is with a real, let's say, rough type, but seeing my sister's enthusiasm for using cosmetics and stuff, well, it's not exactly that he's interested, but he's no longer against it. (Alexander, 32, heterosexual)

Another central female figure who accompanies the man in the construction and practice of his appearance is the mother. Two of the informants mentioned that their mothers bought their underwear. Above all, the maternal figure instills a sense of seeing and being seen and provides an education in the field of appearances and taking care of oneself—an education that values (or does not value) working on appearances. However, I could also observe maternal nonintervention, arising from an absence of mother–son dialogue in the subject of working on one's appearance and taking care of oneself: "My mother never took care of anything like that... She decided that in life when it comes to pointless things like fashion, you can sort yourself out!" (Pedro, 27, homosexual).

However, many anthropologists show the existence of rites of separation whose function is to emancipate the boy from his mother so as to allow his progressive masculinization and to prepare him to face the outside world as a man (cf. "The House of Men" in Mead, 1963, or Welzer-Lang, 2004). Girls, on the other hand, who remain in the realm of women, do not need to be symbolically separated from the woman who brings them into the world. The erasure of these rites and markers in Western societies explains the different constructions of the relationship of young men to masculinity, on the one hand, and to the work of appearances through maternal mediation on the other.

I have shown that women occupy a legitimate status in accompanying men in the area of beauty. One of the central themes that emerged from the discourses of heterosexual lingerie consumers was the interaction within the couple in regard to this recent consumption practice. These interviews were the longest (often around 2 hours) and the most productive. It was a matter, then, of analyzing these interactions as experienced and expressed by these male consumers. We are thus in the context of heterosexual couples where the man (and not simply the woman) wears lingerie.

Men Speaking of Their Interactions Within Couples Around Intimacy-Related Consumption

Through the interviews, I note first that consuming lingerie is also shared by the man's partner. As a result, this practice is often viewed as not solely for himself, as a single individual, but also as something that is engaged in together. It thus creates new interaction within the couple, a new mode of intimate communication. For most informants, these joint practices introduce a novel form of conjugal exchange and play, and they engender a new closeness and intimacy in the partnership, "just between us two":

> We try on stuff together, look at each other in the bathroom, often on the weekend…It's a thing I wouldn't do on my own. It's not much fun. This is a little game between us two. (Pierre-Henry, 37, heterosexual)

> It's enjoyable when it's something private between you and your girl-friend.…It would be no fun to go shopping for lingerie, if I was on my own, and try it on at home. It would be an obligation; I would have to make an effort. Then, afterwards, we'd spend some time together…uh, take a bath together, for example. (Sébastien, 33, heterosexual)

We can identify two types of messages transmitted by the informants as regards the use of "sexy underwear" within the couple: (1) a hedonist mode where "together" is linked to pleasure, enjoyment, and intimacy as opposed to constraint and effort, and (2) a ludic mode where "together" is linked to a little game and playing around as opposed to "on my own" and "not much fun." One may wonder whether the strength of this practice as a couple, this new conjugal intimacy, does not somehow pertain to the fact that it is a "clandestine" male practice taking place in secret, behind closed doors, out of sight of the wider world: "On the other hand, I'm not sure it's something we should share…I don't think I'd be too happy if my girl-friend discussed it with friends over dinner!" (Sébastien, 33, heterosexual).

Male consumption of lingerie seems, because of this sharing, to be valorized by the partner after she's been told about it:

> They liked it. They appreciated it, because they figured since they pay attention to their appearance, it's nice to have a boyfriend who takes care of his too; I mean, they liked it. So there were never any problems. (Pierre, 23, heterosexual)

Another informant notes, "She liked being with someone who takes care of himself and who appreciates nice things. It's still pretty rare. Good thing, too" (Pascal, 28, heterosexual).

In terms of representations, these within-couple practices are under-pinned by a conception of the couple in which the man and the woman must both care about and pay attention to their appearance, in order to show their interest in each other through a shared wish to please. Both partners maintain a balance of attraction:

> In a relationship, personal grooming should be a pleasure…it's part of the fun of being a couple…There are lots of relationships which fall apart because once the two people concerned have got together, they stop making any effort at all.…Taking care of your appearance, well, you do it for yourself, of course, but especially for the person you're with…Both people must be on the same wavelength. (Éric, 25, heterosexual)

However, the balance within the couple may be disrupted when the man engages in more beauty care than the woman:

> The only hitch that might crop up in the relationship is when the man starts to pay more attention to personal care than the woman…It might push the woman into spending more time on it that she would normally. (Sébastien, 33, heterosexual)

This observation tends to show that, even within a couple where the concern for appearances is shared, the woman must nevertheless pay greater attention to how she looks because, traditionally, the woman is defined by the emphasis on appearance, which is in part how femininity is conceived. If this attention is not paid, it seems that a problem may arise as to the respective positions and roles of the woman and the man within the couple. Informants mention this female discomfort in relation to a greater or lesser involvement in the realm of beauty, a domain that was for a long time the monopoly of women, when discussing the reactions of women in general as regards their use of male lingerie:

> [Talking about it with women], [i]t's no longer any fun, for either side (neither from a female nor a male point of view)…The women discover the feminine side to the man, and sometimes the man finds a masculine streak in the woman if she says, "That's horrible! What are you doing? Why do your wear thongs? What's the matter with you?" I think it's just too much for some women. (Pierre, 25, heterosexual)

I don't know any, but I think there must be girls who find it weird because for them it's about femininity...There are no real men left! [laughter] (Alexander, 32, heterosexual)

The wearing of lingerie by men clearly appears to be a mediator of the couple's relations. Like being in love, the emotional climate characteristic of contemporary relationships not only demands telling the loved one about one's steadfast feelings, but also requires that these be enacted (Kaufmann, 2003, 2007). It seems that consumption (in this instance, of lingerie) comes to play a key role in giving the affective relationship a material underpinning.

Indeed, the man who purchases with his wife's guidance or for whom the wife buys everything—suit, ties, shirts, underwear—still exists. The woman ensures that the man is appropriately dressed and that his appearance matches his position; it is partly a duty, as if the body were, above all, a role, a function, a status. Suits are preferably dark for reliability and distinction, even if one sometimes indulges in a light suit and striped shirts. The man dressed by the woman is the acknowledgment that the woman knows, even more than he does, what suits him: He relinquishes his body to her for what he wears and how he looks. She takes care of his needs.

But it is also a relative relinquishment: The man's body to be clothed is only partially the woman's "thing." She is responsible for molding him into the social role that he occupies because the man's body is primarily the corporation's "thing" (the figure of the producer rather than the consumer, as Schroeder & Zwick, 2004, discuss). And as a foil, the man is an object of pride for the wife. For her, who does not work outside the home, he is a way of defining herself socially by proxy. Her identity depends on the status and position of her husband. Nowadays, this mechanism is on the wane. Nonetheless, there is still dependence on the woman or the same-sex partner (when he is viewed as more competent in regard to fashion), especially among informants who wear standard underwear or who are not too concerned about their appearance. The traditional pattern still exists among the older informants as well as the youngest respondent, whose sister or mother continues to choose his clothes.

How do our (young) informants fit into this discussion? The division of roles is less clear-cut. Rather than always expecting the woman to be responsible for his appearance, the man seeks to attract her. Clothes are no longer solely adornment, but also a way of pleasing oneself, out of narcissism and as a game. But it is also a matter of pleasing the woman through a new way of enhancing his physical appearance because she is more able to guide the man's choice. Just as women have learned how to get to know each other better, they have also learned to express what they want at home and they try (our interviewees say) to tell their men what they should do to please them. Older men are not generally independent of women in their clothing practices, but younger men are much more so. Specifically, men in their 30s, after a certain amount of experience of life with a partner, seem more willing to emancipate themselves from socially prescribed roles.

Previously, it was pseudoindependence: the woman dressed the man not to please herself, but for his job and role. Today, although this type of dependence persists, it seems that there is a better match between the woman's desires and those of the man. The criteria of clothing appropriateness are changing. Well-being, as well as aesthetic satisfaction, harmonious bodily movement, and looking stylish, is crucial. Fashion is the instrument that allows men and women to express their desires, including transferring onto their partner what they like and using him or her in their own way. The interviewees indicate their satisfaction with the openness and freedom they now have, but they surrender none of their masculinity as a result.

CONCLUSION

The increased attention paid to the individual, the body, and biographical elements, together with identity and alterity relations, in the study of consumer societies makes the understanding of intimacy an exciting research field. It emphasizes the processes that are constitutive of social relations as well as the subjective and reflexive aspects of social bonds (Bellah, Madsen, Sullivan, Swidler, & Tipton, 1985; Giddens, 1991; Melucci, 1996). In a way, intimacy is replacing the concept of the family as the ideal (de Singly, 2005; Kaufmann, 2003, 2004, 2007). In this context, sex becomes the apogee of intimacy and intimacy is almost impossible without sex (Madelénat, 2009)—which probably explains why seduction rituals are becoming less conventional, more direct, and more ludic. Intimate relationships are increasingly high voltage, both sexually and emotionally.

More specifically, this research reveals that intimacy, as expressed by male consumers, consists conceptually of at least four interrelated dimensions: an emotional dimension that refers to feeling and to concern for the other, a spatial dimension related to proximity and physical interaction, a psychological dimension that implies some intersubjectivity, and a social dimension that includes verbal exchanges of information and knowledge. Hence, this study extends the work of Kimmel and Tissier-Desbordes (1999), Dano et al. (2003), Tuncay (2006), Rinallo (2007), Ourahmoune (2009), and Ostberg (2010) on men's relationship to products associated with the body by specifying their intimate dimensions.

The couple's "between us two" seems to crystallize the informants' interest in this intimate consumption. This "between us" sets the boundaries of outside and inside, of unveiling and the unsayable, and of Us and the Others, and it functions as a stimulus in the couple's private relations in two ways: a hedonic mode (experiencing pleasure) and a ludic mode (playing together). An undeniable easing of the social pressure weighing on traditional masculine norms is reflected in the enjoyment of novel consumer experiences. However, in the process, there also emerge male behavior norms that concern social (and market) injunctions to happiness, pleasure, and aestheticization—injunctions that involve the eroticization of people's lives and summon them to exploit, control, and manage this beauty/seduction capital.

This focus on the theme of intergender interactions in relation to these new forms of male consumption also invites research on how women experience these new male products.

REFERENCES

Altman, Irvin (1975). *The environment and social behavior: Privacy, personal space, territory, and crowding.* Monterey, CA: Books/Cole Publishing Co.

Amy-Chinn, Dee, Christian Jantzen, & Per Østergaard (2006). Doing and meaning: Towards an integrated approach to the study of women's relationship to underwear. *Journal of Consumer Culture, 6* (November), 379–401.

Arnould, Eric J., & Linda L. Price (2002). River magic: Extraordinary experience and the extended service encounter. *Journal of Consumer Research, 20* (June), 24–45.

Baudrillard, Jean (1979). *De la séduction.* Paris, France: Gallimard.

Bawin, Bernadette, & Renée B. Dandurand (2003). De l'intime. *Erudit, 35*(2), 3–231.

Belk, Russell W. (1988). Possessions and the extended self. *Journal of Consumer Research, 14* (September), 139–168.

Belk, Russell W., & Janeen A. Costa (1998). The mountain man myth: A contemporary consuming fantasy. *Journal of Consumer Research, 25* (December), 218–240.

Bellah, Robert N., Richard Madsen, William M. Sullivan, Ann Swidler, & Steven M. Tipton (1985). *Habits of the heart. Individualism and commitment in American life.* Berkeley, CA: University of California Press.

Berlant, Laurent (2000). *Intimacy.* Chicago, IL: University of Chicago Press.

Bourdieu, Pierre (1993). *La misère du Monde.* Paris, England: Seuil.

Bourdieu, Pierre (1998). *La domination masculine.* Paris, France: Editions du Seuil.

Caru, Antonella, Bernard Cova, & Elisabeth Tissier-Desbordes (2004). *Consumerscapes as enclaves of masculinity.* ACR Conference on Gender, Marketing and Consumer Behavior, Madison, WI, June 24–27.

Casey, Emma, & Lydia Martens (2006). *Gender and consumption: Domestic cultures and the commercialization of everyday life.* Aldershot, UK: Ashgate Publishing Limited.

Castelain-Meunier, Christine (1988). *Les hommes aujourd'hui—Virilité et identité.* Paris, France: Acropole.

Castelain-Meunier, Christine (2005). *Métamorphoses du masculin.* Paris, France: PUF.

Damien, Arthur (2006). Hip hop consumption and masculinity. In Lorna Stevens & Janet Borgerson (Eds.), *Gender and consumer behavior* (Vol. 8; p. 12). Edinburgh, Scotland: Association for Consumer Research.

Dano, Florence, Elyette Roux, & Simon Nyeck (2003). Les hommes, leur apparence et les cométiques: Approche socio-sémiotique. *Décisions Marketing, 29* (January–March), 7–18.

de Certeau, Michel (1984). *L'invention du quotidien. T1: Arts de faire, T2: Habiter, cuisiner.* Paris, France: Gallimard.

de Singly, François (2001). Charges et charmes de la vie privée. In Jacqueline Laufer, Catherine Marry, & Margaret Maruani (Eds.), *Féminin-masculin: Question pour les sciences de l'homme* (pp. 149–167). Paris, France: PUF.

de Singly, François (2005). *Libre ensemble. L'individualisme dans la vie commune.* Paris, France: Armand Colin.

Dulac, Germain (2003). Masculinité et intimité. *Sociologie et Sociétés, 35*(2), 9–34.

Eastman, Jacqueline K., Bill Fredenberger, David Campbell, & Stephen Calvert (1997). The relationship between status consumption and materialism: A cross-cultural comparison of Chinese, Mexican, and American students. *Journal of Marketing Theory and Practice, 5*(1), 52–66.

Elliott, Richard, & Christine Elliott (2005). Idealized images of the male body in advertising: A reader-response exploration. *Journal of Marketing Communications, 11*(1), 3–19.

Evans, Mary (2003). *Gender and social theory.* Buckingham, England: Open University Press.

Featherstone, Mike (1991). *Consumer culture and postmodernism.* London, England: Sage Publications, Inc.

Firat, Fuat A., & Alladi Venkatesh (1995). Liberatory postmodernism and the reenchantment of consumption. *Journal of Consumer Research, 22* (December), 239–267.

Fournier, Susan (1998). Consumers and their brands: Developing relationship theory in consumer research. *Journal of Consumer Research, 24* (March), 343–373.

Giddens, Anthony (1992). *Modernity and self-identity, self and society in the late modern age.* Cambridge, England: Polity Press.

Giddens, Anthony (2004). *La transformation de l'intimité* (réédition). Le Rouergue, France: Livre de Poche.

Hefez, Serge (2007). *Dans le cœur des hommes.* Paris, France: Evene.

Héritier, Françoise (1986). *Masculin/féminin, la pensée de la différence*. Paris, France: Odile Jacob.

Holt, Douglas B., & Craig J. Thompson (2004). Man-of-action heroes: The pursuit of heroic masculinity in everyday consumption. *Journal of Consumer Research, 31* (September), 425–440.

Kacen, Jacqueline J. (2000). Girrrl power and boyyy nature: The past, present, and paradisal future of consumer gender identity. *Marketing Intelligence & Planning, 18* (6/7), 345–355.

Kaufmann, Jean-Claude (2003). *Sociologie du couple*. Paris, France: PUF.

Kaufmann, Jean-Claude (2004). *L'invention de soi, une théorie de l'identité*. Paris, France: Armand- Colin.

Kaufmann, Jean-Claude (2007). *Agacements. Les petites guerres du couple*. Paris, France: Le Livre de Poche.

Kimmel, Allan J., & Elisabeth Tissier-Desbordes (1999). Males, masculinity, and consumption: An exploratory investigation. In Bernard Dubois, Tina M. Lowrey, L. J. Shrum, and Marc Vanhuele (Eds.), *European advances in consumer research* (Vol. 4; pp. 243–251). Provo, UT: Association for Consumer Research.

Kozinets, Robert V. (2001). Utopian enterprise: Articulating the meaning of Star Trek's culture of consumption. *Journal of Consumer Research, 28* (June), 67–88.

La Cecla, Franco (2002). *Ce qui fait un homme*. Paris, France: Liana Levi.

Laé, Jean-François, & Bruno Proth (2002). Les territoires de l'intimité. Protection et sanction. *Ethnologie Française, 32*(1), 5–10.

Laqueur, Thomas (1992). *La fabrique du sexe*. Paris, France: Gallimard.

Levinas, Emmanuel (1986). De l'existence à l'existant, Paris: *J. Vrin*.

Levi-Strauss, Claude (2002). *Les structures de la parenté*. Paris, France: Mouton de Gruyter.

Madelénat, Daniel (2009). *Biographie et intimité des lumières à nos jours*. Paris, France: PU Blaise Pascal.

Maffesoli, Michel (1990). *Au creux des apparences. Pour une ethique de l'esthétique*. Paris, France: Plon.

Malossi, Giannino (2000). *Uomo oggetto/material man. Mitologica spettacolo e made de la masculinita*. Bergamo, Italy: Ed Bolis.

Mead, Margaret (1963). *Mœurs et sexualité en océanie*. Paris, France: Plon.

Melucci, Alberto (1996). *Challenging codes—Collective action in the information age*. Cambridge, England: Cambridge University Press.

Molinier, Pascale (2004). Déconstruire la crise de la masculinité. *Mouvements, 31*, 24–29.

Mort, Frank (1988). Boys own? Masculinity, style and popular culture. In Rowena Chapman & Jonathan Rutherford (Eds.), *Male order* (pp. 193–224). London, England: Lawrence and Wishart.

Neuburger, Robert (2000). *Les territoires de l'intime—L'individu, le couple, la famille*. Paris, France: Odile Jacob.

Ostberg, Jacob (2010). Thou shalt sport a banana in thy pocket: Gendered body size ideals in advertising and popular culture. *Marketing Theory, 10* (March), 45–73.

Oswald, Laura R., & Nacima Ourahmoune (2006). Sex for sale: Positioning the eroticized male body in Calvin Klein advertising. In Lorna Stevens & Janet Borgerson (Eds.), *Gender and consumer behavior* (Vol. 8; p. 2). Edinburgh, Scotland: Association for Consumer Research.

Otnes, Cele, & Mary Ann McGrath (2001). Perception and realities of male shopping. *Journal of Retailing, 77*(1), 111–123.

Ourahmoune, Nacima (2009). Intimacy-related male consumption and the masculine identity construction: A consumer point of view. In Sridhar Samu, Rajiv Vaidyanathan, & Dipankar Chakravarti (Eds.), *Asia-Pacific advances in consumer research* (Vol. 8; pp. 130–136). Duluth, MN: Association for Consumer Research.

Ourahmoune, Nacima, & Simon Nyeck (2008). Gender values and brand communication: The transfer of masculine representations to brand narratives. In Stefania Borghini, Mary Ann McGrath, & Cele Otnes (Eds.), *European advances in consumer research* (Vol. 8; pp. 181–188). Duluth, MN: Association for Consumer Research.

Patterson, Maurice, & Richard Elliott (2002). Negotiating masculinities: Advertising and the inversion of the male gaze. *Consumption Markets and Culture, 5*(3), 231–246.

Proshansky, Harold (1973). Theoretical issues in environmental psychology. *Representative Research in Social Psychology, 41,* 93–109.

Rinallo, Diego (2007). Metro/fashion/tribes of men: Negotiating the boundaries of men's legitimate consumption. In Bernard Cova, Robert Kozinets, & Avi Shankar (Eds.), *Consumer tribes: Theory, practice, and prospects* (pp. 76–90). London, England: Elsevier/Butterworth-Heinemann.

Schouten, John, & James H. McAlexander (1995). Subcultures of consumption: An ethnography of the new bikers. *Journal of Consumer Research, 22* (June), 43–61.

Schroeder, Jonathan, & Pierre McDonagh (2005). The logic of pornography in digital print adverts. In Jacqueline Lambiase and Tom Reichert (Eds.), *Sex in consumer culture: The erotic content of media and marketing* (pp. 221–245). Mahwah, NJ: Lawrence Erlbaum Associates.

Schroeder, Jonathan, & Detlev Zwick (2004). Mirrors of masculinity: Representation and identity in advertising images. *Consumption, Markets and Culture, 7* (March), 21–52.

Schwarz, Olivier (1990). *Le monde privé des ouvriers. Hommes et femmes du Nord.* Paris, France: PUF.

Sherry, John F., Jr. (1998). The soul of the company store: Nike Town Chicago and the emplaced brandscape. In John F. Sherry, Jr. (Ed.), *Servicescapes: The concept of place in contemporary markets* (pp. 109–146). Lincolnwood IL: NTC Business Book.

Sherry, John F., Jr., Robert. V. Kozinets, Adam Duhachek, Benét DeBerry-Spence, Krittinee Nuttavuthisit, & Diana Storm (2004). Gendered behavior in a male preserve: Role playing at ESPN Zone in Chicago. *Journal of Consumer Psychology, 14*(1–2), 151–158.

Spiggle, Susan (1994). Analysis and interpretation of qualitative data in consumer research. *Journal of Consumer Research, 21* (December), 491–503.

Thompson, Craig J., & Diana L. Haytko (1997). Speaking of fashion: Consumers' uses of fashion discourses and the appropriation of countervailing cultural meanings. *Journal of Consumer Research, 24* (June), 15–42.

Thompson, Craig J., William B. Locander, & Howard R. Pollio (1989). Putting consumer experience into consumer research. *Journal of Consumer Research, 16* (September), 133–147.

Tisseron, Serge (2001). *L'intimité surexposée.* Paris, France: Hachette Pluriel.

Tuncay, Linda (2005). *How male consumers construct and negotiate their identities in the marketplace: Three essays.* Dissertation, University of Illinois.

Tuncay, Linda (2006). Conceptualizations of masculinity among a "new" breed of male consumers. In Lorna Stevens & Janet Borgerson (Eds.), *Gender and consumer behavior* (Vol. 8; p. 16). Edinburgh, Scotland: Association for Consumer Research.

Tuncay, Linda, & Cele Otnes (2008a). The use of persuasion management strategies by identity-vulnerable consumers: The case of heterosexual male shoppers. *Journal of Retailing, 84* (December), 487–499.

Tuncay, Linda, & Cele Otnes (2008b). Exploring the link between masculinity and consumption. In Tina M. Lowery (Ed.), *Brick & mortar shopping in the 21st century* (pp. 153–168). Mahwah, NJ: Lawrence Erlbaum Associates.

Vigarello, Georges (2004). *Histoire de la beauté: Le corps et l'art d'embellir, de la Renaissance à nos jours.* Paris, France: Seuil.

Wallendorf, M., & Russell W. Belk (1989). Assessing trustworthiness in naturalistic consumer research. In Elizabeth C. Hirschman (Ed.), *Interpretive consumer research* (pp. 69–84). Provo, UT: Association for Consumer Research.

Welzer-Lang, Daniel (2004). *Les hommes aussi changent.* Paris, France: Payot.

XERFI (2010). *La distribution de lingerie et de sous vêtements en France: Décryptage du jeu concurrentiel et opportunités de croissance, Paris.*

13

A Grounded Theory of Transition to Involved Parenting: The Role of Household Production and Consumption in the Lives of Single Fathers

Robert L. Harrison, James W. Gentry, and Suraj Commuri

INTRODUCTION

Married men are rarely responsible for everyday consumption tasks, even mundane tasks such as meal preparation and grocery shopping. Yet, in the case of single fathers, their responsibilities extend from juggling jobs and child care to counseling daughters on feminine hygiene. In doing so, unlike in the case of mothers, fathers must contend with a society that does not equip them for the task or believe that men are naturally disposed to be primary caregivers (Salzman, Matathia, & O'Reilly, 2005). In this chapter, we use data from single fathers to reveal how such men navigate the circuitous path to playing the lead role of a single parent.

Understanding this transition is important because it informs a vital gender transformation against a backdrop of production and consumption. Gender is a central organizing feature of identity (Schroeder, 2003), and it is influential in consumer relationships with consumption rituals, products, and brands. Understanding gender role transitions is crucial to consumer research (Bristor & Fischer, 1993).

Some scholars suggest that gender roles among men are changing fluently, but others argue that changes in actual behavior are slower and more complex (Commuri & Gentry, 2005; LaRossa, 1988; Thompson & Walker, 1989). Some of this complexity is associated with the ambiguity surrounding the normative aspects of men's role. For example, Stern (2003) discusses "men's feelings of powerlessness summoned by a failure to recognize themselves in the powerful male images exposed by feminists" (p. 147). J. Thompson and Fletcher (2005) cite a Leo Burnett Company study finding that 61% of French men, 53% of Brazilian men, and 50% of American men say that expectations of men in society are unclear. Suicide rates among U.S. men aged 25–34 in 2001 were double those in the 1980s, and men now account for one in five cases of anorexia nervosa, up from less than 1 in 10 in 1980 (Salzman et al., 2005).

Such ambiguities resulting from an absence of clear templates of sex roles of the future are compounded in the case of single fathers. When men whose socialization did not necessarily include parenting skills (Pleck & Masciadrelli, 2004) embrace full-time responsibility for their children, how are they to settle into such roles? Our findings indicate that most single fathers in our research are generally successful at making this transition. These findings draw attention to the challenges that most married men are undergoing currently as a result of changing gender norms. The number of single-father households, while constituting less than 5% of households with children, is rapidly rising. In the following sections, we comment on the cultural context of this phenomenon, introduce our research, and discuss a grounded theoretic model of transformation.

CHANGING FAMILY GENDER NORMS

Starting with the continuing increase in the number of women entering the workforce, there have been indications of increasing male participation in the household in general and child care in particular. Yet, the trend has been critically qualified to reveal substantive and subjective differences in the efficacies of men's and women's performances. For example, though it has been shown that men's share in child care is on the rise (Gardyn, 2000), it is also noted that though the father may dress the child in the morning, it is the mother who is responsible for determining what to wear and for purchasing those clothes (DeVault, 1997); that the father's engagement does not entail organizational or managerial tasks such as setting a medical appointment (Marsiglio, 1995); and that fathers are only recruited by mothers as helpers, but seldom determine the direction themselves (Lareau, 2000). As one mother in Russell's (1986) study notes, "I am still the Executive Director of children." This contention is yet to be challenged (Coltrane, 2000).

Therefore, a man's role as father is often discussed in terms of the first three stages of the evolution discussed by Russell (1986)—moral teacher, breadwinner, and sex-role model—but seldom in terms of the fourth stage: the nurturing father. It is repeatedly noted that while fathers see themselves as being involved in their children's lives, their contributions are not hands-on; rather, they involve playfulness, the transmission of life skills, and conversational dominance (Lareau, 2000). This is not to say that fathers do not love and care for their children; however, this does not always include detailed involvement in their children's lives, such as knowing the last names of their children's friends (Lareau, 2000).

Risman (1986, 1987) identifies provision of physical and psychological nurturance to young children as "mothering" and notes that it is primarily a woman's activity—not because of the social organization of work or kinship, but rather because women psychologically desire to mother and men do not. Consistent with this assertion, Coltrane (1989) notes that "traditional tasks of fatherhood are limited to begetting, protecting, and providing for children. While fathers typically derive a gendered sense of self from these activities, their masculinity is even more dependent on *not* doing the things that mothers do" (p. 473). In other words, it is argued by scholars in gender studies that fathers not only are ill-equipped to play the roles that mothers do, but also actively desist from it.

Male identities are structured by themes of differentiation, separation, and autonomy (C. Thompson, 1996). Evidence on the roles of fathers depicted in advertising directed at men indicates that men are indeed often depicted as being stoic and uninvolved fathers. Coltrane and Allan (1994) conclude that "images of autonomous and controlling men were, still are, the norm for television commercials, and emotionally expressive or vulnerable men are a rarity" (p. 55). Gentry and Harrison (2010) suggest that while advertisers claim the emergence of more progressive images of men, such images are rare during television programs targeted toward men. On the contrary, as Tuncay and Otnes (2008) suggest, men are often confronted with conflicting and unattainable notions of masculinity that manifest themselves in the marketplace, often with no attention to a man's ability to embrace roles counter to conventions.

THE SINGLE-FATHER PHENOMENON

Brown (2000) noted that "single father" may take on numerous data-based definitions, including fathers who are actually cohabiting with the mother of their children. Further, he notes that 14% of single fathers live in households headed by their parents or another relative. Eggebeen, Snyder, and Manning (1996) found that nearly 7 out of 10 children living in single-father families shared their home with an adult in addition to their father. Navarro (2008) notes the growing trend of gay men becoming single fathers through artificial insemination. Like many constructs, *single father* may take on numerous contexts, making comparisons of results from studies rather imprecise.

Yet exploring the long-term transition of fathers from relatively uninvolved parent (Lareau, 2000) to highly involved parenting is vital because it offers the potential to reveal how men transform gender roles against the backdrop of production and consumption. It also affords the opportunity to explore in further detail the stresses associated with such transition. R. Thompson (1986) reports loneliness and depression associated with single fathers' efforts to balance work with parenting, in handling household duties and child care largely by themselves, and in providing for the children's emotional needs.

The various testimonies of successful male parenting in extant research do not describe this difficult transition sufficiently. Nor has there been a detailed focus on the consumption experiences and issues required to negotiate this transition. Researchers document that married working women retain most of the traditional responsibilities for care of the household, which includes most forms of shopping, child care, and routine financial activities such as paying bills and balancing financial accounts (Bobinski & Assar, 1994; Hochschild, 1989). In addition, the scant consumer research on the transition to single motherhood suggests that women cope during the initial period by seizing the familiarity of routines and the predictability of well-learned habits to manage risks and uncertainty (Fournier, 1998). Single fathers have no such socialization to fall back on.

METHOD

Consistent with the objective of this research to discover navigation of role transition, we wanted fathers to provide thick descriptions in order to discover a process of transition that is theoretical in its relevance, yet retains the indexicality of its substance. Because of its suitability in generating a general explanation grounded in emic narratives, grounded theory was adopted as the governing methodology. In marketing, grounded theories have been developed in the areas of retailing (Manning, Bearden, & Rose, 1998), advertising and mass media (Hirschman & Thompson, 1997), and consumer behavior (Epp & Price, 2011). Our procedures were consistent with these precedents and particularly with those suggested by Corbin and Strauss (2008), Creswell (2007), Spiggle (1994), and Strauss and Corbin (1998).

We conducted 31 interviews that were obtained by purposive sampling. We used the long interview techniques outlined by McCracken (1988). Men who have full or close to full custody of their children (and no other adult present in the household) were sampled purposively. Informants were located through contacts with clergy, social workers, and acquaintances in four cities in two Midwestern states. We conducted interviews at the informant's place of work, at his residence, or in conference rooms at public libraries. The average length of the interviews was 90 minutes. Typically, interviews started with a discussion of family background and segued into single fatherhood. All interviews were recorded and transcribed verbatim. Names and other personally identifiable information have been disguised to protect the privacy of the informants. A snapshot of the profiles of informants is provided in Table 13.1.

After an initial reading of each transcript, we used open coding techniques described by Corbin and Strauss (2008) to identify key themes, activities, events, and thoughts brought up by informants. We then examined transcripts for common categories across participants in order to categorize the conditions relevant in embedding the narratives in their respective contexts (Auerbach & Silverstein, 2003). Exploratory contexts

TABLE 13.1

Informant Summary

Participant No.	Pseudonym	Age	Years as Single Father	Race	Marital Status[a]	Children
SF01	Brent	49	15	White	Divorced	One girl, 17
SF02	Christopher	42	4	White	Divorced, then ex-wife committed suicide	Two boys, 17 and 21
SF03	David[b]	36	6	White	Divorced, wife in a relationship	Two girls, 7 and 11
SF04	Dan	56	6	White	Divorced	Four adopted kids: boy, 21; two girls (with mother); boy, 14 (with him)
SF05	Donald	45	17	White	Divorced	Three girls, 24, 20, 19; one boy, 18, one stepdaughter, 15
SF06	Douglas	52	4	White	Widower	Two boys, 15 and 17
SF07	Greg	53	3	White	Divorced, later remarried and divorced again	Three girls, 28, 26, 17; two boys, 23 and 21
SF08	Jacob	58	7	White	Widower in second marriage	One boy, 7
SF09	James	42	11	White	Widowed, later remarried and divorced	One boy, 15 (from previous marriage); one girl, 6 (with mother)
SF10	Jason	45	2	Black	Divorced	Two girls, 17 and 15
SF11	Jeff	40	1	White	Divorced	Two boys, 15 and 12; one girl, 8
SF12	Jerry	38	15	White	Divorced	One boy, 16
SF13	Justin	51	18	White	Divorced	One boy, 19

SF14	Kevin	39	6	Black	Divorced, later remarried and divorced again	One girl, 17
SF15	Kip	40	16	White	Divorced	One boy, 19
SF16	Kurt[c]	28	5	White	Divorced	One girl, 6
SF17	Michael	27	2	Black	Unwed, mother incarcerated	One boy, 4
SF18	Milton	46	8	White	Divorced	One boy, 18; one girl, 19
SF19	Mitch	44	7	White	Divorced, later remarried and divorced again	One boy, 5, two girls 17 and 12 (boy from first marriage lived with mother and girl stayed with him); 50/50 custody with youngest girl
SF20	Murray	49	4	White	Widowed	Two boys, 13 and 15
SF21	Noah	46	3	White	Divorced	Two boys, 19 and 17
SF22	Oliver	31	10	Native American/ Latino	Unwed, mother incarcerated	One girl, 10 (three other kids living with mother)
SF23	Ralph	45	10	Black	Divorced	One boy, 15; one girl 13
SF24	Ranto	45	4	Nigerian-American	Divorced	One boy with him; one girl with mother
SF25	Richard	53	10	White	Divorced	Two adopted kids: boy, 18; girl, 17
SF26	Shane	54	6	White	Divorced, later remarried and divorced again	One boy, 17; one girl, 18
SF27	Stan	47	4 ½	White	Widowed, recently remarried	Five kids: boys, 26, 19, and 18; girls, 24 and 8

(continued)

TABLE 13.1 (Continued)

Informant Summary

Participant No.	Pseudonym	Age	Years as Single Father	Race	Marital Status[a]	Children
SF28	Steve	45	2	White	Divorced, wanted wife back	One boy, 16; three girls, 12–18 living with mother
SF29	Terrence[d]	47	2	Black	Divorced	Five kids: three girls and two boys, 10–20
SF30	Timothy	46	2	White	Widower	One boy, 15; one girl, 17
SF31	Walter	68	16	White	Divorced, remarried just recently	Four girls, 28–40

[a] Marital status at the time of the transition.

[b] His ex-wife is supposed to have the girls every other weekend and on Thursday nights (though she is not very reliable).

[c] He does not have full custody; he has his daughter only on weekends.

[d] The court gave him 60/40 custody, but his estimate is that custody is more like 95/5.

were identified in the next stage (Goulding, 2002) and subsequently our attention shifted to relating categories to subcategories along the lines of their properties and dimensions (Strauss & Corbin, 1998). Finally, we synthesized an axial coding model, as advocated by Strauss and Corbin (1998) (Figure 13.1).

FINDINGS

The central phenomenon in the single father's transition into this new role is an adjustment of priorities. The essence of such adjustment deals with placing at center the new role and identity as single father and contemplating the changes required to be successful. The type of reprioritizing process encountered depends in large part upon the conditions existing at the start of the transition.

Surrounding Circumstances

As we will discuss in detail later, we detected four dominant types of reprioritization. It is conceivable that a single father may be reprioritizing more than one of these at the same time (e.g., as a father who may have had to forgo career aspirations as well as to fight stereotypes). Yet, the reason why reprioritization emerges as the central phenomenon is because fathers voluntarily tend to identify one type of reprioritization or another as the archetypical motif of their transition into single parenting. Salient situational conditions explain the variations across single fathers in terms of the respective challenges that call for a respective type of reprioritization.

An important situational condition is the challenge that causes the most disruption in single fathers' lives. In some cases, it is the lack of time to tend to the physical needs of the children. For others, it is a lack of money and, for yet others, it is a lack of skill necessary to be an effective manager of the household. These challenges are not mutually exclusive, but the challenge that first substantively unsettles a new single father appears to play a crucial role in determining the course of subsequent reprioritization.

The lack of time or an inability to manage it effectively is a recurring theme. However, this constraint appears to be most unsettling on fathers who take custody of younger children, typically under the age of 5. Fathers

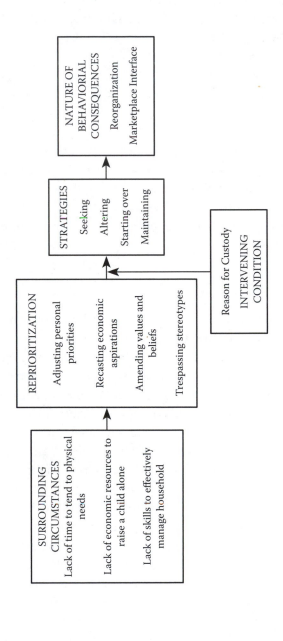

FIGURE 13.1

Axial coding model of reprioritization process.

impuissant with time appear to embark on reprioritization very differently than do those who are not so disenfranchised. When they feel helpless on this dimension, fathers begin to view their task of being a single parent primarily as a two-dimensional zero-sum venture of allocating time to the child or to themselves. A second salient condition is a shortfall of necessary economic resources. In some cases, this shortfall occurs because of a loss of the spouse's income.

But in all cases, it is also a function of the inefficiencies associated with being ill prepared for and abruptly thrust into the role of manager of household finances. Most informants profess to being relatively inexperienced with household shopping. Budgeting and household shopping present new challenges at a time when, in many cases, the loss of a second income is being experienced, thereby escalating the opportunity cost of poorly managed finances. Once fathers realize this situation, it shapes their entire approach toward parenting, beginning with how they manage the critical reprioritization.

A third condition is the lack of skills to manage the household effectively. This condition includes the absence of shopping, cooking, and financial management skills and also the inability to find the skills to tend to the emotional and comfort needs for children. There is much variation in the preparation for household production across the fathers. In sum, when men become single fathers, they are unsettled by one or more of three conditions: lack of time to tend to the physical needs of their children, lack of economic resources, and lack of skills to manage the household effectively.

Reprioritization

The category that holds the most conceptual interest (e.g., most frequently discussed by participants in the study and most saturated with information) is the phenomenon of *reprioritization*—the deliberate reshaping of life space in order to carve out a privileged station for the role of single fatherhood. This central phenomenon subsequently sways decisions ranging from career choice to conformance to stereotypes to more mundane consumption decisions. Following the causal conditions discussed before, four types of reprioritization lie at the core of the transition from being thrust into single parenthood to becoming an involved single father: (a) adjusting personal priorities, (b) recasting economic aspirations, (c) amending values and beliefs, and (d) trespassing stereotypes. Identifying

the route to reprioritization is central to understanding the strategies subsequently chosen in the transition to involved parenting and the extent to
which fathers are successful at it.

Adjusting Priorities

> The most prominent form of reprioritization involves putting the interests
> of the children first. You do not spend money on yourself until you have
> met the needs of your kids. I am very, very thankful that I made the change
> to reduce my cost of living and [to increase] the time required for my chil-
> dren. I am glad that I moved to a job that I can be close to home. If I had it
> all to do over again, the only thing I would have done differently is I'd have
> done it quicker. [Walter]

In the short run, the fathers are clearly giving up more than what may
appear to be a fair share, as evidenced in Richard's following recollection.
Yet irrespective of how fair such reprioritization appears to be, the commitment to and the centrality of this exercise was consistent across informants:

> I told my kids, "Do not worry. Other parents have girlfriends and boy-
> friends over and live-in situations," and the kids hated it and I'd hear about
> it and all this stuff. So I told mine, "Do not worry; I will not date. I will not
> bring in another person; I'm not there for anybody, until you guys are out
> on your own." So, I love them, and I love being a parent, and a single parent,
> and this is my life. [Richard]

Walter said that he never dated when the children were in the house,
though he eventually remarried. Many other informants put their social
lives on hold as well, often viewing dating as just too much to add to their
already overtaxed schedules. Thus, many single fathers forgo interactions
with eligible women that could serve to inflate their self-esteem and possibly restore a more traditional masculine identity.

Recasting Economic Aspirations

Reprioritization can be a single- or multistage exercise. In many cases reprioritization means making new trade-offs between family and work. In Walter's
case above, he also has to reprioritize his economic lifestyle. Whether singly

or multiply staged, there is no doubt among many of the informants that this exercise is the dominant determinant of their success as single fathers:

> [Back] then, I would usually pick him [son] up. I would drop him off about seven and pick him up maybe at five o'clock and then get home and…I did that for about maybe 6 months, maybe not even that long. And finally I just thought, "This just isn't working out real well," and…I felt the need to be with him, real strong…a kind of maternal/paternal instinct there… because he was so little and so I crunched all of the numbers to see if I could financially take like a year off, like a sabbatical. [Jacob]

Along the same lines, Steve talks about how he sets aside the commitment to his career after contemplating its importance vis-à-vis his felt need to be more engaged in his son's life:

> I figure this [(transition] is going to be a long-term thing…[and] what normally they [his company] like to do is have people bust their butt for 2 years and work the weekends and work the nights and work this and I just don't do that.

Associated with the behavioral changes as demonstrated by shifts in working hours is a change in mind-set: "I had to go from being a business person first, if you will, and a home person second, to a home person first and a business person second" [Douglas].

Given the centrality of the provider role to traditional perspectives of masculinity, our informants have difficulty adjusting to the mandated decrement in the importance of their work/career. Further, traditional masculine values such as achievement and competition have to be deemphasized in order to better handle the responsibility for others.

Amending Values and Beliefs

The central phenomenon of reprioritization truly runs deep to the core of the transition to single parenting and emerges in many shades. As is evident in the following excerpt from Oliver's interview, it is not as simple as a decision to spend fewer hours at work. At times it represents a fundamental triage of values and beliefs:

Man! I changed big time. I mean everything changed. I was at the time into like selling drugs and stuff. That was my main source of income. I had a part-time job with my uncle, but that was just kind of to cover up the money....I am glad I got custody of her [daughter] 'cause, it did. It changed everything. I mean I quit that [selling drugs] 'cause I didn't want to risk anything with her. I quit everything and then I got a full time job at a casino.

The sole-parental responsibility casts a very different light upon the dependency of the child on the father for all dimensions of welfare, making risks far less enticing.

Trespassing Stereotypes

In other cases, reprioritization entails a difficult but deliberate abandonment of the comfort of conformance to stereotypes. While most informants observe that their roles as single fathers are respected by others, a few encounter interactions indicating that their roles are inconsistent with doing gender appropriately:

I've had reactions from women in the church that we attend. They've told me that I'm terrible because I raise my girls and that the mother should be raising the girls. And it is wrong for a man to be raising a girl. [David]

A lady in the grocery store asked, "What a beautiful child, yada, yada. Why isn't your wife with you?" I said, "I'm not married, I'm a single parent." She said, "You took this beautiful child away from his mother?" I'm like, "No, his mother walked away." She said, "How could you do that?" [James]

However, the most common phenomenon triggering a need to reevaluate one's definition of what it means to be a male, to be masculine, involves new parental responsibilities:

I tried to be a mother and a father. Like she'd want to play with Barbies... well, her mother might sit and play with Barbies with her, so I did. Not that I wanted to, but I did just because somebody needed to be there with her. After she gets out of the bath, you've got to comb that hair out; you're sitting there on the couch for 20 minutes to half-hour every night combing that long hair out, and a lot of fathers wouldn't do that. Playing with Barbies was hard, but that didn't make me wimpy or womanly because I did it; it's just because I was there for my kid. [Brent]

The marketplace stereotypes fathers. They really do. It's like the fathers are supposed to only know and care about tools and "manly" things. But where I'm at now in my life, I honesty have no use for tools. My daily tasks involve Tupperware dishes to save the leftover macaroni and cheese. Instead of doing the handy work around the house, I'm trying to straighten my daughter's hair. I don't even know how to use a straightener! [Kurt]

As far as talking to other guys...I think a lot of men tend to have homophobia. "Oh my God, you curl hair, what are you, gay?" No, I'm not gay. I'm a dad and I happen to have daughters and that is what they need. [David]

There are many such comments indicating a shift to more feminized roles and that the child's needs had overridden the fathers' preconceptions of "masculine" parenting.

In summary, reprioritization emerges as the central phenomenon because it marks the distinction between being uneasy and being calmer in the role of single parent. Informants' narratives provide clear evidence of a separation of emotional states before and after such reprioritizations. Fathers experiencing extreme time compression appear more likely than others to reprioritize their personal priorities, such as the value they now attach to professional ambition and career progression. These fathers constitute the bulk of the informants who view time as a zero-sum game. Fathers unsettled by the absence of economic resources under single parenting appear more likely than others to reprioritize economic aspirations, where they begin the slow process of accepting the reality that their economic well-being is unlikely to improve in the near- or long term. Finally, fathers most challenged by their inability to tend to the emotional needs of their children appear more likely than others to choose one of the remaining two routes to reprioritization: amending values/beliefs and trespassing stereotypes.

REPRIORITIZATION STRATEGIES

Single fathers reprioritizing their lives, be it through adjustment of personal priorities or trespassing stereotypes, adopt one of four strategies: (a) seeking, (b) altering, (c) starting over, or (d) maintaining. The lives of all informants change tremendously during this period, but some more than others. Some informants seek advice about the needed changes from a wide range of sources, but others seem to "just do it." In part, adhering to a traditional view of masculinity means that the latter group is reluctant to ask for directions and thus avoids possible sources of help, even those made available by marketing institutions. Starting over entails that informants make radical adjustments to certain aspects of their lives.

At the other extreme are those who maintain by trying to keep everyday life the same to the extent possible (often in the case of the death of the mother). But no matter the reason for the absence of the mother from the household, it is impossible to return to what one had before, so change is inevitable. But the magnitude of change is limited in some domains by those who maintain. These strategies are overlapping in nature, as some informants exhibit tendencies to use all four, but across different domains. Milton highlights multiple strategies (maintaining and seeking) used when men learn to take on the sole responsibility for managing the household:

> I started out buying those things that I remembered that she bought, but once you get into it, then you start looking at things differently and you're an involved consumer or...you know...a participant versus a recipient. So you look at different products and try 'em out and you listen to the ads and whatever else. [Milton]

Seeking

Brown (2000) and Eggebeen et al. (1996) note that many single-father households are headed by other adult relatives, often the father's parents. Among our informants, support from the extended family is common, but help is also sought from myriad sources—church, state, neighbors, coworkers, and other single parents. Family support is dominant early in the transition. Reliance on extended family for child care is most common, but friends and even the ex-wife's parents help as well. At one extreme is Jacob, who was in his 50s when his second wife died shortly after the birth of their son. Jacob's parents were dead, and his offspring from his first marriage were somewhat alienated due to a messy divorce.

> Usually, families pull together in a situation like this. Grandmas would get involved and aunts and whatever. I didn't have that. So I had to scramble around and find someone to watch him. He was only 6 weeks old; day care

can't even take him. I did find a lady who[m] I knew and trusted and had the same morals and ethics that I do. I got to her through church. [Jacob]

Jacob is relatively unique among our informants as he could afford to pay sitters if he could find them. Walter's situation is also relatively unique, as his older daughters perform most child care for the younger ones. When he switched jobs from Washington, DC, to Kansas for family reasons, he hired the neighbor, a college student, to take care of his daughters when he traveled during the week.

One unique issue is that of daughters facing puberty. Informants still in touch with their ex-wives seek help from them. For others, help is sought from other women in the family. None of our informants feels sufficiently comfortable with the issue to handle it directly themselves. Consistent with the masculine stereotype that men are reluctant to ask for directions, Greif (1985) notes that single fathers see it as a sign of strength not to ask for help. Thus, the adjustment to seeking information is very challenging, especially because informants do not generally have close friends who are also single fathers. Greif finds that single fathers do not complain much about added responsibilities, in part due to gender norms. Those who have to fight for custody of the children in court have an added incentive not to complain because they fear having that used against them by ex-spouses seeking to regain custody. The decision to handle things on one's own is expressed by many:

> I have friends, you know, and I tell them things, but not a lot…Being a man, still you can't tell them things, feelings and crap, or whatever…It was just figuring it out on my own, not talking to anybody. [Jacob]

Jacob's reaction—essentially that one just adapts quickly—expressed the male tendency not to talk about problems, but just to handle them. In general, much of the learning is from trial and error, as most informants comment that they have no choice, so they just get things done.

Altering

Our informants use multiple coping techniques to handle the challenges facing single fathers during reprioritization. Greg finds that he immediately has to change the family's meal pattern:

> I'd say I more concentrated on meals that I could fix for both of us, instead of buying the separate baby products…you know for my 2-year-old…meals that she would be able to eat…stop buying the steak or the cuts of meat or the adult type foods. [Greg]

Other fathers alter meal patterns even more radically by dining out frequently or by purchasing prepared meals. (We discuss this particular strategy in more detail in a later section.) Several fathers talk about how the family "pulled together" to cope with the reprioritization process: "We were so much reliant and dependent upon each other for help and working together in everything that we did" [David]. Thus, family togetherness in household activities may not be a new phenomenon for the children, but it is new to most fathers.

Starting Over

Some fathers make more radical alterations to their lifestyles, to the point that they encounter completely new environments. Most common among these informants is relocating in direct response to becoming a single father. For Walter and others, relocating the family helps to facilitate the reprioritization process:

> Well, I was going to have to sell the house to have the money and also I figured it would be easier to be a single parent within two blocks of work and within three blocks of the school that she would be going [to] than 45 minutes away.

Others talk about career moves that they made to help in the process. As noted earlier, Oliver changes his entire lifestyle by dropping his illegal activities. David talks about changing shifts:

> I worked twelve and a half hour shifts and I would work a month of days and a month of nights. And then a month of days and a month of nights… it would rotate. So I'd work from 7:30 in the morning until 8 at night and by the time I'd drive home it would be 8:30/9:00. And I know I couldn't do that as a single parent. So I took a day job [at less pay] with the same company.

Jerry became a single father while serving in the Navy in Hawaii. He gave up his naval career and moved to the Midwest, where he had family support. Shane used the change to single parenthood as a stimulus to return to college, and he earned his bachelor's and master's degrees after becoming a single father.

Jacob, despite his ability to pay for sitters for his baby son, found the situation so stressful that, not long after becoming a single father, he took a year off work to take care of his son. Now, 7 years later, he has not returned to work. Thus, for many of our informants, the change in household structures triggers geographical moves, adding to the level of uncertainty faced in terms of adjusting consumption patterns. Further, the changes in priorities in favor of children over career mean compromising masculine values of achievement and competition.

Maintaining

While all households are altered by the loss of the mother, some informants overtly attempt to keep the amount of change as insignificant as possible. As noted earlier, at best this strategy can be implemented in only a few domains. Stan's overriding goal is to maintain the household routine as much as possible after the death of his wife of 20 years:

> I tried to make the transition as smooth as possible. I knew that I could physically handle it and so I went ahead and just continued to do everything that my wife did. Try to keep the routine the same, try to make my life, or my children's lives during the transition, as easy as possible.

Stan intentionally does not ask any of his five children to take on additional chores, though follow-up interviews with two of his offspring indicate that they altered their behaviors to help their father. Brent stays in the city where his child has grown up in order for her to be close to in-laws, though his preference would have been to move elsewhere:

> I think at times it's held me back, I want to see other places…Personally, I really don't like living in X. And if I could have, I would have moved a long time ago, but because of my daughter I could not.

Greg alters his work schedule so that he is home every noon to fix lunch because his children had come to expect it. Though clearly not the majority, some fathers (Douglas, James, Milton, Ranto, and Timothy) try to maintain continuity initially by purchasing the same brands as their wives did.

Intervening Condition

An intervening condition to the strategies selected during the reprioritization process is the circumstance leading to the father being granted custody. The reasons these men become single fathers appears linked to the strategy chosen in reprioritizing their lives (as shown in the model in Figure 13.1). For example, widowers are more likely first to use maintenance, whereas divorcees are more likely to start over. In addition, divorcees appear more likely to alter as opposed to those who gain custody because of abandonment. In some cases, the divorcees continue to fear their ex-wives will contest custody and this fear appears to heighten the attention given to reprioritization.

Nature of Behavioral Consequence

In axial coding, consequences are "the outcomes of the strategies used by participants in the study" (Creswell, 2007, p. 67). The strategies in this study result in reorganization and making use of the market.

Reorganization

Several participants discuss gravitating toward more systematic ways of organizing the macro and micro aspects of their lives, largely in compliance with the financial and time pressures. Greg talks about his revised system of completing housework:

> We have a system of doing the dishes; it goes from youngest to oldest, so when my 17-year-old, when she finishes dishes, cleans the kitchen and puts everything away, then my…next one, he's 20 now…Stan will know that it's his turn…and we usually give it about a 3-day period…ignore the dishes, let them stack up for about 3 days…and after I see that Stan has done his… put them all away, then I know that I've got about 3 days to let them accumulate…so we kind of share in that…they take care of their own room[s] and their bathroom is upstairs right there in the hallway. There [are] two bedrooms upstairs and mine is down[stairs]…and so we all take care of our own individual behavior…I guess vacuuming and dusting the main living areas, I've always just taken care of it.

Along the same lines, Jacob and many others acknowledge the necessity of organizing meals, baths, and time together so that children are in bed at a regular time: "Younger kids thrive on routine. Every night bath time is approximately 8 p.m.; bedtime is at 9. Kids need stability and thrive when they are aware of what is going down" [Jacob].

Some of the support networks discussed previously are instrumental in triggering or enforcing the reorganization. Some enforcement is more hands-on where grandparents are now performing some of the parenting roles on a day-to-day basis. For example, Michael takes his laundry to his mother's house. She also does much of the seasonal shopping for Michael's son. But more often than not, such reorganization gradually starts placing parental burdens and responsibilities, be they minor or major, on the children themselves:

> Yeah...she...sometimes I'll forget...if we are out of something but she'll remember. She'll say, "Yeah we are out of that, remember we cooked it," and [I say], "Oh, yeah...OK, we will get another one." So that is she helps...she reminds me what we need and what we are out of...so she is a big help... that is why I like taking her. [Oliver]

That the loss of an adult (and often the one playing a primary role in household management) results in a redefinition in the organization of household responsibilities and schedules is to be expected. To some extent, though, the nature of the reorganization by single fathers is different from that found previously with single mothers (Bates & Gentry, 1994), as it is possible that children of single fathers are often being asked to do even more than in single-mother households.

Marketplace Interface

One consequence of the reprioritization process is the single father's adaptation to the marketplace. At one extreme, fathers subcontract some consumption decisions directly to the marketplace: "Clothes shopping for her [daughter] was...I never considered it to be a problem, it was just a matter of going in and depending on the clerks to be salesmen, to sell, to convince her about things" [Walter]. Similarly, Jordan learns many of his early consumption patterns from day-care service providers: "By the time he was 9 months old...he was eating some solid stuff, but I was trying to watch what the day care was feeding him."

Douglas finds great joy in shopping for clothes with his teenage sons [he was an anomaly in terms of finding pleasure in shopping] and uses it as a "bonding" experience:

> Clothes shopping has turned into a good experience. About 2 years ago, the little lightbulbs in their heads went on, and, "Yeah, dad, I kind of would like some new clothes." It's kind of neat you know. They had been shopping at the Gap, but I took them to Von Maur. They don't like shopping at Wal-Mart or Target as they tend to be a little bit more fashion oriented than that. Shopping usually isn't fun, but this has been great…We'll go on a trip to a big city and I'll go shopping with them there…They're faster shoppers than I am, but we all have the same sense of style of what we like and what we don't like.

As previously mentioned, many of the fathers rely on support from friends and family. Other fathers resort to less personal sources of advice, in some cases gravitating toward mass media and resources available online. For David, when the distinction between the roles of a parent and a friend blur, he begins to depend on *Super Nanny* on TV for parental guidance on how to establish himself as the father first and then a friend. Jacob says that he could not find any single fathers to talk with, so he frequented multiple websites in the early days of his single parenthood. Having never cooked before, he learns from cooking shows on TV and through experimentation. One informant even suggests that one might learn from commercials: "You'd be amazed at how much commercials will teach you as long as you accept whatever that commercial is trying to show you" [Jerry].

Some informants transfer chores to the market. Instead of preparing meals at home, they eat out because they do not have time between work and their other parental role responsibilities. Another option, used by Matthew, is a food service called Dinner Date, which provides customers a menu and all the ingredients needed to assemble meals to be taken home to freeze.

In addition, we identify two subcategories regarding the father's interface with the marketplace: handling money shortages and meal preparation.

Handling money shortages. For most of the fathers, money is an issue. None of the men report receiving any financial child support from the mothers. Most of the financial discussion deals with grocery shopping.

When shopping, almost all informants report similar attitudes of price consciousness. It may be that their emphasis on price represents attempts to maintain their masculinity when shopping (Patterson & Elliott, 2002). Shopping is recognized as contributing to the creation of self-identity of men and women (Miller, Jackson, Thrift, Holbrook, & Rowlands, 1998; Otnes & McGrath, 2001; Shields, 1992). Reekie (1992) suggests that "it is possible for a man to simultaneously engage in consumer behavior and maintain his masculine identity" (p. 192). On the surface, this statement appears contradictory as shopping is considered a "feminine" domain and the tenets of masculinity mandate shunning it. However, the men in our study—whose masculinity is constantly being challenged as they take on "feminine" roles such as braiding a daughter's hair, doing laundry, preparing meals, playing along with dolls, and dealing with daughters' puberty—appear to use some aspects of consumption to maintain traditional ideas of masculinity:

> The other thing I look for is price…I'm not really big on name brand… you might have mayonnaise here and Miracle Whip: "Hey, mayonnaise is cheaper today" and I'll get mayonnaise. I'm not very big on name brand. Price, the ease or how quick[ly] I can make it, how fast I can make it, and if it is something for my son to eat…those are my three ways for picking things out. [Michael]

As is evident, men for the most part are not brand conscious while shopping, but they exhibit a rational shopping style usually associated with the traditional male ideology (i.e., shopping as a justified need, or useful work) (Campbell, 1997; Miller et al., 1998). Though these men refute many gender stereotypes when they become effective single parents, they maintain some aspects of traditional masculinity; being a "rational," penny-pinching consumer appears to be one of them. An alternative explanation of this frugal shopping orientation is that it may be a situational response to financial constraints. For some of the men in our study, exorbitant shopping is not an option due to lack of resources:

> Where she [ex-wife] would buy the Tide that is real expensive, I might buy something that is on sale. I watch my money a lot closer. Because she was making, when she worked she made pretty good money, so…that is all gone away and I still have the same bills, I've taken everything on except for her credit cards and cell phone, so I pay everything right now. So grocery shopping, I try to watch the food. I do a lot of looking at ads to see what is

on sale—laundry detergent, things like that, I'll buy the stuff that is on sale. Cheaper, you know. [Jeff]

Interestingly, however, when resources became available in some cases, the frugal shopping style does not go away over time. Further, several informants expressed the emphasis on price rather than brand: "As long as it is on sale…we are buying it. That's kinda the way I buy." [chuckle] [Noah]. Others made the following observations:

Shopping was a lot of trial and error. I would try some of the cheaper brands, but if I didn't like it I never bought it again. I'd go back to the name brands. [Are you a price-conscious shopper?] Oh, absolutely, always have been. A couple [of] things I don't scrimp on is meat; I don't buy cheap meat. I just don't think it's as good, or as healthy for that matter. But the rest of it, yeah, I look at price. [Dan]

When we go out to eat, I use coupons, and that embarrasses my son. [Don]

Being single, it was always "conserve." Being on your own, it was always about the financials…There is not a whole lot of junk snack stuff. We still get a lot of fruit; we eat a lot of apples and oranges. He loves pineapples… and watermelon, tons of watermelon. [Do you buy what your wife did?] I did for a while, and then I would go to the cheaper brand. [Steve]

I'll buy more generic stuff than I used to, because everything is so damn expensive these days, and then trying to be a single parent with one income and no child support any more, so we look at cutting corners when we can, and save some money here or there. [Christopher]

I never looked through ads, you know coupons and ads. Now I will go through like that Wednesday paper that has the shopping center ads, grocery store ads, and I note sales….You know I never thought I'd buy milk at Walgreen's, but when it's on sale for $2.29 and I just cross the street to Super Saver I pay $3.59…I think more than actually financially, emotionally, you feel like OK, I've got the best buy for my money and that makes you feel good, as far as managing your budget. [Jason]

You know, being a single parent tends to be on a tight budget, so even my oldest daughter, we'd go to the grocery store and we'd look at items to purchase and she'd be like, "Well, Dad, this one is cheaper." [chuckle] [David]

Given the loss of an adult provider from the household, financial problems are to be expected. However, what was unexpected was the almost universal discussion of attempts to hold down grocery costs. While the literature on single-mother households (Downey, Ainsworth-Darnell, & Dufur, 1998; McLanahan & Sandefur, 1994) indicates the existence of financial constraints, there is no apparent emphasis on spending less on groceries than previously. The relatively new responsibility for grocery shopping may provide a cost-cutting opportunity for the single fathers. On a deeper plane, as Otnes and McGrath (2001) propose, it may be that this new responsibility is also seen as an opportunity to assert their traditional masculinity by focusing on value for price.

Theoretically, this price-sensitive, caring consumer differs from the caring consumer outlined by Thompson, Locander, and Pollio (1990) in their study of working mothers. They find that everyday consumer tasks such as making purchase decisions, grocery shopping, and preparing meals often evoke emotionally charged meanings, grounded in a historical legacy of cultural ideas of motherhood. For the men in this study, such meanings serve as a hurdle to their developing a caring orientation. To develop this caring orientation, the single father must overcome the gender conflict that develops at a very early age; male identities are predisposed toward a self-focused and autonomy-driven orientation. Miller's (1998) theory of shopping takes a traditional woman's perspective of shopping as a labor of love. The identification of nuanced dimensions of cooking, shopping, and brand sensitivity as labors of love does not resonate with these single fathers. Nor do single fathers retain the normative expectations imposed on the ideal mother, who is supposed to be more interested in purchasing the right brands for her family members; this may underlie Coupland's (2005) finding of subconscious brand loyalty even in rather mundane product classes.

Meal preparation. While cooking has been central to the social construction of motherhood (Matthews, 1989; Strasser, 2000), it is not central to the social construction of fatherhood. The fathers often looked to food projects to make meal preparation quick and easy. Frozen pizzas, TV dinners, and microwavable instant meals help save time and energy during mealtime. However, some fathers were conscious of the fact that some of the microwavable instant dinners were more expensive, so they were selective when purchasing such products. Jeff, whose family does not frequently eat out, likes to buy products that are easy to prepare:

Yeah…I like the casserole that you put in a dish, and bake for 30 minutes. I buy chicken breasts, that takes 5 minutes to prepare….pop it in the oven, takes a half hour and we are good to go. I plan like five meals a week and then we'll have leftovers on the weekend most of the time…Not a big change, as the kids' mom wasn't very good at planning stuff like that…I try to stay with stuff that I can fix in 15 minutes tops.

I did all of the grocery shopping myself. What I would look for is…on a box and what was plastered on the box and says, "Can be made in 7 minutes"…I was not organized enough to plan ahead the meal schedule. [Stan]

Meal planning? Not much. I'll start cooking and I won't even know what I want to eat until I start looking in the freezer or fridge. And then just, OK this sounds good. I'll make this. There is no planning. [Oliver]

Terrence mentions that he wants a freezer so that he can cook big meals and freeze them. When he is reinterviewed nearly a year later, he says that he has gotten his freezer, but he has yet to cook any food and then store it in the freezer. The use of technology like a crock-pot evoked mixed reactions: "[I like] the fact that you could fix it ahead of time, the night before, plug it in the morning, and when you got home, it was done" [Mitch]. Likewise, Stan notes: "I should have learned to throw stuff in the crock pot when we left in the morning, but I just didn't get the hang of that one."

This difficulty in managing meal preparation is most easily attributed to lack of experience due to the way that men have been socialized. Fournier (1998) discusses the transition of a new single mother: She handled the new situation by remembering heuristics learned while growing up. Our fathers lack such socialization.

The single fathers adjust to a new responsibility (cooking) under circumstances in which free time was a scarce commodity. To some extent, this is somewhat old news in that middle-class working women have encountered such issues for three decades. However, due to their lack of experience, men handle them somewhat differently.

Meal planning apparently is not a strength of single fathers in general. Our results are in contrast to those of Heslop, Madill, Duxbury, and Dowdles (2007), who find it common for both married mothers and single mothers to cook on weekends, freeze the food, and consume the meals during the week. Only Jerry, among our informants, talks about cooking a roast on the weekend and eating leftovers during the week. Jeff uses the opposite strategy of cooking during the week and eating leftovers on the weekend, but there was little evidence of any long-term (more than a day) planning. Greg says that he would cook large meals and freeze them, but later throws them out as his children prefer store-bought frozen meals. The food industry is well aware of the importance of providing cheap, convenient, healthy offerings, and the segment of single fathers is probably the most appreciative because such offerings are partial, short-run solutions to the provision of what they perceive to be needed.

DISCUSSION

The research reported here investigates the processes involved in the transition to single fatherhood. Although they did not seek it, our informants, with a few exceptions, feel greatly enriched by the opportunity to become more deeply involved with their children. Though it is growing rapidly, the single-father segment may never constitute a viable market segment. Despite the relative infrequency of the single-father phenomenon, we argue that research on single fatherhood provides insight into several areas of theoretical concern.

As noted early in the chapter, American society has generally stacked the deck against fathers assuming the responsible-parent role. However, most of the fathers in this research demonstrate a determination to beat the odds. Our research sheds light on the redefinition of masculinity during the transition to involved parenthood. Some informants learned experientially to parent effectively, as they engaged in what appeared to be on-the-job training. Their gender maintenance does dissipate over time, but it may be a lingering process.

At the same time, marketers are not helping by perpetuating gender norms through advertising. Many informants note that fathers are not presented in nurturing roles on TV, especially in advertising. While firms may be leery of harming the fragile male ego, men experiencing redefinitions of masculinity may appreciate a less virile, less violent male being represented in advertising. Moreover, gender roles within the family may be in a state of flux (Commuri & Gentry, 2005; Gentry, Commuri, & Jun, 2003); to the extent that they are becoming more egalitarian, the barriers faced by single fathers in their transitions may be insightful for broader segments of fathers.

Future research must consider the perceptions of the children as well as those of single fathers. The general path leading to empowerment may reflect efforts on the father's part to justify his efforts, with questionable perceptions existing in terms of his successes. We are unaware of studies in consumer research that evaluate both father and child perspectives in search of convergence and divergence. There have been many calls for investigating the perspectives of all family members (Epp & Price, 2008), and our research suggests we need to be more discriminating in our categorization of families. Daughters present unique challenges to single fathers, especially in terms of issues surrounding puberty. At the same time, daughters generally provide more help with household chores and grocery shopping. Fathers' coping strategies also vary by the age of the children. Those with young children report in far more detail their challenges in terms of finding day care. Obviously, all families are not alike, and more effort is needed to sort these issues.

Another issue needing attention is what happens to the family household system associated with the mundane brands that are repurchased consistently. The subconscious brand loyalty that Coupland (2005) uncovers may not exist if price-conscious men take full responsibility for grocery shopping. We suggest that the shopping heuristics learned, as discussed in the mother–daughter study by Moore, Wilkie, and Lutz (2002), may well be quite distinct from what the informants' children in our study learned, as there is evidence in our data that children may be learning price-conscious perspectives toward shopping. For example, David notes that his older daughter helps him pick out cheaper items in the store. Brent talks about his daughter shopping very little and calling him for permission when she wants to buy an item on sale. Stan's youngest son takes pride in trying to be as fiscally conservative as possible in order to help the family finances. The emphasis on price consciousness in the single-father household may challenge the subconscious brand loyalty finding of Coupland (2005). Future research should also investigate how the transition and changes that these fathers undergo affect the consumer socialization of their children.

REFERENCES

Auerbach, Carl F., & Louise B. Silverstein (2003). *Qualitative data: An introduction to coding and analysis*. New York, NY: New York University Press.

Bates, Myra Jo, & James W. Gentry (1994). Keeping the family together: How we survived the divorce. *Advances in Consumer Research, 21*(1), 30–34.

Bobinski, George S., & Amardeep Assar (1994). Division of financial responsibility in baby boomer couples: Routine tasks versus investments. In Janeen A. Costa (Ed.), *Gender issues and consumer behavior* (pp. 125–141). Thousand Oaks, CA: Sage Publications.

Bristor, Julia M., & Eileen Fischer (1993). Feminist thought: Implications for consumer research. *Journal of Consumer Research, 19*(4), 518–536.

Brown, Brett (2000). The single-father family: Demographic, economic, and public transfer use characteristics. *Marriage & Family Review, 29*(2/3), 203–230.

Campbell, Colin (1997). Shopping, pleasure and the sex war. In Pasi Falk & Colin Campbell (Eds.), *The shopping experience.* Thousand Oaks, CA: Sage Publications.

Coltrane, Scott (1989). Household labor and the routine production of gender. *Social Problems, 36*(5), 473–490.

Coltrane, Scott (2000). Research on household labor: Modeling and measuring the social embeddedness of routine family work. *Journal of Marriage and Family, 62*(4), 1208–1233.

Coltrane, Scott, & Kenneth Allan (1994). New fathers and old stereotypes: Representations of masculinity in 1980s television advertising. *Masculinities, 2*(4), 43–66.

Commuri, Suraj, & James W. Gentry (2005). Resource allocation in households with women as chief wage earners. *Journal of Consumer Research, 32*(2), 185–195.

Corbin, Juliet M., & Anselm Strauss (2008). *Basics of qualitative research: Techniques and procedures for developing grounded theory.* Thousand Oaks, CA: Sage Publications, Inc.

Coupland, Jennifer Chang (2005). Invisible brands: An ethnography of households and the brands in their kitchen pantries. *Journal of Consumer Research, 32*(1), 106–118.

Creswell, John W. (2007). *Qualitative inquiry and research design: Choosing among five approaches.* Thousand Oaks, CA: Sage Publications.

DeVault, Marjorie (1997). Conflict and deference. In Carol Counihan & Penny Van Esterik (Eds.), *Food and culture: A reader* (pp. 180–199). New York, NY: Routledge Press.

Downey, Douglas B., James W. Ainsworth-Darnell, & Mikaela J. Dufur (1998). Sex of parent and children's well-being in single-parent households. *Journal of Marriage and the Family, 60*(4), 878–893.

Eggebeen, David J., Anastasia R. Snyder, & Wendy D. Manning (1996). Children in single-father families in demographic perspective. *Journal of Family Issues, 17*(4), 441–465.

Epp, Amber M., & Linda L. Price (2008). Family identity: A framework of identity interplay in consumption practices. *Journal of Consumer Research, 35*(1), 50–70.

Epp, Amber M., & Linda L. Price (2011). Designing solutions around customer network identity goals. *Journal of Marketing, 75*(2), 36–54.

Fournier, Susan (1998). Consumers and their brands: Developing relationship theory in consumer research. *Journal of Consumer Research, 24* (March), 343–373.

Gardyn, Rebecca (2000). Make room for daddy. *American Demographics,* (June), 34–36.

Gentry, James, & Robert L. Harrison (2010). Is advertising a barrier to male movement toward gender change? *Marketing Theory, 10*(1), 74–96.

Gentry, James W., Suraj Commuri, & Sunkyu Jun (2003). Review of literature on gender in the family. *Academy of Marketing Science Review,* 1–20.

Goulding, Christina (2002). *Grounded theory: A practical guide for management, business and market researchers.* Thousand Oaks, CA: Sage Publications.

Greif, Geoffrey L. (1985). *Single fathers.* Lexington, MA: Lexington Books.

Heslop, Louise A., Judith Madill, Linda Duxbury, & Melissa Dowdles (2007). Doing what has to be done: Strategies and orientations of married and single working mothers for food tasks. *Journal of Consumer Behavior, 6*(2–3), 75–93.

Hirschman, Elizabeth C., & Craig J. Thompson (1997). Why media matter: Toward a richer understanding of consumers' relationships with advertising and mass media. *Journal of Advertising, 26*(1), 43–60.

Hochschild, Arlie (1989). *The second shift: Working parents and the revolution at home.* New York, NY: Viking Penguin.

Lareau, Annette (2000). My wife can tell me who I know: Methodological and conceptual problems in studying fathers. *Qualitative Sociology, 23*(4), 407–433.

LaRossa, Ralph (1998). Fatherhood and social change. *Family Relations, 37,* 451–457.

Manning, Kenneth C., William O. Bearden, & Randall L. Rose (1998). Development of a theory of retailer response to manufacturers' everyday low cost programs. *Journal of Retailing, 74*(1), 107–137.

Marsiglio, William (1995). Fatherhood scholarship: An overview and agenda for the future. In William Marsiglio (Ed.), *Fatherhood: Contemporary theory, research and social policy* (pp. 1–20). Thousand Oaks, CA: Sage Publications, Inc.

Matthews, Glenna (1989). *Just a housewife: The rise and fall of domesticity in America.* New York, NY: Oxford University Press, USA.

McCracken, Grant (1988). *The long interview* (Vol. 13) Newbury Park, CA: Sage.

McLanahan, Sara, & Gary D. Sandefur (1994). *Growing up with a single parent: What hurts, what helps.* Cambridge, MA: Harvard University Press.

Miller, Daniel (1998). *A theory of shopping.* Ithaca, NY: Cornell University Press.

Miller, Daniel, Peter Jackson, Nigel Thrift, Beverley Holbrook, & Michael Rowlands (1998). *Shopping, place and identity.* London, England: Routledge Publishing.

Moore, Elizabeth S., William L. Wilkie, & Richard J. Lutz (2002). Passing the torch: Intergenerational influences as a source of brand equity. *Journal of Marketing, 66*(2), 17–37.

Navarro, Mireya (2008). The bachelor life includes a family. *New York Times,* September 7, 2008.

Otnes, Cele, & Mary Ann McGrath (2001). Perception and realities of male shopping. *Journal of Retailing, 77*(1), 111–137.

Patterson, Maurice, & Richard Elliott (2002). Negotiating masculinities: Advertising and the inversion of the male gaze. *Consumption Markets and Culture, 5*(3), 231–249.

Pleck, Joseph H., & Brian P. Masciadrelli (2004). Paternal involvement by US residential fathers: Levels, sources, and consequences. In Michael E. Lamb (Ed.), *The role of the father in child development* (Vol. 4; pp. 222–271). Hoboken, NJ: John Wiley & Sons, Inc.

Reekie, Gail (1992). Changes in the Adamless Eden. In Rob Shields (Ed.), *Lifestyle shopping: The subject of consumption.* London, England: Routledge Publishing.

Risman, Barbara J. (1986). Can men mother? Life as a single father. *Family Relations, 35*(1), 95–102.

Risman, Barbara J. (1987). Intimate relationship from a microstructural perspective: Men who mother. *Gender and Society, 1*(1), 6–32.

Russell, Graeme (1986). Primary caring and role sharing fathers. In Michael E. Lamb (Ed.), *The father's role: Applied perspectives.* New York, NY: John Wiley & Sons.

Salzman, Marian L., Ira Matathia, & Ann O'Reilly (2005). *The future of men.* New York, NY: Palgrave Macmillan.

Schroeder, Jonathan E (2003). Gender, consumption, and identity. *Family Relations, 37*(6), 1–4.

Shields, Rob (1992). *Lifestyle shopping: The subject of consumption.* London, England: Routledge Publishing.

Spiggle, Susan (1994). Analysis and interpretation of qualitative data in consumer research. *Journal of Consumer Research, 21* (December), 491–503.

Stern, Barbara (2003). Masculinism(s) and the male image: What does it mean to be a man? In Tom Reichart & Jaqueline Lambiase (Eds.), *Sex in advertising: Perspectives on the erotic appeal* (pp. 215–229). Mahwah, NJ: Lawrence Erlbaum Associates.

Strasser, Susan (2000). *Never done: A history of American housework.* New York, NY: Henry Holt and Company.

Strauss, Anselm, & Juliet Corbin (1998). Basics of qualitative research: Techniques and procedures for developing grounded theory. Thousand Oaks, CA: Sage Publications.

Thompson, Craig J. (1996). Caring consumers: Gendered consumption meanings and the juggling lifestyle. *Journal of Consumer Research, 22* (March), 388.

Thompson, Craig J., William B. Locander, & Howard R. Pollio (1990). The lived meaning of free choice: An existential-phenomenological description of everyday consumer experiences of contemporary married women. *Journal of Consumer Research, 17*(3), 346–361.

Thompson, Julie, & Kristin Fletcher (2005). Metros versus retros: Are marketers missing real men? www.leoburnett.com/manstudy/contact/htm

Thompson, Linda, and Alexis J. Walker (1989). Gender in Families: Women and men in marriage, work, and parenthood. *Journal of Marriage and Family, 51*(4), 845–871.

Thompson, Ross A. (1986). Fathers and the child's best interests: Judicial decision making in custody disputes. In Michael E. Lamb (Ed.), *The father's role: Applied perspectives* (pp. 61–102). New York, NY: John Wiley & Sons.

Tuncay, Linda, & Cele Otnes (2008). Exploring the link between masculinity and consumption. In Tina M. Lowery (Ed.), *Brick & mortar shopping in the 21st century.* Mahwah, NJ: Lawrence Erlbaum Associates.

Section V

New Directions

14

(Re)Igniting Sustainable Consumption and Production Research Through Feminist Connections

Susan Dobscha and Andrea Prothero

> Gender relations are a site in which to develop a deeper understanding of environmental issues, and environmental relations offer...a clearer picture of gender politics: what the specific relations are between gender and environmental issues cannot be understood without...situated consideration of the people and places (and non-human beings) involved. (Mortimer-Sandilands, 2008, p. 312)

INTRODUCTION: PATHWAYS TO RESEARCH

This chapter serves as a launching point for new work on sustainability in the consumer research arena by reimagining the work using gender as a theoretical lens. Many consumer researchers who study sustainability have concluded that the discipline has stalled in its approach to the topic and that its impact on the larger debate is therefore minimal (Prothero et al., 2011). Some work has blamed the field's paradigmatic legacy of economics, psychology, and statistics for the inability to analyze problems that are more macro in scope, while other research points to larger, more ideological issues related to capitalism, wealth distribution, and materialism (Durning, 1992; Kilbourne, McDonagh, & Prothero, 1997; O'Connor, 1994). A shift from the dominant social paradigm (DSP) to a new environmental paradigm in marketing (Kilbourne et al., 1997; Prothero et al., 2011) requires a shift in epistemology that includes gender, race, class, and development as key social constructions that impact sustainability research.

Feminist theory successfully integrates these key issues into its discussion of important societal problems such as poverty, public health, education, and, notably here, sustainability. Feminist approaches to sustainability, such as feminist economics, feminist geography, and feminist sociology, can serve consumer behavior to formulate new research questions that will move the sustainable consumption and production (hereafter, SC&P) research agenda forward. SC&P has been defined by the United Nations Environment Program (UNEP, 2009) as

> the use of services and related products, which respond to basic needs and bring a better quality of life while minimizing the use of natural resources and toxic materials as well as the emissions of waste and pollutants over the life cycle of the service or product so as not to jeopardize the needs of further generations. (p. 8)

Research that focuses on SC&P therefore explores

the inseparability of nature and society
an over reliance on "short-termism," rational decision making, and profit maximization
the marginalization of certain groups within society and the social structures that perpetuate this marginalization

Despite efforts by consumer researchers to move the sustainability agenda away from individual consumption patterns to broader objectives (Berg, 2011; Connolly & Prothero, 2008; Hansen & Schrader, 1997; Martens & Spaargaren, 2005) and to forward gender/feminism ideology to a more prominent place within the consumer behavior discipline (Bristor & Fischer, 1993; Hirschman, 1993; Scott, 2005), the general lack of traction on both fronts has left the field devoid of gender research that has had any sustained impact and sustainability research that has made real inroads toward wide-scale change. Indeed, only a few marketing pieces explore the intersection between feminism and sustainability explicitly (Dobscha & Ozanne, 2001; McDonagh & Prothero, 1997).

The gender/sustainability relationship, however, does have a long history in the social sciences, including sociology, geography, feminism, and economics. From areas as diverse as feminist geography (Seager, 2003; Sharp, 2008), rural sociology (Seyfang, 2006), developing nations' sustainable development (Pandey, 2010), the biological sciences (Weasel, 1997), and ecological economics (McMahon, 1997), gender plays an important role in the conceptualization of sustainability.

Feminist theory as a paradigm treats gender as a contested construct that engages structures of power that have historically led to imbalances of power and resources. Furthermore, feminist theory requires that scientists engage their communities of interest in some praxis stage that allows the work of the scientist to improve the conditions of the community under scrutiny (Bristor & Fischer, 1993). While an exhaustive overview of all subgroups of feminist theory would be impossible to accomplish, we have chosen four subfields (sociology, economics, geography, and ecofeminism) that integrate sustainability and feminist theory and further consider how they can help move forward the study of SC&P in consumer research.

Thus, to serve our aim of considering how environmental feminist theory can advance the broad sustainability research agenda in the marketing and consumer research fields, we first highlight the existing deficiencies in the sustainability field within marketing and consumer research. Next we explore four research streams in the social sciences that have successfully integrated sustainability and gender in their research endeavors. We then outline how an infusion of environmental feminist theory can contribute to the current sustainability research initiatives in marketing and consumer research.

At this point, we would like to clarify that we are viewing gender from an implicit versus explicit framework. An explicit discussion of gender focuses on biological differences that may predict certain sustainable attitudes and behaviors (Vinz, 2009). An implicit analysis considers gender as a social construction that perpetuates power and resource imbalances (Vinz, 2009). The field of marketing has primarily engaged in explicit analyses of gender at the expense of implicit analyses of the role gender plays in the perpetuation of unsustainable business and marketing practices.

In their review of gender research in the consumer research field, Bettany, Dobscha, O'Malley, and Prothero (2010) highlighted the gradual move of research in the discipline away from that which focused solely on the biological differences between men and women (the "gender as a variable" research agenda) to more sophisticated and nuanced research exploring the social construction of gender. Sociologists and other fields that focus on gender have long abandoned this "gender as variable" agenda in favor of uncovering the role gender plays in social situations, social structures, and dimensions of power. Their work highlights the underlying principles that govern gender relations and, specifically in connection with sustainability, find that issues of nature and society cannot be studied separately because to do so would be to continue the policies that have led to environmental degradation to date.

SUSTAINABILITY RESEARCH IN MARKETING AND CONSUMER RESEARCH: LACK OF IMPACT OR "BENIGN NEGLECT"?

The fields of marketing and consumer research have seen a renewed interest in the topic of sustainability. There have been several special issues on sustainability in mainstream marketing journals: the *Journal of Macromarketing* and *Journal of the Academy of Marketing Science* in the United States and the *Journal of Marketing Management* in the UK. In addition, sustainability seems to be a staple on the roundtable circuit of the field's most important conferences (Association for Consumer Research, European Association for Consumer Research, American Marketing Association, Transformative Consumer Research). And European scholars have historically tackled this issue with more vigor than their American counterparts.

Thus, there is little doubt that the current academic and popular focus on sustainability is unprecedented: journal special issues, specialty conferences, listservs, topical blogs, and government initiatives. With this massive explosion of information, research, conversations, and energy, it would seem that some sign of progress or forward movement could be seen in terms of changes in consumption and production practices, marked shifts in public policy, and polluting industries attempting to clean up their processes. Yet, shifts in behavior, attitudes, and intentions have, by and large, not surfaced. There appears to be a disconnection between the efforts of the sustainability community and the actions of those stakeholders that could impose the greatest impact on the health of our natural world. There are several alternative explanations for this lack of progress; we will focus our discussion here on the paradigmatic legacy within marketing that has led the field astray.

THE MARKETING PARADIGM'S LEGACY OF UNSUSTAINABLE SUSTAINABILITY RESEARCH

Marketing as an academic discipline was born from a marriage of psychology and economics (Alvesson, 1994; Bartels, 1965; Day & Wensley, 1983; Jones & Monieson, 1990). These paradigms shaped our discipline in myriad ways, notably creating dual foci in consumer decision making and marketing strategy. Research has stayed within these narrow research lanes, leading to what Reibstein, Day, and Wind (2009) have characterized as "marketing losing its way" (p. 1). In particular, they argued that marketing, with its "bifurcated" emphasis on behavioral decision making and marketing strategy, has failed to contribute to the global conversations on "major societal concerns" such as the crumbling financial system, health care, energy conservation, and consumers in developing nations (p. 2). The negative effects for sustainability research particularly are that such a micro-orientation has led to a hyperfocus on individual consumers and failed to address larger societal concerns.

Reviews of the sustainability literature in marketing point to this legacy as being detrimental to the movement of a progressive agenda that would have large impacts on consumption and production practices (Kilbourne & Beckmann, 1998; Prothero et al., 2011). By focusing on the demographics or other predictors of "green" consumption, it allows the biggest polluters—manufacturers—to continue their unsustainable practices. The "market model" has failed to produce wide-scale changes in production and distribution practices; consumers changing to reusable bottles will in the end have only a negligible environmental impact while a ban on plastic water bottles would have a much more substantial impact.

The focus on consumption patterns has had another, unintended negative consequence: blaming consumers for the current state of the environment. This "storyline," defined as a narrative "about social reality combining elements from many different domains...which provide an actor with a set of symbolic references that suggest a common understanding" (Jensen, 2005, p. 169) has served to place consumers as the primary perpetrators in environmental crises such as pollution and waste production. As many have argued elsewhere, this storyline allows the focus to remain on consumer action (or lack thereof) while allowing companies to continue to avoid scrutiny (Vinz, 2009). The only time negative attention is paid to unsustainable companies is the brief period after an environmental crisis, such as the BP oil spill in the Gulf of Mexico and the nuclear plant meltdowns in Japan. This attention is temporary and typically does not result in changes in public policy, public opinion, or consumer behavior.

A lack of sustained focus and pressure on those processes that contribute the most to environmental crises is particularly frustrating given the incredible amounts of academic and policy efforts happening on many fronts. As noted earlier, within marketing, there have been several special issues on sustainability. The most recent effort was published in the *Journal of the Academy of Marketing Science* (*JAMS*) in 2011. This special issue is an excellent window into the weaknesses inherent in the discipline's core coverage of the topic of sustainability. The papers included use established theoretical frameworks (resource theory, market orientation, corporate social responsibility) and come to conclusions consistent with previous work in the area (i.e., consumers and businesses may not act altruistically but can be persuaded to consume sustainably with appropriate incentives).

What is absent from this particular special issue (and, in fact, most of the other special issues on sustainability published in mainstream marketing journals) is application of theories or paradigms with critical perspectives. Therefore, the deficiencies of sustainability research in marketing are replicated in this most recent special issue. This replication continues to perpetuate the problems outlined by Reibstein et al. (2009): "Through a process of benign neglect, academic marketing has left voids that other fields have filled" (p. 1). A similar point about SC&P is made elsewhere (McDonagh, Dobscha, & Prothero, 2011).

Marketing researchers such as Fisk, Kilbourne, McDonagh, and Prothero have spent their careers illuminating the critical topic of sustainability from a broad macroperspective. The latest incarnation of research in the field, however, shows us that even though there has been an enormous renewed interest in the topic, most of this research does not explore how we might redefine the philosophy of consumption and marketing within a global society existing on ever diminishing resources. At the same time, while over the decades marketing and consumer researchers have produced a fair share of research on this topic (albeit, under different guises), sustainability as a research topic has not had the large-scale impact on the field that other concepts, such as culture, globalization, relationship marketing, and branding, have had.

With the increased focus on sustainability within the discipline, there seems to be almost no discussion of the role of gender within the sustainability arena. A recent overview of gender and consumer behavior conferences (Bettany et al., 2010) found that, while much gender and consumer research work has been conducted, sustainability did not figure prominently as one of the topical areas of interest and was virtually absent from the typical list of topics covered by the premier gender scholars in the field of consumer research. Instead, work at these conferences focuses primarily on fashion, family, feminist theory, sports, and, most recently, masculinity.

Fortunately, some important work in consumer research on gender and sustainability has found its way into mainstream journals. In the 1990s, some consumer researchers introduced ecofeminism as a paradigm that illuminated the connection between women and nature in their mutual marginalization (Dobscha, 1993; Lozada & Mintu-Wimsatt, 1995; McDonagh & Prothero, 1997, and, more recently, Littlefield, 2010). These articles have not, however, led to a shift in the discipline on how researchers or organizations view the important connection between the role of men and women in society and the need for sustainable solutions to major issues such as climate change, oil usage, urban sprawl, and factory farming, to name a few. Instead, sustainability research, as discussed before, primarily continues on with its emphasis on measuring individual consumption patterns.

What will it take for marketing to occupy a legitimate and important place in sustainability research? While the recent flurry of attention to sustainability in marketing would indicate that this area is not suffering from "benign neglect," it does continue to be predominantly led by "status quo" research that fails to confront the core assumptions guiding the way in which we conduct research and the topics we choose to study. What, then, will it take for future research to move beyond the micro, managerialist perspectives that are currently dominating the field? This research agenda attempts to "right the ship" by infusing current sustainability research in marketing with perspectives from feminist theory. Specifically, we highlight four branches of feminist theory that deal with environmental issues: ecofeminism, feminist sociology, feminist economics, and feminist geography.

INTEGRATING FOUR BRANCHES OF ENVIRONMENTAL FEMINIST THEORY INTO MARKETING AND CONSUMER RESEARCH ON SUSTAINABILITY

Ecofeminism (Revisited)

We revisit ecofeminism in light of its initial failure to impact the marketing discipline's approach to sustainability (Dobscha, 1993; Lozada & Mintu-Wamsatt, 1995). The ecofeminism literature began to flourish in the 1970s (Daly, 1978; d'Eaubonne, 1974; Griffin, 1978; Ruether, 1974) in fields such as sociology and women's studies. Ecofeminism works within a set of guiding principles. First, it assumes that nature and society are inseparable, instead of embodying a hierarchical relationship where the needs of society are valued over those of nature. Second, a short-term economic outlook favors rational decision making and profit maximization over environmental protection. Third, both women and nature have been marginalized because of existing social structures, and this has resulted in the long-term oppression of women and the long-term destruction of the environment. These issues, which have been further explored explicitly in the diverse ecofeminism literature, are discussed briefly next.

Leppänen (2004) traces the earliest work back to the beginning of the twentieth century and also explores some important developments in the 1940s (Wägner, 1941, in Leppänen, 2004). A number of key works were published in the 1980s (Mies, 1986; Shiva, 1988) when, as with the feminist literature, divergent thoughts and opinions on ecofeminism began to develop, and this continued throughout the 1990s (Agarwal, 1992; Diamond & Orenstein, 1990; Jackson, 1995; Merchant, 1992; Warren, 1990) and into the 2000s (Leppänen, 2004; Moore, 2008a, 2008b; Mortimer-Sandilands, 2008). Some authors have questioned the efficacy of ecofeminism and in particular its contribution to the feminist agenda (Moore, 2008a). Others (Agarwal, 1992; Cuomo, 1997; Jackson, 1995; Sturgeon, 1997) criticize the essentialist nature of some early ecofeminists such as Shiva (1988) and Salleh (1997)—in particular the notion that women are in some way closer to nature than men. More recently there has been a movement within ecofeminism to illuminate men's relationship with nature (Littlefield, 2010).

Moving away from the essentialist works, some authors argue that ecofeminism has the potential to become a "radical liberatory theory" that could add an extra layer to the domination field that normally considers class, gender and race (Leppänen, 2004, p. 38). Moore (2008b) also suggested adding development to this list. In rejecting the essentialist perspective, Plumwood (1993) argues for ecofeminism to take on more political meaning, and Mortimer-Sandilands (2008) suggests that "ecofeminist analysis is at its most powerful when it questions the intersecting dynamics of gender and nature as they occur in concrete and situated places and times" (p. 307). It is these aspects of ecofeminism that are explored further in this chapter.

One of the unfortunate consequences of some of the earlier ecofeminism literature is that it perpetuated the stereotype that women are somehow inherently closer to nature and therefore in charge of its care (i.e., "Mother Nature" and the Gaia principle). The intent was to highlight the joint struggles of women and nature without presupposing women's closeness to nature or excluding men's connection and participation (Sandilands, 1999). The essentializing idea that women are closer to nature, as a result of "biology, spirituality, or nurture" (Lepännen, 2004, p. 43), undermines the central premise that women and nature should be studied jointly because of the commonalities of their domination (Plumwood, 1993).

A common thread that occurs throughout the ecofeminism literature is an acceptance that social structures that impact women negatively are the same ones that impact the natural environment negatively. The "domination of women by men and the domination of the environment by humans are inter-related" (McDonagh & Prothero, 1997, p. 363), and it is changing the social structures that allow these dominations that becomes important (Dobscha & Ozanne, 2001).

In order to move beyond the previous ecofeminist work published in marketing and consumer research, we must set a research agenda that clarifies the message that women are not inherently better able or equipped to care for the earth and that men are somehow biologically driven to pollute and pillage. Instead, ecofeminist research should guide marketing and consumer research by incorporating the idea of mutual domination and look at men's complex and sometimes puzzling relationship to nature (Littlefield, 2010). Specifically,

- How is the mutual domination hypothesis reflected in how markets are formed, created, maintained, and dismantled?

- Are new forms of sustainable consumption, such as prosocial and collaborative consumption, being driven by a new ethos born from deeper connections to nature?
- Will sustainable consumption gain more mainstream acceptance if it taps into consumers' deep connections to nature? Would fostering a connection to nature create a more sustainable consumption pattern among mainstream consumers?

Ecofeminism embraces many important principles that, if applied to marketing and consumer research, would serve to provide richer, more complex solutions to the problem of sustainability. Feminist sociology adds a level of understanding about sustainability by providing critique about the social structures that continue to dominate both women and nature and providing solutions for dismantling them.

Feminist Sociology

Sociology has a long tradition of trying to understand the social structures that impact people's daily lives (Mills, 1959). However, starting in the 1970s, some sociologists began to question the social structures that were studied as well as the people being studied (Acker, 1973; Bart, 1971; Oakley, 1972). These early critics found that the discipline was dominated by the experiences of men and that women's lived experiences were either marginalized or ignored. The field of feminist sociology sought to rectify this omission by considering the content and methodology of mainstream sociology (Ritzer, 1990). Chafetz (1988) defined feminist sociology as embodying research that (1) has gender as a central focus, (2) problematizes gender relations in terms of social and other inequities, (3) recognizes that gender is not immutable, and (4) explores feminist theory that challenges the current status quo that devalues women.

Following from this agenda in the late 1970s, some sociologists began to theorize that nature and society are inseparable and suggest that studying them separately privileges research conducted on human (notably male) domains and ignores or undervalues work that focuses on nature. Thus, by dividing nature and society, it is argued that social structures that have traditionally dominated nature (governments, businesses, religions) will continue the environmental devastation wreaked by industrialized nations. Feminist sociologists continue to confront the traditional paradigm by making clear the connections among the important components of their discipline: "The very definition of environmental degradation varies not only across different societies and cultures, but also by gender, class, and race within a particular society" (Goldman & Schurman, 2000, p. 572).

Feminist sociology alerts us to the discrepancies related to women's participation in structures of power, such as the labor force and government (Hessing, 1995). When viewed through a lens of sustainability, this translates into three problems:

- Women are less represented than men in management due to the male bias that permeates, including the new "green economy."
- Women are still under-represented in government, where environmental policies are written and enacted.
- Women are disproportionately negatively affected by environmental degradation, due to their front-line responsibilities with family and household creation and maintenance.

Feminist sociologists, such as Smith, view these "facts" as evidence of pervasive gender bias in all "relations of ruling," where "ruling apparatuses are those institutions of administration, management and professional authority, and of intellectual and cultural discourses, which regulate, lead and direct contemporary capitalist societies" (Smith, 1990, p. 3). When women are not included in these ruling apparatuses, certain stories are not told and laws are enacted without women's input. The marketing of infant formula to developing nations and laws that were written and voted upon by men that govern women's bodies are but a few examples.

From an employment perspective, even though over 52% of employees in the United States are female, women still make up only a very small percentage of those who hold senior management positions. A global survey showed that in 2010 only 20% of global senior management positions were held by women (Grant Thornton, 2011) and only 15 of the CEOs of the top Fortune 500 companies are female (Fortune, 2010); in Europe only 9.7% of corporate board leaders of the top 300 companies are women (Clark, 2010). At the same time, men's salaries continue to be consistently higher than women's, at both the lower and higher ends of the salary scale.

In the European Union the salary gap is 18% (Spiegel Online International, 2010) and in the United States women earn 20% less than their male colleagues, and women also tend to dominate lower paid and less skilled professions. In the marketing profession women tend to make a considerable percentage of the workforce; in the UK, for instance, it has been classified as roughly 50/50 male and female. However, even though the Institute of Practitioners in Advertising appointed its first female president in 2011, only 22.4% of those in senior management positions are women (Sweney, 2011).

This discrepancy also permeates through to jobs in sustainability fields. Recent work on sustainability employment, for example, shows that women do not fare any better than in more traditional sectors (Masika & Joekes, 1996; Morgenstern, 2010). In both rural environments and organizations, positions of power are still primarily held by men and, in some cases, access to valuable resources is restricted due to prevailing gender biases (Masika & Joekes, 1996). The "green economy" is projected to create 50 million worldwide jobs in the next 20 years (Stevens, 2010) and, while this may seem like a boon for women, about 75% of these jobs will be related to renewable energy and green buildings—two sectors where women have long been marginalized. (Less than 1% of top managers in the energy sector are women and only 9% of construction jobs are held by women.)

Integrating feminist sociology into the current research on sustainability will impact not only the topics covered but also the manner in which the problems of SC&P are addressed. Specifically,

- What impact has the exclusion of women in key sustainable jobs and positions of power in the green economy had on the integration of sustainability practices into business, marketing, and production? Would resources be allocated differently and different questions asked?
- How have marketing's dominant paradigms (economics and psychology), which traditionally favor the masculine experience, served to stifle work in SC&P? Does the application of these paradigms to questions of sustainability leave out standpoints situated in the local and the feminine?
- How does the lack of a feminine standpoint impact sustainability practices within the home and at a local governmental level? What impact does this have on the development of sustainable regulations and public policies?
- How would a more explicit integration of gender, race, class, and development into sustainability research serve to change the marketing discipline's current orientations?

Feminist sociology provides insights into how social structures serve to maintain positions of domination or, as Smith puts it, influences the "relations of ruling" that serve to silence women's viewpoints. What feminist sociology does not adequately address is how these social structures are interwoven with global institutions such as financial and labor markets. Feminist economics adds to our understanding about gender and sustainability by infusing work related to the underlying assumptions guiding financial market activity and labor market valuation.

Feminist Economics

The field of economics plays an important role in the current debates on such pressing environmental issues as climate change and production/ consumption cycles. Some critics point to the false objectivity premise that economists hold related to their role in the uneven distributions of wealth between rich and poor and the valuation of environmental impacts of manufacturing for future generations (Buckingham, 2004). This false objectivity stance has been viewed by some economists as unethical, immoral, and unconscionable (Donath, 2000).

The field of feminist economics illuminates the fissures in mainstream accounts of economics by injecting critical issues such as sustainability into the field's current models. What these scholars find is that the models that dominate economics, those of "competitive production and exchange in markets" (Donath, 2000, p. 116), fail to include the critical unpaid work of child and elder care that is mostly undertaken by women. It is the belief of feminist economics scholars that if these critical social functions continue to be ignored, women will continue to occupy a lower position within the economy.

Feminist economists also lament the way in which environmental costs are accounted for in neoclassical economic models. These models have traditionally emphasized "small changes, monetary valuation, individual self-interest, and individual utility from consumption" (Nelson, 2009, p. 12) with almost no consideration of long-term interests such as pollution, climate change, and energy usage. They claim that this short-sightedness is in fact as unsustainable as the consumption, transportation, and housing patterns that it has perpetuated through the flawed assumptions of "rational decision making" and "profit maximization." Nelson (2009) states: "At this point in our history, and facing the particular problem of climate change, economists need to recognize that our modeling and econometric skills, however hard-earned, may not be what the world most needs right now" (p. 13).

Ecological economists argue for a commitment to developing models that account for the human inputs and consequences of current business practices. Marketing researchers in sustainability would be well served to question the predominant business model of "profit maximization" and go even further to critique commonly accepted marketing canons such as the proliferation of consumer choice ideology, the perpetuation of materialism and overconsumption, and pricing goods using a life-cycle approach. Specifically,

- How do profit maximization models and short-term outlooks impact sustainability research within marketing and consumer research?
- How would an infusion of new accounting principles (human consequences of consumption and current business practices) change the current strategy models used in marketing? How would pricing theory be affected, for example?
- How would new models of economics that embrace what is still primarily "women's work" impact current assumptions that underpin marketing and consumer research?
- With most family consumption activities still performed by female heads of households, would the work required to make sustainable choices be held in higher regard? If this previously invisible work were valued more explicitly in the current models, would it lend legitimacy to these acts and affect how producers think about the impact their products have on their consumers?

Feminist Geography

Feminist geography is a newer subfield of feminism that focuses its energy on key issues related to women and their relations to space (physical and virtual) and social power. Baschlin (2002) lays out their agenda thusly:

> …topics on spatial structures as the relations between access to space and social power from which results dominance or exclusion of social groups; questions about the definition of "labor," production and reproduction, and the gendered division of labor; and topics of social constructions of "nature" and culture. (p. 29)

Gilmartin's (2002) work on the relationship between gender and access to land in rural South Africa provides an excellent window into this branch of feminism. She sought "to understand how geography can be used to resist oppression and to create alternative spaces of belonging" (p. 35). This work serves to illuminate "strategies for maintaining the silence and the strategies for breaking it" (Morrison, 1992, p. 51). Feminist geography also attempts to create and nurture a dialogue that looks at geography through an anticolonial lens, insisting that conquest has been one of the key drivers of the oppression of social and physical space for certain groups. For example, Ni Dhomhnaill (1996) wrote about the Irish practice of naming and owning their physical surroundings in spite of the oppressive colonial control imposed by England. This naming practice gave the Irish people a way of possessing the land around them without the benefit of "titular ownership" (p. 431).

Another application of feminist geography is in the area of women's travel writings, which were ignored in mainstream geography journals in favor of men's work on chronicling the stranger experiencing a foreign and exotic land. This exclusion led to greater fetishization of the "other," ignored the experiences of the "local," and favored the cultural practices of the landscape over the natural connections. Feminist geographers are able to study events, like festivals or farming practices, with the added contextual richness of time and place. These additional elements give rise to the role gender plays in the "power of geographical exclusions" and the "tyranny of space" (Kobayashi, 1997, p. 8).

This ability to report on the experiences of the local and the familiar provides a more complex picture of the negative impacts of environmental degradation on groups formerly hidden or voiceless, such as farmers, mothers, caretakers, and local governments (who are unable to fight off corporate farming initiatives). When large corporate farming companies move into small farming communities and systematically buy out the local farmer, the long-term repercussions from this "tyranny of space" policy are economic, in terms of the decimation of the local labor force, but also environmental, in terms of the increased use of pesticides that lead to increases in cancer and the devastation of local crops in favor of profit-producing crops, such as soybeans and corn (Fearnside, 2001).

Sustainability research in marketing simultaneously privileges and denies culpability in what Vinz (2009) and others describe broadly as "northern economies"—industrialized nations that rely on the natural resources of "southern economies" (see later discussion) to fuel economic growth and daily life. Much of the research at the intersection of gender and sustainability that occurs outside the field of marketing focuses on "southern" economies, which are typically rural communities that exist in developing nations.

Fontagné, Gaulier, and Zignago (2008) define the line between north and south in terms of GDP. Low-producing GDP countries constitute southern economies, while high-producing GDP countries comprise northern economies. Research topics that have southern economies as their focus highlight how women are excluded from land policy decisions (Agarwal, 1992), are disproportionately negatively affected by pesticide use (Ransom, 2002), and are forbidden from participating in market activities (OECD, 2006). Within marketing, we focus almost no attention on these rural economies but instead conduct research on those economies that are most at fault for environmental degradation.

This north/south split is reflected in the geopolitical fairness arguments put forth by Freund and Kilbourne (working paper) and others. They claim that focusing exclusively on the north/south split fails to acknowledge the large middle ground between those nations contributing greatly to the production/consumption cycle. It is also argued that these types of analyses ignore women's experiences in the local food economy and other marketplace activities (Durning, 1992). Applying feminist geography to marketing issues would serve to illuminate Freund and Kilbourne's assertion that "the most dangerous ecological problems, such as climate change, are inherently global and are not contained within the geographical borders of any state" (working paper, p. 1). Feminist geographers would agree and add that focusing on man-made borders creates blindness to the lived experience of women whose everyday interactions with their food supply, the marketplace, and other social structures are impacted by the natural environment.

How, then, can feminist geography aid further research in the field of SC&P? Specifically,

- How have gender, race, class, and development impacted the rise and fall (and possible rise again) of "family" farming? What "relations of ruling" impact the family farm business model and marketplace activities? Do masculine models of "ownership" and "stewardship" overshadow other models that may be better suited to sustainable farming?

- Is the movement to increase SC&P hindered or helped by traditional notions of physical nation-state boundaries? How can researchers begin to bridge the intellectual gap between research that reflects these sometimes arbitrary boundaries and the natural boundaries created by rivers, lakes, oceans, mountains, and valleys? How have man-made boundaries served the sustainability movement? Do we need to think more creatively about the notions of boundaries in order to improve sustainability practices?
- Are there underlying gender readings of the retailing proposition that "bigger is better"? What is the relationship between gender dynamics and retailing practices? How are "big box retailers" a symptom of a lack of understanding of the relationship between physical spacing and sustainability? How would the view of these retailing practices change if viewed through a lens of feminist geography?

CONCLUSION

As discussed in the sustainability section earlier, we posit that much of the current work in sustainability within marketing and consumer research perpetuates old models of consumption and business practices and fails to apply a critical perspective. As such, we argue that within the consumer research field a more nuanced approach to studying the important intersection between gender and sustainability research would produce richer representations in our tackling issues related to sustainability marketing generally and more specifically the fields of SC&P.

Researchers in marketing and consumer behavior must begin to explore the overconsumption patterns of the North that then fuel environmentally devastating manufacturing and distribution practices. Feminist economists advocate for a shift in economic models that would include long-term environmental effects in addition to short-term profit maximization goals. Marketing could work in tandem with this initiative to educate consumers about the full consumption cycle and the negative health effects of not just consuming but also producing toxic products. Americans in particular are disconnected from their waste, bodily and consumption, and this disconnection has perpetuated a "toxic love affair" (Freinkel, 2011, p. 3) with convenience goods, such as plastic water bottles. By (re)connecting consumers from the most wasteful nations with the consequences of their overconsumption, consumers will better understand the consequences of their overconsumption and may be more likely to reduce their personal contributions to the problem.

An important distinction must be made here between previous sustainability research on changing consumption patterns and this research agenda. Blaming consumers for the current environmental crisis is not productive and, in simpler terms, has not worked to change consumer perceptions and behavior. This research agenda proposes that by educating consumers about the full life cycle of products, including how they are produced to how they are disposed of, will serve a greater purpose of putting all the elements of the process on notice that their practices are unacceptable. For example, consumer, NGO, and media pressure, not changes in the law, led to major retailers' decision to discontinue stocking baby bottles lined with BPA. While the bigger issue of why manufacturers continue to use this lining in products looms large, it is the work of public health advocates and other media outlets that raised awareness about the potential dangers and shifted consumer perception.

This chapter has aimed to illustrate how a combination of feminist theory and sustainability, as theorized and debated in other disciplines and discussed briefly earlier, could allow future research to move beyond the narrow, managerial focus pervading current marketing and consumer research discourses. A focus on ecofeminist perspectives has the potential to allow more systemic and macro agendas to emerge and flourish, where future research agendas not only could examine microissues such as the attitude–behavior gap or the willingness-to-pay debate, but also will tackle questions that focus on a critical analysis of existing marketing paradigms and a wider SC&P agenda that moves beyond the "let's blame the consumer" agenda.

REFERENCES

Acker, Joan (1973). Women and social stratification: A case of intellectual sexism. *American Journal of Sociology, 78*(4), 174–183.

Agarwal, Bina (1992). The gender and environment debate: Lessons from India. *Feminist Studies, 18*(1), 119–518.

Alvesson, Matts (1994). Critical theory and consumer marketing. *Scandinavian Journal of Management, 10*(3), 292–313.

Bart, Pauline (1971). Sexism and social science: From the gilded cage to the iron cage, or, the perils of Pauline. *Journal of Family and Marriage, 33*(4), 734–745.

Bartels, Robert (1965). Development of marketing thought: A brief history. In Jagdish N. Sheth & Dennis E. Garrett (Eds.), *Marketing theory: Classic and contemporary readings* (pp. 190–210). Cincinnati, OH: South-Western Publishing Co.

Baschlin, Elisabeth (2002). Feminist geography in the German-speaking academy: History of a movement. In *Feminist geography in practice* (pp. 25–30). Malden, MA: Blackwell Publishers.

Berg, Annukka (2011). Not roadmaps but toolboxes: Analyzing pioneering national programs for sustainable consumption and production. *Journal of Consumer Policy, 34*(1), 9–23. (DOI 10.1007/s10603-010-9129-2).

Bettany, Shona, Susan Dobscha, Lisa O'Malley, & Andrea Prothero (2010). Moving beyond binary opposition: Exploring the tapestry of gender in consumer research and marketing. *Marketing Theory, 10*(1), 3–28.

Bristor, Julia M., & Eileen Fischer (1993). Feminist thought: Implications for consumer research. *Journal of Consumer Research, 19* (March), 518–536.

Buckingham, Susan (2004). Ecofeminism in the twenty-first century. *Geographical Journal, 170*(2), 146–154.

Chafetz, Janet S. (1988). *Feminist sociology: An overview of contemporary theories.* Itasca, IL: F. E. Peacock Publishers.

Clark, Nicola (2010). Getting women into boardrooms, by law. *New York Times Online.* http://www.nytimes.com/2010/01/28/world/europe/28iht-quota.html

Connolly, John, & Andrea Prothero (2008). Green consumption: Life-politics, risk and contradictions. *Journal of Consumer Culture, 8*(1), 117–145.

Cuomo, Chris J. (1997). *Feminism and ecological communities: An ethic of flourishing.* London, England: Routledge.

Daly, Mary (1978). *Gyn/ecology: The metaethics of radical feminism.* Boston, MA: Beacon Press.

Day, George S., & Robin Wensley (1983). Marketing theory with a strategic orientation. *Journal of Marketing, 47* (Fall), 79–89.

d'Eaubonne, Francoise (1974). *New French feminism: An anthology.* New York, NY: Shocken Books.

Diamond, Irene, & Gloria Orenstein (Eds.) (1990). *Reweaving the world: The emergence of ecofeminism.* San Francisco, CA: Sierra Club Books.

Dobscha, Susan (1993). Women and the environment: Applying ecofeminism to environmentally related consumption. *Advances in Consumer Research, 20,* 36–40.

Dobscha, Susan, & Julie Ozanne (2001). An ecofeminist analysis of environmentally sensitive women: Qualitative findings on the emancipatory potential of an ecological life. *Journal of Public Policy and Marketing, 20*(2), 201–214.

Donath, Susan (2000). The other economy: A suggestion for a distinctively feminist economics. *Feminist Economics, 6*(1), 115–123.

Durning, Alan T. (1992). *How much is enough? The consumer society and the future of the Earth.* New York, NY: W. W. Norton and Company.

Fearnside, Philip M. (2001). Soybean cultivation as a threat to the environment in Brazil. *Environmental Conservation, 28*(1), 23–38.

Fontagné, Lionel, Guillaume Gaulier, & Soledad Zignago (2008). Specialisation across varieties within products and north–south competition. *Economic Policy, 23*(53), 51–91.

Fortune, (2010). Women CEOs. *Money Magazine.* http://money.cnn.com/magazines/fortune/fortune500/2010/womenceos/

Freinkel, Susan (2011). *Plastic: A toxic love story.* New York, NY: Houghton Mifflin Harcourt.

Freund, Jim, & William Kilbourne (working paper). *The consumption dilemma and geopolitical fairness.*

Gilmartin, Mary (2002). Making space for personal journeys. In Pamela Moss (Ed.), *Feminist geography in practice* (pp. 31–410). Oxford, England: Wiley Blackwell.

Goldman, Michael, & Rachel Schurman (2000). Closing the "great divide": New social theory on society and nature. *Annual Review of Sociology, 26,* 563–584.

Grant Thornton (2011). Proportion of women in senior management falls to 2004 levels. http://www.gti.org/Pressroom/Proportion%20of%20women%20in%20senior%20 management%20falls%20to%202004%20levels.asp

Griffin, Susan (1978). *Women and nature: The roaring inside her.* London, England: The Women's Press.

Hansen, Ursula, & Ulf Schrader (1997). A modern model of consumption for a sustainable society. *Journal of Consumer Policy, 20*(4), 443–468.

Hessing, Melody (1995). The sociology of sustainability: Feminist eco/nomic approaches to survival. In Michael D. Mehta & Eric Ouellet (Eds.), *Environmental sociology: Theory and practice* (pp. 231–254). North York, ON: Cactus Press Inc.

Hirschman, Elizabeth C. (1993). Ideology in consumer research 1980 and 1990: A Marxist and feminist critique. *Journal of Consumer Research, 19* (March), 537–555.

Jackson, Cecile (1995). Radical environmental myths: A gender perspective. *New Left Review, 210,* 124–142.

Jensen, Hans R. (2005). Environmentally co-responsible consumer behavior and political consumerism. In Klaus G. Grunert & John Thorgerso (Eds.), *Consumers, policy and the environment: A tribute to Folke Olander* (pp. 165–181). New York, NY: Springer.

Jones, D. G. Brian, & David D. Monieson (1990). Early development of the philosophy of marketing thought. *Journal of Marketing, 54* (Jan), 102–113.

Kilbourne, William E., & Susan Beckmann (1998). Review and critical assessment of research on marketing and the environment. *Journal of Marketing Management, 14* (July), 513–532.

Kilbourne, William E., Pierre McDonagh, & Andrea Prothero (1997). Sustainable consumption and the quality of life: A macromarketing challenge to the dominant social paradigm. *Journal of Macromarketing, 17*(1), 4–24.

Kobayashi, Audrey (1997). The paradox of difference and diversity (or, why the threshold keeps moving). In John Paul Jones, III, Heidi J. Nast, & Susan M. Roberts (Eds.), *Thresholds in feminist geography: Difference, methodology, representation* (pp. 3–10). Lanham, MD: Rowman & Littlefield Publishers, Inc.

Leppänen, Katarina (2004). At peace with earth—Connecting ecological destruction and patriarchal civilization. *Journal of Gender Studies, 13*(1), 37–47.

Littlefield, Jon (2010). Men on the hunt: Ecofeminist insights into masculinity. *Marketing Theory, 10*(1), 97–117.

Lozada, Hector, & Alma Mintu-Wimsatt (1995). *Ecofeminism and green marketing: Reconciling nature and hu(man)kind.* Washington, DC: American Marketing Association.

Martens, Susan, & Gert Spaargaren (2005). The politics of sustainable consumption: The case of the Netherlands. *Sustainability: Science, Practice, & Policy, 1*(1), 1–14.

Masika, Rachel, & Susan Joekes (1996). Employment and sustainable livelihoods: A gender perspective. Report No. 37. Brighton, UK: Institute of Development Studies.

McDonagh, Pierre, Susan Dobscha, & Andrea Prothero (2011). Sustainable consumption and production: Challenges for transformative consumer research. In Mick David Glen, Simone Pettigrew, Cornelia Pechmann, & Julie Ozanne (Eds.), *Transformative consumer research for personal and collective well-being* (pp. 267–282). London, England: Routledge.

McDonagh, Pierre, & Andrea Prothero (1997). Leap-frog marketing: The contribution of ecofeminist thought to the world of patriarchal marketing. *Marketing Intelligence & Planning, 15*(7), 361–388.

McMahon, Martha (1997). From the ground up: Ecofeminism and ecological economics. *Ecological Economics, 20*(2), 163–173.

Merchant, Carolyn (1992). *Radical ecology: The search for a livable world.* London, England: Routledge.

Mies, Maria (1986). *Patriarchy and accumulation on a world scale.* London, England: Zed Books.

Mills, C. Wright (1959). *The sociological imagination.* New York, NY: Oxford University Press.

Moore, Niamh (2008a). Eco/feminism, non-violence and the future of feminism. *International Feminist Journal of Politics, 10*(3), 282–298.

Moore, Niamh (2008b). The rise and rise of ecofeminism as a development fable: A response to Melissa Leach's "Earth mothers and other ecofeminist fables: How a strategic notion rose and fell." *Development and Change, 39*(3), 461–475.

Morgenstern, Claire (2010). Is the green jobs movement leaving women behind? www.greeneconomypost.com/green-jobs-women-8669.htm

Morrison, Toni (1992). *Playing in the dark: Whiteness and the literary imagination.* New York, NY: Vintage Press.

Mortimer-Sandilands, Caitriona (2008). Eco/feminism on the edge. *International Feminist Journal of Politics, 10*(3), 305–313.

Nelson, Julie A. (2009). Between a rock and a soft place: Ecological and feminist economics in policy debates. *Ecological Economics, 69*, 1–8.

Ni Dhomhnaill, Nuala (1996). Dinnsheanachas: The naming of high or holy places. In P. Yaeger (Ed.), *The geography of identity* (pp. 408–432). Ann Arbor, MI: University of Michigan Press.

Oakley, Ann (1972). *Sex, gender and society.* London, England: Temple Smith.

O'Connor, James (1994). Is sustainable capitalism possible? In Martin O'Connor (Ed.), *Is capitalism sustainable?* (pp. 152–175). New York, NY: Guildford Press.

OECD (2006). Enhancing women's market access and promoting pro-poor growth. In *Promoting pro-poor growth: Private sector developments,* pp. 63–72.

Pandey, Anupam (2010). Greening Garhwal through stakeholder engagement: The role of ecofeminism, community and the state in sustainable development. *Sustainable Development, 18*(1), 12–19.

Plumwood, Val (1993). *Feminism and the mastery of nature.* London, England: Routledge.

Prothero, Andrea, Susan Dobscha, Jim Freund, William E. Kilbourne, Michael G. Luchs, Lucie K. Ozanne, & John Thørgersen (2011). Sustainable consumption: Opportunities for consumer research and public policy. *Journal of Public Policy and Marketing, 30*(1), 31–38.

Ransom, P. (2002). *Women, pesticides and sustainable agriculture.* Paper presented at the Women's Caucus for the Earth Summit, CSD NGO Women's Caucus.

Reibstein David, George Day, & Jerry (Yoram) Wind (2009). Is marketing academia losing its way? *Journal of Marketing, 73*(4), 1–3.

Ritzer, George (1990). Metatheorizing in sociology. *Sociological Forum, 5*(1), 3–15.

Ruether, Rosemary R. (1974). *New woman new earth*. Minneapolis, MN: Seabury Press.

Salleh, Ariel (1997). *Ecofeminism as politics: Nature, Marx and the postmodern*. London, England: Zed Books.

Sandilands, Caitriona (1999). *The good-natured feminist: Ecofeminism and the quest for democracy*. Minneapolis, MN: University of Minnesota Press.

Scott, Linda (2005). *Fresh lipstick: Redressing fashion and feminism*. New York, NY: Palgrave Macmillan.

Seager, Joni (2003). Rachel Carson died of breast cancer: The coming of age of feminist environmentalism. *Signs, 28*(3), 945–972.

Seyfang, Gill (2006). Ecological citizenship and sustainable consumption: Examining local organic food networks. *Journal of Rural Studies, 22* (October) 383–395.

Sharp, Joanne (2008). Geography and gender: What belongs to feminist geography? Emotion, power, and change. *Progress in Human Geography*, July 11, 1–7.

Shiva, Vandana (1988). *Staying alive: Women, ecology and development*. London, England: Zed Books.

Smith, Dorothy (1990). *Texts, facts, and femininity*. London, England: Routledge.

Spiegel Online International (2010). Salary gap widens between German men and women. http://www.spiegel.de/international/europe/0,1518,682026,00.html

Stevens, Candice (2010). Are women the key to sustainable development? www.bu.edu/pardee/files/2010/04/UNsdkp003fsingle.pdf

Sturgeon, Noël (1997). *Ecofeminist natures: Race, gender, feminist theory and political action*. New York, NY: Routledge.

Sweney, Mark (2011). Women under-represented in senior advertising jobs, says IPA report. http://www.guardian.co.uk/media/2011/jan/20/ipa-women-in-advertising

UNEP (2009). Frequently asked questions: The Marrakech process—Towards a 10-Year framework of programs on sustainable consumption and production. http://www.unep.fr/scp/marrakech/about.htm

Vinz, Dagmar (2009). Gender and sustainable consumption: A German environmental perspective. *European Journal of Women's Studies, 16*(2), 159–179.

Wägner, Elin (1990/1941). *Väckarklocka*. Stockholm, Sweden: Bonnier.

Warren, Karen (1990). The power and promise of ecological feminism. *Environmental Ethics, 12*(2), 125–146.

Weasel, Lisa (1997). The cell in relation: An ecofeminist revision of cell and molecular biology. *Women's Studies International Forum, 20*(1), 49–59.

15

Beyond Gender: Intersectionality, Culture, and Consumer Behavior

Ahir Gopaldas and Eileen Fischer

INTRODUCTION

In this chapter, we show that consumer researchers interested in studying gender, culture, and consumer behavior may benefit from going beyond gender to consider intersectionality. Intersectionality has been diversely described as an analytical tool (Collins, 1998), buzzword (Davis, 2008), concept (Crenshaw, 1989), perspective (Shields, 2008), and even paradigm (Hancock, 2007). At base, intersectionality is the idea that each and every person is positioned in society at the intersection of multiple social axes, such as race, class, and, of course, gender. Consequently, every person is subject to advantages and disadvantages particular to his or her intersectional position.

Intersectionality also denotes an interdisciplinary field of studies that has explicating human phenomena along multiple social axes as a shared objective. Thus, intersectionality researchers may examine social axes as diverse as age and immigration status in research contexts as varied as domestic violence and fashion advertising. This chapter presents the key tenets of the intersectionality literature (first section), highlights intersectionality-oriented work in consumer culture theory (second section), and outlines promising avenues for future research on intersectionality and consumption (third section).

AN OVERVIEW OF THE INTERSECTIONALITY LITERATURE

The idea of intersectionality emerged in Black feminist discourse. In most chronological accounts, theorists identify Kimberle Crenshaw's (1991) essay on the factors perpetuating violence against women of color as the origin of the term *intersectionality* and Patricia Hill Collins's (1990/2000) articulation of Black feminist thought as the tipping point that transformed the marginalized discourse into a major theoretical conversation.

On one hand, the idea of intersectionality has been gaining currency in social theory, education, and practice. It has been hailed as a "spectacular success" (Collins, 1990/2000; Davis, 2008, p. 67)—the most important contribution that critical race theories (for a review, see Crenshaw, Gotanda, Peller, & Thomas, 1995) and feminist standpoint theories (for a review, see Harding, 2004) have made to social science so far (Hancock, 2007; McCall, 2005). Major social science journals now expect intersectional analyses, while race-, class-, or gender-only studies can be seen as "theoretically misguided, politically irrelevant, or simply fantastical" (Davis, 2008, p. 68). Pivotal texts on intersectionality (Collins, 1990/2000; Crenshaw, 1991) have been applied widely across the social sciences from anthropology (Boellstorff, 2007) to psychology (Warner, 2008). Intersectionality is now also taught in introductory sociology courses (Andersen & Collins, 1992; Ritzer & Goodman, 2008).

Finally, though theory is a few steps ahead of practice, awareness of intersectionality is slowly but surely affecting domains such as human rights advocacy, identity politics, and social movements (Aguirre, 2000; Bernstein, 2005; Hurtado, 2005; Padilla, 1997; Verloo, 2006), counseling, psychotherapy, and social work (Edwards, Merrill, Desai, & McNamara, 2008; Kohn & Hudson, 2002; Spencer, Lewis, & Gutierrez, 2000), and workplace diversity training (Konrad, Prasad, & Pringle, 2006).

On the other hand, several theorists observe that the intersectionality literature suffers from too much ambiguity and complexity (Brewer, Conrad, & King, 2002; Davis, 2008; Jordan-Zachery, 2007; McCall, 2005; Nash, 2008; Staunaes, 2003). Accordingly, to mobilize the transdisciplinary utility of the intersectionality literature, we aim to reduce its ambiguity and complexity by organizing its tenets in a systematic manner.

Key Terms

In the intersectionality literature, the term *category*, invoked in phrases such as "analytic category" (Browne & Misra, 2003; McCall, 2005) and "categories of difference" (Bedolla, 2007; Hancock, 2007), is often used at two different levels of abstraction to refer to both classification systems (e.g., gender) and specific classes (e.g., women). For clarity, we use the terms *structure, category,* and *intersection:*

- A social identity *structure* refers to a pervasive system of human classification. Some examples of social identity structures are age, attractiveness, body type, caste, citizenship, education, ethnicity, gender, height and weight assessments, immigration status, income, marital status, nationality, occupation, physical ability, race, religion, sex, sexual orientation, and socioeconomic status.
- A social identity *category* refers to a specific class in a classification system. Some examples of social identity categories are college educated, skinny, Jewish, immigrant, old, married, pretty, Romanian, and short.
- An *intersection* refers to a social identity space demarcated by one or more identity categories (e.g., poor White people). Unlike the more popular metaphor of social location or position that conjures an image of pinpoint precision and permanence, the metaphor of identity space lends itself more easily to conjuring the fuzzy boundaries that categories really draw (Bowker & Star, 1999) and the important possibility of further demarcation or subdivision (e.g., highly educated, poor White people).

The Nature of Social Identity Categories

In the intersectionality literature, as in contemporary sociology, social identity categories are assumed to be constructed by human beings. Categories are not predestined by nature or God or any other conceptualizations of extra-human forces (Berger & Luckmann, 1966; Potter, 1996; Searle, 1995). A corollary of this constructivist proposition is that identity categories are not timeless but rather historical, produced by persons in a sociohistoric moment; hence, all categories can also be said to have a genealogy (Foucault, 1970).

Identity categories are also context specific. Boundaries are drawn differently in different contexts. For example, class may be delineated as diversely as blue-collar/white-collar, lower/middle/upper, or poor/rich in different contexts. Observers of the same context from different vantage points may perceive different social classifications and produce partial and situated knowledge (Haraway, 1988). Hence, any perspective on human phenomena is always standpoint specific (Harding, 2004; Hartsock, 1997). Identity categories are not only historical or originating in specific times, but also dynamic or always changing in time, so any discussion of them is necessarily time specific (Pierson, 2004). There may be considerable variance in the rate at which different categories change. Some may change so gradually as to appear permanent, while others may change so quickly as to appear haphazard. However stable they may appear, categories are continually constructed, reproduced, opposed, and transformed. For example, the boundaries of racial categories have been revised at a relatively rapid rate in Puerto Rico (Loveman & Muniz, 2007) and Brazil (Schwartzman, 2007).

Though specifically formulated to conjure an illusion of homogeneity, an identity category is often, if not always, a polysemic signifier—a signifier with multiple meanings—and each meaning in turn has multiple implications. For example, in popular American discourses, the category of man can signify meanings as diverse as courageous, clumsy, primitive, reserved, rebellious, or virile (Adams & Savran, 2002); which meaning is mobilized often depends on the other categories along with which it is manifested. In summary, intersectionality presupposes that identity categories are constructed, historical, dynamic, context specific, standpoint specific, time specific, and polysemic.

The Notion of Intersectionality

A number of theorists have struggled to define the notion of intersectionality. Ordered chronologically, a selection of some of the best definitions illustrates a gradual movement of the intersectionality literature from the problems of a specific social group to the general problems of social classification:

> "the various ways in which race and gender interact to shape the multiple dimensions of Black women's employment experiences" (Crenshaw, 1991, p. 1244)

"analysis claiming that systems of race, social class, gender, sexuality, ethnicity, nation, and age form mutually constructing features of social organization, which shape Black women's experiences and, in turn, are shaped by Black women" (Collins, 1990/2000, p. 299)

"the dynamic and interdependent matrices of privilege and disadvantage that affect labor market outcomes across social locations" (Browne & Misra, 2003, p. 507)

"the relationships among multiple dimensions and modalities of social relations and subject formations" (McCall, 2005, p. 1771)

"the interaction [among] categories of difference in individual lives, social practices, institutional arrangements, and cultural ideologies and the outcomes of these interactions in terms of power" (Davis, 2008, p. 68)

The intersectionality literature describes social identity structures as coconstitutive, mutually constitutive, interdependent, interlocking, interlinking, or intertwined. In statistical terms, one would say that social identity structures are not always mutually independent variables. For example, one's gender or race categories might affect one's ability to belong to certain education or occupation categories and, in turn, affect one's ability to belong to certain income or class categories. Although this is a frequent claim in the intersectionality literature, advice on how to trace such interdependence is scarce, perhaps because the nature of each link among social identity structures is unique.

Methodological Approaches to Intersectionality Research

Like most scholars, intersectionality researchers must select their research methods in tandem with their theoretical questions. McCall (2005) has begun to simplify this selection process by offering a tripartite typology of methodological approaches based on one high-level criterion: What sort of complexity are researchers trying to explain? According to McCall, an *anticategorical* approach investigates the process of categorization; appropriate methods include deconstruction and genealogy. An *intracategorical* approach investigates the experiential heterogeneity of a group; appropriate methods include case study and (auto)ethnography. An *intercategorical* approach investigates the differences among groups; appropriate methods include factor analysis and hierarchical modeling. Refining this typology, we suggest that there are four possible goals of intersectionality research, which may be pursued in any combination across a stream of research or in a single research project:

Matrix analysis. This type of analysis asks the following questions: "Which social identity structures are operational in the focal context?" "Which categories are salient within each structure?" This type of analysis is most likely to be conducted at the outset of a research project and appropriate research methods are thematic analysis or formal content analysis of textual data such as informant narratives or published blogs.

Among-intersections analysis. This type of analysis asks, "What are the divergent experiences across social groups?" Such analysis must entail purposive sampling of informants or subjects, whether qualitative or quantitative data are being collected. What sets intersectionality research apart from other statistical studies of group differences is the focus on the interaction effects among the structures (Berdahl & Moore, 2006). In other words, intersectionality research of this kind is inherently comparative and more concerned with how multiple social identity structures interactively shape human experience than with analyses involving only one structure.

Within-intersection analysis. This type of analysis often begins by identifying an intersection that has been historically overlooked in a field of research, usually a social group that has been marginalized on two or more counts (e.g., Black women in Collins's [1990/2000] landmark text on intersectionality). It then asks the question, "What are the unique experiences of this marginalized group?" Thereafter, to avoid homogenizing the experience of the group, this type of analysis also asks, "How do the experiences of group members diverge from one another?" Appropriate research methods include participation, observation, interviews, or (auto)ethnography.

Process analysis. This type of analysis asks the following questions: "By what processes are the focal categories constructed, reproduced, opposed, or possibly transformed over time?" What mechanisms might alter the current distribution of power among stakeholders?" Appropriate research methods include genealogy, historical analysis, or longitudinal netnography.

INTERSECTIONALITY IN CONSUMER CULTURE THEORY

We will refer to cultural research on consumer behavior as consumer culture theory (CCT). Although the term intersectionality has not been invoked in CCT thus far, a number of studies examine how social identity structures affect consumer culture. In this section, we review four intersectionality-oriented studies published in the *Journal of Consumer Research* (Crockett & Wallendorf, 2004; Fischer & Arnold 1990; Henry, 2005; Holt & Thompson, 2004). These articles are not directly informed by the intersectionality literature *per se*, but rather are sensitized to some of its logic via precursory and parallel literatures: critical theory, feminism, men's and women's studies, and the works of Pierre Bourdieu. We review key aspects of these studies to highlight how the logics of intersectional research are manifest and indicate how CCT can be conducted with a sensitivity to intersectionality.

"More Than a Labor of Love: Gender Roles and Christmas Gift Shopping"

In this paper, Fischer and Arnold (1990) examine how sex, gender-role attitudes, and gender identity intersect to shape the culture of Christmas gift-shopping. This article exemplifies two of the methodological approaches to intersectionality research: matrix analysis and among-intersections analysis. Fischer and Arnold begin their research with a matrix analysis to identify which social identity structures are salient within the context of Christmas gift-shopping. Through qualitative interviews and extensive literature review, they identify that sex [man, woman], gender-role attitudes [traditional, egalitarian], and gender identity [masculine, feminine] are salient identity structures in Christmas gift-shopping.

Building on this matrix analysis, Fischer and Arnold conduct an among-intersections analysis. They undertake a survey to examine several main and interaction effects. They propose and verify that

women are more involved than men in gift-shopping
women with traditional gender-role attitudes are more involved in gift-shopping than women with egalitarian gender-role attitudes
men with egalitarian gender-role attitudes are more involved in gift-shopping than men with traditional gender-role attitudes

persons with more feminine gender identities (regardless of their sex) are more involved in gift-shopping

Fischer and Arnold define being more involved in Christmas gift-shopping as giving gifts to more recipients, starting one's shopping earlier, spending more time per recipient, and experiencing greater success in gift selection.

Fischer and Arnold's (1990) basic premise—that there is significant heterogeneity within social identity categories (i.e., among men and among women)—is a fundamental notion in the intersectionality literature. It is also worth noting that their quantitative approach to among-intersections analysis is supported by other recent advocates of intersectionality research (Berdahl & Moore, 2006; McCall, 2001a, 2001b).

"The Role of Normative Political Ideology in Consumer Behavior"

This paper by Crockett and Wallendorf (2004) examines the role of political ideology in the domain of everyday provisioning (e.g., grocery shopping). Although theirs is not an analysis that involves gender as a structure, their empirical research nicely illustrates what may be described as a within-intersection analysis because it investigates the unique circumstances and divergent responses of a marginalized social group. In the context of Black Milwaukee, also known as the ghetto, resident consumers have severely attenuated access to marketplace goods and services, "symbolized by rotting fruit, green meat, and shelves without unit pricing in ghetto stores" (p. 525). Drawing on ethnographic data, the authors reveal these consumers' divergent responses to this problem: outmigration, opposition to outmigration, outshopping, neighborhood loyalty, Black entrepreneurship, etc. The authors also show how this diversity of responses aligns with consumers' own political ideologies (Black liberal, Black nationalist).

The authors' theoretical discussion also provides an excellent example of a process analysis that fits well within the tradition of intersectionality research. They develop an intricate recursive model of social relations wherein socioeconomic structures are the foundations for particular ideologies, ideologies are a guiding framework for marketplace behavior, and the marketplace is an alternate political sphere where consumers attempt to reproduce or transform socioeconomic structures to reinforce their worldviews. Finally, researcher reflexivity is a common ethic in intersectionality research and Crockett and Wallendorf's study is an exemplar in this regard. Because gender and race are salient identity structures in their data, the authors detail their own standpoints:

> The first author, a black male...privileges his access to discussions of race with other blacks...because household provisioning is a predominantly female activity, his gender required him to develop sufficient rapport...The second author, a white female, provided analytical distance in both data coding and analysis. (p. 514)

"Man-of-Action Heroes: The Pursuit of Heroic Masculinity in Everyday Consumption"

In this 2004 paper, Holt and Thompson examine the role of gender and class in the domain of everyday lifestyle consumption (i.e., "leisure and hobbies, mass media viewing, the home, autos, clothing, sports, and so on" [p. 437]). This study examines the discourses and practices animating the lives of middle-aged straight White men in smaller American cities—men whose masculinity has been threatened by socioeconomic changes and whose consumption is often characterized as compensatory. A historical analysis of mass-cultural discourses in twentieth century America reveals three models of American masculinity: breadwinner, rebel, and man of action. The difficult choice between the reliable but dull breadwinner model and the exciting but juvenile rebel model is resolved by the exciting and reliable man of action model (e.g., Dirty Harry, James Bond). Holt and Thompson illustrate how their informants employ the breadwinner–rebel dialectic to infuse everyday consumption with dramatic tension and heroic achievement and perform the man of action script to avert economic and social threats to their masculinity.

The authors also use Bourdieu's (1984) theory of habituation to argue that class (working, professional) operates as a "malleable interpretive framework" (p. 438) that men employ to customize the models of masculinity to their socio-economic situation. Accordingly, this study includes both within-intersection analysis (i.e., of the unique experiences of middle-aged, straight White men) and between-intersections analysis (i.e., of working-class vs. professional-class middle-aged, straight White men).

"Social Class, Market Situation, and Consumers' Metaphors of (Dis)Empowerment"

Henry's (2005) paper examines the role of class in the domain of financial planning (e.g., purchasing, investing, and saving practices). Specifically, he compares the behavior of professional- and working-class, employed, young, and childless men in Sydney, Australia. Henry (p. 769) reveals that professional-class socialization fosters perceptions of the self as "potent actor," which in turn encourages intricate investment strategies that allow for financial growth.

On the other hand, working-class socialization fosters perceptions of the self as "impotent reactor," which in turn encourages minimal investment strategies that emphasize financial security and preclude class advancement. Accordingly, this study is both a between-intersections analysis and a process analysis. The process analysis is exemplary in that it illuminates how an otherwise largely invisible set of mechanisms (i.e., one's self-perceptions, sense of [dis]empowerment, and conceptions of the future) reproduces the structure of class. Henry concludes with the following notes for future research, which bolsters our call for more intersectionality-oriented research:

> Bourdieu (1984) thought of social class as one type of class…he included gender and age as other types of classes…Bourdieu argued that…all the properties influencing material conditions and conditioning should be integrated into the analysis…Future studies should examine the intersection of multiple class types on (dis)empowerment. (p. 776)

INTERSECTIONALITY AND CONSUMPTION: AVENUES FOR FUTURE RESEARCH

As we have shown in the prior section, several CCT studies examine how domains of consumption are shaped by social identity structures. In this section, we outline new avenues for future research on intersectionality and consumption.

Overlooked Structures, Categories, and Intersections

One avenue for future research is simply to start examining social identity structures, categories, or intersections that have been relatively or entirely overlooked. For example, although many consumer researchers have examined the role of class (Allen, 2002; Henry, 2005) and gender (Fischer & Arnold, 1990; Thompson, 1996) in consumer culture, to the best of our knowledge, none have examined the role of occupation or physical ability. For example, consumer researchers may conduct an ethnography in a single firm to examine how consumption differs across divisions and levels of a corporate structure. Furthermore, while many consumer researchers have included race in their analyses, the focus has remained on popular American divisions of race (Black, White) (Bradford, 2009; Crockett & Wallendorf, 2004). Classifications of race vary widely across continents and nations.

Finally, researchers will have no difficulty finding overlooked intersections (e.g., wealthy Muslim consumers or physically disabled Chinese consumers) but they may have difficulty legitimating why these intersections matter theoretically. For a helpful example, consider Üstüner and Holt's (2007) study of poor migrant women in Turkey. Although this consumer intersection is far from the archetypal consumer in the mostly Western marketing imaginary, the authors cleverly use this distance to their advantage. They position their sample of informants in stark contrast to the usual samples in consumer acculturation research and build a distinct model of *dominated* consumer acculturation.

From Reproductive to Transformative Processes

A second avenue for future research is to focus on transformative processes in marketer and consumer identity politics. Each of the CCT studies reviewed in the previous section is an account of how social identity structures are reproduced through consumption, with the possible exception of Crockett and Wallendorf's study, which reveals acts of social reproduction and attempts at social transformation. It would behoove a new generation of intersectionality-oriented research to focus not only on how social identity structures are reproduced but also on how they are transformed by marketers and consumers. For example, Thompson and Tian (2008) reveal three strategies that editors of lifestyle magazines use to resignify the identity of the American Southerner: symbolic gentrification, revisionist reclamation, and mythological conflation.

An example of a context in which consumer researchers could explore how marketers and consumers are reconfiguring gender and intersecting structures, such as profession, is the contemporary phenomenon of mother-entrepreneurs, or "mom-preneurs" (Costin, 2011). These women generally develop businesses to retail a product that has been inspired by their own experiences as mothers. The products are then often marketed to other mothers with the assistance of mommy-bloggers. (See relevant discussion of stay-at-home-dads in Chapter 7 in this volume.)

Social Identity Structures in New Media

A third avenue of research is to investigate the selective reproduction of identity structures in matchmaking sites and social media (e.g., eHarmony and Facebook), which promise to reshape the way in which people meet and marry across traditional boundaries (e.g., family and class). Traditional social networks (e.g., family gatherings, community events, religious groups, workplaces, neighborhood bars, etc.) tend to facilitate encounters among members of the same class, ethnicity, or religion. By contrast, new web-mediated networks help maintain traditional ties as well as facilitate encounters by commercial interests (e.g., among fans of the same musician or drivers of the same sports car).

Several questions are raised by these new technologies. To what extent do these new media necessitate representation of oneself according to existing social identity structures? In virtual spaces, where a temporary emancipation from identity categorization is technically feasible, how do marketers facilitate or limit such emancipation? Which identity structures are prerequisites for participation? For example, are identity markers such as religion, race, education, and income required or optional fields in personal profiles for making friends and finding partners? Such research could clarify whether and how social media are producing new patterns of kinship.

Marketer Representation of Multiply Marginalized Groups

A fourth avenue for future research is to examine whether and how marketers feature multiply marginalized groups in their brand communications. Black feminist thought would predict that marketers will deviate from the mythical norm of a "white, thin, male, young, heterosexual, Christian, and financially secure" person (Lorde, 2007/1984, p. 116) on as few counts as possible and only as necessary. Thus, although marketers may feature many marginalized identity categories in association with their brands, persons belonging to multiple marginalized groups (e.g., Black and old) are far less likely to be featured. Such research could produce a theory of when and why marketers include persons belonging to multiply marginalized groups. One reason may be that a sizeable number of their consumers are situated in such intersections.

Another reason may be that such persons serve as multiplicative markers of corporate diversity. For example, a single visual presentation of a female person of color in a wheelchair may signal that the corporation explicitly welcomes employees and customers across categories of gender, race, and physical ability. However, one might also wonder how much corporate commitment such an image suggests if the image is limited to the diversity page of the corporate website, rather than featured in its more visited home pages and shopping catalogs.

Emotions as Links Between Intersectional Identities and Consumer Behavior

A fifth avenue for future research is to investigate whether and how emotions link intersectional identities and consumer patterns. Neither intersectionality theorists nor consumer culture theorists have shown much interest in studying emotions thus far. Consumer culture theorists have tended to conceptualize culture as a system of meaning, focusing on myths and ideologies (Arnould & Thompson, 2005), while forgetting that culture is also a system of emotion norms. Nonetheless, we argue that researching emotions is a worthy avenue of future research. Our argument is based on three premises:

- A rich stream of research on the sociology of emotions demonstrates that different social groups have different emotion norms (Turner & Stets, 2006).
- Consumer research on affect suggests that different emotions have different functional influences on consumer behavior (Griskevicius, Shiota, & Nowlis, 2010).

- Many psychologists concur that emotions collectively constitute the primary system of human motivation or, at the very least, that emotions are an appropriate level of analysis at which to study human motivation (Izard, 2009).

We argue that just as intersectional identity spaces foster certain ideologies, which in turn foster certain consumer patterns (Crockett & Wallendorf, 2004), so too intersectional identity spaces foster certain emotions, which in turn foster certain consumer patterns. In other words, we argue that beyond ideologies and myths, emotions, too, may be important mediators of the link between identity spaces and consumer patterns. For example, social groups that are often shamed in popular culture (e.g., via racist or sexist innuendo) are likely to develop mechanisms for coping with shame, at least some of which are likely to be consumptive in nature (e.g., wearing certain clothes to fit in, moving to multicultural neighborhoods, or buying cars and houses that defy stereotypes).

CONCLUSION

In this chapter, we accomplish three goals. First, we present the key tenets of the intersectionality literature. Identity categories are constructed—historical, dynamic, context-specific, standpoint-specific, time-specific, and polysemic. Intersectionality denotes the sociological condition that each and every person is positioned in society at the intersection of multiple social axes. Each and every person is consequently subject to unique advantages and disadvantages particular to his or her intersection. Methodological approaches to intersectionality research include matrix analysis, among-intersections analysis, within-intersection analysis, and process analysis.

Second, we explicate four exemplary intersectionality-oriented articles in consumer culture theory. Collectively, these articles emphasize that there is considerable behavioral heterogeneity among members of the same identity space or intersection. Furthermore, these articles emphasize that identity structures such as race, class, or gender are not as independent from one another as one might imagine. Finally, these articles show that taking on the complexity of intersectionality is feasible within the scope of a journal article. Readers interested in more exemplars of intersectionality-oriented research may also consider the work of Allen (2002), Bradford (2009), and Üstüner and Holt (2007).

Third, we outline promising avenues for future research on intersectionality and consumption. We encourage researchers to examine social identity structures, categories, and intersections that have been overlooked; imagine how social identity structures can be transformed to empower more consumers; investigate whether and how social media are producing new patterns of kinship; understand when and why marketers feature multiply marginalized groups; and consider the role of emotions in linking intersectional identities to consumer patterns.

REFERENCES

Adams, Rachel, & David Savran (2002). *The masculinity studies reader.* Malden, MA: Blackwell.

Aguirre, Adalberto (2000). Academic storytelling: A critical race theory story of affirmative action. *Sociological Perspectives, 43* (Summer), 319–339.

Allen, Douglas E. (2002). Toward a theory of consumer choice as sociohistorically shaped practical experience: The fits-like-a-glove (FLAG) framework. *Journal of Consumer Research, 28* (March), 515–532.

Andersen, Margaret L., & Patricia H. Collins (1992). *Race, class, and gender: An anthology.* Belmont, CA: Wadsworth.

Arnould, Eric J., & Craig J. Thompson (2005). Consumer culture theory (CCT): Twenty years of research. *Journal of Consumer Research, 31* (March), 868–882.

Bedolla, Lisa García (2007). Intersections of inequality: Understanding marginalization and privilege in the post-Civil Rights era. *Politics and Gender, 3* (June), 232–248.

Berdahl, Jennifer L., & Celia Moore (2006). Workplace harassment: Double jeopardy for minority women. *Journal of Applied Psychology, 91* (March), 426–436.

Berger, Peter, & Thomas Luckmann (1966). *The social construction of reality: A treatise in the sociology of knowledge.* New York, NY: Doubleday.

Bernstein, Mary (2005). Identity politics. *Annual Review of Sociology, 31* (February), 47–74.

Boellstorff, Tom (2007). Queer studies in the house of anthropology. *Annual Review of Anthropology, 36* (April), 17–35.

Bourdieu, Pierre (1984). *Distinction: A social critique of the judgment of taste.* Cambridge, MA: Harvard University Press.

Bowker, Geoffrey C., & Susan Leigh Star (1999). *Sorting things out: Classification and its consequences.* Cambridge, MA: MIT Press.

Bradford, Tonya Williams (2009). Intergenerationally gifted asset dispositions. *Journal of Consumer Research, 36* (June), 93–111.

Brewer, Rose M., Cecilia A. Conrad, & Mary C. King (2002). The complexities and potential of theorizing gender, caste, race, and class. *Feminist Economics, 8* (July), 3–17.

Browne, Irene, & Joya Misra (2003). The intersection of gender and race in the labor market. *Annual Review of Sociology, 29* (June), 487–513.

Collins, Patricia H. (1990/2000). *Black feminist thought: Knowledge, consciousness, and the politics of empowerment.* New York, NY: Routledge.

Collins, Patricia H. (1998). *Fighting words: Black women and the search for justice.* Minneapolis, MN: University of Minnesota Press.

Costin, Yvonne (2011). ICT as an enabler for small firm growth: The case of the mompreneur. *International Journal of E-Politics, 2* (March), 17–29.

Crenshaw, Kimberlé (1989). Demarginalizing the intersection of race and sex: A Black feminist critique of antidiscrimination doctrine, feminist theory and antiracist politics. *University of Chicago Legal Forum, 1989,* 139–167.

Crenshaw, Kimberlé (1991). Mapping the margins: Intersectionality, identity politics, and violence against women of color. *Stanford Law Review, 43* (July), 1241–1299.

Crenshaw, Kimberlé, Neil Gotanda, Gary Peller, & Kendall Thomas (1995). *Critical race theory: The key writings that formed the movement.* New York, NY: New Press.

Crockett, David, & Melanie Wallendorf (2004). The role of normative political ideology in consumer behavior. *Journal of Consumer Research, 31* (December), 511–528.

Davis, Kathy (2008). Intersectionality as buzzword: A sociology of science perspective on what makes a feminist theory successful. *Feminist Theory, 9* (April), 67–85.

Edwards, Katie M., Jennifer C. Merrill, Angeli D. Desai, & John R. McNamara (2008). Ethical dilemmas in the treatment of battered women in individual psychotherapy: Analysis of the beneficence versus autonomy polemic. *Journal of Psychological Trauma, 7* (March), 1–20.

Fischer, Eileen, & Stephen J. Arnold (1990). More than a labor of love: Gender roles and Christmas gift shopping. *Journal of Consumer Research, 17* (December), 333.

Foucault, Michel (1970). *The order of things: An archaeology of the human sciences.* London, England: Tavistock Pub.

Griskevicius, Vladas, Michelle N. Shiota, & Stephen M. Nowlis (2010). The many shades of rose-colored glasses: An evolutionary approach to the influence of different positive emotions. *Journal of Consumer Research, 37* (August), 238–250.

Hancock, Ange-Marie (2007). When multiplication doesn't equal quick addition: Examining intersectionality as a research paradigm. *Perspectives on Politics, 5* (March), 63–79.

Haraway, Donna (1988). Situated knowledges: The science question in feminism and the privilege of partial perspective. *Feminist Studies, 14* (Fall), 575–599.

Harding, Sandra G. (2004). *The feminist standpoint theory reader: Intellectual and political controversies.* New York, NY: Routledge.

Hartsock, Nancy C. M. (1997). The feminist standpoint: Developing the ground for a specifically feminist historical materialism. In Diana T. Meyers (Ed.), *Feminist social thought: A reader* (pp. 462–483). New York, NY: Routledge.

Henry, Paul C. (2005). Social class, market situation, and consumers' metaphors of (dis) empowerment. *Journal of Consumer Research, 31* (March), 766–778.

Holt, Douglas B., & Craig J. Thompson (2004). Man-of-action heroes: The pursuit of heroic masculinity in everyday consumption. *Journal of Consumer Research, 31* (September), 425–440.

Hurtado, Aida (2005). Toward a more equitable society: Moving forward in the struggle for affirmative action. *The Review of Higher Education, 28* (Winter), 273–284.

Izard, Carroll E. (2009). Emotion theory and research: Highlights, unanswered questions, and emerging issues. *Annual Review of Psychology, 60,* 1–25.

Jordan-Zachery, Julia S. (2007). Am I a Black woman or a woman who is Black? A few thoughts on the meaning of intersectionality. *Politics and Gender, 3* (June), 254–263.

Kohn, Laura P. & Kira M. Hudson (2002). Gender, ethnicity and depression: Intersectionality and context in mental health research with African American women. *African American Research Perspectives, 8* (Winter), 174–184.

Konrad, Alison M., Pushkala Prasad, & Judith K. Pringle (2006). *The handbook of workplace diversity.* Thousand Oaks, CA: Sage.

Lorde, Audre (2007/1984). *Sister outsider: Essays and speeches.* Berkeley, CA: The Crossing Press.

Loveman, Mara, & Jeronimo O. Muniz (2007). How Puerto Rico became White: Boundary dynamics and intercensus racial reclassification. *American Sociological Review, 72* (December), 915–939.

McCall, Leslie (2001a). *Complex inequality: Gender, class and race in the new economy.* New York, NY: Routledge.

McCall, Leslie (2001b). Sources of racial wage inequality in metropolitan labor markets: Racial, ethnic and gender differences. *American Sociological Review, 66* (August), 520–542.

McCall, Leslie (2005). The complexity of intersectionality. *Signs: Journal of Women in Culture and Society, 30* (Spring), 1771–1800.

Nash, Jennifer C. (2008). Re-thinking intersectionality. *Feminist Review, 89* (June), 1–15.

Padilla, Laura M. (1997). Intersectionality and positionality: Situating women of color in the affirmative action dialogue. *Fordham Law Review, 66*, 843–930.

Pierson, Paul (2004). *Politics in time: History, institutions, and social analysis.* Princeton, NJ: Princeton University Press.

Potter, Jonathan (1996). *Representing reality: Discourse, rhetoric and social construction.* London, England: Sage.

Ritzer, George, & Douglas J. Goodman (2008). *Modern sociological theory.* New York, NY: McGraw–Hill Higher Education.

Schwartzman, Luisa Farah (2007). Does money whiten? Intergenerational changes in racial classification in Brazil. *American Sociological Review, 72* (December), 940–963.

Searle, John R. (1995). *The construction of social reality.* New York, NY: Free Press.

Shields, Stephanie (2008). Gender: An intersectionality perspective. *Sex Roles, 59* (September), 301–311.

Spencer, Michael, Edith Lewis, & Lorraine Gutierrez (2000). Multicultural perspectives on direct practice in social work. In Paula Allen-Meares & Charles D. Garvin (Eds.), *The handbook of social work direct practice* (pp. 131–150). Thousand Oaks, CA: Sage.

Staunaes, Dorthe (2003). Where have all the subjects gone? Bringing together the concepts of intersectionality and subjectification. *NORA: Nordic Journal of Women's Studies, 11* (June), 101–110.

Thompson, Craig J. (1996). Caring consumers: Gendered consumption meanings and the juggling lifestyle. *Journal of Consumer Research, 22* (March), 388.

Thompson, Craig, & Kelly Tian (2008). Reconstructing the South: How commercial myths compete for identity value through the ideological shaping of popular memories and countermemories. *Journal of Consumer Research, 34* (February), 595–613.

Turner, Jonathan H., & Jan E. Stets (2006). Sociological theories of human emotions. *Annual Review of Sociology, 32*, 25–52.

Üstüner, Tuba, & Douglas B. Holt (2007). Dominated consumer acculturation: The social construction of poor migrant women's consumer identity projects in a Turkish squatter. *Journal of Consumer Research, 34* (June), 41–56.

Verloo, Mieke (2006). Multiple inequalities, intersectionality and the European Union. *European Journal of Women's Studies, 13* (August), 211–228.

Warner, Leah (2008). A best practices guide to intersectional approaches in psychological research. *Sex Roles, 59* (September), 454–463.

16

Gender Research as the Ingénue of Marketing and Consumer Behavior

Janeen Arnold Costa and Gary J. Bamossy

INTRODUCTION

As a starting point for our review of gender literature in marketing and consumer behavior, we have chosen Sidney J. Levy's "Symbols for Sale" (1959). Levy opens a thoughtful section of this classic article by stating, "One of the most basic dimensions of symbolism is gender" (p. 72). Also in 1959, the famous Broadway musical *West Side Story* expanded to a full tour of the United States. The female lead, Maria, carried out her role in the play as the classic ingénue. We contend that, in many ways, research on gender and consumption has played out its role as ingénue in the marketing and consumer behavior literature over the last 50 years, emerging finally in the past decade as less naïve, more independent, more adult, and more secure.

The ingénue analogy in gender research in marketing and consumer behavior extends well beyond the characteristics of the ingénue herself. The classic ingénue is defined by her age—that crepuscular moment between adolescence and adulthood—and also by her innocence. A naïf in a complex, urbane world, she moves unaware of the hypocrisy, duplicity, and exploitation around her. Often thought of as lacking sophistication, an ingénue is credulous and vulnerable, dependent on a protective paternal figure, and living in constant peril of being exploited or corrupted by some lurking cad or villain. This threat is the central tension of her life. The questions of how she will navigate this world and who she will become make her interesting (Chocano, 2011).

In the early years of the marketing discipline, our own important directors and producers, who set agendas and priorities for what should and would be produced, reviewed, and disseminated to the academic and business publics, emerged. Sophisticated competitors also represented their works on other stages and venues. As our discipline matured, though, moments of real opportunity for rigorous gender research were neglected. The emerging story lines of research showed biases and marginalization for some roles, and, sadly, but true to character, the ingénue herself was often her own worst enemy.

Casting, Characters, and Venues

A long-standing formula indicates that many of the best plays and films are based on (life) stories and/or real events ("life imitates art"). In another time-honored tradition, academic research in business has been known to lag behind, rather than to lead, the research efforts of private industry (Levy, 2011). Gender research in the marketing discipline is illustrative. At the end of World War II, not all who emulated the main character in *Rosie the Riveter* (1944) wanted to leave factory labor and return home. But most women did, and Herbert Hoover's 1928 presidential campaign slogan of "a chicken in every pot and a car in every garage" began to take hold in post-WWII America.

At that time, American companies were particularly interested in gendered consumption and marketing: "principally focusing on men for autos and women for food and household products." The cover of Rainwater's (1962) *Workingman's Wife: Her Personality, World and Life Style* proclaimed it to be "the first intimate marketing portrait of the woman who can make or break America's most widely advertised products...who she is, who she is not, what she buys, and why." The book's publisher went on to issue such gender-based magazines as *Physical Culture* (bodybuilding), *Family Weekly, Ladies' Home Journal,* and *The American Home*—all of which were well researched, nicely targeted, and commercially successful.[1]

To the extent that scholars have viewed marketing as an applied discipline, these early industry studies on gendered consumption nicely plotted paths for academics to follow with their own research. However, that early gender focus remained applied and empirical, with few marketing scholars who examined theories underlying, precipitating, or supporting the life-changing events of American life. Significant numbers of women entered the workforce for wartime production, then either remained as industrial labor following the war or, in greater numbers, transitioned back to the role of housewife. These substantial socioeconomic shifts were generally not recognized by the marketing discipline as being of interest for major theoretical inquiry (Kassarjian, 2011).

Sociologists, historians, economists, and anthropologists (cf. Cowan, 1976; Goode, 1964; Honey, 1984; Lerner, 1987; Ogburn & Nimkoff, 1955; Reiter, 1975; Rosaldo & Lamphere, 1974; Trey, 1972; Winch, 1952) critically examined the larger significance of this major gender shift and its impact on the structure and dynamics of capitalism, pushing for new theoretical perspectives and, following the practice of scholars, published books and articles in their own disciplines' outlets.

Meanwhile, marketing focused on the value of applying *segmentation* (Levy, 2011) as a lens for research, leading to some critical theoretical and applied methodological publications regarding Blacks, such as the changing nature of their socioeconomic struggles in the marketplace, and representational styles in media (Bauer, Cunningham, & Wortzel, 1965;[2] Kassarjian, 1969, 1977). Nevertheless, with the exception of Davis (1970, 1971), research on gender/sex roles in the marketing literature remained largely descriptive and empirical, primarily focusing on income disparities (Haberman & Elinson, 1967; Rosen & Granbois, 1983) and spouses' decision-making roles (Park, 1982; Sharp & Mott, 1956; Starch, 1958; Wolgast, 1964; Zober, 1966).

By the 1970s, the marketing discipline's research culture and ethos were decidedly male in orientation. White males dominated faculty memberships at research institutions and on editorial boards. Research topics cast in our journals' headliner roles were framed around quantitative methods and the testing of hypotheses. Rather than theory building and/or critical analysis, theory derived from other disciplines dominated, particularly in the field of decision making and information processing—both topics central to marketing's applied worldview. Thus, borrowing extensively from theories already developed in cognitive and social psychology, the central cast and star roles of marketing involved empirically, testing topics such as attitudes, attitude change, intentions, memory, learning, and perceptions. The role of gender was primarily an afterthought in the story line, generally functioning in a supporting role of covariate to tease out interactive effects.

THE INGÉNUE FINDS HER VOICE

In the early 1990s, the ingénue's role developed. A key venue for gender research began to take shape with the establishment of the ACR-sponsored conferences, which looked specifically at the broad topic of gender and consumption. Janeen Costa founded and chaired the first three "gender conferences," in 1991, 1993, and 1996 at the University of Utah. Held biannually since then, in settings from San Francisco to the UK's Lake District, the conferences provided a new venue for those interested in presenting and publishing their work on gender in consumer behavior and marketing. In the following, Costa reflects on the inception and development of the gender conferences:

> I came into marketing and consumer behavior with a PhD in cultural anthropology. After several years' teaching on a short-term contract in an anthropology department, I undertook a post-doc in marketing at the University of Utah, where I was later hired and eventually obtained tenure. In my first foray into the field, I wrote a paper on material culture and gender in rural Greece, presented at the 1988 ACR conference in Hawaii. Russ Belk previewed the paper and suggested one important change—that I include a section on methods. In anthropology conferences, little mention was made of methods; papers were substantive and theoretical, with an assumption that knowledge was gained in various ways, primarily through ethnographic fieldwork, and that the importance of any given work was its overall contribution to a greater understanding of the human condition. Belk's suggestion that I detail my methods was an early indication of the state of consumer behavior research.
>
> In Hawaii, I found myself confronted with an entirely new vocabulary, as well as novel methods, that came from cognitive psychology. I was stunned by what seemed to me to be a microscopic focus on the individual mind, with knowledge obtained through experiments and quantitative methods that seemed removed from real life. I had entered the field at a time when the approach to investigating a consumer's lived experience, and theorizing about human social behavior more broadly, fit our analogy of the ingénue; this was the case for both gendered approaches and consumer behavior research in general. My work in anthropology had been much more comprehensive than an emphasis on gender. Class, ethnicity, family, and other social groups and systems were all part of human behavior, which was for me primarily social. Thus, any and all aspects of society were

relevant. Nevertheless, my research on gender was a promising avenue for me to explore consumer behavior.

Looking over the published work, I was more than surprised—I was astounded—by the lack of research beyond the quantitative-based studies that found men and women were either different, or the same, with little exploration of why, how, or what it meant in a larger context of consumer behavior and of society. When one of my submissions was rejected for presentation at a Winterthur Museum conference on gender and material culture, I received a letter indicating I might consider holding my own conference, within the academic discipline of consumer behavior. Because I felt there might be others in our field who, like me, sought more exploration of, and emphasis on, gender, the conferences were born. The first gender conference in 1991 drew a variety of submissions, from different disciplines, utilizing various methods, and providing diverse perspectives. Still, the tendency to find that men and women behave differently, and then to *stop* there, was common among the submissions. I hoped the conference, designed to be intimate and interactive, with single sessions that all participants attended together, would expand both the knowledge and the desire to understand what lay behind gendered findings.

I was not disappointed. As I proceeded with the next two conferences in 1993 and 1996, some scholars became loyal and regular participants, and some academics notably absent from the first conference began to attend as well. I continued to hope that more men would come and that topics would expand to include gender-based behavior in males. I expressed my desire that cultural and cross-cultural studies would be submitted, giving us a greater foundation upon which to understand biology-based versus learned (changing, cultural) behaviors. Eventually, I would call for research on LGBT consumption. Moreover, as a cultural anthropologist specializing in economic anthropology, I knew that consumption was only one part of economic behavior, which included, from an anthropological perspective, production, distribution, and consumption. All acts of consumption are simultaneously acts of production, and vice-versa. So, I specifically expanded my call to include gender issues in marketing. While research in gender and advertising had already been presented and was growing, I also hoped for studies on sales, interactions within retail venues, media issues, product design, and so on. Some inroads were made in those areas, with interesting results.

My pleas for someone to take over the gender conferences were (gratefully) realized when Dan Wardlow and Eileen Fischer held the fourth conference in San Francisco in 1998. Since then, the conferences have been held every other year, eventually including European venues as well. This latter development was significant. As a group, the European scholars were already more proficient than were Americans in social approaches, in theory, and in cross-cultural differences. They were less tied to cognitive psychology, its methods and narrow focus. They were aware of, and often resistant to, American ethnocentrism and dominance in approaches to the topic and in publishing in visible outlets. Europeans brought to the field what was to me a very welcome diversity and broadening of the treatment of gender. For some scholars, the conferences and the proceedings functioned as a springboard to presenting and publishing their work in the *Journal of Consumer Research* or other journals, broadening the impact of the topic and its diverse methods, theories, and approaches. In some cases, their research furthered their careers.

In 1994, I served as editor for a Sage book providing a selection of works that had been presented in the first two gender conferences (Costa, 1994). I included some chapters that did not reflect my own preferences for methods or theory. My purpose was to present the field as it was at that time, as well as to show some of the best and newer research that academics were undertaking in both consumer behavior and in contributing disciplines. The book in which this current chapter is published is only the second book, then, to attempt to summarize and present the most interesting work that has taken place since 1994 and that continues to energize the field.

When I attend ACR and other conferences, I am often introduced to young academics as "the founder of the gender conferences." My husband and coauthor, Gary Bamossy, says that I am "Miss Gender." I regret both appellations. While I am happy to have been the instigator of the gender conferences, I failed to produce much of my own work on the topic. Instead, I pushed others to do their own best research and to disseminate their findings. My own research efforts were focused more on economic development and marketing. I started the gender conferences because I found the field to be limited in methods and theory development. I do not claim to have had the insight and skill to be considered an expert in gender and consumer behavior. Rather, I am an anthropologist with a keen interest in all social dimensions of human behavior, including, but not limited to, gender.

This concludes my musings on the early phases and development of the gender conferences. Those who have chaired the conferences since 1996 are numerous and have proven to be dedicated to the topic and to the field. My health and retirement on disability have prevented my involvement in the last few conferences, which I regret. However, since the fourth conference, the first I did not chair, I continue to be delighted by the conference chairs' leadership and guidance in the field and by the participants' work and the direction of their research. Overall, though, I am proud of my role as an early catalyst in the evolution of our discipline's thinking about gender and its many and complex roles in consumption. Each gender conference draws new participants and develops new perspectives.

These reflections on the overall state of marketing and consumer behavior and on gender emphases in the discipline in the late 1980s and early 1990s fit well with our analogy of the ingénue. Costa's personal deliberations suggest that the gender conferences provided a significant venue for the maturation of the ingénue, and we will continue our focus primarily on the gender conferences in the sections that follow.

Diverse Approaches and Emerging Roles of Substance

A key element in the role of the ingénue is how the character unfolds and how the weaknesses and tensions of her storyline develop over time. In the case of gender research as ingénue, the character's diverse approaches to her work and the roles of real substance that have developed have taken the shape of an impressive oeuvre. The past two decades of gender studies in consumer behavior put the "disembodied heads of consumers, which are the focus of the psychological studies, back on their bodies, situate them in a culture and moment, and so provide a rich contextual understanding of consumer behavior" (Deighton, MacInnis, McGill, & Shiv, 2010, p. 1). The following section of this chapter provides a review of and commentary on the different elements of these role developments, focusing on methods, critical social issues, identity, culture, and theory development. Our review focuses on the gender conferences but also includes other notable work.

Methods

The choice of a methodological approach to a research topic depends on what is examined, as different methods better serve particular forms of inquiry. As the ingénue analogy and Costa suggest, the methods used in most gender and consumer behavior research before 1991 were limited to quantitative studies and experiments. These methods do not typically provide the complex understanding of gender and consumer behavior that we and other scholars have sought.

However, gender researchers over the last two decades have used a variety of methodological tools to expand knowledge. For example, many scholars use naturalistic inquiry and depth interviews: D. Park and Deshpande (2004) study video war-gamers. Goulding and Saren (2006) and Goulding, Saren, Maclaran, and Follett (2004) explore androgyny and gender identity and blurring within the Gothic subculture. Dolan and Scott (2009) investigate Avon trading circles and gender empowerment. Woodruffe-Burton and Ireland (2008) are concerned with narcissism. Welsh (2008) examines dieting. Through ethnography, netnography, and content and discursive analyses, Gentry and Harrison (2008) consider market forces that slow the movement of male gender neutrality portrayals in media representations; Jardine (2004) researches advertisements for weight loss pills and Kjeldgaard and Storgaard (2008) delineate tensions of tradition and modernity as played out in Mexican telenovelas.

Similarly, Coleman, Parmentier, Sredl, and Tuncay (2008) investigate gendered discourses of the home as portrayed in *Sex and the City,* Tuncay (2006) studies metrosexuals' conceptions of masculinity, and Hamilton and Hewer (2010) evaluate masculine identities in pop dancing. Using comparable methods, Parmentier and Coleman (2010) explore source cues in online communities, Oswald and Ourahmoune (2006) evaluate the erotized male body in Calvin Klein advertisements, and Ruangwanit and Wattanasuwan (2008) examine ways in which men reestablish their sense of masculinity. Duffy (2010) also uses life-story analysis in assessing male identity construction. McMellon (2005) utilizes introspection and photographic and text analyses to explore how individuals use their past in construction identity. These few exemplars indicate the variety and competent use of methods designed to provide greater and deeper insight into diverse gender topics.

Gender Research of Critical Social Issues

Naiveté and a lack of social/political awareness clearly are *not* characteristics of our ingénue's development over the past 20 years. Compassionate, constructive, comparative, historical, and critical analyses of gendered issues that focus on the levels of the individual, the marketplace, media, society, and the world are all part of the repertoire. A small sample includes obesity/lipophobia (Aaskegaard, 2004; Friend & Westgate, 2006; Welsh, 2008); "feminine" physical activities (Brace-Govan, 2008); hegemonic masculine power in media representation (Kaiser, Looysen, & Hethorn, 2008); drug policy as it relates to gender, ethnicity, and social class (Borrowman & Costa, 2004); the gendered nature and problematic of academia (Maclaran, 2010; Woodruffe-Burton & Peñaloza, 2010); empowerment of women (Dolan & Scott, 2009; Scott & Peñaloza, 2006; Scott, Parmentier, Sredl, & Coleman, 2006); and Third World women, social class, and globalization (da Cruz, Augusto, Vieira, Natt, & Ayrosa, 2010; Rafferty, 2010; Scott, 2010; Venkatesh, 2010).

Feminist theory discussions could be cited here or in the section on theory; we see some of the studies as particularly relevant social critique (Borgerson & Schroeder, 2004; Catterall, Maclaran, Stevens, & Hamilton, 2008; Schroeder & Borgerson, 2004).

Identity

Gender researchers often seek an understanding of the *lived experiences* of consumers, situating them in a specific social and cultural setting and offering analyses that provide a contextual understanding. In an important work, Linda Scott (2006) establishes a guidepost for later scholarship on feminist gender identity in the United States. The stream of gender research over the past two decades clearly illustrates shaping and maintaining identity as a lifelong work in progress for people; consumption and representation provide many of the necessary props and symbolic signals used in that ongoing construction.

Sexual orientation, gender bending, and brands used in these contexts have been analyzed, offering insights into the male "gayz," LGBT representation in mainstream commercials, androgyny, retailing, cyberspace communities, homoeroticism in fashion, fashion magazines, advertising using female nudity, cross-dressing, and gay attire for business professionals (Aiden & Ross, 2006; Azar & Darpy, 2008; Beetles & Harris, 2004; Chen, Aung, Liang, & Sha, 2004; Drinck & Kreienkamp, 2006; Goulding et al., 2004; Oakenfull, 2010; Rinallo, 2006; Rosenbaum & Daunt, 2010; Tsai, 2004, 2006). Of course, Wardlow's (1996) edited work was an important precursor to later developments in LGBT perspectives.

Consumption and representation provided various contexts to explore and critically assess constituted notions of masculinity and femininity in the marketplace. Gentry and Harrison (2008) examine why marketing's role portrayals of males support existing masculine hegemony in the United States, while Bettany (2006) considers how feminist epistemology shapes our understanding of masculinity in marketing. Catterall, Maclaran, and Stevens (2006; see also 2000, 2005) reflect on the transformative potential that a critical feminist perspective might have on our discipline of consumer research. Brace-Govan (2008, 2010) examines body styles, the roles of women's physical activity over the past 120 years in the UK, and what is seen as appropriate viewing of the body; Martens (2008) provides a shorter historical perspective on a broader range of topics in her feminist critique of consumer culture for the period of 1950–1970.

Gender Research and Culture

"The Europeans are coming!" would only capture a portion of the cultural diversity found in gender research over the past two decades. The 2010 gender conference, held in Ambleside in the heart of the UK's Lake District, drew participants from 14 countries, primarily from North America, Europe, and Asia. The range of research on culture goes well beyond the traditional geographic connotation of culture. Scholars explore wedding cultures; food cultures; cultural practices regarding breast feeding; subcultures of sex product enthusiasts, Goths, and Gamers; Sikh online dating sites; the impact of colonial rule on the representation of men and women in Indian advertising; Mediterranean male "consumerscapes;" and metalevel cultural models for constructing notions of male masculinity (Caru, Cova, & Tissier-Desbordes, 2004; Cayla & Koops-Elson, 2006; Cross, 2010; Goulding et al., 2004; Hewer & Brownlie, 2010; Maclaran & Catterall, 2004; Ourahmoune & Özçaglar-Toulouse, 2010; D. Park & Deshpande, 2004; Previt, 2010; Ruangwanit & Wattanasuwan, 2010; Takhar, Parsons, & Maclaren, 2008; Venkatesh, 2010; Walther, 2010; Watson & Helou, 2006).

In assessing gender research in terms of scholarly contributions from around the world, our ingénue has evolved into a global star over the past two decades. While we reviewed some of these studies in previous sections, the cultural and geographic diversity of this stream of research greatly enriches the intellectual culture and ethos of scholars in the field. Studies of symbolic aspects of material consumption range from gendered cultural analysis of coffee chains in India (Venkatesh, 2010) to the meanings of purchasing lingerie among Brazilian women of lower social class, to gendered differences in luxury goods in Turkey (da Cruz et al., 2010; Gul, 2010). Important social issues relating to self-image and self-worth are researched among young women in Ghana (Scott, 2010), women and young housewives in Croatia and China (Bei, Liao, Widdows, & Widdows, 2004; Sredl, 2004), and brides in northern Algeria (Ourahmoune & Özçaglar-Toulouse, 2010). Some scholars review behavior across cultures (Caldwell & Kleppe, 2006). Historical analyses push our understanding of gender across time and associated cultural eras (Minowa & Branchik, 2008; Minowa & Witkowski, 2008).

Theory Extension and Development

While we open this chapter with a prescient quote from Levy (1959) regarding the fundamental symbolic importance of gender, any reflections on gender and theory development within consumer behavior may well start with Stern's (1993) article, which introduced our field to the theoretical lens of feminist literary criticism, using advertisements as its focus. This article, along with Bristor and Fischer's (1993) theoretical overview of how feminist thought can inform our consumer research in meaningful ways, marks the beginning of theory extension in the arena of gender and consumption. To bookend the key works that assess theory development and research in gender and consumer behavior, we point to Fischer, Parmentier, and Scaraboto (2010) and Bettany, Dobscha, O'Malley, and Prothero (2010).

The majority of the articles we mention in our preceding discussions develop and utilize theory as they explore and explicate particular phenomena. As we reflect on theory extension and development, we continue to be both pleased and impressed by scholars' efforts to explicate the complexities of the consumers' lived experiences and to place those works in a larger frame of understanding. Gender and gendered behaviors are deeply rooted in culture and history, and they play out in structural and social hierarchies that are wonderfully complex, contemporary, and chaotic. Over the past two decades, analyses of gendered identities, cultural narratives, and discourses have informed the performance of gender through consumption and explicate the managerial efforts and consequences of marketers. Our ingénue has grown from her humble/simple, male/female dichotomous character to be multidimensional, secure, and mature. Significantly, she continues to aspire to further growth and development.

FINAL REFLECTIONS

Our reflections on gender studies, primarily as presented at the gender conferences over the past two decades, indicate substantial, clear progress toward understanding the variety and complexity of gender and consumption. Still, we would like to see greater focus on the contextual intricacies and on critical social implications. For instance, in the film *Schmatta: Rags to Riches to Rags* (2009), the producers examine development and decline in the American garment industry. Largely monopolized in the past by American blue-collar women, the social, economic, and political milieu for textile and garment production has shifted to the Third World, notably India and China. In the United States, clothing produced in America for sale in America has dropped from 95% in 1965 to 5% in 2009. While production has shifted geographically, in all places it remains gender biased; males dominate management and females dominate labor. At the same time, fashion continues to drive consumption of garments for both men and women in the United States. Moreover, presentation of fashion is accomplished largely and most publicly through the use of men and women who are idealized as largely unobtainable, beautiful, and sexually desirable. In addition, domestic production has dropped amid overall declines in American manufacturing, further exacerbated by the recent jobs recession. As a result, both men and women are no longer able to purchase even less expensive clothing produced in the Third World. In the meantime, Third World women and children are employed in conditions we would consider illegal and immoral in the United States. As a final dramatic and ironic point, Western fashion continues to spread and stimulate consumer desires in the Third World.

With respect both to socially critical topics and to the need to analyze production, distribution, and consumption together, consider the recent revolution in Egypt and the "Arab Spring." Social media, utilized by both men and women, precipitated, maintained, and ultimately succeeded in deposing former Egyptian President Mubarak. The protesters became rebels and then became victors. While the long-term outlook for democracy remains uncertain in Egypt, democratic reforms and freedom were the revolutionary goals. Just a few weeks later, on the 100th anniversary of International Women's Day, Egyptian women protested again, this time citing their crucial participation in the revolution and urging a place at the table for women seeking democratic reform. These women were met with men's voices that told them to return home, where they belonged. Women participated in producing the revolution and in distributing information that led to effective demonstrations and rebellion, yet are barred from full involvement in consuming the fruits of their labor.

More Nomo...ing

Despite notable progress over the last few decades, we see a need for greater and more consistent nomothetic and nomological thinking. Since the 1991 advent of the gender conferences, calls have been answered for greater emphasis on cultural and cross-cultural studies, on males, and on increased research on those with different sexual or bodily orientations (e.g., LGBT). For both of us, the purpose of these appeals has been not only to increase knowledge specific to each of these phenomena, but also to move in the direction of understanding what gender and male–female–other mean on a more general level.

Thus, specific research should lead to generalizations and to nomothetic and nomological assertions and theory. As indicated earlier, some of this progress has been accomplished. Still, we believe studies of specific situations and topics should always lead to a greater understanding of gender and consumer behavior at a higher level. For example, ethnography should lead to ethnology; that is, a specific study or group of studies should lead to broader understanding. As an example using one of the authors' early works, Costa (1989) describes the ways in which Greek space and tools or implements are divided along male–female lines. In this case, the gender dimensions reflect cultural dichotomies of clean/dirty, outside/inside, sacred/profane, exterior/interior, business/home, public/private, and so on. While it may be interesting to read the descriptions, to understand the depth and extent of such divisions, and to see the way in which gender is woven into Greek culture in various ways, the analysis cannot stop there and still be considered as useful and pioneering. Rather, theoretical considerations must be pushed to a higher level, seeing if and how the data generate insights into universals of gender. Thus, along nomological and ethnological lines, does this ethnographic Greek case suggest any social or biological "rules" that would apply in other or in all societies? If so, what would those be? If not, why? We suggest that both generalizations and specificities, nomothetic and idiographic, must be developed, with clear divisions between the two and with explanations of where, how, and why they converge or diverge.

Thus, like Fischer et al. (2010), we applaud the recent developments in the field of gender and consumer behavior. Fischer and her coauthors suggest further study along certain lines, while we have chosen other areas we deem to be in need of expanded development. We believe that any scholar will find ellipses in the field and new directions for significant research. The important book in which this chapter appears illustrates the extant state of scholarship and provides inspiration for future research in our discipline. We applaud the work of the contributors and, significantly, the efforts of Otnes and Zayer to bring the publication to fruition.

ACKNOWLEDGMENTS

We would like to thank Hal Kassarjian, Sid Levy, and John Sherry for taking the time to allow us to interview them for this chapter. All three of them immediately saw the importance of this volume and expressed appreciation to us (!) for being part of our reflections chapter. It doesn't get any better than that.

NOTES

1. For an interesting overview of this era, see *Brands, Consumers, Symbols and Research: Sydney J. Levy on Marketing,* 1999, compiled by Dennis W. Rook, Sage Publications, Thousand Oaks, CA.

2. The opening paragraph of this 1965 *Journal of Marketing* article reads: "The distinctive nature of the Negro revolution is…[not] to overthrow the established order so much as…to achieve full membership in that order. Because material goods have such an important symbolic role in American society [their] acquisition…should be

symbolic to the Negro of his achievement of full status." The article then goes on to be quite empirical/descriptive and, in retrospect, makes some assumptions about Negroes that would now be viewed as alarming.

REFERENCES

Aaskegaard, Søren (2004). Consumer culture at large: Cacophony, lipophobia, lipophilia and the quest for identity. In Linda Scott & Craig Thompson (Eds.), *Gender and consumer behavior* (Vol. 7). Madison, WI: Association for Consumer Research (online version, n.p.).

Aiden, Alexander J., & Frances Ross (2006). Masculinity, fashion consciousness and homo-erotic from a spatial angle. In Lorna Stevens & Janet Borgerson (Eds.), *Gender and consumer behavior* (Vol. 8). Edinburgh, Scotland: Association for Consumer Research (online version, n.p.).

Azar, Salim L., & Denis Darpy (2008). Moving beyond binary oppositions: Exploring brand sexual associations. In Shona Bettany, Susan Dobscha, Lisa O'Malley, & Andrea Prothero (Eds.), *Gender and consumer behavior* (Vol. 9). Boston, MA: Association for Consumer Research (online version, n.p.).

Bauer, Raymond A., Scott M. Cunningham, & Lawrence H. Wortzel (1965). The marketing dilemma of Negroes. *Journal of Marketing, 29* (July) 1–6.

Beetles, Andrea, & Lloyd C. Harris (2004). Female nudity in advertising: An exploratory study. In Linda Scott & Craig Thompson (Eds.), *Gender and consumer behavior* (Vol. 7). Madison, WI: Association for Consumer Research (online version, n.p.).

Bei, Lien-Ti, Tsai-Ju Liao, Kealoha Widdows, & Richard Widdows (2004). The influences of women's self-perceptions on their household contributions: A comparison of three Chinese cities. In Linda Scott & Craig Thompson (Eds.), *Gender and consumer behavior* (Vol. 7). Madison, WI: Association for Consumer Research (online version, n.p.).

Bettany, Shona (2006). Feminist epistemology meets the masculinity of marketing and consumer knowledge: A contemporary rendering of a decade-long debate. In Lorna Stevens & Janet Borgerson (Eds.), *Gender and consumer behavior* (Vol. 8). Edinburgh, Scotland: Association for Consumer Research (online version n.p.).

Bettany, Shona, Susan Dobscha, Lisa O'Malley, & Andrea Prothero (2010). Moving beyond binary opposition: Exploring the tapestry of gender in consumer research and marketing. *Marketing Theory, 10* (March), 3–28.

Borgerson, Janet L., & Jonathan E. Schroeder (2004). Identity and iteration: Marketing and the constitution of consuming subjects. In Linda Scott & Craig Thompson (Eds.), *Gender and consumer behavior* (Vol. 7). Madison, WI: Association for Consumer Research (online version, n.p.).

Borrowman, Mary Ann, & Janeen Arnold Costa (2004). Consuming illicit drugs: Disproportionate disadvantage and poor women of color. In Linda Scott & Craig Thompson (Eds.), *Gender and consumer behavior* (Vol. 7). Madison, WI: Association for Consumer Research (online version, n.p.).

Brace-Govan, Jan (2008). The historically vexatious question of physical activity and women: Restrictions, malleability and resistance. In Shona Bettany, Susan Dobscha, Lisa O'Malley, & Andrea Prothero (Eds.), *Gender and consumer behavior* (Vol. 9). Boston, MA: Association for Consumer Research (online version, n.p.).

Brace-Govan, Jan (2010). Bodystyle, physicality and bodywork. Introducing a typology of embodiment for women. In Lisa Peñaloza & Helen Woodruffe-Burton (Eds.), *Gender and consumer behavior* (Vol. 10; pp. 91–94). Ambleside, UK: Association for Consumer Research.

Bristor, Julia M., & Eileen Fischer (1993). Feminist thought: Implications for consumer research. *Journal of Consumer Research, 19* (March) 518–527.

Caldwell, Marylouise, & Ingeborg Astrid Kleppe (2006). Gender identity and perceptions of femininity in everyday life: A multi country study of contemporary young female achievers. In Lorna Stevens & Janet Borgerson (Eds.), *Gender and consumer behavior* (Vol. 8). Edinburgh, Scotland: Association for Consumer Research (online version, n.p.).

Caru, Antonella, Bernard Cova, & Elisabeth Tissier-Desbordes (2004). Consumerscapes as enclaves of masculinity. In Linda Scott & Craig Thompson (Eds.), *Gender and consumer behavior* (Vol. 7). Madison, WI: Association for Consumer Research (online version, n.p.).

Catterall, Miriam, Pauline Maclaran, & Lorna L. Stevens (Eds.) (2000). *Marketing and feminism: Current issues and research*. London, UK: Routledge.

Catterall, Miriam, Pauline Maclaran, & Lorna L. Stevens (2005). Postmodern paralysis: The critical impasse on feminist perspectives on consumers. *Journal of Marketing Management, 21*(5–6), 489–504.

Catterall, Miriam, Pauline Maclaran, & Lorna L. Stevens (2006). The transformative potential of feminist critique in consumer research. In *Advances in consumer research* (Vol. 33; pp. 222–226). Boston, MA: Association for Consumer Research.

Catterall, Miriam, Pauline Maclaran, Lorna L. Stevens, & Kathy Hamilton (2008). Materialist feminism: Reinstating a wider social critique in research on gender and consumer behavior. In Shona Bettany, Susan Dobscha, Lisa O'Malley, & Andrea Prothero (Eds.), *Gender and consumer behavior* (Vol. 9). Boston, MA: Association for Consumer Research (online version, n.p.).

Cayla, Julien, & Mark Koops-Elson (2006). Global men with local roots: Representation and hybridity in Indian advertising. In Lorna Stevens & Janet Borgerson (Eds.), *Gender and consumer behavior* (Vol. 8). Edinburgh, Scotland: Association for Consumer Research (online version, n.p.).

Chen, Joseph, May Aung, James Liang, & Tina Sha (2004). The dream market: An exploratory study of gay professional consumers' homosexual identities and their fashion involvement and buying behavior. In Linda Scott & Craig Thompson (Eds.), *Gender and consumer behavior* (Vol. 7). Madison, WI: Association for Consumer Research (online version, n.p.).

Chocano, Carina (2011). Thelma, Louise, & all the pretty women. *The New York Times*, April 21 (online version, n.p.).

Coleman, Catherine A., Marie-Agnes Parmentier, Katherine Sredl, & Linda Tuncay (2008). Gendered discourses of the home as portrayed in the media: An examination of *Sex and the City* and *Entourage*. In Shona Bettany, Susan Dobscha, Lisa O'Malley, & Andrea Prothero (Eds.), *Gender and consumer behavior* (Vol. 9). Boston, MA: Association for Consumer Research (online version, n.p.).

Costa, Janeen Arnold (1989). On display: Social and cultural dimensions of consumer behavior in the Greek Saloni. In Thomas K. Srull (Ed.), *Advances in consumer research* (Vol. 16; pp. 562–566). Provo, UT: Association for Consumer Research.

Costa, Janeen Arnold (Ed.) (1994). *Gender issues and consumer behavior.* Thousand Oaks, CA: Sage.

Cowan, Ruth Schwartz (1976). The "Industrial Revolution" in the home: Household technology and social change in the 20th century. *Technology and Culture, 17*(1), 1–23.

Cross, Samantha N. N. (2010). Food, gender and consumption compromises in the home. In Lisa Peñaloza & Helen Woodruffe-Burton (Eds.), *Gender and consumer behavior* (Vol. 10; pp. 132–136). Ambleside, UK: Association for Consumer Research.

da Cruz, Zuleica, Cleiciele A. Augusto, Francisco G. D. Vieira, Elisângela Natt, & Eduardo A. T. Ayrosa (2010). Symbolic consumption and transfer of meanings in the purchase of lingerie by low-income women in Brazil. In Lisa Peñaloza & Helen Woodruffe-Burton (Eds.), *Gender and consumer behavior* (Vol. 10; pp. 103–107). Ambleside, UK: Association for Consumer Research.

Davis, Harry L. (1970). Dimensions of marital roles in consumer decision making. *Journal of Marketing Research, 7* (May), 168–177.

Davis, Harry L. (1971). Measurement of husband–wife influence in consumer purchase decisions. *Journal of Marketing Research, 8* (August), 305–312.

Deighton, John, Debbie MacInnis, Ann McGill, & Baba Shiv (2010). Broadening the scope of consumer research. *Journal of Consumer Research, 36* (April), v–vii.

Dolan, Catherine, & Linda M. Scott (2009). Lipstick evangelism: Avon trading circles and gender empowerment in South Africa. *Gender and Development, 17* (July), 203–218.

Drinck, Barbara, & Eva Kreienkamp (2006). Reactions to the gender and queer perspective: Market research is empowered by accepting gender and sexual orientation as consumer categories. In Lorna Stevens & Janet Borgerson (Eds.), *Gender and consumer behavior* (Vol. 8). Edinburgh, Scotland: Association for Consumer Research (online version, n.p.).

Duffy, Deirdre (2010). The village voice: Masculine identity construction within an interpretive community. In Lisa Peñaloza & Helen Woodruffe-Burton (Eds.), *Gender and consumer behavior* (Vol. 10; pp. 40–44). Ambleside, UK: Association for Consumer Research.

Fischer, Eileen, Marie-Agnès Parmentier, & Daiane Scaraboto (2010). We've come a long way, baby: But where to next in research on gender, markets, marketers, and consumption? In Lisa Peñaloza & Helen Woodruffe-Burton (Eds.), *Gender and consumer behavior* (Vol. 10; pp. 246–253). Ambleside, UK: Association for Consumer Research.

Friend, Lorraine A., & Lori S. Westgate (2006). Is fat still a feminist issue? The selling of hope, fear, and resistance at the movies. In Lorna Stevens & Janet Borgerson (Eds.), *Gender and consumer behavior* (Vol. 8). Edinburgh, Scotland: Association for Consumer Research (online version, n.p.).

Gentry, James, & Robert L. Harrison (2008). Marketing forces slowing male movement toward gender neutral. In Shona Bettany, Susan Dobscha, Lisa O'Malley, & Andrea Prothero (Eds.), *Gender and consumer behavior* (Vol. 9). Boston, MA: Association for Consumer Research (online version, n.p.).

Goode, William J. (1964). *The family.* Englewood Cliffs, NJ: Prentice Hall.

Goulding, Christina, & Michael Saren (2006). "Performing" gender: Multiple gender identities within the gothic subculture. In Lorna Stevens & Janet Borgerson (Eds.), *Gender and consumer behavior* (Vol. 8). Edinburgh, Scotland: Association for Consumer Research (online version, n.p.).

Goulding, Christina, Michael Saren, Pauline Maclaran, & John Follett (2004). Into the darkness: Androgyny and gender blurring within the Gothic subculture. In Linda Scott & Craig Thompson (Eds.), *Gender and consumer behavior* (Vol. 7). Madison, WI: Association for Consumer Research (online version, n.p.).

Gul, Misra (2010). Gender differences in purchase of luxury brands, materialism and social consumption: An exploratory study in Turkey. In Lisa Peñaloza & Helen Woodruffe-Burton (Eds.), *Gender and consumer behavior* (Vol. 10; pp. 224–229). Ambleside, UK: Association for Consumer Research.

Haberman, Paul W., & Jack Elinson (1967). Family income reported in surveys: Husbands versus wives. *Journal of Marketing Research, 4* (May), 191–194.

Hamilton, Kathy, & Paul Hewer (2010). Gender in motion: Dancing salsa and masculine identities. In Lisa Peñaloza & Helen Woodruffe-Burton (Eds.), *Gender and consumer behavior* (Vol. 10; pp. 16–20). Ambleside, UK: Association for Consumer Research.

Hewer, Paul, & Douglas Brownlie (2010). Nigella.com: Celebrity brands and gastrocommunities. In Lisa Peñaloza & Helen Woodruffe-Burton (Eds.), *Gender and consumer behavior* (Vol. 10; pp. 230–233). Ambleside, UK: Association for Consumer Research.

Honey, Maureen (1984). *Creating Rosie the Riveter: Class, gender, and propaganda during World War II.* Amherst, MA: University of Massachusetts Press.

Jardine, Andrew (2004). A discursive analysis of a television advertisement: The I'd like advertisement for Xenical. In Linda Scott & Craig Thompson (Eds.), *Gender and consumer behavior* (Vol. 7). Madison, WI: Association for Consumer Research (online version, n.p.).

Kaiser, Susan, Ryan Looysen, & Janet Hethorn (2008). Un(mark)eting hegemonic masculine fashion: On the politics of cultural (in)visibility. In Shona Bettany, Susan Dobscha, Lisa O'Malley, & Andrea Prothero (Eds.), *Gender and consumer behavior* (Vol. 9). Boston, MA: Association for Consumer Research (online version, n.p.).

Kassarjian, Harold H. (1969). The Negro and American advertising, 1946–1965. *Journal of Marketing Research, 6* (February), 29–39.

Kassarjian, Harold H. (1977). Content analysis in consumer research. *Journal of Consumer Research, 4* (June), 8–18.

Kassarjian, Harold H. (2011). Phone interview with Gary J. Bamossy, June 5.

Kjeldgaard, Dannie, & Kaj Storgaard (2008). Global local gender identities in market places of transition: Marianismo and the consumption of the telenovela *Rebelde*. In Shona Bettany, Susan Dobscha, Lisa O'Malley, & Andrea Prothero (Eds.), *Gender and consumer behavior* (Vol. 9). Boston, MA: Association for Consumer Research (online version, n.p.).

Lerner, Gerda (1987). *The creation of patriarchy.* Oxford, England: Oxford University Press.

Levy, Sidney J. (1959). Symbols for sale. *Harvard Business Review, 37* (July–August), 117–124.

Levy, Sidney J. (2011). Phone interview with Gary J. Bamossy, June 6.

Maclaran, Pauline (2010). The gendered nature of academic culture. In Lisa Peñaloza & Helen Woodruffe-Burton (Eds.), *Gender and consumer behavior* (Vol. 10; pp. 99–100). Ambleside, UK: Association for Consumer Research.

Maclaran, Pauline, & Miriam Catterall (2004). Techno-erotics and DIY masculinity. In Linda Scott & Craig Thompson (Eds.), *Gender and consumer behavior* (Vol. 7). Madison, WI: Association for Consumer Research (online version, n.p.).

Martens, Lydia (2008). Feminism and the critique of consumer culture, 1950–1970. In Shona Bettany, Susan Dobscha, Lisa O'Malley, & Andrea Prothero (Eds.), *Gender and consumer behavior* (Vol. 9). Boston, MA: Association for Consumer Research (online version, n.p.).

McMellon, Charles (2005). In the land of the morning calm: Exploring how ex-American soldiers construct and maintain identity by recycling past experiences. In Karin M. Ekstrom & Helene Brembeck (Eds.), *European advances in consumer research* (Vol. 7; pp. 201–207). Goteborg, Sweden: Association for Consumer Research.

Minowa, Yuko, & Blaine J. Branchik (2008). Eros, Thanatos, and androgyny: Gendered consumption of religions and rituals in classical Greece. In Shona Bettany, Susan Dobscha, Lisa O'Malley, & Andrea Prothero (Eds.), *Gender and consumer behavior* (Vol. 9). Boston, MA: Association for Consumer Research (online version, n.p.).

Minowa, Yuko, & Terrence H. Witkowski (2008). Voluptuous dialogues from a gathering in the garden: Women to consume, women to be consumed in 17th century Persia. In Shona Bettany, Susan Dobscha, Lisa O'Malley, & Andrea Prothero (Eds.), *Gender and consumer behavior* (Vol. 9). Boston, MA: Association for Consumer Research (online version, n.p.).

Oakenfull, Gillian (2010). Gay consumers and their brands: The gender-bending role of gay identity. In Lisa Peñaloza & Helen Woodruffe-Burton (Eds.), *Gender and consumer behavior* (Vol. 10; pp. 191–195). Ambleside, UK: Association for Consumer Research.

Ogburn, William F., & M. F. Nimkoff (1955). *Technology and the changing family.* Cambridge, MA: Greenwood Press.

Oswald, Laura R., & Nassima Ourahmoune (2006). Sex for sale: Positioning the eroticized male body in Calvin Klein advertising. In Lorna Stevens & Janet Borgerson (Eds.), *Gender and consumer behavior* (Vol. 8). Edinburgh, Scotland: Association for Consumer Research (online version, n.p.).

Ourahmoune, Nacima, & Nil Özçaglar-Toulouse (2010). Gender, fashion consumption and the Kabyle exogamic wedding ceremonies. In Lisa Peñaloza & Helen Woodruffe-Burton (Eds.), *Gender and consumer behavior* (Vol. 10; pp. 123–126). Ambleside, UK: Association for Consumer Research.

Park, C. Whan (1982). Joint decisions in home purchasing: Muddling through process. *Journal of Consumer Research, 9* (September), 151–162.

Park, David, & Sameer Deshpande (2004). Seeking entertainment through battle: Understanding the meaning of consumption processes for male Warhammer enthusiasts. In Linda Scott & Craig Thompson (Eds.), *Gender and consumer behavior* (Vol. 7). Madison, WI: Association for Consumer Research (online version, n.p.).

Parmentier, Marie-Agnès, & Catherine Coleman (2010). Reading source cues in online communities. In Lisa Peñaloza & Helen Woodruffe-Burton (Eds.), *Gender and consumer behavior* (Vol. 10; pp. 144–148). Ambleside, UK: Association for Consumer Research.

Previt, Josephine (2010). Women's lived and embodied experiences of breastfeeding: A critique of a social marketing approach. In Lisa Peñaloza & Helen Woodruffe-Burton (Eds.), *Gender and consumer behavior* (Vol. 10; pp. 76–80). Ambleside, UK: Association for Consumer Research.

Rafferty, Karen (2010). The emotional benefits of feeling feminine: How class-based emotions and gender conceptions shape self-fashioning practices. In Lisa Peñaloza & Helen Woodruffe-Burton (Eds.), *Gender and consumer behavior* (Vol. 10; pp. 87–90). Ambleside, UK: Association for Consumer Research.

Rainwater, Lee (1962). *Workingman's wife: Her personality, world and life style.* New York, NY: MacFadden-Bartell (now MacFadden Communications Group).

Reiter, Rayna R. (Ed.) (1975). *Toward an anthropology of women.* New York, NY: Monthly Review Press.

Rinallo, Diego (2006). The male gaze and the queer eye: Male consumers' reading strategies of media representations of men. In Lorna Stevens & Janet Borgerson (Eds.), *Gender and consumer behavior* (Vol. 8). Edinburgh, Scotland: Association for Consumer Research

Rosaldo, Michelle, & Louise Lamphere (Eds.) (1974). *Woman, culture, and society.* Stanford, CA: Stanford University Press.

Rosen, Dennis L., & Granbois, Donald H. (1983). Determinants of role structure in family financial management. *Journal of Consumer Research, 10* (September), 253–258.

Rosenbaum, Mark S., & Kate L. Daunt (2010). People as virtual products: Analyzing human exchanges on craigslist and gumtree.com. In Lisa Peñaloza & Helen Woodruffe-Burton (Eds.), *Gender and consumer behavior* (Vol. 10; pp. 108–112). Ambleside, UK: Association for Consumer Research.

Rosie the riveter (1944). dir. Joseph Santley, Republic Pictures (film).

Ruangwanit, Nopporn, & Kritsadarat Wattanasuwan (2008). Empowering consumption: A narrative of reestablishment of the masculine self. In Shona Bettany, Susan Dobscha, Lisa O'Malley, & Andrea Prothero (Eds.), *Gender and consumer behavior* (Vol. 9). Boston, MA: Association for Consumer Research (online version, n.p.).

Ruangwanit, Nopporn, & Kritsadarat Wattanasuwan (2010). Cultural masculinity: A narrative to reaffirming men's masculinity through cultural capitals. In Lisa Peñaloza & Helen Woodruffe-Burton (Eds.), *Gender and consumer behavior* (Vol. 10; pp. 44–68). Ambleside, UK: Association for Consumer Research.

Schmatta: Rags to riches to rags (2009). prods. Daphne Pinkerson & Mark Levin, Blowback Productions for HBO (film).

Schroeder, Jonathan E., & Janet Borgerson (2004). Judith Butler, gender theorist: Philosophical and phenomenological insights into marketing and consumer behavior. In Linda Scott & Craig Thompson (Eds.), *Gender and consumer behavior* (Vol. 7). Madison, WI: Association for Consumer Research (online version, n.p.).

Scott, Linda (2006). *Fresh lipstick: Redressing fashion and feminism.* Hampshire, England: Palgrave Macmillan.

Scott, Linda (2010). Attending to power: Sanitary provisions and female education in Ghana. In Lisa Peñaloza & Helen Woodruffe-Burton (Eds.), *Gender and consumer behavior* (Vol. 10; pp. 95–96). Ambleside, UK: Association for Consumer Research.

Scott, Linda, Marie-Agnès Parmentier, Katherine Sredl, & Catherine A. Coleman (2006). Women's empowerment and the positive role of the market. In Lorna Stevens & Janet Borgerson (Eds.), *Gender and consumer behavior* (Vol. 8). Edinburgh, Scotland: Association for Consumer Research (online version, n.p.).

Scott, Linda, & Lisa Peñaloza (2006). Matriarchal marketing: A manifesto. *Journal of Strategic Marketing, 14* (March), 57–67.

Sharp, Harry, & Paul Mott (1956). Consumer decisions in the metropolitan family. *Journal of Marketing, 21* (October), 149–156.

Sredl, Katherine C. (2004). Balkan Barbie: Women and consumer culture in post-socialist Croatia. In Linda Scott & Craig Thompson (Eds.), *Gender and consumer behavior* (Vol. 7). Madison, WI: Association for Consumer Research (online version, n.p.).

Starch, Daniel (1958). *Male vs. female. Influence on the purchase of selected products.* Greenwich, CT: Fawcett Publications.

Stern, Barbara B. (1993). Feminist literary criticism and the deconstruction of ads. *Journal of Consumer Research, 19* (December), 556–566.

Takhar, Amandeep, Elisabeth Parsons, & Pauline Maclaran (2008). Gender, self discovery and identity conflict on a Sikh dating website. In Shona Bettany, Susan Dobscha, Lisa O'Malley, & Andrea Prothero (Eds.), *Gender and consumer behavior* (Vol. 9). Boston, MA: Association for Consumer Research (online version, n.p.).

Trey, J. E. (1972). Women in the war economy—World War II. *Review of Radical Political Economics, 4* (July), 40–57.

Tsai, Wan-Hsiu Sunny (2004). Gay advertising as negotiations: Representations of homosexual, bisexual and transgender people in mainstream commercials. In Linda Scott & Craig Thompson (Eds.), *Gender and consumer behavior* (Vol. 7). Madison, WI: Association for Consumer Research (online version, n.p.).

Tsai, Wan-Hsiu Sunny (2006). Interpreting gay window advertising. In Lorna Stevens & Janet Borgerson (Eds.), *Gender and consumer behavior* (Vol. 8). Edinburgh, Scotland: Association for Consumer Research (online version, n.p.).

Tuncay, Linda (2006). Conceptualizations of masculinity among a "new" breed of male consumers. In Lorna Stevens & Janet Borgerson (Eds.), *Gender and consumer behavior* (Vol. 8). Edinburgh, Scotland: Association for Consumer Research (online version, n.p.).

Venkatesh, Alladi (2010). Food marketing, gender discourses in the Indian context—A visual cultural analysis of an Indian coffee chain, "Café Coffee Day." In Lisa Peñaloza & Helen Woodruffe-Burton (Eds.), *Gender and consumer behavior* (Vol. 10; pp. 136–140). Ambleside, UK: Association for Consumer Research.

Walther, Luciana (2010). Automatic lover—Cultural texts about the vibrator and consumers' interpretive strategies. In Lisa Peñaloza & Helen Woodruffe-Burton (Eds.), *Gender and consumer behavior* (Vol. 10; pp. 196–223). Ambleside, UK: Association for Consumer Research.

Wardlow, Daniel L. (Ed.) (1996). *Gays, lesbians, and consumer behavior: Theory, practice, and research issues in marketing.* New York, NY: Haworth Press, Inc.

Watson, Joel, & Mary Helou (2006). Men's consumption fears and spoiled identity: The role of cultural models of masculinity in the construction of men's ideals. In Lorna Stevens & Janet Borgerson (Eds.), *Gender and consumer behavior* (Vol. 8). Edinburgh, Scotland: Association for Consumer Research (online version, n.p.).

Welsh, Talia (2008). Dualism, disembodiment, and dieting women. In Shona Bettany, Susan Dobscha, Lisa O'Malley, & Andrea Prothero (Eds.), *Gender and consumer behavior* (Vol. 9). Boston, MA: Association for Consumer Research (online version, n.p.).

Winch, Robert F. (1952). *The modern family.* New York, NY: Holt McDougal.

Wolgast, Elizabeth H. (1964). Do husbands or wives make the purchasing decisions? *Journal of Marketing, 23* (October), 151–158.

Woodruffe-Burton, Helen, & Katie Ireland (2008). Scrutinizing the female body: Narcissism, bodily discourse and women's pursuit of the body beautiful. In Shona Bettany, Susan Dobscha, Lisa O'Malley, & Andrea Prothero (Eds.), *Gender and consumer behavior* (Vol. 9). Boston, MA: Association for Consumer Research (online version, n.p.).

Woodruffe-Burton, Helen, & Lisa Peñaloza (2010). Embodying gender in consumption and markets: Advancing gender problematics in market and consumption research and careers. In Lisa Peñaloza & Helen Woodruffe-Burton (Eds.), *Gender and consumer behavior* (Vol. 10; pp. 7–15). Ambleside, UK: Association for Consumer Research. 7–15.

Zober, Martin (1966). Determinants of husband–wife buying roles. In Steuart H. Britt (Ed.), *Consumer behavior and the behavioral sciences* (pp. 224–225). New York, NY: Wiley.

Glossary

Agapic love: love that is characterized by self-sacrifice and unselfishness, often equated with God's love for mankind.

Alterity: a feeling of "otherness," or the ability to distinguish between the self and the nonself.

Alternative gender performances: consumers' deployment of gender capital in a way that creates new gender ideologies and/or challenges the dominant gender ideology.

Antinomical: contradictory.

Cathexis: the investment of emotion or energy in an object, activity, or idea.

CGA: consumer-generated advertising refers to publicly disseminated, brand-related messages that consumers create on their own or in response to company contests.

Consumer collectives: groups of consumers who are joined by a common consumption interest.

Consumer culture: a cultural system whose members share the belief that the consumption of marketplace-mediated goods, services, and experiences is a preeminent and meaningful act.

Cosmogonies: theories of how the universe was created.

Coven: a gathering of witches, vampires, or Wiccans.

Cultural imaginary: the intersection of fantastical images and discourses that serve as a reference for the collective identity formation of a culture (from Lykke, 2000).

Dialogic ethics: various ethical stances that are rooted in community and relationship to community and that treat all parties involved in a communication as constitutive of the communication itself; thus, power is not only in the hands of the speaker but in all parties through dialogic exchange; an ethics rooted in social, cultural, and historical circumstances.

Discourse: a more or less formalized way of understanding the world that is translated into language; for example, the "discourse of gender" implies the ways that understandings of gender are communicated in society.

Discursive strategy: an active, goal-oriented way of using language in order to depict a specific version of the world. This strategy, in turn, serves the purpose of those who produce the discourse.

Ecofeminism: a branch of feminism that explicitly focuses on the connection between how society treats women, people of color, and the underclass and its treatment of the nonhuman natural environment.

Empowerment: in the context of vulnerability in consumer contexts, the opportunity for expression and voice that does not simply emanate, but has a constitutive role in the development of meaning and position.

Feminist economics: a branch of economics that questions how traditional economic models value traditionally feminine sectors of the marketplace such as childrearing, eldercare, and housework.

Feminist sociology: a branch of sociology that observes gender in relation to power, both individually and within society at large.

Fingerspitzengefühl: a German term that translates to "fingertips feeling"—or an exquisite, almost intuitive sense for some phenomenon.

Gender: a characteristic that results from cultural and social processes that pertain to expectations of masculinity and femininity, which are culturally, sociologically, and psychologically—rather than biologically—constructed.

Gender capital: a form of embodied cultural capital that may be utilized as a resource to gain advantage in various markets (the labor market, the marriage market, the educational market, etc.).

Gender identity: the way individuals identify with a gender category— that is, the degree or extent to which individuals think of themselves as possessing masculine or feminine personality traits; how individuals identify themselves with the gender associated with their biological sex.

Gender norms: the expected expression of gender in a society.

Gender roles: norms or culturally derived behaviors and activities of individuals, based on their socially identified masculine or feminine gender. These behaviors and activities originate from social learning and experiences programmed differently for each gender.

Grounded theory: theory that is generated by a process of inductively determining findings from data, rather than using data to test or support an existing theory deductively.

Hedonism: dedication to the experience of pleasure as the highest good in life.

Hegemony: a social scientific concept attributed to the late Antonio Gramsci, an Italian leftist academic. The concept refers to the subtle mechanism through which dominating forces in society operate to maintain the status quo. Hegemony works through limiting the conceivable life-worlds of ordinary people so they will not be able to oppose those in power.

Hermeneutic: interpretive or explanatory.

Heteronormative: the cultural predilection that favors relationships between members of the opposite sex.

Homoerotic: the tendency to be sexually aroused by a member of the same sex.

Hypersexualization: the accentuation of sexuality.

Ideology: a prevailing belief system for an individual, social class, or culture.

Intersectionality: a field of studies that aims to explicate human phenomena along multiple social axes.

Liminality: a transitional period during which a person is suspended between two different states of social identity or social rank (e.g., an engaged person is neither single nor married).

Media literacy: an ability to think critically about mass media programming and the ways such programming—film, television shows, advertising, videogames, and more—is created, produced, and disseminated.

Narcissist: someone who expertly manages the impressions he or she imparts to others, who craves admiration but has contempt for those who offer it, someone who seeks emotional experiences to fill the inner void, someone terrified of ageing and death (based on Lasch, 1979).

North/South divide: the dilemma presented by the split of those economies that are developed and industrialized ("the North") and those that are developing, including socialist and communist nations ("the South"). Northern economies operate with skilled labor in skill-intensive jobs and high consumer demand. Southern economies operate with unskilled labor in labor-intensive jobs and low consumer demand.

Objectification: a concept, usually associated with feminist theory, that accounts for the ways humans see other people or treat other people as simply anatomy—as a body or body part.

Operand resources: physical resources that are typically tangible, finite, and static in nature, and acted upon to produce effects and create value.

Operant resources: human, organizational, informational, and relational resources that are typically invisible, intangible, dynamic, and infinite in nature and capable of producing effects and creating value.

"The Other": in anthropology, a group perceived as different and as the object of observation, data collection, and theorizing; often associated with the idea of dominating non-Western people.

Phenomenology: a form of qualitative research that is guided by the first-person point of view of the research participant ("informant") and that encourages the informant to guide the unfolding of the research process, rather than to follow a preestablished research plan.

Plat du jour: a French expression used in restaurants that translates as "dish of the day." In English, it connotes something from which everyone chooses; a common choice.

Projection: techniques used to discover meanings that are sometimes inaccessible by direct measurement and that enable people to attribute or acknowledge characteristics they might otherwise overlook.

Reprioritization: the deliberate reshaping of life space in order to carve out a privileged station—for example, the role of single fatherhood.

Retrosexual: term coined as a reaction to the buzzword "metrosexual." As opposed to a metrosexual, a retrosexual adheres to classical masculine ideals—for example, not caring too much about his appearance.

Salaryman masculinity: a hegemonic form of Japanese masculinity characterized by an intense work ethic, loyalty to the firm, and a breadwinner mentality. During postwar Japan's economic boom, salarymen were heroic embodiments of the nation's economic growth; more recently, they are often portrayed as figures of ridicule.

Sartorial: term used for matters relating to clothes, especially more finely tailored garments.

Selectivity hypothesis: a model based on the notion that men and women use different strategies to process information. It posits that men use heuristic devices or single cues that are highly available, salient, and relevant to the self, while women engage in effortful and comprehensive processing, attempting to assimilate all available cues relevant to the self and to the others.

Sex: sexual behaviors and physiological characteristics and differences (e.g., chromosomes, hormonal profiles, internal and external sex organs) that define men and women.

Sexism: a term formed during the women's rights movement of the 1960s and 1970s meaning that one gender is perceived as superior to the other.

***Shinjinrui* ("the new breed"):** the generation of Japanese who came of age during the 1970s or after and grew up in the prosperous times of the economic boom. Many shinjinrui are only children and are described as lazier and more self-centered than previous generations.

Social-desirability bias: a phenomenon in psychological research that reflects the tendency of study participants to provide responses to stimuli that they believe are most desired by the researchers.

***Soushokukei danshi* ("grass-eating-type men") masculinity:** a recent form of hegemonic Japanese masculinity characterized by feminine consumption practices (e.g., fashion, beauty work) and preference for comfortable lives (vs. intense corporate careers). Soushokukei danshi are heterosexual men, but are purportedly uninterested in relationships with the opposite sex.

Sustainable consumption and production: the use of services and related products that respond to basic needs and proffer a better quality of life while minimizing the use of natural resources and toxic materials, as well as the emissions of waste and pollutants over the product/service life cycle so as not to jeopardize the needs of further generations.

Sustainable marketing: the practice of marketing whereby feasible trade-offs between business and environmental concerns are attempted, time lines are lengthened, and systems reflect the lifetime cost of production rather than the short-term cost of use.

Symbolic body: the notion that the body is a symbol of individual status and individual consumption power.

Taxonomy: the outcome of the structured classification of phenomena.

Traditional gender performances: consumers' deployment of gender capital in a way that supports, strengthens, and/or perpetuates the dominant gender ideology.

Triangulation: in qualitative research, the tendency to conduct research so that multiple researchers study the same phenomena or use different methods to study them, in order to enhance validity of the findings.

WOMM: the use of consumer testimonials and opinions in professional marketing activity through such forms as "buzz," blogs, viral marketing, and other consumer-driven discourses.

Zeitgeist: a German word meaning a key spirit or mood of a particular historic period reflected in the dominant ideas of beliefs of the time.

Name Index

A

A Theory of Shopping, 183
Abu Dhabi, 73–74, 76, 79, 81
ACNE, 266
Advertising Age, 19, 93
Advertising Research Foundation, 133
Advertising Women of New York, 19
Afterimage: The Journal of Media Arts and Cultural Criticism, 139
Air Force (U.S.), 95
Aikawa, 298
Algeria, 167, 313, 421
Amazon, 165
American Academy of Pediatrics, 13
American Behavioral Scientist, 139
American College of Obstetricians and Gynecologists, 13, 15
American Girl Place, 177
American Home, The, 412
American Marketing Association, 374
American Medical Association, 13
American Public Health Association, 13
Apple Newton, 166
"Arab Spring," 423
Aristotle, 23
Arnault, Bernard, 274
Association for Consumer Research, 374
AT&T, 180
Austen, Jane, 39
"Average Joe," 255–256
Avon, 187–188, 418

B

Bakuman, 297–298
Bamossy, Gary, 416
Bank of Japan, 291
Barr Pharmaceuticals, 11, 13
Belk, Russ, 414
Bleuler, Eugen, 66
Body Parts (advertising campaign), 22

Bond, James (character), 401
Bowflex, 96, 102
Bono, Chaz, xv
Brady (character in *Sex and the City*), 72–73
Brody, Adrian, 274
Brooks, Vincent (character), 299
Brooklyn (NY), 18, 72
Brothers (store), 270
Brown, Helen Gurley, 64, 83
Buber, Martin, 24
Buffy the Vampire Slayer, 33
Burke, Kenneth, 144, 149, 153
Burning Man (festival), 178
Butler, Rhett, 74

C

Calvin Klein, 418
Campaign for Real Beauty, 22, 180
Carlyle (character in *Twilight*), 53, 49
Carrefour, 325
Carrie (character in *Sex and the City*), 70, 72–74, 76–80, 83
Carrie's Closet (iPhone app), 80
Casablanca, 33
CBS, 13, 17, 133
Center for Drug Evaluation and Research, 13
Charlotte (character in *Sex and the City*), 70, 72–74, 76–77, 81
Cheap Monday, 266
Cheerios, 121
Choki, 299
Clinton, Senator Hillary, 14
Cohen, Andy, 69
"Cohort 3," 295
Color Me Mine, 37
Cosby Show, (The), 18
Costa, Janeen Arnold, xv, 414
Crenshaw, Kimberle, 394
Collins, Patricia Hill, 394

Subject Index